A WOMEN'S LECTIONARY FOR THE WHOLE CHURCH

Praise for *A Women's Lectionary for the Whole Church*

"Here is revealed Gafney's pastoral sensibilities and her wisdom in dealing with hard issues within worship. Her lectionary always has the worshipper in mind, and any preacher aiming at a similar sensitivity will find much to stimulate in her writing."

—*The Preacher*

"Gafney's innovation is to be explicit in her point of view and singularly dedicated to her hermeneutic for selection and translation. She seeks to tell the story of salvation through the voices of the marginalized, and the project is arguably more necessary now than ever."

—Episcopal Preaching Foundation

"Gafney's commentaries overflow with learned discussion of the ancient contexts of scripture and its history of consequences. Individual readers, Bible study groups, and preachers will all benefit from the insights of this volume, even if their congregations never adopt the lectionary itself."

—*Anglican Theological Review*

"Gafney's lectionary resources are a wonderful addition for worship planning, congregational or personal devotional practices, a Bible or book study, or even for use in a theological education setting."

—*Christian Feminism Today*

"In her stunning new lectionary series, Wilda Gafney has restaged the old, old story by recentering it on those who lived mostly at the edges—women with their own stories to tell, now blinking in bright lights long trained on the men in their lives."

—Barbara Brown Taylor
Coeditor, *Feasting on the Word*

"Gafney's resource will transform how the Bible gets read and preached in our churches, bringing us closer to the totality of God's love."

—Rev. Karoline M. Lewis, PhD,
The Marbury E. Anderson Chair of Biblical Preaching, Luther Seminary,
and Program Director, *Festival of Homiletics*

"This lectionary is so powerful we will finish each reading saying out loud, 'The word of God! Thanks be to God!'"

—Cláudio Carvalhaes, Associate Professor of Worship,
Union Theological Seminary, New York

"With scholarly rigor and pastoral embrace, a painter's attention to detail and a sculptor's care for craft, Gafney has given the Church a tremendous gift."

—Jeff Chu
Author, *Does Jesus Really Love Me:
A Gay Christian's Pilgrimage in Search of God in America*

"For anyone wanting to read and meditate on scripture and be nurtured by the word without being harmed, this text is indispensable."

—Willie James Jennings, Associate Professor of Systematic Theology
and Africana Studies, Yale Divinity School

"In a predominantly patriarchal world that still diminishes the lives, gifts, contributions, and voices of women, Professor Wil Gafney offers a distinct, bold, women's lectionary for the whole church and academy."

—The Rev. Dr. Luke A. Powery, Dean, Duke University Chapel,
and Associate Professor of Homiletics, Duke Divinity School

"*A Women's Lectionary for the Whole Church* challenges the androcentric landscape of our most common readings, upending customary theological constructs to uncover the presence of the feminine Divine."

—Rev. Traci D. Blackmon, Associate General Minister,
Justice & Local Church Ministries, The United Church of Christ

"Reading Wil Gafney's work is not unlike listening to a gifted jazz musician. She knows the tradition yet has the ability to weave multiple genres together to create a powerful and beautiful new song."

—Rev. Otis Moss III, Senior Pastor,
Trinity United Church of Christ, Chicago, Illinois

"Dr. Gafney has written a series of volumes that laypeople and clergy can read easily and be blessed by mightily as their souls cry out in ecstasy, "Finally comes the poet!" I commend her work to those who will use this Lectionary. And I encourage you to read it carefully and prayerfully."

—The Rev. Dr. Jeremiah A. Wright Jr., Pastor Emeritus,
Trinity United Church of Christ, and author of *What Makes You So Strong?*

"I did not know how much my soul needed *A Women's Lectionary for the Whole Church* until I began reading it, but now I suspect that I will never prepare another sermon or devotional without consulting it. Every pastor, indeed every Christian, needs this among their collection."

—Chanequa Walker-Barnes, PhD,
author of *I Bring the Voices of My People: A Womanist Vision for Racial Reconciliation*
and *Too Heavy a Yoke: Black Women and the Burden of Strength*

"As someone who has learned so much from the Rev. Dr. Wil Gafney, I commend it to every congregation and classroom. It is a prime example of revolutionary scholarship."

—Brian D. McLaren,
author of *Faith After Doubt*

"*A Women's Lectionary for the Whole Church* is an essential tool for all 'who seek to know God more clearly and to follow God more nearly.'"

—Kelly Brown Douglas
Interim President, Episcopal Divinity School and author,
Stand Your Ground: Black Bodies and the Justice of God

"I could sit at the feet of Wil Gafney for days and soak up her wisdom and knowledge. She has offered the church a treasure in this *Women's Lectionary*, and we would do well to make use of it quickly and thoroughly."

—Rev. Nadia Bolz-Weber, author

"*A Women's Lectionary for the Whole Church* is not only a resource for liturgy and preaching. I believe it is also a tool for contemplation on the mighty works of God on behalf of all people."

—The Rt. Rev. C. Andrew Doyle, Episcopal Bishop of Texas
and author of *Embodied Liturgy*

"This resource will be a great blessing and useful to all who seek to loose the shackles and set free the voices of the religiously oppressed and suppressed."

—Rev. Dr. Yvette A. Flunder, Presiding Bishop,
The Fellowship of Affirming Ministries,
and Senior Pastor, City of Refuge UCC in Oakland, California

YEAR C

A WOMEN'S LECTIONARY FOR THE WHOLE CHURCH

WILDA C. GAFNEY

Copyright © 2024 by Wilda C. Gafney

All rights reserved. No part of this book may be reproduced, stored in a retrieval system, or transmitted in any form or by any means, electronic or mechanical, including photocopying, recording, or otherwise, without the written permission of the publisher copyrights@cpg.org.

Church Publishing
19 East 34th Street
New York, NY 10016
www.churchpublishing.org

Cover art by Pauline Williamson
Cover design by Tiny Little Hammers
Typeset by Nord Compo

Library of Congress Control Number: 2024935209

Names: Gafney, Wilda, 1966- author.
Title: A Women's Lectionary for the Whole Church: Year C / Wilda C.
   Gafney.
Description: New York, NY : Church Publishing, [2024-] | Contents: Year C

ISBN 978-1-64065-572-0 (paperback)
ISBN 978-1-64065-573-7 (ebook)

*For those who have searched for themselves in the scriptures
and did not find themselves in the masculine pronouns.
May these words of mine please you.**

---

* Psalm 104:35, *BCP*, adapted

CONTENTS

Acknowledgments xiii
About the Cover Images xv
Abbreviations xvii
Biblical Resources xix
Introduction.. xxi
Text Selection xxv
Using A Women's Lectionary xxvii
About the Translations xxix
The Lessons with Commentary 1

    Advent I / 1
    Advent II / 5
    Advent III / 9
    Advent IV / 13
    Christmas I / 17
    Christmas II / 20
    Christmas III / 23
    First Sunday after Christmas / 26
    Feast of the Holy Name, January 1 / 29
    Second Sunday after Christmas / 32
    Feast of the Epiphany / 36
    Epiphany I / 39
    Epiphany II / 43
    Feast of the Presentation, February 2 / 47
    Epiphany III / 50
    Epiphany IV / 53
    Epiphany V / 56
    Epiphany VI / 61
    Epiphany VII / 67
    Epiphany VIII / 71
    Last Week of Epiphany (Transfiguration) / 75
    Lent—Ash Wednesday / 78
    Lent I / 81
    Lent II / 86
    Lent III / 89
    Lent IV / 93

Lent V / 97
Feast of the Annunciation, March 25 / 101
Palm Sunday—Liturgy of the Palms / 104
Palm Sunday—Liturgy of the Word / 106
Monday in Holy Week / 114
Tuesday in Holy Week / 117
Wednesday in Holy Week / 121
Maundy Thursday / 123
Good Friday / 127
Holy Saturday / 136
Easter—The Great Vigil / 141
Easter Day—Early Service / 152
Easter Day—Principal Service / 152
Easter Day—Evening Service / 158
Monday in Easter Week / 162
Tuesday in Easter Week / 164
Wednesday in Easter Week / 166
Thursday in Easter Week / 168
Friday in Easter Week / 170
Saturday in Easter Week / 172
Saturday in Easter Week / 172
Second Sunday of Easter / 174
Third Sunday of Easter / 179
Fourth Sunday of Easter / 184
Fifth Sunday of Easter / 190
Sixth Sunday of Easter / 194
Feast of the Ascension / 199
Seventh Sunday of Easter / 201
Pentecost Vigil (or Early Service) / 206
Pentecost Principal Service / 211
Trinity Sunday / 216
Season after Pentecost / 218
Proper 1 (Closest to May 11) / 219
Proper 2 (Closest to May 18) / 223
Proper 3 (Closest to May 25) / 228
Proper 4 (Closest to June 1) / 232
Proper 5 (Closest to June 8) / 236
Proper 6 (Closest to June 15) / 240
Proper 7 (Closest to June 22) / 244
Proper 8 (Closest to June 29) / 248

Proper 9 (Closest to July 6) / 251
Proper 10 (Closest to July 13) / 256
Proper 11 (Closest to July 20) / 260
Feast of Mary Magdalene, July 22 / 265
Proper 12 (Closest to July 27) / 268
Proper 13 (Closest to August 3) / 272
Proper 14 (Closest to August 10) / 276
Feast of the Ever-Blessed Virgin Mary, August 15 / 281
Proper 15 (Closest to August 17) / 284
Proper 16 (Closest to August 24) / 288
Proper 17 (Closest to August 31) / 291
Proper 18 (Closest to September 7) / 296
Proper 19 (Closest to September 14) / 300
Proper 20 (Closest to September 21) / 303
Proper 21 (Closest to September 28) / 306
Proper 22 (Closest to October 5) / 310
Proper 23 (Closest to October 12) / 313
Proper 24 (Closest to October 19) / 316
Proper 25 (Closest to October 26) / 321
Feast of All Saints, November 1 / 326
Proper 26 (Closest to November 2) / 329
Proper 27 (Closest to November 9) / 333
Proper 28 (Closest to November 16) / 337
Majesty of Christ (Closest to November 23) / 341

Appendix: Divine Names and Titles 345
Bibliography 349
Scripture Index 353

ACKNOWLEDGMENTS

YEARS B AND C

Many thanks to the Rev. Dr. Mark Bozzuti-Jones and Ms. Summerlee Staten for the hospitality of the Trinity Retreat Center. I am grateful for the reading and consultation of Bishop Yvette Flunder, the Rev. Dr. Pamela Lightsey, the Rev. Dr. Martha Spong, and the Rev. Dr. Eric Thomas as I remain ever mindful of the sacred responsibility to write for all of God's children. Particular thanks to Ms. Leah Jordan for her excellent editorial work.

PREVIOUS VOLUMES

I would like to thank the Louisville Institute for the 2019 Sabbatical Grant for Researchers; the trustees, administration, faculty, and staff of Brite Divinity School for a twelve-month sabbatical in 2019; and the rector, Mike Kinman, vestry, and members of the All Saints Episcopal Church in Pasadena for ongoing material, spiritual, and temporal support during this project and for committing to a year-long trial use of the lectionary in 2020–2021.

Special thanks to the former RevGalBlogPal community and Martha Spong for an early hearing of the work and a collaborative digital space in which to try out lesson and translation choices. For valuable feedback, support, and inspiration, many thanks to the women, nonbinary persons, and men who attended collaborative consultation sessions across the country, including Martha Simmons of the African American Lectionary Project. Thanks to Alicia Hager for administrative support in the first year and to NaShieka Knight, my research assistant at Brite.

I remain grateful for translations and translators that have inspired me to take up the text: Marcia Falk, Everett Fox, Hugh Page, and Joel Rosenberg. I am appreciative of the *Wisdom Psalter* by Laura Grimes; it was an early resource, and she an early collaborator. The psalms in these volumes are shaped by that interaction.

I am deeply grateful for all who have expressed support and encouragement, and impatience for delivery in person, through correspondence, and on social media. I am profoundly grateful for all of you who have purchased, given, recommended, and assigned *A Women's Lectionary for the Whole Church, Year A* and *Year W*.

Lastly, I mourn those who will not see this project, especially those who died due to Covid 19 and its complications. They are legion.

ABOUT THE COVER IMAGES

I first saw Wil Gafney in chapel at Candler School of Theology in October of 2016, during a service where Leea Allen read an amazing poem, "Heart Matters," and Dr. Gafney preached a sermon entitled "Love God Herself," drawn from Beyoncé's song "Don't Hurt Yourself." I was inspired. I didn't have anything that day other than a regular piece of paper and my colored pens—this was before I unapologetically carted my markers into services because I do most of my work in situ—but I drew the image of a woman standing proud, brown face crowned with locks of dark hair, clothed in green, and holding up the world. She speaks to me of triumph.

This was not the last time that Dr. Gafney's words would inspire my art.

In a Queer and Feminist Theology course I took, we read Dr. Gafney's article "Don't Hate the Playa, Hate the Game." In it, she refocused our attention on the fullness of Delilah's story, teasing out details and possibilities of connection that reframed both Delilah's motivations and power. If you haven't read it, I suggest you do. It spoke to me of honey, and fire, and memory, and love, and retribution, and these things all shaped the piece I created in response: "Remembering the Fire."

Since then, I've been inspired many times over.

When I was beginning a Lenten series, I read Dr. Gafney's article "Ritualizing Bathsheba's Rape" and drew, in response, "In the Ashes." The piece depicts Bathsheba sitting by a fire in ashes, weeping and cradling her dead child while David laments outside. I also did a series of pieces of the women in Saul's life that were inspired by what Dr. Gafney wrote in her incredible *Womanist Midrash*. Time and time again, I know that if I want to be schooled in a text, brought closer to the nuances and truths contained therein, and inspired by those truths, I will find that wisdom in Dr. Gafney's works. Without a doubt, the volume you currently hold in your hands contains this wisdom, and I hope you are similarly inspired.

My pieces for the *Women's Lectionary* were created in the same theme and seek to center and lift up the power that Black Women have in these stories of salvation. I drew "Queen of Heaven" (the cover image for Volumes A, B, and C) in June of 2017 using Tombow Watercolor Markers on Bristol Vellum paper. It shows Mary, enthroned and crowned with all the planets of the solar system and the wonders of the Universe bearing witness, clothed in life and light, and holding the Christ Child in her arms. She is the guardian and the bearer of God—Theotokos; she is the creation honored by the Creator.

The next work, "No Longer Lost" (the cover image for Volume W), speaks of the parable where God is imaged as a woman, the woman who loses her coin and finds it. She celebrates with all of her neighbors as God celebrates with the host of heaven when the lost ones come home. Surrounding her in these coins are us, connecting, praying, studying, dancing. You can also see the dove, and the lost sheep, and the broom, because some things need cleaning up, not the least of which are our misconceptions and our preconceived notions, which have grown dusty as we have let them sit.

Let the words of the Rev. Dr. Wil Gafney clear up some of those misconceptions and open windows to shed light on truth in a way you have never before seen. Sit with these words. Let them sink in. Feel their power and be empowered by the story of the Good News told in ways you may have never experienced before. May the luminous wisdom of the Word find a home within you, and may it spark your inner fire.

Pauline Williamson, creating as Seamire

ABBREVIATIONS

Alter	*The Hebrew Bible: A New Translation with Commentary*, trans. Robert Alter
AYBD	*Anchor Yale Bible Dictionary*
BigS	*Bibel in gerechter Sprache*
BDAG	*A Greek-English Lexicon of the New Testament and Other Early Christian Literature*, revised and edited by Frederick William Danker
BDB	*Brown-Driver-Briggs Hebrew and English Lexicon*
CEB	*Common English Bible*
DCH	*Dictionary of Classical Hebrew*
DSS	Dead Seas Scrolls
Fox	*The Five Books of Moses*, trans. Everett Fox
GSJPS	*A Gender-Sensitive Adaptation of the JPS Translation*
HALOT	*Hebrew and Aramaic Lexicon of the Old Testament*
IB	*The Inclusive Bible*
JPS	Jewish Publication Society *TANAKH*
KJV	King James Version
LXX	Septuagint
MT	Masoretic Text
NRSV	New Revised Standard Version
RCL	Revised Common Lectionary
SP	Samaritan Pentateuch

BIBLICAL RESOURCES

Original Language Texts
Dead Sea Scrolls
Hebrew Masoretic Text
Nestle-Aland Greek New Testament, 28th ed.
Peshitta (both testaments)
Samaritan Pentateuch
Septuagint
Targums
Vulgate

Bibles in Translation
Bishops Bible, 1568
Common English Bible, 2011
Dead Sea Scrolls Bible, 1999
Douay-Rheims Bible, 1582 (NT), 1610 (HB)
The Early Prophets: Joshua, Judges Samuel, Kings, Everett Fox, 2014
Five Books of Moses, Everett Fox, 1995
A Gender Sensitive Adaptation of the JPS Tanakh, 2006
Geneva Bible, 1599
The Hebrew Bible: A Translation with Commentary, Robert Alter, 2018
Inclusive Bible, 2007
Jewish Publication Society Tanakh, 1985
King James Version, 1611
A New English Translation of the Septuagint, 2000
New Revised Standard Version, 1989
Revised Standard Version, 1971
Tyndale's (incomplete) translation, 1525
Wycliffe Bible, 1384

Commentaries
Hermeneia
Jewish Publication Society Torah Commentary
The Torah, A Women's Commentary
The Wisdom Commentary
Women's Bible Commentary
The Yale Anchor Bible Commentary

INTRODUCTION

What does it look like to tell the Good News through the stories of women who are often on the margins of scripture and often set up to represent bad news? How would a lectionary centering women's stories, chosen with womanist and feminist commitments in mind, frame the presentation of the scriptures for proclamation and teaching? How is the story of God told when stories of women's brutalization and marginalization are moved from the margins of canon and lectionary and held at the center in tension with stories of biblical heroines and heroes? More simply, what would it look like if women built a lectionary focusing on women's stories? These were my initial questions when I sat down to draft a proposal for a women's lectionary, a lectionary designed by women—or an individual woman—for the whole church. I do not imagine that my questions and perceptions are the questions and perceptions of all other women. But I do believe that my questions and perceptions invite women, men, and nonbinary readers and hearers to engage the scriptures in new ways, and in that engagement, they might find themselves and their questions represented.

The lectionary is a catechetical tool. There are more than two billion Christians in the world, according to the Pew Research Center's Forum on Religion and Public Life (Global Religious Landscape). As of 2015, there were nearly 2.3 billion Christians representing slightly more than 31 percent of the world's total population. With Roman Catholics making up an estimated 1.2 billion and accounting for Orthodox Christians, Anglicans, Episcopalians, Methodists, Presbyterians, Lutherans, and other Reformed traditions, along with some Baptist and congregational churches that use a lectionary, the overwhelming majority of Christians receive their scripture mediated through a lectionary; that would be nearly 1.4 billion persons whose customary exposure to the scriptures occurs through a lectionary. Based on the numbers in the Pew Research Center's May 12, 2015, report, "America's Changing Religious Landscape," as many as 60 percent of American Christians attend services in churches that use lectionaries.

The scriptures are androcentric (male-focused), as are the lectionaries dependent upon them. Those lectionaries are not simply *as* androcentric as are the scriptures, but in my experience as a congregant and priest, women are even less well represented in them than they are in the biblical text. For example, there are at a minimum one hundred and eleven named women in the Hebrew Scriptures—which is itself underrepresented in preaching lectionaries and not always preached upon or even read—that reckoning does not account for the numbers of unnamed women and girls. Yet not many of my students or parishioners can name even ten women in the Hebrew Scriptures or even the entire biblical canon. The extent lectionaries do not introduce us to even a tithe of them. As a result, all many congregants know of the Bible is the texts they hear read from their respective lectionary.

As a biblical scholar, it is my hope to see congregants exposed to the Bible more broadly and deeply and see them equipped to engage the sacred texts of their tradition critically and with nuance. As a Hebrew biblical scholar, it is my hope to see congregations embrace the Hebrew Scriptures as a full and sufficient canon of scripture, revealing God and her word in conversation with, but not subject to, the Christian scriptures that follow, honoring the ancient texts and *their* contexts. As a professor, priest, and preacher, I am keenly aware that it is the stories of women and girls, female characters and their names (when given), that are most likely to be unknown by congregants and seminarians and, all too often, clergy. A more expansive, more inclusive lectionary will remedy that by introducing readers and hearers of scripture to "woman story" in the scriptures. (Adapted from April D. Westbrook, *"And He Will Take Your Daughters . . .": Woman Story and the Ethical Evaluation of Monarchy in the David Narrative.*)

Biblical women are often generalized as a monolith of oppressed biblical womanhood. In my years teaching in theological classrooms and Jewish and Christian congregations, I find scripture readers unfamiliar with women prophets (the subject of my first book, *Daughters of Miriam: Women Prophets in Ancient Israel*) or the more than twenty named Israelite and Judean queens preserved in the text (addressed in my most recent monograph, *Womanist Midrash: A Reintroduction to the Women of the Torah and the Throne*), or the female assassins who execute their would-be rapists, or many other texts in which women have unexpected power and agency. A significant aim of this project is to increase biblical literacy, beginning with scripture's most neglected population.

Recognizing that the scriptures are an androcentric collection of documents steeped in patriarchy, this lectionary grapples with the gender constructs of the text rather than romanticizing admirable heroines. Indeed, it questions "admirable" constructs of womanhood rooted in birthing and mothering. The extent to which women's narratives uphold the patriarchal agendas of the scriptures is held in tension with those passages in which women demonstrate agency, wielding power and authority. Sometimes those are the same texts. The degree to which the scriptures are (and are not) liberating for all of their characters and claimants will be, hopefully, more accessible to preacher and reader and other interpreters and exegetes.

Biblical values and norms around gender occupy a central place in biblical interpretation, providing an opportunity for preachers to engage them and their impact on the construction of gender norms in the world in which these texts are interpreted. I believe it is crucial to reframe the texts so that women and girls are at the center of the story, even though they are, to one degree or another, literary creations of premodern men. It is important that women who are often second-class citizens in the text and in the world in which the text is interpreted have a text selection and reading paradigm that centers the interests and voices of women in the text, no matter how constructed. The task of preachers is to proclaim a word—of good news, of liberation, of encouragement, of prophetic power, of God-story, and sometimes, of lament, brokenness, and righteous rage. These lectionaries will provide a framework to do that and attempt to offer some balance to the register in which the word has often been proclaimed.

A significant aspect of the work of shaping a lectionary and preaching from it is hermeneutical. I was (and remain) convinced it ought to be possible to tell the story of God and God's people through the most marginalized characters in the text. That is my practice as a preacher. This project, *A Women's Lectionary for the Whole Church*, intends to do that in a three-year lectionary accompanied by a standalone single-year lectionary. The three-year cycle, Years A, B, and C, will feature the Gospels of Matthew, Mark, and Luke, respectively, with John interwoven, as is the case in the Revised Common Lectionary (RCL) and Episcopal Lectionary (similar to the RCL but with the inclusion of deuterocanonical texts not deemed canonical by churches outside of the Anglo-Catholic and Orthodox streams). Year W (for "Women") covers all four Gospels.

Specifically, the *Lectionary* includes:

1. companion texts in the traditional four-fold model, first lesson, generally Hebrew Bible, Psalm (or other Canticle), Christian Testament lesson, and Gospel appropriate to the liturgical season;
2. fresh translation of the lessons for each Sunday, the Principal Feasts, Holy Week, and the Feasts of the Ever-Blessed Virgin Mary and Mary Magdalene, using gender-expansive language and, in the case of the Psalms, explicitly feminine God-language (see "About the Translations");
3. brief text commentaries on each day's lections, and
4. brief preaching commentaries on each day's lections.

The lectionary *does not* include collects. The lack of collects—prayers that tie together the readings that open the Liturgy of the Word—is intentional, that clergy and lay liturgists might develop their own in conversation with the lectionary.

A final word about gendered language: as a women's lectionary, this project specifically and intentionally makes women visible in these lectionary texts. This will inevitably seem strange to some hearers and readers. Some will find it welcome and a signifier of inclusion. Some will find it discordant, and I invite those to think deeply about what that discomfiture signifies. These responses may well be multiplied when reading and hearing the Psalms using feminine pronouns. And some will find the language in these volumes insufficiently inclusive, particularly with regard to nonbinary and a-gender persons. While there is nonbinary language for human and divine subjects, the purpose of this project is to make women and girls more visible. Nonbinary and inclusive language can obscure women and girls. The commitment to the visibility of women and girls is not in conflict or competition with the commitment to the visibility of nonbinary persons; this language, my language, like all language, is simply inadequate to express the fullness of God in and beyond the world or even in human creation.

Most simply, these translations seek to offer and extend the embrace of the scriptures to all who read and hear that they might see and hear themselves in them and be spoken to by them. Similarly, taking seriously that we are all created in the image of God, these translations seek to display a God in whose Image we see ourselves reflected and reflecting.

TEXT SELECTION

I crafted lectionaries that centered the telling of the stories of scripture on the stories of women and girls in the text, without regard to whether they are named or voiced in the text or whether their experiences of and with God support the narrative and theological claims made by and on behalf of the text or not. Specifically, I prioritize passages in which women and girls are present, whether named or not, whether speaking or not. In addition, I selected passages in which women and girls are present but obscured in plurals and other groupings, e.g., "children," "Israelites," "people," "believers," etc. As is the case with all lectionaries, some passages recur, and others are omitted altogether. None of the extant Christian lectionaries offers a comprehensive reading of any of the canons of scripture. This lectionary is no exception.

My methodology was broadly as follows:

1. First, I established a female canon within the broader canons of scripture by using Accordance Bible Software to identify passages in which there is explicit language for female persons. I designed a Boolean search to capture as many terms as possible in singular and plural constructions and varied grammatical forms (mother* <or> daughter* <or> sister* <or> wom*n <or> wife <or> wives <or> widow* <or>*maid* <or> mistress* <or> lady <or> ladies <or> prostitute* <or> prophetess* <or> princess* <or> queen* <or> sorceress* <OR> womb <OR> pregnan* <or> midwi*e*.) My search terms were not necessarily exhaustive, but they were more than sufficient for the task. I used the *Dictionary of Women in Scripture,* edited by Carol Meyers et al., to supplement this list.

2. Then, beginning with the liturgical season and its themes, I identified Hebrew biblical or deuterocanonical texts from the female canon. (Year W does not use the deuterocanonical texts apart from select readings during one or more of the Principal Feasts, such as Judith during the Great Vigil of Easter).

3. Next, I looked for readings that shared thematic language or specific words that related to the liturgical season and first lesson. I saved my Boolean search results in text groups: Hebrew Bible, Psalms, books that make up the New Testament lesson—Acts, the Epistles, and Revelation—and the Gospels. That meant I did not have to search the entire canon each time I worked on a specific reading. One nontraditional aspect of these lectionaries is that I occasionally use the Acts of the Apostles as the New Testament lesson, expanding the options for readings with female characters.

4. Sometimes a specific passage in a Gospel, psalm, or Epistle would suggest itself. Other times, I would move through the lesson categories looking for connective language. Most often, the selection sequence was Hebrew Bible followed by a psalm, then the Gospel and the New Testament lesson last.

Text selection was one of the most time-consuming aspects of the project, second only to translating the text. I was greatly facilitated in this world by collaboration circles, in person in Atlanta, Chattanooga, Chicago, Dallas, Fort Worth, Pasadena, Richmond (VA), and in Kapaa, Kilauea, and Wailua, Kauai (HI) in addition to international trips to Managua (Nicaragua) and a continuing education event for clergy on a Central and South American cruise where the *Lectionary* was one of the teaching topics. There is also an ongoing digital collaboration through a closed Facebook working group.

My conversation partners included sixty-three participants from across the United States, United Kingdom, Scotland, Canada, and New Zealand in one setting, Episcopal parishes in Kauai and Pasadena during separate one-month residencies, and a series of individual and small group consultations, some seventeen collaborations, some of which were composed of multiple sessions. Denominations represented included: African Methodist Episcopal, Anglican, Baptist (of various sorts), Disciples of Christ, Episcopal, the Fellowship of Affirming Ministries, Lutheran, Presbyterian, Unitarian Universalist, United Church of Canada, United Church of Christ, United Church of Scotland, and United Methodist.

I deliberately engaged potential users of the *Lectionary,* including clergy, seminarians, and lay leaders, with a range of gender identities and expressions. I also held a specific session for queer-identifying and nonbinary readers and hearers of the text focusing on the use and implications of binary language, even in service to womanist/feminist work, in an increasingly post-binary world.

I am beyond grateful for the contributions, questions, and suggestions of all of these conversation partners, including their assessment of wording and translation choices in addition to text pairings.

USING A WOMEN'S LECTIONARY

The *Women's Lectionary* is designed for congregational and devotional life. It will also serve well in theological classrooms in preaching, worship arts, liturgy, and spiritual formation. The *Lectionary* is also suitable for clergy lectionary study groups. Individuals and congregations will have a number of options for use. Each set of readings is accompanied by text and translation notes and a preaching commentary. In addition, the *Lectionary* comes with a list of the divine names and titles used for God in these translations that might be used in public liturgy and private prayer. There is also an index of all of the passages of scripture in the lectionary, making them available for individual study. Suggested practices for public reading follow in the "About the Translations" section.

CONGREGATIONAL USE

The gender-expansive translations throughout the *Women's Lectionary* and explicit feminine God language in the Psalter provide an opportunity for Christian education and formation on matters of biblical authority and translation issues, oft-neglected conversations in congregations (beyond creedal statements).

- Adopt the *Lectionary* fully, Years A, B, and C, for three years using these lessons in this translation.
- Adopt the *Lectionary* for a single year, using Year W for representation from all four Gospels. This would be especially suitable for churches that do not use a multiyear lectionary.
- Adopt the *Lectionary* to replace a year in the three-year lectionary currently in use.
- Adopt the *Lectionary* readings using another translation of the scriptures for public proclamation. (This may be a useful option in a congregation that might balk at hearing feminine pronouns used for God in scripture proclamation.)
- Use the *Lectionary* for substitute readings for the same day and liturgical season in a particular year (for example, when the Episcopal or RCL lessons are unsatisfactory).
- Use the *Lectionary* for Bible study, whether preaching from the *Lectionary* or not. The preaching prompts may be used as conversation starters.
- Use the list of divine names and titles for God to enrich the theological language of the community in liturgy, corporate, and personal prayer.

DEVOTIONAL USE

The *Lectionary* is designed for oral reading; read it out loud. Use the *Lectionary* for devotional reading, daily or weekly, whether your congregation uses the *Lectionary* or not. The four lessons can be read together every day of the week in their liturgical setting or spread out over the course of the week. The index can be used to identify individual passages for study, and the list of divine names in the appendix can be used to augment the vocabulary of prayer.

THEOLOGICAL EDUCATIONAL USE

As a resource in the theological classroom, the *Lectionary* offers a much-needed alternative to the long-standing Episcopal and Revised Common Lectionaries for the study of liturgy and worship planning, offering a relevant and expansive vocabulary at a time when many clergy, congregations, and denominations are looking for liturgical alternatives, and some are considering revisions of prayer books and hymnals for this very purpose.

These translations make a specific contribution to the oft-neglected but necessary conversation about the nature, function, and scope of biblical translation beyond the standard rubric of formal literalism and dynamic flexibility.

ABOUT THE TRANSLATIONS

Gender matters. Gender matters in the text, in the world, in the world of the text, and in the world of the translator. Gender matters to me and to countless numbers of women hearers and readers of the biblical text for whom it is Scripture. Gender matters significantly to those who have been and are marginalized because of gender, especially when it is done in the name of God, appealing to the Scriptures. And gender matters to men. Gender matters to hearers and readers of the Scriptures who are privileged to share the gender of the dominant portrayal of God, the majority of biblical characters, the majority of biblical characters who have speaking parts, the majority of translators of biblical texts, and the majority of interpreters of biblical texts.

(Wilda Gafney, *Womanist Midrash:
A Reintroduction to the Women of the Torah and the Throne*, 289).

While prompted in part by my experience of hearing the scriptures read and proclaimed in nearly exclusively masculine language, multiplied in effect by equally, if not more, male liturgical language, this *Women's Lectionary* is a lectionary for the whole church. Androcentrism, sexism, and misogyny in the scriptures, in their translation, and in their preaching and liturgical use hurt men and boys and nonbinary children and adults as much as it does women and girls. Exclusively masculine language constructs and reinforces the notion that men are the proper image of God and women are secondary and distant. Further, the simple reality that men and boys have always heard their gender identified with God cannot be overlooked as a source of power and authority, and security in terms of their place in the divine household and economy. Many, if not most, women and girls have not heard themselves identified by their gender as and with the divine, and for those who have had that experience, it has been profoundly moving, rare, and even sometimes profoundly disturbing. The translation choices employed in the *Women's Lectionary* offer an opportunity to hear the scriptures in public and private settings in a different timbre, a feminine vocal register. Specific translation choices are annotated in the text notes that follow each set of readings. Italicized text indicates First Testament quotations in the Second Testament.

The *Women's Lectionary* is a multilayered work. In addition to the compilation of entirely new lectionary readings for the three-year cycle and single composite year, the production of entirely new gender-expansive translations and, in the Psalms, explicitly feminine translations distinguish this lectionary. Gender-expansive means expanding collections of people, e.g., Israelites, children, nations, and even "people" to reflect gendered subgroups such as "the women, children, and men of Israel." (These translations generally place women before men in translation.) In every place where it can be reasonably inferred a group is composed of persons of more than one gender, I reflect that in the translation. Where gender-neutral or inclusive language is used, it is used for male subjects; for example, "child" is used preferably to "son."

In genealogies, gender expansiveness means that lineages are presented matrilineally. For example, rather than "the God of Jacob," the *Lectionary* uses "the God of Rebekah's line." When supplemental language is added to establish the maternal genealogy, it is placed in brackets, i.e., "[Rachel-born] Benjamin." In each case, the original reading and translation choices are clearly identified in the text notes. For this project, explicitly feminine language is preferable to inclusive and neuter language, which obscures and erases women and girls. In addition, singular neuter gender and inclusive plurals do not disrupt the learned gender patterns, as many readers and hearers interpret them through their previously learned gender patterns and experience them as male. There is also some nonbinary language for human beings and God throughout the *Lectionary*; erasure of any gendered minority is contrary to the aims of this project.

Because so many readers pray the Psalms devotionally, I wanted to offer an opportunity to hear those compositions speaking to, by, and about women and girls primarily and to encounter God in explicitly feminine language so readers of all genders will have the experience of praying to God in the feminine gender. Therefore, these translations of the Psalms use feminine pronouns for God primarily, supplemented by nonbinary pronouns.

Following the practice of translators before me, I have adopted the practice of choosing descriptive expressions for the name of God and other divine names and titles. Given the most commonly used title for God in the Hebrew Scriptures, LORD (with the large and small caps indicating it is a substitutionary word for God's unpronounceable Most Holy Name represented by the letters YHWH) is the common male human slaveholding title; it is not used for God in the *Lectionary*. The *Lectionary* preserves the ancient biblical and rabbinical practice of substituting something that can be said for that which cannot. (In some places, the Hebrew Masoretic Text uses Elohim, "God," as a substitute.) In rabbinic and subsequent practice, *HaShem*, "the Name," is a common substitution; there are others.

Dr. Joel Rosenberg of Tufts University translated selected psalms for the Kol Haneshamah Reconstructionist prayer book. He renders the divine name using choices such as "THE ETERNAL," "THE ONE," and in Psalm 29, "THE ONE WHO CALLS over many waters." I was deeply impacted by these translations during the time I spent as a member of the Dorshei Derekh Reconstructionist minyan of the

Germantown Jewish Centre in Philadelphia and adopted and expanded the practice in my own translations for teaching, preaching, and publication. The translations in *Lectionary* draw from a robust list of options for naming God listed in an appendix. Some examples include: Ark of Safety, Dread God, Fire of Sinai, Rock Who Gave Us Birth, She Who Is Holy, etc. The list numbers more than one hundred and twenty. I preserve "Lord" for human beings, as that is the origin of the title and respectful address, and functionally the title refers to a slaveholder or other hierarchical role.

Similarly, in the Second Testament, I also reserve "Lord" for human beings—apart from Jesus. There are two sets of divine names and titles for the Christian Testament in the appendix. For Jesus, I use: Anointed, God-born, Messiah, Rabbi, Redeemer, Savior, Son of Woman, Teacher, and Woman-Born. Son of Woman and Woman-Born both derive from the expressions previously and commonly translated as "son of man" (in the KJV) and more recently as "mortal" or "the human one" in translations like the NRSV and CEB. The underlying Greek expression, *huios tou anthropou*, means "son [male offspring] of a human" ("person of either sex" according to the standard authoritative BDAG lexicon); it also means "humankind" collectively. Whether one speaks or writes from a human, biological perspective or a theological one, the humanity of Jesus stems from his mother. Grammatically, Son of Woman and Woman-Born are both correct. Inasmuch as the generic "man" is no longer used to represent humanity in totality, an argument can be made that Son of Woman is more theologically correct. The expression *huios tou anthropou* is not *de novo* to the Second Testament; it occurs in the First Testament in both Hebrew as *ben adam* and the same Greek expression in the LXX. *Ben adam* means son (and generic child) of humanity. In the First Testament and deuterocanonical books, I use woman-born where there is a human title signifying mortality. In at least one occurrence, in a poetic text, I translate it as "children of earth and Eve," given that the root of *adam* is *adamah*, "earth" (soil).

There is a second list of divine titles for God (apart from Jesus) used in the Second Testament. Those names and titles are: Creator, Creator of All, Dread God, Faithful One, Father, Holy One, Living God, Majesty, (our) Maker, Most High, One Parent, Provider, Shepherd-Of-All, Sovereign, and Weaver (of lights). While I do preserve "Father" in some places, I employ it much less frequently than it occurs in the text. I reserve it for places where the parentage of Jesus is being addressed specifically. As it pertains to God's whereabouts and way of being in this world and the world beyond this one, I eschew "king" and "kingdom" in the *Lectionary*. As with all human attempts to describe God, monarchal language is inadequate; it is particularly unsuitable in that it stems from a rather brutal human system of governance that is unnecessary in the space where God is. Instead, I utilize "reign" and "realm" individually or in combination and "majesty." (The latter is feminine in Greek and functions as a divine title in Hebrews 1:3 and 8:1). When translating from the Hebrew Bible and deuterocanonical texts, I use "ruler" preferentially.

I take special care with translation choices for the Christian Testament because of the long history of anti-Judaism and anti-Semitism in biblical translation and interpretation and, in some cases, in the texts themselves. This lectionary intentionally excludes texts that blame Jews for the death of Jesus. The expression "the Jews" in Christian literature, including scripture, and in broader Christian discourse is very often negative. In the Greek New Testament, *Ioudaioi* can mean Jews, Judeans (people from Judea), or Jewish Christians in distinction from Gentile Christians. I use Judeans preferentially. In addition, because "scribes" can be easily misunderstood as simple copyists, I translate them as "biblical scholars" to make their underlying expertise more readily apparent.

Because scripture is read and heard and understood contextually, I am mindful of the ways in which the Scripture has been read and heard and understood in the broader Western and specifically American contexts. Across both testaments and the writings in between, slavery is ubiquitous, including on the lips of Jesus. While many translations use "servant" preferentially, I find that to be dishonest given that the persons so named were owned, controlled, raped, impregnated, bred, sold, maimed, and killed. Even when the bondage was of short *durée* or to pay off a debt, the lord and master had complete control of the subjugated person's body and sometimes retained their children after their liberation. So while it is certain to produce discomfort in the reader and hearer, I preserve "slave" and invite the reader and preacher to wrestle with that term and its influence on and in crafting and defending the American slavocracy. Minimizing the footprint of slavery in the scriptures weakens the link between them and subsequent slaveholding societies and the churches that unite them and us. Readers are welcome to replace the word "slave" with "servant," knowing that doing so writes over the degree to which the scriptures are slaveholding texts with no imagination of the possibility of abolition. I would encourage congregations to talk about that language and why they will or will not retain it.

Also, bearing in mind the American context in which these translations were produced and the related contexts in which they will be read, I chose to disrupt the traditional biblical language of light and white to mean good and dark and black to mean something negative or even evil. While there is no concept of race in the Hebrew Bible or Christian Testament, and people and nations are not assessed based on skin color and physical characteristics, that language has been mapped onto human bodies in the postbiblical world, justifying dehumanizing treatment, including slavery and legalized discrimination, including in the Church. Not all dark/black language in the biblical text is negative. Where it indicates something positive or holy, I retain it; for example, "God dwells in thick darkness" throughout the Scriptures.

As I move to complete Year C and make final edits to Year B, I return to my early definition of translation as "art and science," more specifically, as a "mysterious and nearly indefinable process, which is both art and science" and as *poiesis*,* creation. Creation in this sense means the creation of a new text in a new language out of the elements of the original text, its original language content and context/s and, out of the receiving language and context/s of the intended reader hearers (including the translator). I find translation to be a dance between all of these components. Language is not static; thus, translation is fluid—hence so many translations of the biblical text and other classic volumes and their revisions. What that means for this project is that successive iterations of individual passages may be revised between volumes and some small number were, challenging the recent (in millennial terms) insistence on a literal inflexible, unchanging text and singular interpretation for all time, common among evangelical and fundamentalist strains of Christianity that cast a long shadow. In these translations, I dance with the Spirit, following her lead, acknowledging that this dance is not the only dance; (indeed, I dance other dances in other projects).

In sum, the translations in the *Lectionary*:

- Identify original language and translation choices in accompanying text notes.
- Identify supplemental expansive translations with brackets.
- Expand people groups to make the presence of women and girls explicit.
- Use feminine and nonbinary pronouns for God in the Psalms.
- List genealogical information maternally.
- Use expansive descriptive language for the name of God instead of "Lord."
- Limit use of "Father" to texts addressing Jesus's parentage.
- Replace "kingdom" with "reign" and "realm" or with "majesty" (ruler is used preferentially in the Hebrew Bible).
- Use "Judeans" rather than "Jews" preferentially where appropriate.
- Maintain slave language rather than weaken or minimize with "servant."
- Modulate "dark/black" negative language as "shadow" and "bleak/ness."

It is my hope that this lectionary will enrich the experience of hearing and reading scripture and invite readers and hearers into deeper study of the scriptures, their

---

* *Poiesis* is Greek for creation out of some kind of starting material, particularly the creation of art, poetry, out of words. Contemporarily it is used to name the creation of blood cells out of material within the human body: hematopoiesis. I develop this concept in the appendix "A Note on Translating" in *Womanist Midrash: A Reintroduction to the Women of the Torah and of the Throne* (Louisville: Westminster/John Knox Press, 2017), 281–84.

translation, and interpretation. It is also my hope that liturgy, the work of the people in service to God, will be a place where all people can experience themselves as fully created in the image of God whose words they hear through the scriptures and in prayer and preaching.

THE LESSONS WITH COMMENTARY
Year C

ADVENT I

Zechariah 8:1–13; Psalm 46; 1 John 4:13–21; Luke 1:5–19

Zechariah 8:1 The word of the Sovereign of heaven's legions came to me, saying: ² Thus says the Commander of heaven's vanguard: I am jealous for Zion with great jealousy, and with great wrath am I jealous for her. ³ Thus says the Ruler of the multitudes of heaven: I will return to Zion and will dwell in the midst of Jerusalem, and Jerusalem shall be called "The Faithful City" and the mountain of the Sovereign of the vanguard of heaven shall be called "The Holy Mountain." ⁴ Thus says the Holy One of heaven's armies: Elder women and elder men shall again sit in the streets of Jerusalem, each with staff in hand because of their great age. ⁵ And the streets of the city shall be full of girls and boys playing in its streets.

⁶ Thus says the Majesty of the Heavens: Though it seems miraculous in the eyes of the remnant of this people in these days, should it also seem miraculous to me, says the Commander of winged warriors? ⁷ Thus says the Sovereign of heaven's legions: It is I who will save my people from the east land and from the west land. ⁸ Then I will bring them to dwell within Jerusalem; they shall be my people and I will be their God, in faithfulness and in righteousness.

⁹ Thus says the Commander of heaven's legions, "Strengthen your hands—you all who hear in these days these words from the mouths of the prophets, female and male, who were present when the foundation was laid for the rebuilding of the temple, the house of the Ruler of the Multitudes of Heaven. ¹⁰ For before those days the wages of human [labor] was nothing and of animal [labor, less]; as for those coming and going, there was no security from the enemy and I set every single person against their neighbor. ¹¹ Yet now I will not deal with the remnant of this people as in the former days, says the Sovereign of heaven's legions. ¹² For there shall be a sowing of peace: the vine shall yield its fruit, the earth shall yield its produce, and the heavens shall yield their dew; and I will inherit the remnant of this people with all these things. ¹³ And it will be that just as you have been a cursing among the nations, house of Judah and house of Israel, so it will be that when I save you all, you shall be a blessing. Fear not; strengthen your hands.

Psalm 46

¹ God is for us a refuge and strength,
 a help in trouble, easily found.
² Therefore we shall not fear, though the earth should change,
 though the mountains quiver in the heart of the sea;

3 its waters roar and churn,
   the mountains tremble with its swell.
4 There is a river whose streams make glad the city of God,
   the holy habitation of the Most High.
5 God is in the midst of her, she shall not be moved;
   God will help her when the morning unfurls.
6 The nations roar, dominions quiver;
   God puts forth her voice, the earth melts.
7 The Warrior Protectrix is with us;
   a stronghold for us is the God of Rebekah's line.
8 Come, behold the works of the Fire of Sinai;
   see what desolations she has set on the earth.
9 She makes wars cease to the end of the earth;
   she breaks the bow, and shatters the spear,
   she burns chariots with fire.
10 "Be still and know that I am God!
   I am exalted among the nations,
   I am exalted in the earth."
11 The Warrior Protectrix is with us;
   a stronghold for us is the God of Rebekah's line.

1 John 4:13 By this we know that we abide in God and God in us, because God has given us God's own Spirit. 14 And we have seen and so testify that the Father has sent the Son of God as the Savior of the world. 15 God abides in those who confess that Jesus is the Son of God, and they abide in God. 16 So we have known and have believed the love that God has for us.

God is love, and those who abide in love abide in God, and God abides in them. 17 Love has been perfected among us in order that we may have boldness on the day of judgment, because as God is, so are we in this world. 18 There is no fear in love, rather perfect love casts out fear, for fear relates to punishment, and whoever fears has not reached perfection in love. 19 We love because God first loved us. 20 If someone says, "I love God," and hates their sister or brother, they are a liar; for those who do not love a sister or brother whom they have seen, cannot love God whom they have not seen. 21 The commandment we have from God is this: those who love God must love their sisters and brothers also.

Luke 1:5 And it was in the days of Herod king of Judea, there was a priest named Zechariah, who belonged to the lineage of Abijah. His wife was a descendant of Aaron, and her name was Elizabeth. 6 Both of them were righteous before God, living according to all the commandments and righteous requirements of the Sovereign God blamelessly. 7 Now they had no child because Elizabeth was barren, and they both were advanced in age.

8 And it happened that when Zechariah was serving as priest and his order had the service before God, 9 according to the custom of the priesthood, he was chosen by lot to offer incense

and he entered the sanctuary of the Holy God. [10] The whole assembly of the people was praying outside at the time of the incense offering. [11] There appeared to Zechariah a messenger of the Living God, standing to the right of the altar of incense. [12] Now Zechariah was shaken when he saw the messenger and fear overwhelmed him. [13] But the messenger said to him, "Fear not, Zechariah, for your prayer has been heard. Your wife Elizabeth will give birth to a son for you, and you will call his name John. [14] You will have joy and gladness, and many at his birth will rejoice, [15] for he will be great in the sight of the Sovereign God. Wine and strong drink he must not drink. He will be filled with the Holy Spirit from his mother's womb. [16] He will turn many of the women and men of Israel to the Holy One their God. [17] He will go before the Holy God with the spirit and power of Elijah *to turn the hearts of parents to their children*, and the disobedient to the wisdom of the righteous, to prepare for the Redeeming God a people made ready." [18] Then Zechariah said to the messenger, "How shall I know this? For I am an old man and my woman is getting old herself." [19] The messenger answered him saying, "I am Gabriel. I stand before God and I have been sent to speak to you and to proclaim to you this good news."

PROCLAMATION
Text Notes

The title "Lord of Hosts" may be familiar, particularly from hymnody—"Lord Sabaoth" in *A Mighty Fortress*—but is not always understood. "Hosts," *tzavaoth*, is a measure of armed forces like a legion or battalion; God's celestial army is often portrayed as stars and other heavenly bodies. See Deuteronomy 4:19; 1 Kings 22:19; Nehemiah 9:6. The title is repeated in nearly every verse of the first lesson. As with "Lord," I translate the title in a variety of ways to limit repetition and facilitate theological imagination. A list of those names can be found in the appendix.

Zechariah 8:10 is quite awkward. Most literally, it is "wages (singular collective) of humankind there was not and of animalkind there was nothing."

The abundance of masculine actors (characters or gendered nouns) and masculine pronouns throughout the scriptures regularly makes identifying specific referents difficult. In 1 John 4:21, it is unclear whether the "he" who taught us is intended to be read as God or Jesus. Arguably, either is appropriate.

It may be important to note that Elizabeth was barren in spite of being blameless. To some, it will matter to hear that infertility and other undesired conditions are not punishments and cannot be reversed through increased piety.

In Luke 1:15, the Greek presents John's rule of life "from his mother's womb." Both the NRSV and CEB omit mother and womb and use "from before his birth." This is not only an erasure of Elizabeth, but it disembodies birth, very much at odds with the coming Incarnation. For this reason, I translate both Hebrew Greek verbs for childbirth as "to give birth" rather than "to bear." Lastly, the language around her seclusion is quite strong; "she hid herself," a potentially powerful sermon prompt.

Luke 1:17 quotes Malachi 4:5–6 (3:23–24, Hebrew): Look! I will send you all the prophet Elijah before the great and terrible day of the HOLY ONE OF OLD comes. ⁶ He will turn the hearts of parents to their children and the hearts of children to their parents, so that I will not come and strike the land with destruction. Sirach 48 is a paean of praise to Elijah and includes in verse 10 the turning of a parent's heart to their child as a result of Elijah's prophetic work. The expectation of the return of Elijah—perhaps via the same flaming heavenly chariot—to signal the beginning of this coming messianic age led to the reading of John the baptizer as the Elijah figure signifying the messianic age that began with the advent of Jesus. There is still some expectation of Elijah's return in some traditions of Judaism where the cup of Elijah, left for him at Passover seders, signifies the possibility of his return.

Preaching Prompts

"Fear not." These are the words that signal the advent of a new age. The first lesson ends, "Fear not. Strengthen your hands (for the work to come)." Because God is with us, in the psalm, we shall not fear. The author of the Epistle teaches that God is perfect love who casts out all fear from our lives, defining fear as guilt and expectation of punishment from which we have been delivered and saved and thus have no need to fear. A divine messenger from the throne of God bids the Zachariah of the Gospel reading, "Fear not." Something is coming. Someone is coming. It will be wondrous, and it will also be terrifying. God is at work in human bodies, in the bodies of women, building the families through which God's saving love will be known.

Today we have two Zachariahs. The first, the prophet, proclaims a God who will gather up the tattered remnants of her savaged people in the aftermath of their near destruction by their conquerors and oppressors. This ingathering of exiles culminates in a return to the holy space that had been desecrated then abandoned. This passage is also about the advent of renewal and restoration. The immediate change to their circumstances means persons of every gender, women, men, and those that fall between the poles of the binary, will be safe in public at every age. In the binary linguistic structure of the text, the verse could be read to also say that women and girls are safe in public from harassment and assault to the same degree that men have always been safe in public. The passage concludes with the prophet receiving the call and responsibility to facilitate intergenerational restoration and healing. To turn the hearts of each generation toward the other, using the language of parents and children. This is reiterated in the Gospel. The advent of the messianic age is a relational paradigm.

The psalm professes a powerful God with the cosmos at her fingertips. It comes from a time when the temple shone in splendor, and it was inconceivable that it, the city or the nation, could ever fall. Reading it with a post-conquest and post-fall (of Jerusalem) text makes the claim that God is unchanged, undiminished, undefeated.

By the time of the Epistle, the messianic age has begun with the advent of the totality of God's love knitted into human flesh, and we are called to live in that relational reality demonstrating it with our love. First John 4 makes clear that the treatment of women and girls is a fit metric for whether we individually or collectively love God. We cannot love God whom we have seen and hate (abuse, discriminate against) her children. This holds true for all marginalized populations.

In the Gospel, the story takes place in a family, in a community. There will be a familial relationship between Jesus and John, Mary and Elizabeth. There will also be a spiritual familial relationship between the disciples of John and the disciples of Jesus. John will inherit the prophetic mantle of Elijah and pick up his work turning the hearts of one generation toward the other and turning the hearts of human beings back to God. We are all called to turn to the love of God and be that love of God in relationship with those in our families and communities in a way that continues to reflect that love.

We are told to "fear not" and "strengthen our hands (for the work to come)." The work of living out the love of God in our relationships, in our families, in our congregation, in our communities, and in the world is an overwhelming call. To the fear that we cannot love the world into wholeness, God says, "Fear not." To the fear that we cannot eradicate patriarchy in the church, God says, "Fear not." To the fear that we cannot live in peace in the fullness of who we are, publicly and privately, God says, "Fear not."

ADVENT II

Isaiah 41:4–5, 8–10, 17–20; Psalm 27:4–5, 7–10, 13–14; 1 Peter 3:13–17; Luke 1:26–38

Isaiah 41:4 Who has worked and done this,

> calling the generations from the beginning?
> I, God Whose Name is Holy am the beginning
> and will be with the end; I am that one.

⁵ The coastlands seen and fear,
> the ends of the earth tremble;
> they have drawn near and come.

⁸ Now you, Israel [born of Rebekah], my slave,
> Jacob, who I choose, seed of [Sarah and] Abraham my dear friend;

⁹ who I snatched from the ends of the earth,
> and called from her farthest edges,
> saying to you, "You are my slave,
> you I chose and I will not reject you.

¹⁰ Fear not, for I am with you,
> be not afraid, for I am your God;
> I will strengthen you, truly will I help you,
> I will uphold you with my victorious right hand."

17 The poor and needy seek water and there is none,
   and their tongue is parched with thirst;
   I the God Who Provides will answer them,
   I the God of Israel will not forsake them.
18 I will open the bare heights, rivers,
   and in the midst of the valleys, fountains;
   I will situate the wilderness as a pool of water,
   and the dry land as springs of water.
19 I will put in the wilderness the cedar,
   the acacia, the myrtle, and the olive;
   I will place in the desert the cypress,
   the elm, and the box tree together.
20 So that they may see and know,
   may consider and comprehend,
   that the hand of the Mighty God has done this,
   the Holy One of Israel has created it.

Psalm 27: 4–5, 7–10, 13–14

4 One thing I asked of the Fount of Life,
   that [one thing] will I seek:
   to live in the house of the Womb of Life
   all the days of my life,
   to behold the beauty of the Wellspring of Life,
   and to inquire in her temple.
5 She will shield me in her shelter
   when the day is evil;
   she will cover me under the cover of her tent;
   she will raise me high on a rock.
7 Hear my cry, Faithful One, when I cry aloud,
   be gracious to me and answer me!
8 To you my heart says, "Seek my face!"
   Your face, Just One, do I seek.
9 Do not hide your face from me.
   Do not send your slave away in anger;
   you have been my help.
   Do not abandon me, do not forsake me,
   God of my salvation!
10 If my mother and father forsake me,
   the Compassionate God will gather me in.
13 If I but believe, I shall see the goodness of She Who is Faithful
   in the land of the living.

¹⁴ Wait for the LIVING GOD;
   be strong, and let your heart take courage;
   wait for GOD WHOSE NAME IS HOLY!

1 Peter 3:13 Now who will harm you if you all are zealots for good? ¹⁴ Yet if you suffer because of righteousness, you all are blessed: "Do not fear what they fear, and do not be intimidated." ¹⁵ Rather, "sanctify as Sovereign," Christ in your hearts. Always have ready a defense for anyone who asks from you an account for the hope that is in you. ¹⁶ Yet do so with gentleness and reverence, maintaining a good conscience, so that when you are maligned, they who abuse you for a good way of life in Christ may be put to shame. ¹⁷ For suffering for doing good is better, if suffering should be God's will, than to suffer for doing evil.

Luke 1:26 In the sixth month the angel Gabriel was sent by God to a town of Galilee, Nazareth, ²⁷ to a virgin betrothed to a man whose name was Joseph, of the house of David. And the name of the virgin was Mary. ²⁸ And the angel came to Mary and said, "Rejoice, favored one! The Most High God is with you." ²⁹ Now, she was troubled by the angel's words and pondered what sort of greeting this was. ³⁰ Then the angel said to her, "Fear not Mary, for you have found favor with God. ³¹ And now, you will conceive in your womb and give birth to a son, and you will name him Jesus. ³² He will be great and will be called the Son of the Most High, and the Sovereign God will give him the throne of his ancestor David. ³³ He will reign over the house of Jacob forever, and of his sovereignty there will be no end." ³⁴ Then Mary said to the angel, "How can this be, since I have not known a man intimately?" ³⁵ The angel said to her, "The Holy Spirit, She will come upon you, and the power of the Most High will overshadow you; therefore the one born will be holy. He will be called Son of God. ³⁶ And now, Elizabeth your kinswoman has even conceived a son in her old age, and this is the sixth month for she who was called barren. ³⁷ For nothing will be impossible with God." ³⁸ Then Mary said, "Here am I, the woman-slave of God; let it be with me according to your word." Then the angel left her.

PROCLAMATION

Text Notes

The specific identities of the trees in Isaiah 41:19 are unable to be clearly identified and vary across translation. This is true of all ancient flora and fauna to some degree.

Psalm 27:8 is often revised in translation to read seek "his" or "God's face" (see NRSV and CEB). However, it is sensible as is: the psalmist longs to be seen by God even as she seeks God's face.

Preaching Prompts

These lessons and the stories behind them offer a potent reminder that there was great risk in saying "yes" to God, choosing Christ as child or as the Crucified one. Elizabeth's blessing can be seen as words of protection. The psalm portrays God as a safe place to hide when the world and even members of one's family are against you. The Epistle calls us to bear witness to our faith no matter what may come, making clear that suffering, justified and unjustified, is the expected lot in life. In the Gospel, heaven and earth conspire to overturn the levers of power.

Elizabeth is from a religiously active family. She is named for the mother of the priesthood, Elisheba, whose descendants with Aaron are the only legitimate priests in Israel. Perhaps her closeness to the temple and its rituals facilitated the knowledge of scripture and ancestors she demonstrates in her blessings by drawing on the words of Deborah (to Ja'el) in Judges 5:24: "Most blessed of women . . . of tent-dwelling women most blessed." And those spoken in blessing to Judith (13:18), "O daughter, you are blessed by the Most High God above all other women on earth. . . ."

Mary and Judith are linked in those words of blessing, "among" and "above other" women in Luke 1:42. Both Judith and Mary have their virtue attested—Judith's piety as a widow (Judith 8:4–6) and Mary's virginity (Luke 1:26ff)—and both will use their bodies in scandalous ways to effect salvation. Judith entices an enemy general who seeks to seduce her—but with a maid present to testify to her virtue—and beheads the man with his own sword (Judith 13:4–10). Like her textual sisters, Jael's story is framed by scandal, assassinating an enemy general after welcoming him to hide; a man who was so well known as a rapist, his mother imagines his delay is caused by his proclivities (Judges 4:17–24; 5:24–30). His position at his death, between (not "at" per NRSV) Jael's legs, would seem confirmation.

The blessings of Jael and Judith, with their histories of violence, worry the apparent innocence of the annunciation with the reminder of the violence to which Mary is at risk now and the violence she will live to see enacted on the body of her son. In the words of another holy person, "a sword will pierce her soul" (Luke 2:35).

Mary agrees to the divine pregnancy, risking being ostracized and perhaps stoned for the appearance of breaking faith with Joseph. For some readers, there will always be a question of the degree to which Mary was free to refuse. That she affirmatively consents is clear: "Let it be with me according to your word." But could she refuse? Before she consents, Gabriel says: "You will. . . ." The timing is crucial, helping readers and hearers grapple with consent issues in the text and the gulfs between ancient and contemporary ethical standards.

Where Judith is an older widowed woman when she puts her body on the line to save her people, Mary, named for the prophet Miriam like all of the "Marys," was young and on the cusp of marriage. Each woman has her bona fides established in a lengthy genealogy. Judith's is the longest of any woman in the canon, stretching from the time of Nebuchadnezzar to Simeon, Leah's son by Jacob (Judith 8:1; 9:2), though some argue against her historicity. While Judith's husband is folded into *her* genealogy, "Her husband Manasseh, who belonged to her tribe and family," Mary's genealogy is *Joseph's* genealogy (in Matthew).

Returning to the Epistle, Mary's "yes" is why there is such a sure hope. It is that hope which sustains us in the world that is waiting for the return of Christ, the world in which suffering endures.

ADVENT III

Isaiah 12:1–6; Psalm 118:1–9; 14–21;
Revelation 1:4–6, 8, 12–18; Luke 1:39–45

Isaiah 12:1 You will say in that day,

"I will give thanks to you, REDEEMING ONE,
for though you were angry with me,
your anger turned away,
then you comforted me.

2 Behold! God is my salvation;
I will trust and I will not fear,
for Yah [She Who Is] GOD is my strength and my might
and has become my salvation."

3 Then you all shall with joy draw water from the wells of salvation.

4 And you all shall say in that day,
"Give thanks to the GOD OF OUR SALVATION,
call on God's Name;
acclaim God's deeds among the nations;
make known that God's Name is exalted."

5 Sing praises to the MIGHTY GOD, who has done gloriously;
let this be made known in all the earth.

6 Shout [daughter]! Sing [daughter]! [Daughter,] you who dwell in Zion!
For great in your midst [daughter] is the Holy One of Israel!

Psalm 118:1–9; 14–21

1 Give thanks to the ANCIENT OF DAYS who is good;
God's faithful love is everlasting!

2 Let the children of Rachel, Leah, Bilhah, and Zilpah say,
"God's faithful love is everlasting!"

3 Let the house of Elisheba's descendants say,
"God's faithful love is everlasting!"

4 Let those who revere the FIRE OF SINAI say,
"God's faithful love is everlasting!"

5 Out of my distress I called on YAH, THE ARK OF SAFETY;
the FAITHFUL GOD answered me and set me in a broad place.

⁶ With the Dread God on my side I do not fear.
   What can the children of earth and Eve do to me?
⁷ The Fearsome God is for me, to help me;
   I shall look [down] upon those who hate me.
⁸ Better is it to shelter in the Saving God
   than to trust in the woman-born.
⁹ Better is it to shelter in the Saving God
   than to trust in the high-born.
¹⁴ The Mighty God is my strength and my might
   and has become my salvation.
¹⁵ The sound of song and of salvation is in the tents of the righteous:
   "The right hand of the Most High is mighty;
¹⁶ the right hand of the Mighty God is exalted;
   the right hand of the Most High is mighty."
¹⁷ I shall not die, but I shall live,
   and recount the deeds of the Ancient Of Days.
¹⁸ The Merciful God has punished me severely,
   but to death did not hand me over.
¹⁹ Open to me the gates of righteousness,
   that I may enter through them
   and give thanks to the Fount of Justice.
²⁰ This is the gate of the Living God;
   the righteous shall enter through it.
²¹ I thank you for you have answered me
   and have become my salvation.

Revelation 1:4 John to the seven churches that are in Asia: Grace to you all and peace from the One who is and who was and who is to come, and from the seven spirits who are before God's throne, ⁵ and from Jesus Christ, the faithful witness, the firstborn of the dead, and the ruler of those who reign on the earth.

To Jesus who loves us and freed us from our sins by his blood ⁶ and made us to reign, priests serving his God and Father, to Christ be glory and power forever and ever. Amen.

⁸ "I am the Alpha and the Omega," says the Sovereign God, "who is and who was and who is to come, the Almighty."

¹² And I turned to see whose voice spoke with me and turning, I saw seven golden lampstands. ¹³ And in the midst of the lampstands I saw one like the Son of Woman, wearing a robe (down to the feet) and with a golden sash wrapped around their chest. ¹⁴ Their head and hair were white as wool, white as snow and their eyes were like a flame of fire. ¹⁵ Their feet were like fine bronze, like that refined in a furnace, and their voice was like the sound of many waters. ¹⁶ And they had in their right hand seven stars and from their mouth a sharp two-edged sword came and their face was like the sun shining with all its power.

[17] Now when I saw [the one like the Son of Woman], I fell at their feet as dead. Then they placed their right hand on me, saying, "Fear not; I am the First and the Last [18] and the Living One. I was dead, and look! I am alive forever and ever! And I have the keys of Death and of Hades."

Luke 1:39 Mary set out in those days and went to the hill country with haste, to a Judean town. [40] There she entered the house of Zechariah and greeted Elizabeth. [41] Now when Elizabeth heard Mary's greeting, the baby leaped in her womb and Elizabeth was filled with the Holy Spirit. [42] Elizabeth exclaimed with a loud cry, "Blessed are you among women, and blessed is the fruit of your womb. [43] From where does this [visit] come to me? That the mother of my Sovereign comes to me? [44] Look! As soon as I heard the sound of your greeting in my ear, the baby in my womb leaped for joy. [45] Now blessed is she who believed that there would be a fulfillment of those things spoken to her by the Holy One."

PROCLAMATION

Text Notes

"Yah" (as in "hallelujah/hallelu-yah") is, according to grammatical form, feminine, though it takes masculine verbs in biblical Hebrew and successive literature. In some contemporary Jewish feminist practices and prayer, it is used as a feminine name for God, with the grammar modified accordingly. It is also the first syllable of the unpronounceable divine name, the Tetragrammaton, YHWH, which, when translated, "I Am/Will Be who I Am/Will be"; there are no strictures on pronouncing the one syllable. In Isaiah 12:2, I offer a feminine reading option in brackets for those who so choose.

The grammar of the instructions in Isaiah 12:6 is second person feminine. I use "daughter" each place the feminine singular ending is used to enable the reader and hearer to experience the text as it was written.

In the psalm, "Let Israel say . . ." and "Let the house of Aaron say . . ." are replaced by female equivalents, the enslaved and free women who gave birth to the twelve tribal heads and Aaron's wife. Verse 5 combines "Yah" with the unpronounceable divine Name. In verse 6, I replace *adam*, meaning "humanity" (and including a reference to the soil of the earth, *adamah*), with "children of earth and Eve" to preserve the sense of the scope of humanity and the physical earth and its soil as well. "Woman-born" in verse 8 serves the same purpose.

In Revelation 1:5, the original language is "ruler of kings," a grammatical plural that would include female monarchs like Israel's own last sovereign before Roman rule, Salome Alexandra, also known as Shlomzion, the Peace of Zion. (Her sons' refusal to accept her rule—her husband passed the throne to her knowing their character—resulted in them drawing Rome into the dispute, Pompey on one side, Caesar on the other, leading to the installation of the Herods.) Likewise, "kingdom" is modified in verse 6, which has been translated as "a kingdom [and] priests" in the Vulgate, Wycliffe, RSV, NRSV, and CEB, and as "kings and priests" in Tyndale, Geneva,

Bishop, and KJV. And as is the rule in this lectionary, whenever Father is used to signify the parentage of Jesus, it is retained. *Kratos*, "power" in verse 6, is variably translated as "might," "strength," and "dominion." In verse 13, the name of the garment, *podere*, signifies its length to the feet and includes the root of the word for foot.

The one "like the Son of Woman" is, at some levels, recognizably human. But that one has transcended the limitations of the human body, including death; in so doing, that one has transcended the gender binary and continuum, indicated by the use of the pronouns they/them/their.

Preaching Prompts

In each lesson, there is trust in God for salvation from varying degrees of vulnerability and precarity. In each case, the bid or vow to fear not comes from a place of hope. Isaiah 12 offers, perhaps, the most profound statement of trust in God; set in the aftermath of the Assyrian devastation, the world as it had been known simply no longer exists. This is an example of what we say in the Black Church, "Don't wait till the battle is over; shout now." Verse 4 indicates that the day of salvation has not yet come, but the poet-prophet will praise and trust and hope anyway.

The psalm offers a liturgy for a festival day (traditionally associated with Passover). It articulates an intentional choice to celebrate at an appointed time, no matter the circumstances surrounding the people. The longer version acknowledges the danger that surrounds, but instead of bowing to fear, the community offers praise in the midst of the terror and violence that surround them.

The apocalyptic writer is in extreme danger and thus writes in code. The divine one comes to him in a form that can be apprehended by the human mind and its eyes. The one who radiates like the sun has hair like white wool, and has feet made of the most finely refined bronze, eviscerates fear and any imagined reason to fear, having transcended death and holding the keys to Death and Hades.

In the Gospel, Elisabeth and Mary are heirs to the promises in Isaiah, and in the psalm, the hope of salvation no matter the threat of their current circumstances, personally or politically. On the one hand, there is much to fear in their world: abandonment in the wake of a disreputable pregnancy, pregnancy complications, death, and the encroaching power of the empire, which includes police harassment and brutality, and physical and sexual violence. On the other hand, there is a hope for salvation that is more than hope. Their story is the story of their people, the people who have been delivered and redeemed from oppressors in the past. They know that God can, and hope that God will, do it again.

As advent lessons, these readings provide space for the preacher, readers, and hearers to articulate what is the hope of advent in this world and how that hope may be a buffer against the very real fears of the present age. It is also an opportunity to talk about the vulnerability of women in systems of power and times of turmoil and change. And when miraculous pregnancies are celebrated, acknowledging the painful reality often found outside of the text—an opportunity for social action and education around pregnancy complications and maternal mortality.

ADVENT IV

Exodus 20:1–21; Psalm 91; Romans 8:14–25; Luke 1:46–56

Exodus 20:1 Now God declared all these declarations:
² I am the HOLY ONE your God, who brought you out of the land of Egypt, out of the house of slaves. ³ There shall be no other gods for you in my face.
⁴ You shall not make for yourself an idol of any form that is in the heavens on high, or that is on the earth below, or that is in the waters under the earth. ⁵ You shall not bow down to them or serve them: I the THUNDER OF SINAI your God am a jealous God, visiting the iniquity of parents upon children to the third and the fourth [generation] of those who hate me. ⁶ And faithfully loving to the thousandth [generation] of those who love me and keep my commandments.
⁷ You shall not lift up as a trifling thing the Name of the MAJESTY OF THE AGES your God, for the JUDGE OF ALL FLESH will not acquit anyone who lifts up as a trifling thing the Name of the FIRE OF SINAI.
⁸ Remember the sabbath day and keep it holy. ⁹ Six days shall you labor and do all your work. ¹⁰ Now the seventh day is a sabbath to the WOMB OF CREATION your God; you shall not do any work—you, your daughter or your son, your female slave or your male slave, your livestock or the or your immigrant [neighbor] in your towns. ¹¹ For in six days the CREATOR OF ALL made the heavens and the earth and the sea and all that is in them; and God rested the on the seventh day; therefore the EVER-LIVING GOD blessed the sabbath day and consecrated it.
¹² Honor your mother and your father, so that your days may be long in the land that the FAITHFUL ONE your God is giving you.
¹³ You shall not murder.
¹⁴ You shall not commit adultery.
¹⁵ You shall not steal.
¹⁶ You shall testify against your neighbor [as] a lying witness.
¹⁷ You shall not covet your neighbor's house; you shall not covet your neighbor's woman, or female slave or male slave, or ox, or donkey, or anything that is your neighbor's.
¹⁸ When all the women, children, and men saw the thunder and the lightning—and the sound of the trumpet!—and the mountain smoking, the people were afraid and they trembled, and they stood far off. ¹⁹ And the people said to Moses, "You speak to us, and we will listen, yet do not let God speak to us or we shall die." ²⁰ Then Moses said to the people, "Fear not for it is only to test you that God has come, and for the sake that the fear of God would be upon you all so that you do not sin." ²¹ Then the women, children, and men stood far off while Moses drew near to the thick darkness where God was.

Psalm 91

1 She who settles in the shelter of the Most High,
   who stays in the shadow of Shaddai [at her breast]:
2 She will say to the SHELTERING GOD,
   "My refuge and my stronghold; my God, in her I trust."
3 For she will deliver you from the snare of the huntress
   and from the devastating pestilence.
4 She will cover you with her pinions,
   and under her wings shall you find refuge;
   a shield and buckler are her faithfulness.
5 You shall not fear the terror of night,
   or the arrow that flies by day;
6 nor even the pestilence that stalks in darkness,
   or the destruction that ravages at noonday.
7 A thousand may fall at your side,
   and ten thousand at your right hand,
   yet near you, it shall not approach.
8 Only glance with your eyes
   and see the punishment of the wicked.
9 For you, the SAVING GOD is your refuge,
   the Most High, your habitation.
10 No evil shall befall you,
   no plague come near your tent.
11 For her angels will she command for you,
   to keep you in all your ways.
12 On their hands shall they carry you,
   lest you strike your foot against a stone.
13 On the lion and the adder shall you tread;
   you will trample the young lion and the serpent.
14 For she who is bound to me, I will deliver her;
   I will exalt her, for she knows my Name.
15 When she calls me, I will answer her.
   I will be with her in trouble;
   I will rescue her and honor her.
16 With long life shall I satisfy her,
   and show her my salvation.

Romans 8:14 Now as many as are led by the Spirit of God are daughters and sons of God. 15 For you all did not receive a spirit of slavery to fall again into fear, but you have received a spirit of adoption through which we cry, "Abba! Father!" 16 It is that same Spirit who bears witness with our spirit that we are daughters and sons of God. [17] And if daughters and sons, then heirs, heirs of God and heirs with Christ, if it is true that we suffer with Christ so that we may also be glorified with Christ.

[18] I consider that the sufferings of this present time are not worth comparing with the glory about to be revealed to us. [19] For the creation waits with eager longing for the revealing of the daughters and sons of God; [20] for the creation was subjected to futility, not of its own will but by the will of the one who subjected it, in hope [21] that the creation itself will be set free from its bondage to decay and will obtain the freedom of the glory of the daughters and sons of God. [22] We know that the whole creation has been groaning in labor pains until now; [23] and not only the creation, but we ourselves, who have the first fruits of the Spirit, groan inwardly while we wait for adoption, the redemption of our bodies. [24] For in hope we were saved. Now hope that is seen is not hope. For who hopes for what is seen? [25] But if we hope for what we do not see, we wait for it with patience.

Luke 1:46 "My soul magnifies the Holy One,
- [47] and my spirit rejoices in God my Savior,
- [48] for God has looked with favor on the lowliness of God's own womb-slave.
  Surely, from now on all generations will call me blessed;
- [49] for the Mighty One has done great things for me,
  and holy is God's name.
- [50] God's loving-kindness is for those who fear God
  from generation to generation.
- [51] God has shown the strength of God's own arm;
  God has scattered the arrogant in the intent of their hearts.
- [52] God has brought down the powerful from their thrones,
  and lifted up the lowly;
- [53] God has filled the hungry with good things,
  and sent the rich away empty.
- [54] God has helped God's own child, Israel,
  a memorial to God's mercy,
- [55] just as God said to our mothers and fathers,
  to [Hagar and] and Sarah and Abraham, to their descendants forever."
- [56] And Mary remained with Elizabeth about three months and then returned to her home.

PROCLAMATION

Text Notes

Hebrew parallelism is often difficult to translate fully into English. There are often repeating words and sounds, such as "teachers teach" and "preachers preach." The opening line of Exodus 20 includes one such pair. God "spoke all these speakings." In verse 2, God brings the people out of the house of enslaved persons, not out of the house of the institution of slavery. The root for "slave" (vv. 2, 10, 17) is also the root for "serve" in verse 4 (Fox and JPS; it also means "worship" as in NRSV, CEB, and Alter). Neither "generation" nor any other noun is present after the counting in verses 5–6. The sojourner in verse 10 belongs to the Israelite community among whom they reside. The translation "resident alien" correctly establishes their residency but portrays them as "alien." The text is clear they are "your" sojourner or immigrant [neighbor]; they belong to the community.

The alliteration in this translation of this song is an artifact of English but adds a nice poetic touch. The choice to use explicitly feminine language for the one who prays and the one to whom prayer is directed mirrors and inverts the language of the text and its traditional translation in which God and the psalmist boutique masculine pronouns. I invite readers to pray the song reflecting on any perceived barriers in the use of feminine language as universal language.

In Psalm 91:1, the divine title "Shaddai" means "the Breasted one"; a *shad* is a woman's breast in Hebrew. The accompanying bracketed expression gives voice to this. In verse 14, the verb *ch-sh-q* means to love and be bound by desire, to cling to the beloved.

Preaching Prompts

Fear not! That is one of the messages of Advent and one on which all of the Advent lessons in Year C focus. These Advent readings conclude with the invitation of God to approach her in the holy darkness in which she resides, a terrifying prospect for mere mortals. That deep darkness is one of the primary metaphors of Advent. It is not in opposition to the light that has long been associated with Christ coming into the world. Rather, it is the source of that light. Light and dark are not antithetical, one good, one bad. That binary understanding does not represent the fullness of how light and dark are portrayed in the scriptures. It does represent a fundamental vehicle of white supremacy, the mapping of the binary understanding onto black, brown, peach, and beige bodies.

The psalm is a testimony to the faithfulness of God as a protector in a world that is regularly unpredictable and frightening. When read with the first lesson, it proclaims the safety of the reader/hearer under the wings of a God who restrains the majesty, power, and holiness of their presence among their people and has the ability to protect them from any danger that might arise from another source.

Paul is in danger yet considers the hope of what is to come, the hope of glory in Christ through the resurrection and the return of Christ for which we also long, for which this Advent is preparation; that hope is incomparable. And we are heirs to the promise in which he trusts, more than heirs, for we have been adopted into the family of God. And in the Gospel, a virginal expectant mother is defiant in her hope and fearlessness in a world that seemed designed to crush her as a woman, as a woman whose reproductive choices were at odds with the expectations of her people, as a woman living under occupation, as a Jewish woman in a world that was already hostile to the similarities of Jewish culture and religion.

We live in a world that can be equally frightening for women, ethnic and sexual minorities, immigrants, and gay and trans folk. Yet we have it within us to choose hope and fearlessness like our scriptural forebears. We wait for the same hope and trust in the same promise. And we have the same comfort: God is with us. Emmanuel. Soon come. Come, holy Jesus.

CHRISTMAS I

Isaiah 26:16–19; Psalm 68:4–11;
1 Thessalonians 4:13–18; Luke 2:1–14 or 2:1–20

Isaiah 26:16 HOLY ONE, in distress they sought you,
> they pressed out a whispered prayer
> when your chastening was on them.
17 Just as an expectant mother
> writhes-in-labor and cries out in her pangs
> when her birthing time is near;
> thus were we because of you, Holy One.
18 We too were expectant, we writhed-in-labor,
> but it was as though we birthed only wind.
> No victories have we won on earth,
> neither do the inhabitants of the world fall.
19 Your dead shall live; their corpses shall rise.
> Awake and sing for joy you who dwell in the dust!
> For your dew is a radiant dew,
> and the earth shall release those long dead.

Psalm 68:4–11

4 Sing to God, sing praises to her Name;
> exalt her who rides upon the clouds;
> HOLY is her Name, rejoice before her!

⁵ Mother of orphans and defender of widows,
   is God in her holy habitation!
⁶ God settles the solitary in a home bringing prisoners into prosperity;
   while the rebellious shall live in a wasteland.
⁷ God, when you marched before your people,
   when you moved out through the wilderness,
⁸ the earth shook, even the heavens poured down,
   at the presence of God, the One of Sinai,
   at the presence of God, the God of Israel.
⁹ Rain in abundance, God, you showered abroad;
   when your heritage grew weary you prepared rest.
¹⁰ Your creatures found a dwelling in her;
   God, you provided in your goodness for the oppressed.
¹¹ The Author of Life gave the word;
   the women who proclaim the good news are a great army.

1 Thessalonians 4:13 Now we do not want you to be ignorant, sisters and brothers, about those who have fallen asleep, so that you might not grieve as those do who have no hope. ¹⁴ For since we believe that Jesus died and rose, even so they who sleep, will God by Jesus, bring with him. ¹⁵ For this we declare to you by the word of the Most High God, that we who are alive, who remain until the coming of Jesus, will not precede those who have fallen asleep. ¹⁶ For Jesus himself, with a command, in the voice of the archangel and with the trumpet of God, will descend from heaven, and the dead in Christ will rise first. ¹⁷ Then we who are alive who are left, together with them, will be caught up in the clouds to meet Jesus in the air; and so we will be with Jesus forever. ¹⁸ Therefore comfort one another with these words.

Luke 2:1 Now it happened in those days that a decree went out from Caesar Augustus that all the world should be registered (for taxation). ² This was the first registration and occurred while Quirinius was governor of Syria. ³ So all went to be registered; each to their own towns. ⁴ Joseph also went up from Galilee, out of the city of Nazareth into Judea, to the city of David called Bethlehem, for he was from the house and heritage of David. ⁵ He went to be registered with Mary, to whom he was betrothed and who was pregnant. ⁶ So it was, that, while they were there, the time came for her to birth her child. ⁷ And she gave birth to her firstborn son and swaddled him, and laid him in a manger, because there was no place for them in the inn.

⁸ Shepherds were in that region there staying in the fields, keeping watch over their flock by night. ⁹ Then an angel of the Most High God came upon them, and the glory of the Living God shone around them, and they were greatly terrified. ¹⁰ But the angel said to them, "Fear not. Look! For I proclaim to you good news of great joy for all the people: ¹¹ For there is born to you this day a Savior who is the Messiah, the Sovereign God, in the city of David. ¹² This will be a sign for you: you will find a baby swaddled and lying in a manger." ¹³ And immediately there was with the angel a multitude of the heavenly array, praising God and saying,

[14] "Glory to God in the highest heaven,
and on earth peace among peoples whom God favors!"

[15] And it happened when the angels had departed from them into heaven, the shepherds said to one another, "Let us go now to Bethlehem and see this thing that has come to be, which the Sovereign God has made known to us." [16] So they came hurrying and found Mary and Joseph, and the baby lying in the manger. [17] Now seeing this, they made known what had been spoken to them about this child. [18] And all who heard marveled at what was spoken by the shepherds to them. [19] But Mary preserved all these words and pondered them in her heart. [20] The shepherds returned, glorifying and praising God for all they had heard and seen, it was just as it had been told them.

PROCLAMATION

Text Notes

The psalm portion ends with women proclaiming the good news of deliverance using the verbs that will come to mean "proclaim the gospel" in Hebrew and Greek (the LXX uses *euaggelizo*). Unfortunately, NRSV, RSV, CEB, and KJV obscure that this "company of preachers" is exclusively female.

The Epistle uses "Lord" repeatedly in such a way that it is not clear whether the author means God or Jesus. The translation above seeks to clarify the referents; however, the reader should be aware of the likely intentional ambiguity.

Preaching Prompts

The Hebrew Scriptures offer a variety of positions on life after death, including "sleep," to which all succumb, and none rise (see Job 14:10–12, 14). This unit of Isaiah uses the language of pregnancy and birth to speak of life beyond death. This first reading for Christmas brings images of a heavily pregnant woman in conversation with the heavily pregnant and laboring Virgin in the Gospel—though the text and tradition gloss over or minimalize her travail. The pregnant woman is the people who have not been able to deliver themselves or have someone to deliver them—rather than a deliverer, they have only produced wind. God is perhaps midwife here. Because of God's response to her people's prayers across the ages, the equally heavily pregnant earth will one day give birth to the dead.

In both the first lesson and psalm, there is water that renews and refreshes dry places. In the re-gendered psalm, God is the mother of orphans (fatherless children in Hebrew idiom), protector of widows, and provides homes (families) for the lonely. She is also sovereign of the skies, source of rain, and shepherd of her people. The women who functioned as town criers, proclaiming good news of victory in times of war, proclaim the good news of God's providence.

The Epistle takes up the theme of the dead rising and makes it a promise guaranteed by Jesus's own resurrection. Each of these texts, with its focus on birth, life, and life beyond, frames the Gospel and its presentation of the good news of Mary's child and the portents of his birth, which she pondered.

CHRISTMAS II

*Isaiah 66:10–13; Psalm 103:1–17;
1 Peter 1:22–2:3; Luke 2:15–20 or 2:1–20*

Isaiah 66:10 Rejoice with Jerusalem, and celebrate with her
  all you who love her;
  rejoice with her in joy,
  all who mourn deeply over her;
 ¹¹ in order that you all may nurse and be satisfied
  from her comforting breast;
  that you all may drink deeply and delight yourselves
  from the glory of her breast.
 ¹² For so says the Holy One of Old:
  Watch! I will extend to her flourishing like a river,
  and the wealth of the nations like an overflowing stream;
  and you all shall nurse and be carried on her arm,
  and you all shall be bounced on her knees.
 ¹³ As a mother comforts her child,
  so will I comfort you all;
  you all shall be comforted in Jerusalem.

Psalm 103:1–17

 ¹ Bless the FOUNT OF WISDOM, O my soul,
  and all that is within me, bless her holy Name.
 ² Bless the FOUNT OF WISDOM, O my soul,
  and forget not all her benefits.
 ³ She forgives all your sins
  and heals all your infirmities;
 ⁴ She redeems your life from the grave
  and crowns you with mercy and loving-kindness;
 ⁵ She satisfies you with good things,
  and your youth is renewed like an eagle's.
 ⁶ SHE WHO IS WISDOM executes righteousness
  and judgment for all who are oppressed.

7 She made her ways known to Miriam and Moses
    and her works to the children of Israel.
8 WISDOM's womb is full of love and faithfulness,
    slow to anger and overflowing with faithful love.
9 She will not always accuse us,
    nor will she keep her anger forever.
10 She has not dealt with us according to our sins,
    nor rewarded us according to our wickedness.
11 For as the heavens are high above the earth,
    so indomitable is her faithful love upon those who revere her.
12 As far as the east is from the west,
    so far has she removed our sins from us.
13 As a mother's love for her children flows from her womb,
    so too does WISDOM's love for those who revere her flow from her womb.
14 For she herself knows whereof we are made;
    She remembers that we are but dust.
15 Our days are like the grass;
    we flourish like a flower of the field;
16 When the wind goes over it, it is gone,
    and its place shall know it no more.
17 But the faithful love of SHE WHO IS WISDOM endures forever
    on those who revere her,
    and her righteousness on children's children.

1 Peter 1:22 Now that you have purified your souls by your obedience to the truth so that you have the love without pretense of children raised together; from a pure heart love one another persistently. 23 You have been born again, not of corruptible seed but of incorruptible seed through the living and enduring word of God. 24 For:

All flesh is like grass
and all its glory like the flower of grass.
The grass withers,
and the flower falls,
25 *but the word of the Living God abides forever.**

This is the word that was proclaimed to you as good news. *2:1* Lay aside, therefore, all malice, and all deceit, pretense, envy, and all slander. 2 Like newborn babies, long for the pure spiritual milk, so that by it you may grow into salvation—3 if you have tasted that the Sovereign God is good.

See Gospel Reading in Christmas I.

---

* Italicized text indicates First Testament quotations in the Second Testament.

PROCLAMATION

Text Notes

The poet responsible for Isaiah 66 seems to have reached beyond the Hebrew language for the expression "glory of her breast" in verse 11. The underlying expression "teat" or "udder" of glory may well have come from Akkadian and has an Arabic cognate (see the corresponding entry in the *Dictionary of Classical Hebrew*). In verse 12, "flourishing" is a better, less-materialistic reading of *shalom* than "prosperity."

The one comforted by their mother in Isaiah 66:13 is a man; the grammar of his passive comforting relegates his mother to the end of the sentence and makes him the focus: "As a man is comforted by his mother. . . ." Common convention (JPS, NRSV, CEB) inverts the sentence, "As a mother comforts. . . ." Mother-love in Psalm 103:13 is attributed to a father: "As a father mother-loves his children" (using the verbal form of the noun "womb"). The verse could be translated: "As a father loves his children with a mother's love. . . ." As with Isaiah 66, the maternal image, here womb-love, is also attributed to God.

First Peter 1:22 uses *philadelphia*, sibling-love, where I have translated "children raised together" rather than "sisters and brothers" to avoid excluding reader-hearers who do not identify with a binary understanding of gender. The divine mother's milk is described as "spiritual," a somewhat elliptical rendering of *logikos*, which has to do with "carefully thought through, thoughtful" deliberations, particularly in religious contexts. It also connotes "spiritual" in contrast with "literal." (See the corresponding entry in *A Greek-English Lexicon of the New Testament and Other Early Christian Literature* [known as BDAG for its authors].)

Preaching Prompts

These Christmas lessons center an image rarely proffered in liturgy or preaching but common in art and culture, the nursing mother as an icon of love. In Isaiah 66:11, Jerusalem is the nursing mother with abundant "comforting" breasts that are her "glory." (In the CEB, she is full-breasted). In Psalm 103, God's love is womb-love suggesting but not articulating an accompanying abundance of breastmilk (vv. 8, 13). In 1 Peter 2:2–3, God's children are to long for the Gospel as babies long for milk and at the breast of God, "taste and see that God is good"—offering a new way to hear that very common refrain. In Luke 2, the newly delivered Virgin Mother nurses her holy child through the visits of mortals and angels without notice in the text.

In Isaiah 66:13, the poet-prophet uses the image of a mother—clearly nursing in light of the earlier verses—as an image of God. This intersects in interesting ways with the parental image in the Psalms; mother-love of human and divine parents in verses 8 and 13 provides the lexicon for divine imagery. Even with some masculine grammatical language in the texts, the dominant divine images are feminine, rooted in birthing, nursing, and mothering, a reversal of the more common dominant masculine and male imagery. Similarly, the Gospel presents a woman-born Sovereign God swaddled in human flesh, nourished at his mother's breast. Of all the changes that the Christmas miracle births into the world, the ability to experience and name God more richly can be easily neglected.

The imagery of pregnancy, birthing, nursing, and mothering is integral to the Christmas story. It is also the primary trope for women in the scriptures, often reducing them to one dimension. It is not, however, the universal experience of women, and biblical portrayals of women can be painful for those who cannot mother, were not mothered, or were poorly mothered. These images can also be frustrating for those who choose not to mother.

CHRISTMAS III

Wisdom 9:1–6, 9–11; Psalm 33:1–9; Colossians 1:15–20; John 1:1–14

Wisdom 9:1 "O God of my ancestors and Author of mercy,
   who have made all things by your word,
² and by your wisdom have formed humankind
   to govern the creatures you have made,
³ and oversee the world in holiness and righteousness,
   and renders judgment as the soul of righteousness:
⁴ Give me the wisdom that sits by your throne,
   and do not reject me from among your children.
⁵ For I am your slave, the child of your slave girl,
   one who is weak and short-lived,
   with little understanding of judgment and laws;
⁶ for even one who is perfect among human beings
   will be regarded as nothing without the wisdom that comes from you.
⁹ With you is Wisdom, she who knows your works
   and was present when you made the world;
   she knows what is pleasing in your sight
   and what is right according to your commandments.
¹⁰ Send her forth from the holy heavens,
   and from your throne of glory send her,
   that she may labor with me,
   and that I may learn what is pleasing to you.
¹¹ For she knows and understands all things,
   and she will guide me wisely in my actions
   and guard me with her glory.

Psalm 33:1–9

1. Rejoice in the ALMIGHTY, you righteous;
   it is good for the just to sing praises.
2. Praise SHE WHO IS MAJESTY with the harp;
   play to her upon the psaltery and lyre.
3. Sing for her a new song;
   sound a fanfare with all your skill upon the trumpet.
4. For the word of WISDOM is right,
   and all her works are sure.
5. She loves righteousness and justice;
   the faithful love of the MOTHER OF ALL fills the whole earth.
6. By the word of WISDOM were the heavens made,
   by the breath of her mouth all the heavenly hosts.
7. She gathers up the waters of the ocean as in a water-skin
   and stores up the depths of the sea.
8. Let all the earth revere SHE WHO IS WISDOM;
   let all who dwell in the world stand in awe of her.
9. For she spoke, and it came to pass;
   She commanded, and it stood fast.

Colossians 1:15 Jesus is the image of the invisible God, the firstborn of all creation; 16 for in him all things in the heavens and on earth were created, things visible and invisible, whether thrones or dominions or rulers or powers—all things have been created through him and for him. 17 Jesus himself is before all things, and in him all things hold together. 18 Jesus is the head of the body, the church; he is the beginning, the firstborn from the dead, so that he might come to have preeminence in everything. 19 For in Jesus all the fullness of God was well pleased to dwell, 20 and through Jesus God was well pleased to reconcile to Godself all things, whether on earth or in heaven, by making peace through the blood of his cross.

John 1:1 In the beginning was the Word, and the Word was with God, and the Word was God. 2 The Word was with God in the beginning. 3 Everything came into being through the Word, and without the Word not one thing came into being that came into being. What has come into being 4 in the Word was life, and that life was the light of all people. 5 The light shines in the bleakness, and the bleakness did not overtake it.

6 There was a man sent from God, whose name was John. 7 He came as a witness to testify to the light, so that all might believe through him. 8 He himself was not the light, but he came to testify to the light. 9 The true light, which enlightens everyone, was coming into the world.

10 He was in the world, and the world was created through him; yet the world did not know him. 11 To his own he came and his own did not receive him. 12 But to all who did

accept him, who believed in his name, he empowered to become children of God—¹³ that is, those who were born, not of blood or of the will of the flesh or of the will of a human person, but of God.

¹⁴ And the Word became flesh and lived among us, and we have seen his glory, glory as of a parent's only child, full of grace and truth.

PROCLAMATION

Text Notes

The Greek word *pais* used in Wisdom 9:4 means both child and enslaved person. I choose the easier reading here and preserve the slave language in the following verse, where two different words for an enslaved person occur.

Colossians uses the masculine pronoun repeatedly and does not include the name of Jesus in the Greek text. I have substituted it for some of the pronouns for smoothness and clarity.

Preaching Prompts

Today's Christmas readings focus on Wisdom and the Word. Both are invoked in the creation of the world; Wisdom in Wisdom 9:2 and Psalm 33:6, and the Word in John 1:1–2. Jesus is the word incarnate, unnamed in the Gospel portion. The Colossians reading names Jesus explicitly and links him to the creation of the world. This Sunday has traditionally focused on the preexistent Christ of John's Gospel, a concept expressed in grammatical gender (masculine for the Word and feminine for Wisdom in a similar portrayal), but ontologically beyond gender. These lessons present an opportunity to think about why we and our spiritual ancestors, in our languages and theirs, gender things the way we do and what that really means.

The Wisdom reading also offers an opportunity to discuss the ubiquity of slavery in the biblical world and text. The scriptures use the language of slavery as more than a metaphor. Its normalcy is something with which we must contend. Many translations soften slave language to "servant." That seems dishonest given the total control—physical, sexual, reproductive, financial—over the lives and bodies of the persons at stake. Yet it is hard to use slave language in scripture, prayer, and liturgy; doubly so for Black folk.

FIRST SUNDAY AFTER CHRISTMAS

1 Kings 8:12–13, 27–30, 41–43; Psalm 68:15–17, 19–20, 24–27, 31–35;
Revelation 22:10, 22–27; Luke 2:41–51

1 Kings 8:12 Now Solomon [son of Bathsheba] said,

"The Majesty of the Heavens said that God would dwell in thick darkness."

¹³ I have built an exalted house for you, a place for you to dwell for all time.

²⁷ "Yet truly, will God indeed dwell upon the earth? The heavens and the heavens beyond the heavens cannot contain you, much less this house that I have built. ²⁸ Incline toward the prayer of your slave and his supplication, Holy One of Old my God, heeding the cry and the prayer that your slave prays to you today. ²⁹ That your eyes may be open toward this house night and day, toward the place of which you said, 'My Name shall be there,' that you may heed the prayer that your slave prays toward this place. ³⁰ Hear the supplication of your slave and of your people Israel when they pray toward this place; hear in your dwelling place the heavens; hear and forgive.

⁴¹ And also, as for a foreigner who is not of your people Israel and comes from a distant land because of your Name ⁴²—for they shall hear of your great Name, your mighty hand, and your outstretched arm—when a foreigner comes and prays toward this house, ⁴³ hear then in the heavens, your dwelling place, and do according to all that the foreigner calls to you, so that all the peoples of the earth may know your Name and revere you, as do your people Israel, and so that they may know that your Name has been invoked upon this house that I have built.

Psalm 68:15–17, 19–20, 24–27, 31–35

¹⁵ Mountain of God, mountain of Bashan;
  Mountain of many peaks, mountain of Bashan.
¹⁶ Why do you look with envy, many-peakéd mountains,
  at the mountain that God desired for her abode?
  Indeed, the Mother of the mountains will dwell there for all time.
¹⁷ God's chariot corps is ten thousand doubled, and doubled again,
  the Sovereign is in their midst, [as at] Sinai, in holiness.
¹⁹ Blessed be She who bears us up day by day,
  the God of our salvation.
²⁰ Our God is the God of salvation;
  The Source of Life is God, to whom belongs escape from death.
²⁴ They see your processions, God,
  the processions of my God and my Sovereign into the holy place.
²⁵ Before go singers, after, musicians follow,
  in between them young women drum.
²⁶ In great congregations bless God;

bless THE SOURCE OF LIFE, from the fountain of Israel.
27 There is [Rachel-born] Benjamin, the little one, ruling;
then the sons of the royal women of Judah in their crowd;
with royal mothers' sons from Zebulon and Naphtali.
31 Let tribute be brought out of Egypt;
let Nubia stretch out her hands to God.
32 Sing to God, dominions of the earth;
sing praises to SHE WHO IS WORTHY.
33 To the one who rides in the heavens beyond the heavens from before time.
Attend! God gives voice to thunder, a mighty voice.
34 Ascribe power to God!
Upon Israel is her majesty,
and her power is in the skies.
35 Awesome is God,
from your sanctuary, God of Israel:
She gives power and strength to her people.
Blessed be God!

Revelation 21:10 Now the angel carried me away in the spirit to a great, high mountain and showed me the holy city Jerusalem coming down from the heavens, from God. 22 I saw no temple in the city, for the Sovereign God, the Almighty with the Lamb is its temple. 23 And the city has no use of sun or moon to shine in it, for the glory of God is its light, and its lamp is the Lamb. 24 And the nations will walk by its light and the queens and kings of the earth will bring their glory into it. 25 And its gates will not be shut by day and there will be no night there. 26 Women, children, and men will bring into it the glory and the honor of the nations. 27 Now there shall not enter it anything unclean or anyone who does what is detestable or untrue, but only those who are written in the Lamb's book of life.

Luke 2:41 Now, the parents of Jesus went yearly to Jerusalem for the festival of Passover. 42 And when he was twelve years old, they went up as customary for the festival. 43 And when the days of the festival were completed, they returned while the boy Jesus stayed in Jerusalem, and his parents did not know it. 44 Thinking he was in the group of travelers, they went a day's journey and then they started to look for him among their kin and those who knew him. 45 And when they did not find him, they returned to Jerusalem to search for him. 46 Then after three days passed they found him in the temple, sitting among the teachers, listening to them and asking them questions. 47 And all who heard him were amazed at his understanding and his answers. 48 Then when his parents saw him, they were shocked and his mother said to him, "Child, why have you treated us thus? Look! Your father and I have been tormented in searching for you." 49 Then Jesus said to them, "Why were you searching for me? Did you not know that I must be in the house of my Abba?" 50 And they did not understand the thing he said to them. 51 And then, he went down with them and came to Nazareth and was subject to them. And his mother treasured all these things in her heart.

PROCLAMATION

Text Notes

Araphel, thick darkness, is the traditional abode and familiar companion of God, see Deuteronomy 4:11 (NRSV omits its translation), 2 Samuel 22:10, Psalm 18:9, Psalm 97:2, and Job 38:9.

Bashan in the psalm invokes Israel's legendary victory of King Og in the wilderness and the transfer of his verdant trans-Jordan land (oft associated with cattle, see Deuteronomy 32:14) to the Manassites, Deuteronomy 3:14; 4:43, 47; 29:7. The reference dramatizes God's victory by God taking up residence in the home of the now deposed God of the region.

The singers and musicians in Psalm 68:25 could have been a mixed-gender group; the hand-drum, often mistranslated as a tambourine (or timbrel), was solely a woman's instrument. In verse 27, I offer the option of naming Benjamin in the line of Rachel (which connects with the Gospel) and have replaced "princes" with the "sons of the royal women/mothers."

In Revelation 21:26, those who bring glory are unidentified; the subject is included in the verb, inclusive plural. When cities or nations offered tribute in hospitality or conquest, representatives from each section of the populace often participated. The choice of "women, children, and men" rather than the "people" of the NRSV or "they" in the CEB make the population of heaven visible.

Preaching Prompts

Where does God live? These lessons offer a panoply of views found throughout the scriptures to hold in conversation with the Christmastide promise of Immanu-El, God with us. If we take the promise of Immanu-El seriously, we must ask what that means in our world. Is there evidence that God is with us—if we are not US citizens, middle class or upward, white, cis-sexual, heterosexual, or able-bodied? Liberation theologians have long proclaimed that God has a preferential option for the poor. Have our professions become a theological romance of poverty? What does it mean to say God dwells with us? What does it require of us? And what shall we do about it once the Twelve Days of Christmas are past?

FEAST OF THE HOLY NAME, JANUARY 1

Isaiah 7:3–16; Psalm 89:1–8, 14; Philippians 2:5–11; Luke 2:15–21

Isaiah 7:3 The HOLY ONE said to Isaiah, "Go out now to meet Ahaz, you and She'ar-jashub your son, at the end of the conduit of the upper pool on the highway to the Fuller's Field, ⁴ and say to him, 'Watch, hush, and fear not, and let not your heart faint on account of these two smoldering stumps of firebrands, because of the rage of Rezin and Aram or the son of Remaliah.' ⁵ For indeed, Aram has plotted evil against you—with Ephraim and the son of Remaliah—saying, ⁶ 'Let us go up against Judah and cut off Jerusalem and conquer it for ourselves and make the son of Tabeel king in it'; ⁷ therefore thus says the Sovereign GOD:

'It shall not stand,
and it shall not come to pass.
⁸ For the head of Aram is Damascus,
and the head of Damascus is Rezin.'

(In about sixty-five years, Ephraim will be shattered, no longer a people.)

⁹ 'The head of Ephraim is Samaria,
and the head of Samaria is the son of Remaliah.
If you do not stand firm in faith,
you shall not stand firm at all.'"

¹⁰ Again the HOLY ONE spoke to Ahaz, saying, ¹¹ "Ask a sign of the HOLY ONE your God; from the deep of Sheol or the height of what lies above." ¹² Yet Ahaz said, "I will not ask, and I will not test the HOLY ONE." ¹³ Then Isaiah said, "Hear now, House of David! Is it not enough that you exhaust mortals, that you must exhaust my God also? ¹⁴ Therefore the self-same Creator will give you a sign. See, the young woman is pregnant, and she shall give birth to a son, and she shall name him Immanu-El. ¹⁵ He shall eat curds and honey when he knows how to refuse the evil and choose the good. ¹⁶ For before the child knows how to refuse the evil and choose the good, the land before whose two kings you dread will be deserted.

Psalm 89:1–8, 14

¹ I will sing of the faithful love of the FOUNT OF LIFE forever;
with my mouth I will make known your faithfulness from across the generations.
² When I declare that your faithful love is established forever;
your faithfulness is established in the heavens,
³ [you responded,] "I have inscribed a covenant with my chosen one;
I have sworn an oath to the descendants of Bathsheba:
⁴ 'I will establish your line forever,
your throne that I will build, will be to all generations.'"
⁵ The heavens confess your wonders, O WOMB OF CREATION,

and to your faithfulness in the congregation of the holy ones;
⁶ For who in the skies can be compared to the Womb of Life?
who is like the Mother of All among the children of the gods?
⁷ a dread God in the council of the holy ones,
great and terrible above all who surround her.
⁸ Warrior Protectrix, who is mighty like you?
You Who Are, your faithfulness surrounds you.
¹⁴ Righteousness and justice are the foundations of your throne;
enduring love and faithfulness go before your face.

Philippians 2:5 Let the same mind be in you all that was in Christ Jesus,

⁶ who, though he was in the form of God,
did not regard equality with God
as something to be seized,
⁷ but emptied himself,
taking the form of a slave,
being born in human likeness;
then being found in human form,
⁸ he humbled himself
and became obedient to the point of death,
even death on a cross.
⁹ Therefore God also highly exalted Jesus
and gave him the name
that is above every name,
¹⁰ so that at the name of Jesus
every heavenly and earthly knee should bend,
along with those under the earth,
¹¹ and every tongue should confess
that Jesus Christ is Savior,
to the glory of God the Sovereign.

Luke 2:15 And it happened when the angels had departed from them into heaven, the shepherds said to one another, "Let us go now to Bethlehem and see this thing that has come to be, which the Sovereign God has made known to us." ¹⁶ So they came hurrying and found Mary and Joseph, and the baby lying in the manger. ¹⁷ Now seeing this, they made known what had been spoken to them about this child. ¹⁸ And all who heard marveled at what was spoken by the shepherds to them. ¹⁹ But Mary preserved all these words and pondered them in her heart. ²⁰ The shepherds returned, glorifying and praising God for all they had heard and seen; it was just as it had been told them.

²¹ After eight days had passed, it was time to circumcise the child; and he was called Jesus, his name was the name given by the angel before he was conceived in the womb.

PROCLAMATION

Text Notes

Isaiah's son's name means "a remnant will survive." He is a prophetic sign in the text. The stem that means "cut off" in Isaiah 7:6 also means "terrorize." Hebrew hearers would have recognized both meanings. The young woman, an *almah*, in 7:14, is not identified as a virgin, *betulah*. The text does not even stipulate that this is her first child. Many scholars, myself included, consider it possible that she was also the mother of Isaiah's (other) children with equally portentous names, She'ar Yashuv in 7:4 and Maher Shalal Hash Baz in 8:4. The woman's pregnancy is contemporaneous with Isaiah; she *is* pregnant, a descriptive adjective. The word "virgin" and the use of a future tense come from the LXX rather than the Hebrew text, effectively transforming the text to read more easily as a prediction of Jesus.

In the traditional language of Psalm 89:3, God swears an oath to "David, my servant." Note that Bathsheba indeed has her own throne, symbolically if not literally, passed down to the Judean Queen Mothers (see 1 Kings 2:19). The children of the gods refer to any number of divine or semidivine beings, from other gods to angels depending on the age and redaction of the text. Warrior Protectrix, in verse 8, is God of "hosts" or warriors.

Preaching Prompts

Biblical prophecy can include prediction; it is at its heart contemporaneous, interpreting the present and speaking to the people for God as well as speaking to God on behalf of the people. While the framers of the New Testament, and likely the followers of Jesus, interpreted Isaiah 7:14 with reference to Jesus, they did not negate its original meaning in its original context. They interpreted it in their contemporary context as we ought, affirming both interpretations.

Read in context, Isaiah 7:14 is not a prediction but a demonstration of God's reliable fidelity, available in each generation. The young woman in Isaiah is already pregnant. By the time her child is eating soft foods, the two nations threatening Judah will be gone. The presence of Isaiah's son, "A Remnant Shall Survive," is a promise that Judah will not be destroyed while those two nations decline. The promise is faithful, as is the God who made it.

Psalm 89 celebrates the eternal faithfulness of God, in this translation, expressing that *through* Bathsheba rather than *to* David. Such a reading does not redeem her rape; it does keep her centered in the story in which she continues to play a part.

Philippians 2 and Luke 2 are each traditional readings for the Feast of the Holy Name of Jesus observed on January 1. They celebrate the majesty of the name given by angels and the humble majesty of its bearer.

SECOND SUNDAY AFTER CHRISTMAS

Wisdom 3:13–15, 4:1–2; Psalm 143;
1 Corinthians 6:12–20; Luke 3:1–6, 15–23

Wisdom 3:13b Now then, blessed is the barren woman who is undefiled,

> who has not known transgressive intercourse;
> she will have fruit at the assessment souls.

14 And [also blessed] is the eunuch whose hands have worked no wickedness,
> who has not contemplated evil against the Holy One;
> for special grace will be given them for their faithfulness,
> and a place of great delight in the temple of the Most High.

15 For the fruit of good labors is renowned,
> and the root of understanding is unfailing.

4:1 Better is childlessness with excellence of character,
> for in the memory of [such excellence] is immortality,
> because it is known by God and the woman-born.

2 When it is present they imitate it,
> and they long for it when it has gone;
> throughout eternity it is crowned, marching,
> victorious in the contest for prizes that are undefiled.

Psalm 143

1 Saving One hear my prayer;
> give ear to my supplications in your faithfulness;
> answer me in your righteousness.

2 Do not enter into judgment with your slave,
> for none is righteous before you, [none] among all living.

3 For the enemy chased after my life,
> crushed my soul to the ground,
> made me sit in darkness like the eternal dead.

4 Now my spirit faints within me;
> within me my heart is appalled.

5 I remember the days of old,
> I contemplate all your deeds,
> on the works of your hands I meditate.

6 I stretch out my hands to you;
> my soul is like a weary land to you. *Selah*

7 Hurry [and] answer me Holy Protector;
> my spirit is failing.

> Hide not your face from me,
> else I shall be like those who go down to the Pit.
> ⁸ In the morning let me hear of your faithful love,
> for in you I put my trust.
> Teach me the way I should go,
> for to you I lift up my soul.
> ⁹ Save me, SHELTERING GOD, from my enemies;
> with you I am covered.
> ¹⁰ Teach me to do your will,
> for you are my God.
> Your good Spirit,
> may she lead me on a level path.
> ¹¹ For the sake of your Name MERCIFUL GOD, save my life.
> In your righteousness deliver my soul from affliction.
> ¹² In your faithful love, end my enemies,
> and destroy all who afflict my soul;
> for I am your slave.

1 Corinthians 6:12 "Everything is possible for me," but not everything is beneficial. "Everything is possible for me," but I will not be under the power of anything. ¹³ Food is for the stomach and the stomach for food, yet God will destroy each. The body is not for sexual immorality but the Christ, and the Christ for the body. ¹⁴ And God raised the Messiah and will also raise us by the power of God. ¹⁵ Do you all not know that your bodies are members of Christ? Should I therefore take the members of Christ and make them members of a sexually immoral person? Never! ¹⁶ Do you not know that whoever is conjoined to a sexually immoral person becomes one body with that person? For it is said, "*The two shall become one flesh.*" ¹⁷ But anyone conjoined to the Messiah becomes one spirit with Christ. ¹⁸ Shun sexual immorality! Every sin that a person commits is outside the body; but the sexually immoral person sins against the body itself. ¹⁹ Or do you all not know that your body is a sanctuary of the Holy Spirit within you, which you have from God, and that you are not your own? ²⁰ For you were purchased with a price; therefore glorify God in your body.

Luke 3:1 In the fifteenth year of the rule of Emperor Caesar, Pontius Pilate ruled Judea, and Herod governed Galilee as tetrarch and his brother Philip governed the region of Ituraea and Trachonitis as tetrarch, and Lysanias governed Abilene as tetrarch. ² Then, during the high priesthood of Annas and Caiaphas, the word of God came to John the son of [Elizabeth and] Zechariah in the wilderness. ³ He went into the whole region around the Jordan, proclaiming a baptism of repentance for the forgiveness of sins: ⁴ As it is written in the scroll of the words of the prophet Isaiah,

A voice crying out in the wilderness:
"Prepare the way of the MOST HIGH,
make God's paths straight.
⁵ *Every valley shall be filled,*
and every mountain and hill shall be brought low,
and the crooked, straight,
and the rugged, smooth;
⁶ *and all flesh shall see the salvation of God."*

¹⁵ The people were filled with expectation and every woman and man was questioning in their hearts concerning John, whether he might be the Messiah. ¹⁶ John answered all of them, saying, "I baptize you in water; but one more powerful than I am is coming. I am not worthy to loosen the strap of his sandals. He will baptize you in the Holy Spirit and fire. ¹⁷ His winnowing fork is in his hand, to clear out his threshing floor and to gather the wheat into his storehouse; but the chaff he will burn with unquenchable fire."

¹⁸ Thus with many other exhortations John proclaimed the good news to the people. ¹⁹ But Herod the tetrarch (who governed Galilee) who had been rebuked by him concerning Herodias, the wife of his brother and because of all the evil things that Herod had done— ²⁰ he added to them all and shut up John in prison.

²¹ Now when all the women and men were baptized, and when Jesus also had been baptized and was praying, the heavens were opened! ²² And the Holy Spirit descended upon Jesus bodily, like a dove. And a voice came from the heavens, "You are my Child, the Beloved; with you I am well pleased."

²³ Now Jesus was about thirty years old when he began his work. He was the child of [Mary, and] as was thought, of Joseph the child of Heli.

PROCLAMATION

Text Notes

The baptismal feast of Jesus traditionally occurs after Epiphany; however, in the Gospel of Luke, it occurs so early as to require reading out of sequence to hold this Gospel reading until then.

In Wisdom 3, the verb is missing in verse 14; similarly, the object is missing in 4:1. In 4:1, "woman-born" replaces *anthropos*, humanity.

In verse 3 of the psalm, I switched the positions of "soul" and "life" for smoother reading in English.

In 1 Corinthians 6:12, *exestin* means "right," "possible," and "within one's power" (CEB) but is not related to the Law as in NRSV ("lawful"). Verses 15 and 16 use a female sex-worker, *pornes*, to make the point. The following verses use the related term *porneian* (in nominal and verbal forms) to refer to unauthorized or culturally unacceptable sexual intercourse. Both words are used broadly and rhetorically, i.e., slut shaming any woman such as the whore/harlot language in Revelation 17:15 and to describe infidelity to God in Hosea 9:1; Jeremiah 3:6; Ezekiel 23:19; 1 Chronicles 5:25; and Revelation 17:2; 18:3, 9. *Porneia*, traditionally translated as "fornication" here, is also used for marital infidelity in Matthew 5:32; 19:9; a man living with his father's wife in 1 Corinthians 5:1. I use various forms of "sexual immorality" to indicate the breadth of the underlying terms and the continual reconceptualization of what is moral and culturally accepted sexual practices across time in the Church and the surrounding culture. Verse 16 of the Epistle quotes Genesis 2:2.

The verbs for the conversion of the "crooked" to "straight" and the "rugged" to "smooth" are missing from Luke 3:5.

Preaching Prompts

While Jesus has the longest childhood in Luke, it ends quickly. (We will return to his infancy for the Feast of the Presentation.) These Christmastide lessons take an unflinching look at the world into which the Redeemer was born, focusing on women as the barometer of liberation (or the lack thereof) and as recipients of the gospel. The first lesson, from Wisdom, may be unfamiliar. It offers the rare presentation of a barren woman as blessed and includes the person who does not fit easily into the gender binary, the eunuch. The woman (and presumably the eunuch as well) is blessed for sexual purity. The Epistle holds a rare bit of body positivity—though with significant caveats—as the sanctuary of the Holy Spirit. The caveats are that the Christian conform to the expected sexual mores. The Gospel reading presents a woman caught up in a sexual scandal against the background of the baptism of Jesus and those who received John's preaching and baptism—"the people" who would have included women. The scandal of Herod's (Antipas) marriage to his (half) brother (Herod) Phillip's wife Herodias—who was the daughter of their brother in common Aristobulus, making her each of their niece is elaborated upon in *Antiquities 18.5.1*. I selected the psalm to give Herodias a voice and invite the reader, hearer, and preacher to hear and present it as her prayer.

In these lessons, women are trapped to no small degree by social, cultural, and religious understandings of sexuality that in theory apply to men, but not to the same degree. And at the same time, women were hearing and responding to the gospel and getting baptized, but rising up out of the water to a world in which they were no more free, even with the Holy Spirit resident in the sanctuary of their bodies. These lessons offer an opportunity to reflect on the sexual and other moral ethics it upholds and commends and how those expectations are communicated and applied unevenly.

FEAST OF THE EPIPHANY

Isaiah 60:1–6, 11; Psalm 67; 2 Timothy 1:5–10; Matthew 2:1–12

Isaiah 60:1 Arise, daughter; shine, daughter; for your light has come, daughter,
>and the glory of the Holy One has risen upon you, daughter.
>² For—watch now, daughter!—bleakness shall cover the earth,
>and thick bleakness the peoples;
>and upon you, daughter, the Holy One will arise,
>and over you, daughter, God's glory will appear.
>³ Nations shall come to your light, daughter,
>and royalty to the brightness of your dawn, daughter.
>⁴ Lift your eyes round about, daughter, and see;
>all of them gather, they come to you, daughter;
>daughter, your sons shall come from far away,
>and your daughters shall be carried on their nurses' hips.
>⁵ Then, daughter, you shall see and be radiant;
>your heart, daughter, shall tremble and swell,
>because the abundance of the sea shall turn toward you, daughter,
>the wealth of the nations shall come to you, daughter.
>⁶ A multitude of camels shall cover you, daughter—
>young camels of Midian and Ephah—
>all those from Sheba shall come.
>They shall bring gold and frankincense,
>and shall proclaim the praises of the Holy One.
>¹¹ Your gates shall always be open, daughter;
>day and night they shall not be shut,
>so that nations shall bring you their wealth, daughter,
>being led by their royals.

Psalm 67
>¹ May God be merciful to us and bless us,
>show us the light of her countenance and come to us.
>² Let your ways be known upon earth,
>your saving health among all nations.
>³ Let the peoples praise you, O God;
>let all the peoples praise you.
>⁴ Let the nations be glad and sing for joy,
>for you judge the peoples with equity
>and guide all the nations upon earth.

⁵ Let the peoples praise you, O God;
   let all the peoples praise you.
⁶ The earth has brought forth her increase;
   may God, our own God, give us her blessing.
⁷ May God give us her blessing,
   and may all the ends of the earth stand in awe of her.

2 Timothy 1:5 Considering the recollection of your faith without pretense, a faith that lived first in your grandmother Lois and your mother Eunice, now I am persuaded that faith lives in you. ⁶ For this reason I remind you to reignite the gift of God that is within you through the laying on of my hands; ⁷ for God did not give us a spirit of cowardice, but one of power and of love and of self-control.

⁸ Be not ashamed, then, of the testimony of our Savior or of me Christ's prisoner, rather share in suffering for the sake of the gospel, do so through the power of God, ⁹ who saved us and called us with a holy calling, not according to our works, rather according to God's own purpose and grace which was given to us in Christ Jesus before the ages began. ¹⁰ Now it has been revealed through the appearing of our Savior Christ Jesus, who negated death and brought life and immortality to light through the gospel.

Matthew 2:1 Now Jesus was born in Bethlehem of Judea in the days of King Herod. Suddenly sages from the East came to Jerusalem, ² asking, "Where is the one born king of the Judeans? For we have seen his star at its ascent and have come to reverence him." ³ When King Herod heard this, he was shaken, and all Jerusalem with him; ⁴ then calling together all the chief priests and religious scholars of the people, he inquired of them where the Messiah would be born. ⁵ They said to him, "In Bethlehem of Judea; for it has been written by the prophet:

⁶ '*And you, Bethlehem, in the land of Judah,*
   by no means are least among the rulers of Judah;
   for from you shall come a ruler
   who is to shepherd my people Israel.'"

⁷ Then Herod secretly called for the sages and learned from them the time when the star had appeared. ⁸ Then he sent them to Bethlehem, saying, "Go, search diligently for the child, and when you have found him bring me word so that I may also go and reverence him." ⁹ When they had heard the king, they left, and there suddenly was the star that they had seen at its ascent going before them until it stopped over the place where the child was. ¹⁰ When they saw that the star had stopped, they rejoiced; their joy was exuberant. ¹¹ On entering the house, they saw the child with Mary his mother; and they fell down and reverenced him. Then, opening their treasure, they offered him gifts of gold, frankincense, and myrrh. ¹² And having been warned in a dream not to return to Herod, they left for their own country by another road.

PROCLAMATION

Text Notes

Isaiah 60 speaks to a feminine entity, Zion, Jerusalem, frequently styled as God's daughter; each "you" and "your" is explicitly feminine and singular, rhythmic and repetitive in Hebrew. I have added "daughter" each place this occurs for the English speaker-reader-hearer. The daughters in verse 4 were already delineated; "hips" here is actually "side."

Bleakness: The thick bleakness of Isaiah 60:2 is the same (word) as the thick darkness in which God is veiled in other texts, i.e., Exodus 20:21; Deuteronomy 4:11, 5:22; 2 Samuel 22:10; 1 Kings 8:12.

"Spirit of fear" is a familiar and common translation of 2 Timothy 1:7. *Deilia* is cowardice, an important distinction. Fear is not a failing. It is a natural and healthy response. It is harmful to tell folks not to feel what they feel. What matters is how folk respond to fear.

Grammatically speaking, not all of the *magoi* need be male, only one; note: no number of sages is specified. "Religious scholars" is preferable to scribes, which can suggest copyists. The Gospel famously quotes Micah 5:2 that a ruler with ancient origins shall come from Bethlehem of Judah. There is a variant to that text which states that out of Bethlehem of Judah "one shall not come forth" to rule. It is worth considering that both traditions were known at the times of the setting and production of the Gospel. The line "least among the rulers" is specific to the Gospel; it is among the "thousands," i.e., clans in Hebrew and Aramaic (Targum and Peshitta). A different word for ruler is used in the LXX, *archon* vs. *hegemon*.

The word *Ioudaioi* is regularly translated "Jews" but also means "Judeans" in an age where an ethnic name referred to a people, their land, language, and religion(s). "Judean" is often a preferable reading to "Jew" or "the Jews," which in contemporary discourse have often become an epithet in the mouths of anti-Semites. Further, the distinction is a helpful reminder that the Gospels refer to the Judeans of its world and not the Jewish communities of ours.

Preaching Prompts

These lessons frame a number of epiphanies: God's self-revelation and that of Christ to the world beyond Israel in Isaiah 60 and Psalm 67, in the traditional Epiphany Gospel, Matthew 2, and in 2 Timothy 1. These epiphanies are manifest in or accompanied by light, sometimes set in opposition to darkness, sometimes paired with it, requiring thoughtful exegesis in a world in which darkness and blackness are regularly equated with black and brown people set in opposition to whiteness and white people.

In the commentary on Isaiah 60 in the *Jewish Study Bible,* Benjamin Sommer observes a shift from the traditional pattern centering on a male monarch as a royal figure. Rather God's daughter-city Zion is the locus of liberation wrought by God without human delegation. This is a helpful alternative to the common veneration of monarchy and the fallible members of David's lineage. Similarly, it is God and not a human who judges women and men, "the peoples," with equity, in the psalm.

It is worth asking how the women in and behind these texts experienced and articulated their epiphanies. The promises of restoration and reunification to daughter Jerusalem can be heard as the promises to the daughters of Jerusalem, the mothers, wives, sisters, and daughters of those who are in exile and captivity. Lois and Eunice in 1 Timothy have their own stories of faith. What might they have told us in their own Epistle if they had not been relegated to grandmother and mother? (Note the absence of Timothy's male lineage.) These texts offer an opportunity to proclaim the ways in which God is manifest in the world in and beyond the scriptures, in old ways and new.

EPIPHANY I

Genesis 21:14–19; Psalm 34:1–14; 2 Corinthians 9:6–13; Luke 4:1–15

Genesis 21:14 So Abraham rose early in the morning, and took bread and a skin of water, and gave it to Hagar. He placed it on her shoulder, along with the child, and sent her away. Then she walked away and wandered in the wilderness of Beer-Sheba.

¹⁵ When the water in the skin was gone, she thrust the child under one of the bushes. ¹⁶ Then she went and sat herself down before him some way off, about the distance of a bow-shot; for she said, "Let me not see the death of the child." So, she sat before him and she lifted up her voice and she wept. ¹⁷ And God heard the voice of the boy, and the messenger of God called to Hagar from the heavens, and said to her, "What troubles you, Hagar? Fear not, for God has heard the voice of the boy where he is. ¹⁸ Rise, lift the boy and hold him with your hand, for a great nation of him I will make." ¹⁹ Then God opened her eyes and she saw a well of water. She went, and filled the skin with water, and let the boy drink.

Psalm 34:1–14

¹ I will bless SHE WHO IS GOD at all times;
  her praise shall ever be in my mouth.
² I will glory in SHE WHO IS STRENGTH;
  let the humble hear and rejoice.
³ Proclaim with me the greatness of SHE WHO IS EXALTED
  and let us exalt her Name together.
⁴ I sought SHE WHO SAVES, and she answered me
  and delivered me out of all my terror.
⁵ Look upon her and be radiant,
  and let not your faces be ashamed.

⁶ I called in my affliction and SHE WHO HEARS heard me
and saved me from all my troubles.
⁷ The messenger of SHE WHO SAVES encompasses those who revere her,
and she will deliver them.
⁸ Taste and see that SHE WHO IS DELIGHT is good;
happy are they who trust in her!
⁹ Revere SHE WHO IS GOD, you that are her saints,
for those who revere her lack nothing.
¹⁰ The young lions suffer want for food and starve,
but those who seek SHE WHO PROVIDES lack no good thing.
¹¹ Come, children, listen to me;
I will teach you the reverence of SHE WHO IS MAJESTY.
¹² Who is the woman or man that desires life,
and would love long days to enjoy good?
¹³ Keep your tongue from evil,
and your lips from speaking deceit.
¹⁴ Turn from evil, and do good;
seek peace, and pursue it.

2 Corinthians 9:6 Now hear this: The one who sows sparingly, sparingly will also reap, and the one who sows in abundance, in abundance will also reap. ⁷ Each one must give as decided in your heart, not out of reluctance or under pressure, for "God loves a cheerful giver." ⁸ And the power of God is able to grant you every gift abundantly, so that always having enough of everything, you all may abound in every good work. ⁹ As it is written,

> "God scatters generously, and gives to the poor;
> God's righteousness endures forever."

¹⁰ The one who supplies seed to the sower and bread for food will supply and multiply your seed and increase the harvest of your righteousness. ¹¹ Enriched in every way for every kind of generosity which will yield through us thanksgiving to God, ¹² for the offering of this ministry does not only supply the needs of the saints but also overflows with many thanksgivings to God. ¹³ Through the character of this ministry you all glorify God by your obedience to the confession of the gospel of Christ and by the generosity of your companionship with them and with all others.

Luke 4:1 Now Jesus, full of the Holy Spirit, returned from the Jordan and was led by her, the Spirit into the wilderness. ² Forty days was he tempted by the devil. And nothing ate he, not one thing in those days, and when they were at an end he was ravenous. ³ And the devil said to him, "If the Son of God you are, command this stone that it become bread." ⁴ Jesus answered him, "It is written, *Not by bread alone do the children of earth live.*"

⁵ Then it raised Jesus up and showed him all the dominions of the world in a moment of time. ⁶ And the devil said to him, "To you will I give all their authority and their glory; for to me has it been given, and as I will, I give it to anyone. ⁷ Thus, if you will worship me, it shall all be yours." ⁸ And Jesus answered, saying to it, "It is written:

The Holy One your God shall you worship, and God only shall you serve."

⁹ Then it took Jesus to Jerusalem and placed him on the highest point of the temple, saying to him, "If the Son of God you are, throw yourself down from here. ¹⁰ For it is written:

God's own angels will God command on your account, to protect you,

¹¹ and that,

On their hands shall they bear you up lest you strike your foot against a stone."

¹² Then Jesus answered, saying to it, "It is said, *Do not put the Holy One your God to the test."*
¹³ And when every test was at an end, the devil departed from Jesus for a season.

¹⁴ And Jesus returned, in the power of the Spirit, to Galilee and a report about him spread through all the surrounding country. ¹⁵ And he began to teach in their synagogues and was praised by every woman and man.

PROCLAMATION
Text Notes

The baptismal feast of Jesus traditionally occurs after Epiphany; however, in the Gospel of Luke, it occurs so early as to require reading out of sequence to hold this Gospel reading until then. Today's Gospel is the second portion of the baptismal account. Readers and preachers may wish to refer back to the account of the baptism in the readings from the second Sunday after Christmas to connect the stories.

Biblical Hebrew does not have a word that means simply "divine winged being," what many conceive when they read or hear the word "angel." Instead, Hebrew uses a word, *mal'akh,* that means "messenger," whether the one bearing the message is human or divine. Further, these messengers are distinct from cherubim and seraphim—consider them different species; they are never interchanged—and, as in the story of Jacob's ladder, do not have wings. Greek *aggelos* has the same sense of human or divine messenger, and none of the angels of the New Testament are described with wings. There is one distinct angel among the host of heaven, the angel of God (or the Lord) in other translations, here in Genesis 21:17 and Psalm 34:7, the angel of Wisdom. Many scholars understand this angel to be God in disguise so that she can be among her people without her holiness harming them. (I say it is God in drag.)

Verse 9 of the Epistle quotes Psalm 112:9.

Luke 4:4 uses *anthropos,* translating *ha'adam* in quoting Deuteronomy 8:3; both mean "humanity." I use the more poetic choice "children of earth" to avoid the awkwardness resulting from the sentence structure "does humanity live." The passage also quotes Deuteronomy 6:13, 16, and Psalm 91:11–12.

I render "the devil" gender neutral to signify the otherness of the literary, cultural, and cosmic character that is, in some texts, the embodiment of evil and, in others, an oppositional or slandering voice.

Preaching Prompts

In this holy season, immediately on the heels of Christmas, God, her agents, and adversaries show up in supernatural ways. There are epiphanies under virtually every bush. Some who read, hear, and preach these lessons will have their own stories of supernatural intervention, but not everyone will. Yet in many of the difficulties we face, supernatural intervention is not required. Abraham found himself in a difficult marriage in part because of his own actions and in part because of the actions of his first wife, Sarah. While we can see that although God was not going to let Hagar and Ishmael die (suggested by God telling Abraham to let Sarah have her way and abandon them to the wilderness), abandonment is a horrific solution to family strife. There was an opportunity for human beings to choose and do better so that no supernatural force was necessary to preserve life. Living with the consequences of their actions and creating a safe home for the children of their blended polygamist marriage was the harder, fully human choice.

The psalm celebrates the God who provides in the cycle of nature and, on occasion, through divine intervention. Yet at the conclusion, human well-being is tied to human well-doing. In the Epistle, the teaching that God provides is also tied to the work of human affairs: we reap what we sow, faithfully or faithlessly, abundantly or scarcely.

The trials and temptations of Jesus are without peer. However, his response is not supernatural. His reliance on more than the words of scripture—their principles and the God whom they reveal—is paradigmatic for we who, I dare say, will never be snatched up to architectural heights to debate the embodiment of an ancient evil.

While God and their angels appear in our lives on their own schedules, we can be the messenger of God and angels to each other in times of need. An enduring lesson of the first reading is that when their social structures begin to break down, women and children are the most vulnerable and most expendable, and when there is any national, ethnic, racial, or cultural difference, those who are different than the larger or dominant society will be the first to be sacrificed and in need of angels manifesting the love and saving help of God.

EPIPHANY II

1 Kings 17:8–16; Psalm 40:1–11, 13, 16–17; Romans 12:9–18; Luke 4:16–27

1 Kings 17:8 The word of the Holy One to Elijah was, ⁹ "Get up, go to Zarephath, which is part of Sidon, and settle there; watch now, I have commanded a widow woman there to provide for you." ¹⁰ And Elijah got up and went to Zarephath. Then he came to the gate of the town, and look! a widow woman was there gathering sticks; so he called to her and said, "Bring me, please, a little water in a vessel, that I may drink." ¹¹ She went to bring it, and he called to her and said, "Bring me, please, a bit of bread in your hand." ¹² Then she said, "As the Holy One your God lives, if I had a cake. There is only a handful of flour in a jar, and a little oil in a jug. Now look, I am gathering two sticks, then I will go home and prepare the oil and flour for myself and for my child; we will eat it, and we will die." ¹³ Then Elijah said to her, "Fear not; go and do as you have said, only make me a little cake of it and bring it to me first, then make something for yourself and your child afterwards. ¹⁴ For thus says the Holy One the God of Israel: The jar of flour will not empty and the jug of oil will not decrease until the day that the Holy One grants rain upon the earth." ¹⁵ She went and she did as Elijah said, and she and he, and her household, ate for many days. ¹⁶ The jar of flour did not empty and the jug of oil did not decrease according to the word of the Holy One that God spoke through Elijah.

Psalm 40:1–11, 13, 16–17

¹ I waited expectantly for the Saving God;
   she inclined toward me and heard my cry.
² She raised me up from the roaring pit,
   out of the muck and mud
   and settled my feet upon a rock,
   making firm my steps.
³ She put a new song in my mouth,
   a song of praise to our God.
   Many will see and reverence,
   and put their trust in She Who is Worthy.
⁴ Blessed is the woman who makes
   the Magnificent One her trust,
   who does not turn to the proud,
   to those who turn to lies.
⁵ Many are the things you have done,
   you, Majestic One my God;
   your wonders and your thoughts toward us—
   none can compare with you.
   Were I to proclaim and name [them],
   they would be beyond counting.

⁶ Sacrifice and offering you do not desire,
 instead, my ears you have dug open for me.
 For burnt offering and sin offering
 you have not asked.
⁷ Then I said, "Here am I come,
 as in the scroll of the book it is written of me.
⁸ To do your will, my God, is my delight;
 your teaching is in my belly."
⁹ I have proclaimed the good news of vindication
 in the great congregation.
 Look! My lips I have not restrained,
 JUST GOD, you know [it is so].
¹⁰ Your vindication I have not hidden within my heart,
 of your faithfulness and your salvation have I spoken;
 I have not concealed your enduring love
 or your faithfulness from the great congregation.
¹¹ May you, MOTHER OF ALL,
 withhold not your mother-love from me;
 let your enduring love and your faithfulness always keep me.
¹³ Be pleased, FAITHFUL GOD, to deliver me;
 LOVING GOD, hasten to help me.
¹⁶ May they rejoice and be glad in you, all who seek you;
 may they say continually, "Great is the GLORIOUS ONE!"
 those who love your salvation.
¹⁷ Though I am poor and needy,
 may the Sovereign take thought for me.
 My help and my deliverer are you;
 my God, do not delay.

Romans 12:9 Let love be sincere. Abhor what is evil, cling to what is good. ¹⁰ Love one another as family; lead the way in showing honor to one another, ¹¹ in zeal not idle, fervent in spirit, serving the Messiah. ¹² In hope rejoice, in suffering endure, in prayer persevere. ¹³ Take part in meeting the needs of the saints; practice hospitality.

¹⁴ Bless those who persecute you; bless and do not curse them. ¹⁵ Rejoice with those who rejoice and weep with those who weep. ¹⁶ Live in harmony with one another; do not think highly [of yourself], sit with the lowly; do not claim to be wiser than you are. ¹⁷ Do not repay anyone evil for evil, but contemplate what is good in the sight of all persons. ¹⁸ If possible for you, live peaceably with all.

Luke 4:16 Now Jesus came to Nazareth, where he had been nurtured and went, according to his practice on the day of the sabbath, to the synagogue. And he stood up to read. ¹⁷ Then was given him the scroll of the prophet Isaiah. He unrolled the scroll and found the place where it was written:

18 *"The Spirit of the Most High is upon me,*
because God has anointed me
to proclaim good news to those who are poor.
God has sent me to preach liberation to those who are captives
and recovery of sight to those who are blind,
to liberate those who are oppressed,
19 *to proclaim the year of the Most High's favor."*

20 Then Jesus rolled up the scroll, gave it back to the attendant, and sat down and every eye of all in the synagogue looked intently at him. 21 Then he began to speak to them, saying, "Today this scripture has been fulfilled in your hearing." 22 And all bore witness to him and marveled at the gracious words that came from his mouth. They said, "Is not this Joseph's son?" 23 Then Jesus said to them, "Of course you all will quote me this proverb, 'Doctor, cure yourself!' And you all will say, 'The things we have heard you did at Capernaum, do here in your hometown.'" 24 And Jesus said, "Truly I tell you, no prophet is accepted in their hometown. 25 But I speak truth to you all, there were many widows in Israel in the days of Elijah, when the heavens were closed three years and six months, and there was a severe famine over all the land. 26 Yet Elijah was sent to none of them, rather to Zarephath in Sidon, to a widow woman. 27 And there were also many lepers in Israel in the time of the prophet Elisha, and none of them was cleansed except Naaman the Syrian."

PROCLAMATION

Text Notes

"The word was/happened to . . ." the prophet; throughout the Hebrew Bible, the word of God "happens" to prophets; it is an encounter.

In biblical Hebrew, "hope in" [God] and "wait for" [God] are the same word; see Psalm 40:1. My preference for "wait" is shaped by my identity and culture. Black folk have learned to wait on God even when hope is thin.

In verse 4 of the psalm, I chose to replace "blessed/happy is the man" (JPS, Alter) with "happy is the woman" rather than a plural inclusive such as "blessed/happy are they" (NRSV, CEB). While men have had the experience of hearing someone with their gender as the subject of and petitioner in psalms, women have not as singular subjects. In addition to using explicitly feminine language for God in the Psalms in this volume, I will occasionally use the feminine singular for the human person praying, praising, or lamenting in the psalm reading. "Blessed" is a stronger choice and preferable here. In addition, "blessed" is the translation that extends beyond the Hebrew Bible into the New Testament, i.e., the Beatitudes.

Torah, in Psalm 40:8, is broad, meaning "teaching," according to its root. There is no sense of Torah scrolls being available throughout most of the First Testament.

The verb *basar* in Psalm 40:9 means to preach or proclaim good news and is the literary and cultural root of what becomes the proclamation of the gospel in the Second Testament.

In Psalm 40:11, "mother-love" translates *racham*, love that emanates from the womb, the *rechem*. ("Belly" in verse 8 often functions as a synonym for womb.)

Romans 12:16 uses a verb that means "condescend" to describe Paul's instruction that Christians spend time with the "lowly." I translate it "sit with" here.

"Nurtured" in Luke 4:16 has the particular sense of having been nourished, specifically, fed. Jesus's literacy is noteworthy in an age where illiteracy was more common than not. In comparison, very few of Israel's prophets were recorded as writing their oracles; Jeremiah was famously illiterate, relying on Baruch to read and write his scrolls. Jesus quotes Isaiah 61:1–2 and 58:6 in inverse order. The evangelist has him citing the LXX version, "the acceptable year of the Holy One," where the MT has "year of the Holy One's favor." Translations like the NRSV, CEB, and the present one use "favor" given Jesus would have been reading the Hebrew text (though whether it corresponded to the MT or LXX cannot be ascertained). Notably, Jesus or the author attenuates the Isaiah reading, omitting "the day of vengeance." In verse 25, I expand the pronoun in Jesus's proverb to reflect the inclusivity of the prophetic tradition in each canon.

Preaching Prompts

Jesus's declaration of the gospel to which he was called should come with the reminder that that gospel, that good news, was already in the world. He took up the call issued by Isaiah or one of his disciples, writing in Isaiah's name. A call we can also see at work in God's interaction with Elijah and Elijah's interaction with the widow. In each of these lessons, good news is concrete—as it is in the Epistle. It is food on the table for you and your child, it is welcome and hospitality, and it is liberation from an unjust carceral system. It is a gospel that does not leave anyone out because of their gender, class, social location, or ethnicity.

God sends Elijah to a foreign woman, a scandalous proposition; more than that, her people are ancient enemies, the Philistines. In that sending, their roles become reversed; he is the foreigner, and she is the citizen. He is at her mercy, but they are both in need. Their story is one of the mutual aid.

I have translated the psalm to be heard as her prayer. (I discuss the specific translation choices in the previous section.) I address her and their encounter more fully in the second volume of *Womanist Midrash: A Reintroduction to the Women of the Former Prophets*, (Westminster/John Knox Press, forthcoming). The psalmist does more than pray for help in their time of need. They have already internalized the Torah, the teaching of God, so that it is deep in their belly, in their body, including their womb. And they, too, are a preacher of the good news.

In each of these lessons, God is manifest in human flesh, more, in human actions. The old saying that we are the hands of God applies here. We are the ones called to make the good news of God's love and justice manifest in the world, and that comes with more than the words we preach. We are called to live good news and bring good news physically to the hurting, hungry, isolated, and confined people who need to hear it and receive its liberation. But a gospel that seeks to change the social and economic status of everyone it encounters is unwelcome in many spaces. We may not receive the welcome the widow gave to Elijah. We may experience the rejection that Jesus did.

FEAST OF THE PRESENTATION, FEBRUARY 2

(The Feast falls variably in early Epiphany. For simplicity and consistency, it is placed after the Second Sunday of Epiphany in these volumes.)

Leviticus 12:1–8; Psalm 48:1–3, 9–14; 1 John 5:1–5; Luke 2:22–38

Leviticus 12:1 The HOLY ONE OF SINAI spoke to Moses, saying, [2] Speak to the women and men of Israel, saying:

When a woman conceives and gives birth to a male, she shall be taboo seven days; as during the days of her menstruation, she shall be taboo. [3] On the eighth day the flesh of his foreskin shall be circumcised. [4] Then, thirty and three days shall she sit in blood purification; she shall not touch any holy thing, or come into the sanctuary, until the days of her restoration are fulfilled. [5] Now, if she gives birth to a female, she shall be taboo two weeks, as in her menstruation; her time of blood purification shall be sixty-six days.

[6] On completing the days of her purification for a daughter or for a son she shall bring a yearling lamb for a burnt offering—and a pigeon or a turtledove for a sin offering—to the priest at the entrance of the tent of meeting. [7] Then he shall offer it before the FIRE OF SINAI and make atonement on her behalf and she shall be restored from her flow of blood. This is the teaching for the woman who gives birth to a female or male. [8] If she cannot afford a sheep, she shall take two turtledoves or two pigeons, one for a burnt offering and the second for a sin offering; and the priest shall make atonement on her behalf, and she shall be restored.

Psalm 48:1–3, 9–14

[1] Great is the AGELESS GOD and greatly praised,
in the city of our God is God's holy mountain.
[2] Beautiful in elevation, the joy of all the earth,
Mount Zion, in the far north,
is the city of the great Sovereign.
[3] Within her citadels God

has made herself known as a bulwark.
9 We contemplate your faithful love God,
in the midst of your temple.
10 Like your Name, God, your praise,
reaches to the ends of the earth.
Your right hand is filled with righteousness.
11 Let Mount Zion be glad,
let the towns of Judah rejoice
because of your judgments.
12 Go about Zion, go all around her;
count her towers.
13 Set your hearts upon her ramparts;
go through her citadels,
that you may recount to the next generation:
14 For this God is our God, our God forever and ever.
She will be our guide until we die.

1 John 5:1 Everyone who believes that Jesus is the Messiah is born of God, and everyone who loves the parent loves the child of the parent. ² By this we know that we love the children of God, when we love God and undertake God's commandments. ³ For the love of God is this, that we keep God's commandments. And God's commandments are not difficult, ⁴ for anything born of God conquers the world. And this is the victory that conquers the world, our faith. ⁵ Who is it that conquers the world but the one who believes that Jesus is the Son of God?

Luke 2:22 Now when the days of their purification were fulfilled according to the teaching of Moses, they brought Jesus up to Jerusalem to present him to the Holy One: ²³ As it is written in the teaching of the Sovereign God, "Every male who opens the womb [as firstborn] shall be called holy to the Sovereign One." ²⁴ So they offered a sacrifice according to what is stated in the teaching of the Holy One, "a pair of turtledoves or two young pigeons."

²⁵ Now, there was a man in Jerusalem whose name was Simeon; this man was righteous and devout, waiting to welcome the consolation of Israel, and the Holy Spirit, she rested on him. ²⁶ It had been revealed to him by the Holy Spirit that he would not see death before he had seen the Messiah of the Most High God. ²⁷ Led by the Spirit, Simeon came into the temple. When the parents brought in the child Jesus, to do for him what was customary under that which was taught, ²⁸ Simeon took him in his arms and praised God, saying,

29 "You release now your slave in peace, Master,
according to your word;
30 for my eyes have seen your salvation,
31 which you have prepared in the presence of all peoples,

³² a light for revelation to the Gentiles
and for glory to your people Israel."

³³ And the child's mother and father were amazed at what was being said about him. ³⁴ Then Simeon blessed them and said to his mother Mary, "This child is set for the falling and the rising of many in Israel, and to be a sign provoking contention; ³⁵ also, your own soul a sword will pierce so that the true hearts of many will be revealed."

³⁶ There was also a prophet, Anna the daughter of Phanuel, of the tribe of Asher. She was of a great age, having lived with her husband seven years after her marriage, ³⁷ then as a widow to the age of eighty-four. She never left the temple but worshiped there with fasting and prayer night and day. ³⁸ At that moment she came and began to praise God, and to speak about the child to all who were looking for the redemption of Jerusalem.

PROCLAMATION

Text Notes

The traditional language "clean" and "unclean" is deeply implicated in the biased treatment of women and girls, particularly after the onset of menstruation. The language lends itself easily to a debased understanding of women and girls that is inconsistent with full humanity and the image of God. These two distinct words, which are not antonyms, have the sense of being temporarily taboo, not ready to rejoin community, and restoration to a communally appropriate state (see Ilona Rashkow's *Taboo or Not Taboo*). The "purification" requires time, ritual bathing, and an offering. The use of the word "atonement" in verse 8 has made it easier to construct women's bodies and reproductive acts as in some way tainted. However, even moderating the language does not ameliorate the ways in which women and their bodies and reproductive biology are treated as dangerous and in need of control.

In the world of the Hebrew Scriptures, women are impregnated; in verse 2, the Hiphil verb is causative, "she is seeded / caused to bear seed." Contemporary translations tend to use "conceive," reflecting subsequent understanding.

In Psalm 48, Zion's superlatives hail from other cultures identifying their God as God of all the earth using the specific vocabulary of surrounding nations: *nof* signals "elevation" but is also the Egyptian name of Memphis, the capital city (and may also mean "fair," see JPS). Zaphon is the home of the Canaanite gods and is in the farthest northern reach, unlike Zion/Jerusalem. In verse 14, God will be our God "until death"; "until we die" makes clear that it is not God who will die.

Luke 2:22 makes Mary's obligation under the Torah "theirs," Joseph's as well; this is counter to the text and practice between Leviticus and Luke and subsequent rabbinic and contemporary Jewish practice.

Preaching Prompts

When overlaid with the androcentrism, patriarchy, and occasional misogyny of the text, the ritual and language for the restoration to the community sounds harsh and discriminatory to many contemporary and non-Jewish ears. It is helpful to remember that biblical Hebrew has a much smaller vocabulary than English and uses some words in ways that extend far beyond their literal meaning. In Leviticus 12, the "purify," "atone," and "sin offering" apply to cleansing the woman and her physical spaces, including the sanctuary, from blood taboo, which was not a matter of sin or transgression. Arguably this period afforded the new mother rest and bonding time; the additional time for the female infant may account for the occasional vaginal discharge (or appearance of such) observable in newborn girls.

The *Churching of Women* is a Christian rite likely derived from these Leviticus and Luke texts, previously practiced in Catholic and Anglican congregations where a new mother refrained from attending church for four to six weeks and, upon her return, prayed a prayer of thanksgiving and received a blessing. However, some women experienced isolation and stigma and were treated as unclean until they were "churched." The ritual has fallen into disuse.

While all spilled blood requires purification with both ritual and hygienic components, women and girls were subject to blood taboo and purity regulations. Contemporarily, our society seems obsessed with which bodies bleed and bear which organs to categorize and gender and assign identities and restrooms. Without either passing judgment on another culture or co-opting the specific practice of another religion, we can make physical and ritual space for human bodies in all of their life-stage changes and welcome and re-welcome folk to and back to the community upon and after significant transitions. This text can provide an opportunity to think about how we reintegrate a transperson into the congregation.

EPIPHANY III

Isaiah 2:1–5; Psalm 119:10–18; 1 Peter 1:22–25; Luke 4:38–44

Isaiah 2:1 The word that Isaiah son of Amoz envisioned about Judah and Jerusalem:

² And it will be in coming days,
 the mountain of God's home
 shall be the highest of the mountains,
 and shall be elevated beyond the hills,
 all the nations shall stream to it.
³ Many peoples shall come and say,
 "Let us go and ascend the mountain of the Holy One of Sinai,
 to the home of the God of Jacob [of the line of Rebekah];

>   that God may teach us God's ways
>   and that we may walk in God's paths."
>   For out of Zion shall go forth instruction,
>   and the word of the Holy One from Jerusalem.
> 4 God shall judge between the nations,
>   and shall decide justly for many peoples;
>   they shall beat their swords into plowshares,
>   and their spears into pruning hooks;
>   nation shall not lift up sword against nation,
>   neither shall they learn war any more.
> 5 O house of Jacob [of the line of Rebekah]
>   come, let us walk
>   in the light of the Holy One of Old!

Psalm 119:10–18

> 10 With my whole heart I seek you;
>   let me not stray from your commandments.
> 11 In my heart I treasure your word,
>   that I might not sin against you.
> 12 Blessed are you Ageless One;
>   teach me your statutes.
> 13 With my lips I recount
>   all the judgements of your mouth.
> 14 Over the way of your testimony I delight
>   as much as over all riches.
> 15 On your precepts I meditate,
>   and I gaze upon your paths.
> 16 In your statutes I delight;
>   I will not forget your word.
> 17 Reward your slave,
>   that I may live and keep your word.
> 18 Open my eyes, so that I may gaze upon
>   wondrous things from your teaching.

1 Peter 1:21 Through Christ you have come to faith in God who raised Jesus from the dead and gave him glory, so that your faith and hope are upon God. 22 Now that you have purified your souls by your obedience to the truth so that you have the love—without pretense—of children raised together; from a pure heart love one another persistently. 23 You have been born again, not of corruptible seed, but of incorruptible seed through the living and enduring word of God. 24 For:

> *All flesh is like grass*
> *and all its glory like the flower of grass.*
> *The grass withers,*
> *and the flower falls,*
> ²⁵ *but the word of the Living God abides forever.*

Luke 4:38 Coming up after leaving the synagogue, Jesus entered Simon's house. Now Simon's mother-in-law was suffering from a high fever, and they asked him about her. ³⁹ Then Jesus stood over her and rebuked the fever and it left her. Immediately she got up and ministered to them.

⁴⁰ As the sun was setting, all the women and men who had any who were sick with various kinds of diseases brought them to him and he laid his hands on each of them and healed them. ⁴¹ And demons came out of many, crying out and saying, "You are the Child of God!" And Jesus rebuked them and would not permit them to speak, because they knew that he was the Messiah.

⁴² As it became morning, Jesus departed and went into a deserted place. And the crowd of women, children, and men were looking for him and they came to him and held him, keeping him from leaving them. ⁴³ Then Jesus said to them, "To the other cities must I proclaim the good news of the realm of God also; for this purpose was I sent." ⁴⁴ And he preached in the Judean synagogues.

PROCLAMATION

Text Notes

The word "teach" in Isaiah 2:3 and Psalm 119:18 provides the root for Torah, which is more teaching than law.

Slavery is ubiquitous in the canons of scripture. While enslavement may have been periodical for some, lasting an agreed-upon number of years, it still entailed full ownership and control of a human person, including their labor, sexuality, and reproduction. Many persons in the scriptures identified themselves as the slave of someone with more power than they as a means of self-abasement. This is common in the Psalms, where persons portray themselves as the slave of God as in Psalm 119:17.

The healing of Peter's (invisible) wife's mother varies slightly among the synoptic gospels: in Mark 1:29–31, the disciples *tell* Jesus about her; he takes her by the hand and lifts her up. In Matthew 8:14–15, Jesus sees her and touches her and she gets up on her own. In Luke 4:38–39, the disciples *ask* Jesus about her; he rebukes the fever without touching her and she gets up on her own. In all of the accounts of the mother-in-law's healing, I translate *diakoneo* as "ministry" to maintain the fuller sense in which acts of service and hospitality are acts of [religious] ministry, illustrated by a government minister as a public servant.

First Peter 1:22 uses *philadelphia*, sibling-love (or brother-love), where I have translated "children raised together" rather than "sisters and brothers" to avoid excluding reader-hearers who do not identify with a binary understanding of gender.

Preaching Prompts

In this week's reading, God is made manifest through the word; the prophetic word, the contemplative word, the living, risen, and enduring Word, the healing word, and the preached word. In Advent, we celebrated the first coming of Christ, bearing witness to the promise of his return. Part of the joy of Christmas—sometimes lost in consumerism—is the down payment on the promise that the world will be conformed to the image of God, a down payment in the form of a holy child through whom God will be made manifest. Now, in the season of Epiphany, receive the glory of God breaking out in the world through Jesus; his words, his touch, his love, and his power over the things that cause injury, harm, and death.

The Isaiah lesson offers a vision of the world fully redeemed and made over into the image of God. It is a world of justice and peace. One is not possible without the other. The psalm bears witness to the epiphany an individual may receive when contemplating the word of God. In the Epistle, God is made manifest in the life of the believer, a life that transcends the fading of mortal flesh which fades like grass. In all of the Gospels, the primary way that Jesus establishes his bona fides is through his healing ministry. Luke is the "Christmas gospel," uniquely presenting stories of the conception of Jesus. But all of the Gospels have a prolonged set of healing stories demonstrating the power of God operating through Jesus to negate the powers of death and disease.

Such healing stories can be difficult to hear in the contemporary world where death and disease abound, including among those who have received and proclaim this gospel. It is important to remember that their abundance is not a promise or a guarantee. And that everyone who is healed would die, perhaps even from another disease. The promise of the Gospel is not a disease-free life but a life that transcends disease and even death. That promise, that future is our sure and trustworthy hope.

EPIPHANY IV

1 Kings 17:17–24; Psalm 146; 1 Corinthians 15:12–26; Luke 7:11–17

1 Kings 17:17 After [the miracle multiplying the meal and oil], the child of the woman—the owner of the house—became ill and his illness was so overwhelming that there was no breath left in the child. [18] And she said to Elijah, "What is between me and thee, man of God? You have come to me to bring my sin to remembrance and to kill my child!" [19] Then he said to her, "Give me your child," and he took the child from her bosom and carried the child up into the room upstairs where he, Elijah, was staying and laid the child on his own bed. [20] Then he cried out to the Holy One of Old, "Holy One my God, have you actually wrought evil upon the widow with whom I sojourn by killing her child?" [21] And Elijah stretched himself upon the child three times, and cried out to the Most High, "Holy One my God, let this child's soul come into him again." [22] And the Most High God listened to the voice of

Elijah and the soul of the child came into him again, and he revived. ²³ Then Elijah took and brought the child down from the house's upstairs room, and gave the child to the mother and said, "Look! Your child lives." ²⁴ So the woman said to Elijah, "Now this I know, you are a man of God and that the word of the HOLY ONE OF OLD in your mouth is truth."

Psalm 146

1 Halleluyah! Praise the AGELESS ONE, O my soul!
   I will praise the EVER-LIVING GOD all my life;
2 I will sing praises to my God throughout my living.
3 Put not your trust in the great, nor in any child of earth,
   for there is no help in them.
4 When they breathe their last, they return to earth,
   and in that day their thoughts perish.
5 Happy are these for whom the God of Rebekah's line is their help,
   whose hope is in the CREATOR OF ALL, their God.
6 Maker of heavens and earth, the seas, and all that is in them;
   keeping faith forever.
7 Bringer of justice to the oppressed,
   bringer of bread to the hungry.
8 The COMPASSIONATE GOD sets the prisoners free,
   the ALL-SEEING GOD opens the eyes of the blind,
   the JUST GOD lifts up those who are bowed down.
9 The RIGHTEOUS GOD loves the righteous,
   the MOTHER OF ALL cares for the stranger,
   orphan and widow she bears up,
   but confounds the way of the wicked.
10 The MAJESTIC ONE shall reign forever,
   your God, O Zion, from generation to generation.

1 Corinthians 15:12 Now if Christ is preached as raised from the dead, how can some of you say there is no resurrection of the dead? ¹³ For if there is no resurrection of the dead, then Christ has not been raised; ¹⁴ and if Christ has not been raised, then our preaching has been in vain along with your faith. ¹⁵ Then we are even found to be false witnesses of God, because we bore witness of God that God raised Christ—whom God did not raise if the dead are not raised. ¹⁶ For if the dead are not raised, then Christ has not been raised. ¹⁷ And if Christ has not been raised, your faith is useless and you are yet in your sins. ¹⁸ And therefore those who have died in Christ have been destroyed. ¹⁹ If for this life we have only hoped in Christ, we are of all people most pitiable. ²⁰ But now indeed Christ has been raised from the dead, the first fruits of those who have died.

²⁰ But now the Messiah has been raised from the dead, the first fruit of those who have fallen asleep. ²¹ For because through a mortal came death, then also through a mortal

resurrection of the dead has come. ²² For just as in Adam all die, thus, in the Messiah, all will be made alive; ²³ but each person in their own order: The first fruit is the Messiah; afterward, they that are the Messiah's at his coming. ²⁴ Then comes the end, when he hands over the sovereignty to Abba God, after the Messiah has destroyed every ruler and every authority and power. ²⁵ For the Messiah must reign until having *put all enemies under foot*. ²⁶ The last enemy to be destroyed is death.

Luke 7:11 The day after [healing a centurion's slave] Jesus went to a town called Nain, and his disciples and a large crowd went with him. ¹² He had just approached the gate of the town and suddenly, being carried out was a man who had died, his mother's only son and she was a widow; with her was a large crowd from the town. ¹³ When the Messiah saw her, he had compassion on her and said to her, "Do not weep." ¹⁴ Then Jesus came forward and touched the coffin, and the bearers stood still. And he said, "Young man, I say to you, rise!" ¹⁵ The dead man sat up and began to speak and Jesus gave him to his mother. ¹⁶ Fear seized all of them; and they glorified God, saying, "A great prophet has risen among us!" and "God visited God's people!" ¹⁷ This word about Jesus spread throughout Judea and all the surrounding country.

PROCLAMATION

Text Notes

"Lord/master" language indicates home ownership (Exodus 22:8; Judges 19:22–23); unfortunately, "mistress" reads as subordinate in English and does not convey the same sense of mastery or ownership; therefore, I use "owner" in 1 Kings 17:17.

In Psalm 146:2, "throughout my living" is derived from "in my continuing," where "continue" is the adverb meaning "longer," *'od*, with the first possessive suffix, "my" attached—a very complex idiomatic saying. The "great" in verse 3 are "nobles," sometimes royal offspring, hence "princes" in other translations. In verse 5, "Rebekah's line" replaces "Jacob." The nature of God's support for the widow and orphan in verse 9 is unclear; the verb there is only used there, and its derivation is unclear. NRSV's "uphold" derives from the LXX and provides the basis for my "bear up." Similarly, the Peshitta has "nourish/support."

In 1 Corinthians 15:24, the language used for Jesus handing over the sovereignty of earth and heaven, *paradidomi*, is the same as that for Judas handing over Jesus to be crucified (Matthew 20:18; 26:2; Mark 10:33; Luke 18:32; 24:7) and for Saul handing over women and men to prison in Acts 8:3. Verse 25 quotes Psalm 110:1.

Jesus's deep compassion for the bereaved widow emanates from deep within him. At the heart of the verb *splagchnizomai*, "to have compassion," is its root *splagchnon*, innards or guts, the locus of emotion.

Preaching Prompts

Jesus revealed God in his person, through the elements and circumstances of his life, through his choices, through his love, through his teaching and feeling, through his death, and through his resurrection. All of these revelations are congruent with and continuations of the revelations of God in the sacred storied past of Jesus and his people, in their scriptures, which have become our scriptures. God has a long history with death. And she has lent her servants her power to raise the dead long before Jesus was miraculously conceived by a woman without the help of a man. Some have wanted to minimize Elijah's power, seizing on the language of "revival" rather than "resurrection," a term that is not used in the Hebrew Bible. "Revive" here means to "return to life." Therefore, it should be understood as a resurrection; it is further indicated by the lack of breath, which, in the ancient world, signified death, as in verse 4 of the psalm.

The psalmist praises God as creator and sovereign of heaven and earth and land and sea. And in more mortal and mundane and concerns, she recognizes that none is so trustworthy or competent to save, heal, and deliver as God. The Epistle establishes the resurrection of Jesus as a cornerstone of faith in him and surety that God is there to raise us as well.

In this Gospel, and in other accounts, Jesus reveals God, not just by the power he wields, but by who he lavishes with God's love—the widow, orphan, and poor of the psalm. Not many, if any, are given the power over life and death that Jesus and some of the prophets wielded. But we all have the ability to manifest God's love and priorities.

EPIPHANY V

Proverbs 8:1–4, 10–17; Psalm 111; James 3:13–18 ; Luke 7:18–35

Proverbs 8:1–4, 10–17

1. Does not Wisdom call,
   and Understanding put forth her voice?
2. On the highest heights, beside the way,
   at the crossroads she takes her stand.
3. Beside the gates at the entry of the town,
   at the opening of the entryway she sings out:
4. "To you, the woman-born, I call,
   and my cry is to all earth's children.
10. Take my instruction and not silver,
    and knowledge but not choice gold.
11. For better is Wisdom than jewels,
    and not even every delight can compare with her.

12 I, Wisdom, dwell with prudence,
   and knowledge and discretion I find.
13 The fear of the Fount of Wisdom is to hate evil;
   pride and arrogance and the way of evil
   and perverse speech I hate.
14 Wise counsel and sound wisdom are mine;
   I am Understanding, might is mine.
15 By me royals reign,
   and rulers decree what is just.
16 By me governors govern,
   and nobles, all who judge rightly.
17 I love those who love me,
   and those who seek me diligently shall find me."

Psalm 111:1–10

1 Praise the Living God!
   I will give thanks to the One God with my whole heart,
   in the assembly of the upright, in the congregation.
2 Great are the works of God,
   contemplated by all who delight in them.
3 Splendor and majesty are her work,
   and her righteousness stands forever.
4 She has gained renown for her wonderful deeds;
   the Womb of Life is gracious and abounds in mother-love.
5 She provides fresh meat for those who revere her;
   she remembers her covenant perpetually.
6 She has declared the strength of her works to her people,
   giving them the heritage of the nations.
7 The works of her hands are truth and justice;
   trustworthy are all her precepts.
8 They stand fast forever and ever,
   Executed in truth and uprightness.
9 She sent redemption to her people;
   she has ordained her covenant forever.
   Holy and awesome is her Name.
10 Awe of the Ageless God is the beginning of wisdom;
    all those who do have good understanding.
    Her praise endures forever.

James 3:13 Who is wise and understanding among you? Show it through a way of life that is good, through works that are done with gentleness born of wisdom. 14 But if any of you have bitter jealousy and selfishness in your hearts, do not boast and bear false witness against the truth. ¹⁵ That is not the wisdom that comes down from above; rather, it is terrestrial, unspiritual, demonic. ¹⁶ For where there is jealousy and selfishness, there will also be turmoil and everything vile. ¹⁷ But the wisdom from above is first of all pure; then peaceable, gentle, reasonable, full of mercy and good fruits, impartial, and sincere. ¹⁸ Yet the fruit of righteousness is sown in peace for they who make peace.

Luke 7:18 Now, the disciples of John brought news of all these things [about Jesus raising the widow's son from the dead] to John. And John called two in particular among his disciples. ¹⁹ He sent them to the Messiah to ask, "Are you the One Who is Coming, or shall we wait for another?" ²⁰ When the men had come to Jesus, they said, "John the Baptizer has sent us to you to ask, 'Are you the One Who is Coming, or are shall we wait for another?'" ²¹ At that moment he, Jesus, healed many people of diseases, illnesses, and evil spirits and to many blind persons he gave sight. ²² Then Jesus answered them, "Go and take this news to John, what you have seen and heard:

those who were blind receive sight,
those who were lame walk,
those who were diseased-in-skin are cleansed,
those who were deaf hear,
those who were dead are raised,
those who are poor have good news proclaimed to them.

²³ And blessed is the woman or man who is not scandalized by me."

²⁴ When John's messengers had gone, Jesus began to speak to the crowds about John: "What did you all go out into the wilderness to see? A reed shaken by the wind? ²⁵ What then did you go out to see? A person dressed in luxurious robes? Look, those whose clothing is lavish and who live in self-indulgence are in royal palaces. ²⁶ What then did you all go out to see? A prophet? Yes, I tell you, and more than a prophet. ²⁷ This is the one about whom it is written,

'*Look, I am sending my messenger ahead of you,*
who will prepare your way before you.'

²⁸ I tell you, among those born of women no one is greater than John; yet the least in the reign of God is greater than he." ²⁹ Now all the people who heard this, including the tax collectors, professed the righteousness of God, being baptized with the baptism of John. ³⁰ But by refusing to be baptized by him, the Pharisees and the legal scholars rejected God's counsel for themselves.

³¹ "To what then will I compare the people of this generation, and what are they like? ³² They are like children in the marketplace sitting and calling to one another,

'*We played the flute for you all, and you did not dance;*
we wailed, and you all did not weep.'

33 For John the Baptizer has come eating no bread and drinking no wine, and you all say, 'He has a demon.' 34 The Son of Woman has come eating and drinking, and you all say, 'Look, a glutton and a drunkard, a friend of tax collectors and sinners!' 35 Yet Wisdom is vindicated by all her children."

PROCLAMATION

Text Notes

I discuss translation as "art and science" in the "Note on Translating" appendix in *Womanist Midrash: A Reintroduction to the Women of the Torah and of the Throne* (Westminster/John Knox, 2017, pp. 281–84). This understanding explains why translations, such as scriptures that originate in different languages, are not static. Readers and hearers of Year W in this series will notice that the material in Luke 7 is translated differently in this volume. (This has been the case for other passages as well; sometimes the changes are very small.)

In Proverbs 8:4, "woman-born" replaces "people/men" as "earth's children" does "children/sons of humanity." Earth, *adamah*, and *adam*, humanity (or person), share the same root. We are earth-crafted earthlings, humus-sourced humans.

In Psalm 111:3, I replaced the nouns "honor and majesty" with the adjectives "glorious and majestic" for smoother English grammar, following JPS in part. God's *tzedakah* primarily means "righteousness" but also has the sense of "beneficence," including generosity to the poor, as in JPS. In verse 4, God's love is articulated with *racham,* which has the womb, *rechem,* as its grammatical root, informing the choice of MOTHER OF ALL as the divine name. The "meat" God provides is literally "prey"; God is apparently quite the huntress. In verses 5 and 10, the verb *y-r-'* is translated "revere," well within the semantic range and preferable to "fear."

There is some uncertainty regarding the translation of *eritheia* in James 3:14 and verse 16; it communicates ambition and strife, both of which are born of self-centeredness.

Jesus uses the expression "woman-born" as shorthand for humanity, while he is presented as the Son of Woman, son of humanity, human child, mortal one. The old "Son of Man" translation misses that *anthropos* means human, not male, and "man" is not generic. Where KJV and RSV use "son of man" throughout both testaments, NRSV has dropped it from the First Testament altogether; CEB follows suit. Instead, they use versions of "mortal (one)," "human one," and "human being." This has the effect of limiting the expression to Jesus, misrepresenting its widespread use in the Hebrew Scriptures. As the title primarily emphasizes humanity, I use Son of Woman to emphasize Jesus's woman-born humanity, which is its primary use in the New Testament (see its use throughout Ezekiel, where it is translated "mortal").

In contrast, in Daniel 7:13, the term has a more supernatural connotation, which can also be found in regard to Jesus (see Matthew 19:28 and 24:30).

In Luke 7:19, "Messiah" replaces "Lord" in keeping with the translation principles of his project; "Lord" is the title associated with slaveholding and patriarchal hierarchy. The One Who is Coming, or more literally, "the Coming One," is a title reflecting expectations based on prophecies of one who will come to lead Israel, such as in Isaiah 61:1; Zechariah 9:9; 14:5, and Malachi 3:1–2. (See Joseph A. Fitzmeyer, *Luke*, Yale Anchor Bible Commentary, p. 666.) Verse 22 blends and cites a number of prophetic texts: Isaiah 26:19; 29:18; 35:5; 61:1.

Jesus's response to John's disciples in Luke 7:22 is a series of paired words with the occasional conjunction, lacking even direct objects:

blind receive-sight,
lame walk,
lepers clean,
and deaf hear,
dead raised,
poor good-news-proclaimed.

The translator must supply the connective tissue of grammar and syntax. These word pairs suggest a highly performative delivery like spoken word poetry, rap, or the preaching tradition of the black church. "Diseased-in-skin" acknowledges the full range of skin disorders included under the ancient understanding of leprosy.

John's messengers in Luke 7:24 are *aggelōn*, but not "angels," which is an anglicized transliteration of the same Greek word. In Greek as well as in Hebrew, the term for messenger refers to human as well as supernatural envoys; as a result, this project uses "messenger" nearly exclusively. God's divine messenger in verse 27, quoting Malachi 3:1, is articulated with the same term. In Luke 7:25 (and Matthew 11:8), John's robe is described with a word that can mean "soft," "fancy," or, with regard to men, one who is sexually penetrated. (I avoid "homosexual" contra to the dominant Greek lexicon, BDAG; that is a contemporary understanding of sexual orientation not applicable to the ancient world.) Unlike the disciples of Jesus, there is no indication that they were women among the disciples of John; the two emissaries to Jesus are explicitly identified as men. But as is the case with all biblical languages, women could be obscured in the plurals of the larger group.

Preaching Prompts

Jesus is the Word enfleshed, and the embodiment of Wisdom personified, a feminine construct in his scriptural tradition.

It is this tradition in which Jesus positions himself as the child of Wisdom; her deeds are his deeds. In so doing, Jesus offers expansive language for the Divine

Mother. His words also remind me of a practice from my own culture: some Black parents will say to a partner when a child is being particularly precocious, "That's *your* child." What behaviors does Jesus associate with his divine Mother? A life full of joy and celebration, including those who, in the words of Paul, are low-status and despised. Yet he does not disdain the ascetic's path John follows; indeed, he commends John with unparalleled praise. There is no single way to follow Jesus.

Finally, in Luke 7:30, there is a layer of the anti-Pharisee tradition that has yielded, and in some cases, still does yield anti-Semitic interpretation. It is critical to remember and reject the harm supersessionist rhetoric in and out of the text does, especially as anti-Semitic attacks are recently resurgent.

EPIPHANY VI

Numbers 5:11–24, 27–28; Psalm 7:1–8, 14–17;
1 Corinthians 7:1–17; Luke 7:36–50

Numbers 5:11 Now the JUDGE OF ALL FLESH spoke to Moses, saying: ¹² Speak to the women and men of Israel and say to them: If the wife of any man goes astray and betrays him with a betrayal, ¹³ and a man lies with her [yielding] an emission of seed yet it is hidden from the eyes of her husband and she conceals [it], and she has rendered herself unacceptable and there is no witness against her and she was not forced . . . ¹⁴ And if a spirit of jealousy comes upon him and he is jealous on account of his wife and she has rendered herself unacceptable, or if a spirit of jealousy comes on him and he is jealous on account of his wife and she has not rendered herself unacceptable . . . ¹⁵ Then the man shall bring his wife to the priest and he shall bring the offering for her: one-tenth of an ephah of barley flour [about two quarts] and he shall not pour oil on it and he shall not put frankincense on it, for it is an offering of jealousy, an offering of remembrance, for remembering iniquity.

¹⁶ Then the priest shall bring her near and set her before the JUDGE OF ALL THE EARTH. ¹⁷ The priest shall take holy water in an earthen vessel, and from the dust that is on the floor of the tabernacle, the priest shall take and put into the water. ¹⁸ Then the priest shall make the woman stand before the DREAD GOD, unbind the hair of the woman and place upon her hands the offering of remembrance; it is an offering of jealousy. And in the hand of the priest shall be the curse begetting waters of bitterness. ¹⁹ Then the priest shall make her swear, saying, "If no man has lain with you and if you have not turned aside to that which is unacceptable while under [subject to] your husband, be uninjured from the curse begetting waters of bitterness. ²⁰ But if you have turned aside while under [subject to] your husband, if you have rendered yourself unacceptable, and a man has lain with you who is not your husband . . ." ²¹ Now the priest makes the woman swear the imprecation [oath of cursing] and says to the woman, "May the ALL-SEEING GOD make you an imprecation and an execration [a ritual cursing and the curse itself] among your people when the FOUNT OF JUSTICE makes your

uterus collapse and your womb swell. ²² Now may these curse-begetting waters of bitterness go into your innards and make your womb swell, your uterus collapse!" And the woman shall say, "Amen. Amen." ²³ Then the priest shall write these curses in a scroll and dissolve them in the waters of bitterness. ²⁴ He shall make the woman drink the curse-begetting waters of bitterness and the curse-begetting waters shall enter her, creating bitterness.

²⁷ When he has made her drink the waters, then, if she has rendered herself unacceptable and has betrayed her husband with an act of betrayal, the curse-begetting waters shall enter into her and cause bitterness and her womb shall swell and her uterus collapse, and the woman shall become an imprecation among her people. ²⁸ But if the woman has not rendered herself unacceptable and is pure, then she shall be uninjured and be able to be sown with seed.

Psalm 7:1–8, 14–17

¹ SHELTERING ONE my God, in you I take refuge;
  save me from all who pursue me and deliver me.
² Else like a lion they will rip me, body and soul, apart;
  they will tear and no one will deliver.
³ RIGHTEOUS ONE my God, if I have done this,
  if there is iniquity in my hands,
⁴ if I have repaid my ally with harm
  or plundered my foe without cause,
⁵ then let the enemy pursue me and overtake me,
  and trample my life to the ground
  and lay my glory in the dust. *Selah*
⁶ Rise up, THUNDERING GOD, in your anger;
  raise up in opposition to the wrath of my enemies;
  wake on my behalf the justice you have appointed.
⁷ Let the congregation of the peoples be gathered around you,
  and above it return [to your place] on high.
⁸ The RIGHTEOUS GOD judges the peoples;
  judge me, RIGHTEOUS ONE, according to my righteousness
  and according to my integrity.
¹⁴ Look! He is pregnant with iniquity,
  having conceived troublemaking,
  and births lies.
¹⁵ A pit he dug and enlarged it,
  then fell into the hole he made.
¹⁶ His troublemaking returns upon his own head,
  and on his head does their violence descend.
¹⁷ I will give thanks to the JUDGE OF ALL FLESH according to her righteousness,
  and I shall sing praise to the Name of the HOLY GOD, the Most High.

1 Corinthians 7:1 Now, about what you have written: It is good for a man not to take hold of a woman. ² But because of sexual immorality, each man should have his own woman and each woman her own man. ³ For the wife, the husband should do his duty and likewise the wife for her husband. ⁴ For the wife does not have authority over her own body, rather the husband does; likewise the husband does not have authority over his own body, yet the wife does. ⁵ Do not ever defraud each other except by agreement for a time to devote yourselves to prayer, and then come together again so that Satan may not tempt you because of your lack of self-control. ⁶ This I say as a concession, not a command. ⁷ I wish that all were as I myself am. But each has their own gift from God, indeed one to one and another to another.

⁸ To the unmarried and the widows I say that it is good for them to remain so. ⁹ But if they are not showing self-control, they should marry; for it is better to marry than to burn. ¹⁰ To the married I give this command—not I but the Most High—a woman should not separate from her man, ¹¹ though if she does separate, let her remain unmarried or else be reconciled to her man; also a man should not divorce his woman. ¹² To the rest I say—I and not the Most High—that if a believer has a woman who is an unbeliever and she agrees to live with him, he should not divorce her. ¹³ And if a woman has a man who is an unbeliever and he agrees to live with her, she should not divorce him. ¹⁴ For the unbelieving man is made holy through his woman, and the unbelieving woman is made holy through her man. Otherwise, your children would be unclean, yet now they are holy. ¹⁵ Now if the unbeliever leaves, let them leave; a sister or brother is not bound in such circumstances. It is to peace that God has called you. ¹⁶ For woman, how do you know whether you will save your man, and how do you know, man, whether you will save your woman? ¹⁷ However let each walk through life as the Holy One has designated and as God has called them. This is what I instruct all the churches.

Luke 7:36 Now one of the Pharisees asked Jesus to eat with him and he went into the Pharisee's house and was seated. ³⁷ And suddenly, a woman who was in the city [known as] a sinner, having learned Jesus was eating in the Pharisee's house, brought an alabaster jar of perfumed ointment. ³⁸ She stood behind him at his feet, weeping, and began with her tears to bathe his feet and with the hairs of her head dried them. And she kissed his feet and anointed [them] with ointment. ³⁹ Now when the Pharisee who had invited Jesus saw it, he said to himself, "If this man was ever a prophet, he would know who and what kind of woman this is who is touching him—that she is a sinner." ⁴⁰ Then Jesus replied [to his thoughts] and said to him, "Simon, I have something to say to you." "Teacher," he replied, "Speak." ⁴¹ "Two debtors had a certain moneylender had: one owed five hundred denarii [more than a year's earning], and the other fifty [almost two month's earning]. ⁴² When they could not pay the moneylender canceled both debts. Now which of them will love their creditor more?" ⁴³ Simon replied and said, "I suppose the one for whom the moneylender forgave the greater debt." And Jesus said to him, "You have judged rightly." ⁴⁴ Then turning toward the woman Jesus said to Simon, "Do you see this woman? I entered your house; water for my feet you gave not, but she with her tears has bathed my feet and with her hair, dried them. ⁴⁵ No kiss [of peace] did you give me, but from when I came in she has not stopped kissing my feet. [46] Oil for my head you did not prepare, but with perfumed ointment she has anointed my feet. [47] That is why I say to you, forgiven are her sins, which were many, thus she loves deeply. But the one to whom little is forgiven, loves little." [48] And Jesus said to her, "Your sins are forgiven." [49] Then those who were reclining at the table with him began to say among themselves, "Who is this who even forgives sins?" [50] And Jesus said to the woman, "Your faith has saved you; go in peace."

PROCLAMATION

Text Notes

The ritual challenge and potential cursing of a woman suspected of adultery is referred to as the Sotach, based on the verb for "turning" or "going astray," *s-t-ch*. The passage is heavily ritualized and repetitive. I have preserved those elements while laboring to make them comprehensible to a wide audience. Contemporary readers and hearers may experience the passage as arcane and deeply troubling for its treatment of a woman who is merely suspected based on a husband's feelings of jealousy. It is important to note that this ritual safeguards a woman from false accusation and subsequent stoning. The cost of the ritual is born by the husband and the woman's fate is theoretically left up to God—though some scholars consider that the water was biologically active, an abortifacient.

The expression in Numbers 5:12 is literally "sinned a sin" but contextually refers to marital infidelity, hence "betrayed a betrayal" here. Everett Fox understands the husband's jealousy to be "jealous-rage" in verse 14 and throughout the passage. Rabbinic commentator Ibn Ezra suggests the emphasis on "seed" in verse 13 indicates she was discovered through pregnancy, since she was not caught in the act, and there were, of course, no witnesses. That raises the possibility that ignorance about conception and pregnancy could have contributed to false accusations.

Verses 13–14, 19, and 27 use *tamei*, traditionally translated "unclean" and verse 28 uses its counterpart, *tahorah*, commonly translated as "clean." However, they are not an inverted word pair; they are not the same word, or root. Ilona Rashkow (*Taboo or Not Taboo: Sexuality and Family in the Hebrew Bible*, Augsburg Fortress, 2000) and Rabbi Phyllis Berman (separately in her own teaching) propose the translation "taboo" and "not taboo" to mitigate the stigma that comes with a scriptural text, proclaiming women "unclean" for regular human, biological occurrences, such as menstruation and other vaginal discharge, birth, and sexual intercourse. In this passage, I use "render herself unacceptable" because of the awkwardness of rendering oneself "taboo."

There are claims that the first and second temples had a designated area on the floor from which the dust used in the ritual in verse 17 was to be taken. The water used in the ritual was taken from the laver used for priestly ablution made from the mirrors of women in Exodus 38:8. (I have previously argued that they served as a signal corps in *Daughters of Miriam*, Fortress, 2008.) In 18, the "unbinding" has been understood as being a veil, braids, or hair in general. The translation "curse-begetting waters of bitterness" in verse 19ff reflects the alliteration in the Hebrew phrase. It is not known whether the ink was biologically active or whether there was any other unnamed element in the potion. The woman may be proclaimed innocent if she has no subsequent miscarriage or aborted pregnancy; however, verse 28 intimates that she may not be in the clear until a later successful pregnancy.

In verse 2 of the psalm (v. 3 in Hebrew), "soul," *nephesh*, represents the living person, "body and soul." In the latter portion of the psalm, the antagonist is singular; some translations use the plural as a gender neutral. In verse 14 (Heb v. 15), I have preserved the masculine singular to highlight the contrast with the language of conception, pregnancy, and birth in the binary framework of the world of the text.

Neither Hebrew nor Greek has distinct words for wives or husbands. Both languages use the expressions "her man" and "his woman" to indicate conjugal relationships. In 1 Corinthians 7, Paul first says that each *woman or man* should have their own spouse. Then using the same wording, he means that each *wife or husband* should do their duty by their spouse. Paul uses *anthropos*, which means "human" and "man" for man and *aner*, male person, for "husband" while using the most common term for women, *gune*, for both women and wives. Having used *anthropos* for male initially, it is not clear whether Paul means "all males" or "all people" have their own gift of God in verse 7.

The word "sinner" in Luke 7:37 and verse 39 is suggestive. However, no specific sin is named, and centuries of patriarchal and misogynistic interpretation have presumed the woman's sins were sexual in nature. The ointment was likely perfumed, as "ointment" and "perfume" are the same word, *muron*. Her physical position in verse 38 indicates his position, reclining on a dining couch, as well as the practice.

Preaching Prompts

Epiphany is a season of focusing on revelations and manifestations of God, particularly in and through Jesus. But while some folk are experiencing God, breaking into their Monday in the world, others are asking where is God? Female characters in the scriptures rarely experience God in the same way as do male characters, and certainly not with the same frequency. This combination of characters provides an opportunity to wrestle with the questions: Where is God? Where is she revealing herself in spaces where cultural, ethnic, gender, and other biases constitute the dominant narrative, including the dominant religious narrative?

While the scriptures reflect their cultures of origin, including predilection for associating women and our bodies with sin and sinfulness, God is not only not limited to these biases, but present in and in spite of these texts; though, it may call for us to read against a text. The first lesson normalizes male jealousy and possessiveness; that kind of jealous rage continues to be normalized by men who stock, control, batter, and even murder their partners and families, leaving many to ask, where Is God? God is the ultimate arbiter of the accused woman's innocence. In the psalm, which may be read from the perspective of the accused woman, God is the author of salvation and the righteous judge.

The Epistle documents Paul's attempt to extend his manner of life to all of the followers of the way of Jesus, a way of life that is also deeply rooted in an unhealthy fixation on women and our bodies. Read with the previous lesson, it provides an opportunity to talk about the ways in which we understand gender and partnership in healthy, consensual, egalitarian terms in spite of the models of our spiritual ancestors. It also provides an opportunity to talk about how we read and understand scripture and that we are not called to imitate all of its cultural constructs and practices. Read with the Gospel, it illustrates how much Pauline theology diverges from the example Jesus set with women in public and in private.

The Lukan Jesus is characterized by close relationships with women from his miraculous conception. The God incarnate in Jesus in Luke is fully human, fully gendered, and deeply connected to the women and men who surround him in living and dying and rising. Yet the worlds in which and to which he writes continue to put strictures and expectations on women about how we look, including what we do to our hair, largely from the perspective of men whose objectification of women and girls and emotional motivation are normalized. This patriarchal social programming is all too often enforced by other women. Where, indeed, is God in this?

Lastly, there is attention to women's hair as an extension of themselves and as a boundary marking intimate access in the first lesson and in the Gospel. Hair continues to function for many in this way in Eastern and Western cultures, whether it is covered or not. And hair loss can be deeply traumatizing. Women with bald heads or closely shaved hair continue to be stigmatized in some contexts via appeals to other biblical passages, i.e., 1 Corinthians 11:6, 15; 1 Timothy 2:9. Billion-dollar industries exist to profit off the ways in which black women's hair functions as extensions of us while being traditionally excluded from dominant cultural notions of beauty, and many black women suffer the unwanted touch of white women, crossing that intimate barrier, to satisfy their curiosity about the texture and feel of our hair.

All of these lessons offer space to ask where it is we see God and seek her in places and persons that have not been designated as worthy of her habitation.

EPIPHANY VII

Genesis 47:13–25; Psalm 107:1–3, 35–43; Acts 5:1–11; Luke 8:1–15

Genesis 47:13 Now there was no food in all the land, for the famine was very severe and the land of Egypt and the land of Canaan languished because of the famine. ¹⁴ Then Joseph gathered up all the money that was found in the land of Egypt and in the land of Canaan for the grain that they bought, and Joseph brought the money into the house of Pharaoh. ¹⁵ When the money from the land of Egypt and from the land of Canaan was spent, then all the Egyptians came to Joseph, saying, "Give us food! For why should we die in front of you? For our money is gone!" ¹⁶ And Joseph answered, "Bring me your livestock and I will give you all food for your livestock if your money is gone." ¹⁷ So they brought their livestock to Joseph and Joseph gave them food for the horses and livestock: the flocks, the herds, and the donkeys; thus Joseph provided them with food that year for all their livestock. ¹⁸ When that year was ended, they came to him the following year and said to him, "We cannot hide from my lord that our money is ended and the herds of cattle are my lord's; there is nothing left before my lord except our bodies and our lands. ¹⁹ Why should we die before your eyes, both we and our land? Buy us and our land for food and we with our land will become slaves to Pharaoh; now give us seed that we may live and not die and that the land not become desolate."

²⁰ Thus Joseph bought all the land of Egypt for Pharaoh and every Egyptian sold their fields because the famine pressed down upon them and the land became Pharaoh's. ²¹ As for the people, he moved them to cities [and made slaves of them] from one end of the border of Egypt to the other end. ²² Only the land of the priests did he not buy, for it [their land] was a statutory holding for the priests from Pharaoh, and they ate on the statutory holding that Pharaoh gave them; therefore, they did not sell their land. ²³ Then Joseph said to the people, "Look here! I have bought you all this day along with your land for Pharaoh; here is seed for you: seed the land. ²⁴ And at the harvests you shall give one-fifth to Pharaoh and four-fifths shall be your own as seed for the field and for food for yourselves and whoever is in your households and as food for your little ones." ²⁵ They said, "You have saved our lives; may it find pleasure in your eyes my lord, we will be slaves to Pharaoh."

Psalm 107:1–3, 35–43

¹ Give thanks to SHE WHO IS MAJESTY, for she is good,
 and her faithful love endures forever.
² Let the redeemed of SHE WHO SAVES proclaim
 that she redeemed them from the hand of the foe.
³ And she has gathered them from [all] the lands;
 from the east and from the west, from the north and from the south.
³⁵ She turns desert into pools of water,
 and dry ground into springs of water.
³⁶ And there she settles the hungry,

and they establish a town to inhabit.
³⁷ They sow fields and plant vineyards,
and they yield a fruitful harvest.
³⁸ She blesses them and they multiply even more,
and their cattle, she does not let diminish.
³⁹ Then they [themselves] are diminished and humbled
through oppression, trouble, and sorrow.
⁴⁰ So, she pours contempt on princes
and makes them wander in empty places where there is no path;
⁴¹ Then she elevates the needy from affliction,
and makes their families like flocks.
⁴² The upright see it and are glad
and every wicked thing shuts its mouth.
⁴³ Who is the wise one who observes to these things?
They will come to understand the faithful love of the S<small>HEPHERDING</small> G<small>OD</small>.

Acts 5:1 Now a certain man named Ananias, with his wife Sapphira, sold some property. ² And he kept back some of the proceeds, with the knowledge of his wife, and brought only a part and placed it at the feet of the apostles. ³ "Ananias," Peter asked, "why has Satan filled your heart to lie to the Holy Spirit and to withhold from the proceeds of the land? ⁴ Was it not [both of] yours while it remained unsold, and in your power? Why have you contrived this in your heart? You did not lie to [mere] mortals but to God!" ⁵ Now when Ananias heard these words, he fell down dying. And great fear came upon all who heard. ⁶ The young men came and wrapped him up, then carried him out and buried him.

⁷ And it happened after about the space of three hours, his wife came in not knowing what had happened. ⁸ Peter said to her, "Tell me whether you two sold the land for such and such." And she said, "Yes, that was the price." ⁹ Then Peter said to her, "How is it that you two have conspired to put the Spirit of the Holy One to the test? Look! The feet of those who have buried your husband are at the door, and they will carry you out." ¹⁰ And she fell down immediately at his feet and died. Then the young men came in and found her dead, and they carried her out and buried her beside her husband. ¹¹ And great fear came upon the whole church and all who heard these things.

Luke 8:1 Now after [a woman anointed his feet] Jesus went on through cities and villages, proclaiming and bringing the good news of the reign of God. The twelve were with him. ² There were also some women who had been cured of evil spirits and infirmities: Mary, called Magdalene, from whom seven demons had gone out, ³ and Joanna, the wife of Herod's steward Chuza, and Susanna, and many others, who provided for them out of their resources.

⁴ Now a great crowd of women, children, and men gathered, coming to Jesus town by town and he said in a parable: ⁵ "A sower went out to sow seed and while sowing some fell on the path and was trampled on, and the birds of the air devoured it. ⁶ And another batch fell on

rock and as it grew up, it withered having no moisture. ⁷ And other seed fell among thorns, and the thorns grew up with it and choked it. ⁸ Yet more fell onto good ground, and when it grew, it produced a hundredfold." As Jesus said this he called out, "Let anyone with ears to hear listen!"

⁹ Then his disciples [including the women who supported him] asked him what this parable meant. ¹⁰ Jesus said, "To you all has it been given to know the mysteries of the majesty of God, but to others, through parables, so that [they would be]:

looking yet not seeing,
and listening but not understanding.

¹¹ "Now the parable is this: The seed is the word of God. ¹² Those on the path are they who have heard; then comes the devil and takes away the word from their hearts in order that they not believe, that they not be saved. ¹³ Those on the rock are they who, when they hear, receive the word with joy, however, they have no root; they believe for a season and then in a time of testing, defect. ¹⁴ The ones that fell among the thorns, they are the ones who hear and they are choked by the cares and riches and pleasures of life as they go their way and they do not produce mature fruit. ¹⁵ But that on good ground, they are those who through a good and honest heart hear the word, hold fast, and bring forth fruit through persistence.

PROCLAMATION

Text Notes

In Genesis 47:14, Joseph "scrapes up" or "gleans" all the money in Egypt. Verse 21 exists in multiple forms. The Masoretic Text and Peshitta have "he moved them to the city." However, the Samaritan Pentateuch and Septuagint have "he made them slaves." The Vulgate lacks either phrase. I have elected to include both phrases.

In Psalm 107:2, "woman-born" renders the euphemism for humanity, "human children/children (or sons) of men." The "empty places" of verse 40 is *tohu*, the empty chaotic space of creation in Genesis 1:1.

Many have broken this passage in Luke 8 after the first three verses, treating the parable of the sower as a separate reading from the account of the women who provide for Jesus and his *other* disciples. Reading the two sections together as a larger unit not only keeps the women among the disciples but offers space for their voices among those who asked Jesus questions, participating fully in Torah and other study with Jesus along with their male comrades.

In Luke 8:3, the women provide for "them" in most manuscripts, indicating significant funding to provide for themselves, other disciples, and Jesus in addition to family obligations. "The disciples" in verse 9 includes the women, emphasized in this translation; see also Joseph Fitzmeyer in the Anchor Bible Commentary volume on Luke, p. 707. Verse 10 loosely quotes Isaiah 6:9–10. I use "majesty" of God to replace "kingdom" in verse 10 to signify the larger grandeur of God's being in Godspace; in other places, such as in verse 1, I use reign or realm as contextually appropriate.

Preaching Prompts

Money is a thorny issue, to borrow an image from the Gospel. Money, wealth, and other resources are not evil; money is a tool. Our financial practices reveal our priorities, our character, our theology, our faith, and our worldview. Joseph—who was culturally Egyptian at this point with an Egyptian name, an Egyptian wife, and virtually a part of the first family in addition to being the chief executive officer of Egypt (Genesis 41:45)—saw the severe famine and poverty that resulted from it as an opportunity to enrich the empire at the expense of its most vulnerable residents. In so doing, he set up, or perhaps, better maximized the efficiency of the system that would enslave his descendants.

In the time of the matriarchs and patriarchs represented by the Joseph story, wealth was on the hoof as the Israelites were not yet agriculturalists. In the subsequent lessons, money, wealth, and resources are represented by having seed to sow and having a successful harvest. In the psalm, God displays God's power and love by providing for the oppressed, afflicted, hungry, and those needing a place to live in which the soil is rich and where they will be able to grow food to feed themselves.

The second lesson and gospel are somewhat antithetical. In the reading from Acts, a couple describes the burgeoning beloved community. It is a crime without an occasion because there was no requirement to give any of their wealth, though that was the common practice. In the Gospel, women who appear to have great wealth lavish it upon this wandering rabbi and their brother disciples, whose fishing enterprises appear to be insufficient to fund their travels. "Wealth" gets redefined in the Gospel. It is no longer limited to the physical resources necessary to sustain life, but through the parable, includes the word of God preached by Jesus, food for our souls.

Running through all of these lessons is the good gift of God's handcrafted earth. It is the cosmic seed vault. It is an inheritance that requires tending. And it is an inheritance that is being squandered. Human action, inaction, and the resulting consequences are rendering our planet less able to receive seed and generate a life-sustaining harvest. Ecology or creation care is also a financial issue that reveals character and commitment, theology, and faith.

EPIPHANY VIII

This Sunday in Epiphany is optional, pending the fall of Easter.

Isaiah 11:1–5; Psalm 33:6–9, 13–22; Romans 15:7–13; Luke 9:18–27

Isaiah 11:1 A sprig shall sprout from the stump of Jesse,
>   [from the line of Ruth]
>   and a shoot shall blossom from those roots.
> ² The spirit of SHE WHO IS WISDOM, she shall rest on that one,
>   the spirit of wisdom and understanding,
>   the spirit of counsel and might,
>   the spirit of knowledge and the reverence of the HOLY ONE OF OLD.
> ³ That one shall delight in revering the HOLY ONE.
>   Not by what their eyes see, shall that one judge,
>   and not by what their ears hear, shall that one decide.
> ⁴ Rather, that one shall, with righteousness, judge the poor,
>   and decide with justice for the oppressed of the earth;
>   that one shall strike the earth with the rod of their mouth,
>   and with the breath [the spirit] of their lips, that one shall kill the wicked.
> ⁵ Righteousness shall gird their inner organs,
>   and faithfulness their loins.

Psalm 33:6–9, 13–22

> ⁶ By the word of WISDOM were the heavens made,
>   by the breath of her mouth, all the heavenly hosts.
> ⁷ She gathers up the waters of the ocean as in a water-skin
>   and stores up the depths of the sea.
> ⁸ Let all the earth revere SHE WHO IS WISDOM;
>   let all who dwell in the world stand in awe of her.
> ⁹ For she spoke, and it came to pass;
>   she commanded, and it stood fast;
>   she commanded, and it stood firm.
> ¹³ From the heavens the MOST HIGH looks down;
>   she sees all the woman-born.
> ¹⁴ From her eternal throne she gazes upon
>   all the inhabitants of the earth.
> ¹⁵ She who fashions their hearts alike
>   is the one who discerns all their doings.
> ¹⁸ Look! The eye of the FAITHFUL ONE is on those who revere her,
>   on those who hope in her faithful love,

¹⁹ to deliver their soul from death,
   and to keep them alive in famine.
²⁰ Our soul waits for SHE WHO SAVES;
   she is our help and shield.
²¹ In her is our heart glad,
   because we trust in her holy Name.
²² Let your faithful love, COMPASSIONATE GOD, be upon us,
   for it is you in whom we trust.

Romans 15:7 Accept one another, therefore, just as Christ has accepted you, for the glory of God. ⁸ I tell you that the Messiah has become a minister to the circumcised for the sake of truth to confirm the promises given to the ancestors [to the mothers and fathers] ⁹ and in order that the Gentiles might glorify God on account of God's mercy. As it is written,

*"Therefore, I will confess you among the Gentiles,
and sing praises to your name,"*

¹⁰ and again it says,

"Rejoice, O Gentiles, with God's people,"

¹¹ and again,

*"Praise the Most High, all you Gentiles,
and let all the peoples praise God,"*

¹² and again Isaiah says,

*"The root of Jesse shall come,
and the one who rises to rule the Gentiles,
in whom the Gentiles shall hope."*

¹³ May the God of hope fill you with all joy and peace in believing, so that you may abound in hope by the power of the Holy Spirit.

Luke 9:18 Now it happened when Jesus was praying alone, the only ones present were the disciples that Jesus asked them, "Who do the crowds of women and men say that I am?" ¹⁹ And they responded, saying, "John the Baptizer, but others, Elijah, and yet others, that one of the prophets of old has arisen." ²⁰ Now Jesus said to them, "But who do you all say that I am?" And Peter answered, "The Messiah of God."
   ²¹ Jesus rebuked them and commanded them not to tell anyone, ²² saying, "The Son of Woman must undergo great suffering, and be rejected by the elders, chief priests, and scholars and be killed and on the third day be raised." ²³ Then Jesus said to them all, "If anyone wants to come after me, let them deny themselves and take up their cross every day and follow me. ²⁴ For those who want to save their life will lose it, and those who lose their life for my sake will save it. ²⁵ For what does it profit any mortal if they gain the whole world, but

lose themselves or are destroyed? ²⁶ As for those who are ashamed of me and of my words, of them will the Son of Woman be ashamed when he comes in his glory and the glory of the Creator and of the holy angels. ²⁷ But truly I tell you, there are some standing here who will not taste death before they see the majesty of God."

PROCLAMATION

Text Notes

"Spirit," "breath," and "wind" are the same word in Hebrew, *ruach*, a feminine noun no matter the (imagined or supposed) gender of the noun/person/entity with which it is linked. The association of *ruach* with "lips" in Isaiah 11:4 makes clear that "breath" is intended. That double meaning continues with Greek *pneuma* in the successive readings. Because ancient readers and hearers would have elucidated both meanings, I have shaped the translation to provide both sets of meetings as they occur. The decision of whether and when to capitalize "spirit" is complicated by the lack of capital letters in Hebrew. (Some Greek manuscripts employ no capital letters.) When "spirit" is functioning as an animate being, a "person," I capitalize it, sparingly in the text, more frequently in the commentary.

There is a vast lexicon of terms for impoverished persons in the Hebrew Bible. The *anavim*, "oppressed" in Isaiah 11:4, are translated elsewhere as "meek" (NRSV) and "lowly" (JPS, Alter). However, their abject state is due to oppression. Verse 5 employs two different words for "loins" in a traditional biblical Hebrew poetic couplet. I have chosen the generic but suggestive "inner organs" for one of these synonyms.

In Psalm 33:14, God's "eternal throne" is "the fixed place [where] God sits." In verse 15, human hearts are *yachad*, "together" or "as one"—the cardinal number is the root word.

Since *pateron* in Romans 15:8 can be inclusive of "ancestors" or "fathers" and God's promises were not and are not limited by gender, I use the most inclusive option. In verse 9, Christ takes up the same diaconal ministry with which the women who follow him are credited. Verses 9–12 quote Psalm 18:49, Deuteronomy 32:43, Psalm 117:1, and Isaiah 11:10 from the LXX. There are some variances between the Greek and Hebrew of Deuteronomy 32:43: In the Hebrew text, "the nations, God's people" are called to rejoice, while in the Greek, the heavens are called to rejoice *with* God's people. (For more on the divergence between the manuscript traditions on this verse, see the annotations and comparisons in *The Dead Seas Scrolls Bible*, ed. Abegg, Flint, and Ulrich.)

Throughout this passage and throughout Luke (and the other Gospels), "disciples" should be understood as inclusive of women. In verse 18, "women and men" makes the gendered composition of "crowds" apparent. The "rebuke" of Jesus in verse 21 has been verbally understood; there is some consensus that he was rebuking the utterance of the messianic title and its explicit political claims and implications, even when only spoken aloud among a presumably trustworthy small group.

Preaching Prompts

In its original context, Isaiah 11 describes a longed-for monarch to restore the sovereignty of ancient Israel. It is messianic in that it looks with hope for a monarch who will be God's chosen servant. In a profoundly Christian reading, Jesus exemplifies all of the virtues expressed in his ancestral scripture, the full measure of the six-fold expression of God's abiding spirit in verse 1. In this often omitted week of readings, the passage provides a final opportunity to marvel at God's appearance among us in Jesus. The Spirit that is upon and within the one who is to come in Isaiah 11:1 is the same spirit that spoke creation into being in Psalm 33:6.

There is an association between "the spirit" and "the word" in the first reading and in the psalm that is carried through into the understanding and identification of Jesus as the Word. Isaiah 11:4 the word is a word of terror, death to the wicked. In the psalm, the word is a word of life, a word of creation. The breath that gives utterance to the word of generativity in Psalm 33:6 and 9 is the very spirit of these readings. In the Epistle, Paul offers his prooftexts that Jesus is this unique manifestation of God's word and spirit and human flesh, including the first reading. But rather than appearing as the master of the universe, Paul points out that Jesus appears as a servant, ministering, not lording.

We skip ahead for this Gospel reading so that if this is a year with Epiphany VIII (which does not occur every year due to the vagaries of the 365 days solar calendar), the last lesson before the Transfiguration will be one of prayer and contemplation, illuminating the path into the coming Lenten season. In the Gospel reading, the matter of the identity of Jesus and his relationship to the hopes and claims of his people, his ancestors, and his ancestral prophets has come to a crux. Peter connects the dots and says out loud what many of the women and men around Jesus are thinking and likely have been for some time. As though he knows he is under surveillance and his words will be used against him, Jesus neither explicitly confirms nor denies Peter's conclusion. As we prepare to go into Lent, we are left with a choice: Do we believe Jesus is the Messiah, and will we follow him through the difficult days ahead? Will we follow Jesus? Will we take up our cross every day? In keeping with the spirit of this lectionary, we might further ask what crosses women and sexual and gender minorities take up for themselves and what crosses are imposed upon them, even, to what crosses are they nailed?

LAST WEEK OF EPIPHANY (TRANSFIGURATION)

Judges 4:5–10; Psalm 46; 2 Peter 1:16–21; Luke 9:28–36

Judges 4:5 Now, Deborah sat [as judge] under the Palm of Deborah between Ramah and Bethel in the hill country of Ephraim and the women and men of Israel came up to her for judgment. ⁶ And she sent and called for Barak ben Abinoam from Kedesh of Naphtali and said to him, "Did not the Sovereign God, the God of Israel, command you? Go! March on Mount Tabor and take ten thousand men from the tribe of Naphtali and the tribe of Zebulun. ⁷ Now, I will draw out for you—toward the Wadi Kishon—Sisera, the commander of Jabin's army along with his chariots and his troops and I will give him into your hand." ⁸ Then Barak said to her, "If you will go with me, I will go; but if you will not go with me, I will not go." ⁹ And Deborah said, "Indeed I will go with you however, there will be no glory for you on the path you are taking, for into the hand of a woman will She Who Is Mighty sell Sisera." Then Deborah got up and she went with Barak to Kedesh. ¹⁰ And Barak called up Zebulun and Naphtali to Kedesh and ten thousand warriors went up behind him, and Deborah went up with him.

Psalm 46

1. God is for us a refuge and strength,
   a help in trouble, easily found.
2. Therefore we shall not fear, though the earth should change,
   though the mountains quiver in the heart of the sea;
3. its waters roar and churn,
   the mountains tremble with its swell.
4. There is a river whose streams make glad the city of God,
   the holy habitation of the Most High.
5. God is in the midst of her, she shall not be moved;
   God will help her when the morning unfurls.
6. The nations roar, dominions quiver;
   God puts forth her voice, the earth melts.
7. The Warrior Protectrix is with us;
   a stronghold for us is the God of Rebekah's line.
8. Come, behold the works of the Fire of Sinai;
   see what desolations she has set on the earth.
9. She makes wars cease to the end of the earth;
   she breaks the bow, and shatters the spear,
   she burns chariots with fire.
10. "Be still and know that I am God!

I am exalted among the nations,
I am exalted in the earth."
¹¹ The Warrior Protectrix is with us;
a stronghold for us is the God of Rebekah's line.

2 Peter 1:16 For we did not follow sophisticated mythologies when we made known to you all the power and coming of our Redeemer Jesus Christ, rather we had been eyewitnesses of his majesty. ¹⁷ For Christ from God the Sovereign received honor and glory, a voice came to him from the Majestic Glory, saying, "This is my Son, my Beloved, with whom I am well pleased." ¹⁸ And we ourselves heard this voice that came from heaven, while we were with him on the holy mountain.

¹⁹ Thus we have a sure prophetic word; you all would do well to be attentive to this as to a lamp shining in a shadowy place, until the day dawns and the morning star rises in your hearts. ²⁰ First this you must understand, that of all written prophecy, none is a matter of individual interpretation. ²¹ For not by human will ever came any prophecy, rather women and men moved by the Holy Spirit spoke from God.

Luke 9:28 Now about eight days after the teachings [about the cost of discipleship], Jesus took with him Peter and John and James and went up on the mountain to pray. ²⁹ And while he was praying, the appearance of his face changed and his clothing lit up white like lightning. ³⁰ And suddenly! They saw two men, Moses and Elijah, speaking to Jesus. ³¹ They appeared in glory and were speaking of his exodus, which he was about to complete in Jerusalem. ³² Now Peter and those with him were weighed down with sleep, but since they were awake, they saw his glory and the two men with him. ³³ And just as they were departing from him, Peter said to Jesus, "Master, it is good for us to be here; so let us make three tent-tabernacles: one for you, one for Moses, and one for Elijah," not knowing what he said. ³⁴ While he was saying this, a cloud came and overshadowed them and they were terrified as they entered the cloud. ³⁵ Then a voice came from the cloud that said, "This is my Son, the Chosen One; listen to him!" ³⁶ And while the voice was still speaking, Jesus was found alone. And they kept silent and told no one in those days anything they had seen.

PROCLAMATION

Text Notes

The Deborah texts exist in poetry (ch. 5) and prose (ch. 4). The poetic version is the most ancient and occurs in multiple manuscripts; some are nearly indecipherable due to their age, generating multiple diverse translations. There are two Septuagint versions, LXX-A (Alexandrinus) and LXX-B (Vaticanus). In both, Deborah is portrayed as God's messenger, a term frequently translated as "angel" but used for both human and divine messengers. This reading confers additional authority upon the woman who is already prophet and judge, following Moses, to be followed only by Samuel. Thus, Deborah's seat in Judges 4:5 was an official judicial seat. With Everett Fox, I also add the context in brackets.

Luke 9:31 employs the noun *exodos* for Jesus's mortal departure, which I translate with its English cognate to preserve the wordplay. Verse 35 has the voice from the heavens, here from a cloud, identify Jesus as "the Chosen [One]" rather than as the beloved as in Luke 3. However, there are some manuscript traditions that maintain Beloved.

Preaching Prompts

The Feast of the Transfiguration marks the "mountaintop moment" in which the veil between heaven and earth, time and eternity, and mortality and immortality parted to allow Jesus to commune with his cultural ancestors visibly on the physical plane in the sight of two of his disciples, granting the experience "legal" attestation, having two witnesses. In today's readings, the mountains themselves are characters. Mount Tabor in the first reading and though unnamed, most likely in the Gospel, represents salvation and deliverance. First, salvation comes at the hand of Deborah, leading Barak and their troops and then, at the feet of Jesus, the mountain may also signal that the saving work of Jesus will also come at the cost of shed blood.

At the Transfiguration, Moses and Elijah can be interpreted as the ancestral figures whose mantles Jesus inherits and surpasses in teaching and working miracles or as representing the Torah and the Prophets. One might wish to note the legacies of female prophets that Jesus also embodies: Miriam, who led people to freedom (Exodus 15:20), Deborah, who won the mountain (Tabor, considered the site of the Transfiguration) in battle (Judges 5:7, 12), and Huldah, who first proclaimed a written word the word of God (2 Kings 22:14–16).

Lastly, verse 32 of the Gospel says that Peter and John were able to witness the transfiguration because they had stayed awake. When the Black Lives Matter movement moved into the mainstream, one of its rallying cries was, "Stay woke!" This was a call to black folk primarily to keep our eyes open to what was going on around us when so much misinformation was being communicated by official sources and some media outlets. The expression was adopted during Advent as the basis for devotional material and sermon development. It has recently been co-opted by ridicule in an attempt to undermine its power. But it remains powerful language, regularly occurring in the scriptures.

LENT—ASH WEDNESDAY

Joel 2:1, 12–17, 21–22; Psalm 90:1–10, 12;
1 Corinthians 15:45–49; Matthew 6:1–6, 16–18

Joel 2:1 Blow the trumpet in Zion!
  Cry the alarm on my holy mountain!
  Let all the inhabitants of the land quake,
  for the day of the Holy God is coming, it is near.
  ¹² Yet even now, says the Holy One,
  return to me with all your hearts,
  with fasting, with weeping, and with lamenting.
  ¹³ Tear your hearts and not your clothing.
  Return to the Holy One, your God,
  for God is gracious and loves as a mother,
  slow to anger, and abounds in faithful love,
  and reluctant to impose harm.
  ¹⁴ Who knows whether God will not turn and relent,
  and leave a blessing behind,
  for a grain offering and a drink offering
  to the Holy One, your God?
  ¹⁵ Blow the trumpet in Zion;
  sanctify a fast;
  call a solemn assembly.
  ¹⁶ Gather the people:
  Sanctify the congregation;
  assemble the aged;
  gather the children,
  even breastfeeding babies.
  Let the bridegroom leave his room,
  and the bride her canopy.
  ¹⁷ Between the portico and the altar
  let the priests, the ministers of the Holy One, weep.
  Let them say, "Spare your people, Holy One,
  and do not offer your heritage as a mockery,
  a byword among the nations.
  Why should it be said among the peoples,
  'Where is their God?'"
  ²¹ Fear not, O land!
  Be glad and rejoice,
  for the Holy One has done great things!

22 Fear not, O animals of the field!
   For the pastures of the wilderness are green;
   the tree lifts up its fruit,
   the fig tree and vine give their riches.

Psalm 90:1–10, 12

1 MOTHER OF THE MOUNTAINS, you have been our refuge
   from one generation to another.
2 Before the mountains were born,
   or you writhed the land and the earth into birth,
   from age to age you are God.
3 You turn mortal flesh back to the dust and say,
   "Turn back, you who are woman-born."
4 For a thousand years in your sight are like yesterday when it is past
   and like a watch in the night.
5 You sweep them aside; they are an illusion;
   In the morning flourishing and in the evening wilting and withering.
6 In the morning it is green and flourishes;
   in the evening it is dried up and withered.
7 For we are consumed in your displeasure;
   we are afraid because of your wrathful indignation.
8 Our iniquities you have set before you,
   and our hidden sins in the light of your countenance.
9 When you are angry, all our days are gone;
   we bring our years to an end like a sigh.
10 The span of our life is seventy years, perhaps in strength even eighty;
   yet the sum of them is but labor and sorrow,
   for they pass away quickly and we are gone.
12 So teach us to number our days
   that we may apply our hearts to Wisdom.

1 Corinthians 15:45 Thus it is written, "The first human, Adam, became a living soul"; the last Adam became a spirit that gives life. 46 But it is not the spiritual that is first, but the physical, and then the spiritual. 47 The first human was from the earth, dust; the second human is from heaven. 48 As was the one of dust, so are those who are of dust; and as is the one of heaven, so are those who are of heaven. 49 Just as we have borne the image of the one of dust, we will also bear the image of the one of heaven.

Matthew 6:1 [Jesus said,] "Now, beware of practicing your justness before other people in order to be seen by them; surely, lest you have no reward from your Creator in heaven.

² "So when you give alms, do not trumpet before yourself, as the hypocrites do in the synagogues and in the streets, in order that they may be praised by other people. Truly I tell you, they have received their reward. ³ But when you give alms, do not let your left hand know what your right hand is doing, ⁴ in order that your alms may be secret; and your Creator who sees in secret will reward you.

⁵ "And when you pray, do not be like the hypocrites; for they love to stand and pray in the synagogues and on the street corners, in order that they may be seen by other people. Truly I tell you, they have received their recompense. ⁶ But whenever you pray, go into your room and shut the door and pray to your Creator who is in secret; and your Creator who sees in secret will reward you.

¹⁶ "And when you fast, do not be sullen like the hypocrites, for they disfigure their faces in order to show other people that they are fasting. Truly I tell you, they have received their reward. ¹⁷ But when you fast, put oil on your head and wash your face, ¹⁸ in order that your fasting may be seen, not by others, but by your Creator who is in secret, and your Creator who sees in secret will reward you."

PROCLAMATION

Text Notes

"Land" in Joel 2:1 and 21 is soil, not the nation. The hearts of the people in Joel 2:12–13 form a collective one, "the heart of you all."

In Psalm 90:2, God's grammatical gender is masculine, and the imagery used for God is feminine, birthing imagery (in the cis-gender ancient Israelite world), yielding the name for God in verse 1. "Turn" in verse 3 means both "turn around" and "repent." Also, in verse 3, "mortal flesh" renders "man," and "woman-born" renders "children / descendants of humanity / humankind" or "mortals."

1 Corinthians 15:47 quotes Genesis 2:7; throughout the passage, Paul uses *anthropos*, "human," rather than *aner*, "man," following Genesis, where the first earthling is "human," not "man."

In Matthew 6:1, "justness/justice," "uprightness," and "righteousness" are all translations of *dikaiosynēn*. Those righteous acts include far more than the alms-giving, prayer, and fasting in the following verses. The prayer room in verse 6 is an inner one, making one's prayer less likely to be seen.

Preaching Prompts

Joel 2 is a call to solemn assembly in fasting and repentance in response to a locust infestation and resulting economic loss and famine seen as divine punishment. It will be important to unravel the blame language. The text is explicitly inclusive across gender and age categories. The image of God as the mother of the mountains in Psalm 90:2 builds nicely on the maternal imagery present in God's mother-love in Joel 2:13.

The people of the land are to quake at God's power and presence (Joel 2:1), but the land itself (herself) should not fear, verse 21. Notably, God addresses the earth and her creatures in verse 21–22 (excluded from the designated verses in the BCP). God cares for them and whether humanity repents or not, God will care for them.

God's essential characteristics delineated in Joel 2:13—graciousness, loving from her womb (the noun and verb share a root), slow to anger, abounding in faithful love, and being slow to inflict retribution—recur in Exodus 34:6, Deuteronomy 4:31, and Jonah 4:2, and throughout the Psalms.

The Epistle makes clear that we are all both earthly dust and the stuff of heaven. We are all equally bearers of the divine image now, and even more so in the age to come. Paul's use of a paradigm distinguishing the spiritual from the physical in 1 Corinthians 15:46 lends itself easily to body/soul dichotomies and hierarchies; it also seems to unhelpfully deemphasize the Incarnation.

As with the Epistle, the implicit gender claims in the Gospel will need to be made explicit. Oiling the head, actually hair, is a common grooming practice for those of African descent like the Afro-Asiatic Israelites and their descendants; it is common in some Asian and other cultures as well. It is less comprehensible in the European culture that has colonized the text and its iconography.

In Matthew 6:6–7, omitted from the reading, Jesus tells his disciples not to pray like Gentiles who essentially babble repeatedly, and in that context introduces the Lord's Prayer. It is worth remembering that Jesus initially understood his ministry to be only to "the lost sheep of the house of Israel" (see Matthew 10:4; 15:6). After his encounter with the Syro-Phoenician woman, his ministry extended to the Gentiles.

A final note, when reciting Psalm 51 in the liturgy of the day, consider recentering Bathsheba's abduction, rape, and forced impregnation along with the murder of her husband.

LENT I

Ezekiel 37:1–14; Psalm 49:1–2, 5–15; Ephesians 1:15 –21; John 3:1–8

Ezekiel 37:1 The hand of GOD WHO DWELLS ABOVE THE CHERUBIM came upon me and God brought me out through the Spirit of GOD WHOSE NAME IS HOLY and rested me down in the middle of a particular valley—and it was full of bones. ² And God brought me over, above them, round and around and look! There were very many in the mouth of the valley and they were very dry. ³ Then God said to me, "Child of earth, can these bones live?" I answered, "Sovereign ALL-KNOWING GOD, you are the one who knows." ⁴ Then God said to me, "Prophesy upon these bones and say to them: Dry bones, hear the word of the ANCIENT OF DAYS. ⁵ Thus says the Sovereign HOLY GOD to these bones: Look! I will cause spirit-and-breath to enter you all and you all shall come to life. ⁶ And I will place sinews upon you all and I will make flesh come upon you all, and I will cover you all over with skin and put spirit-and-breath in you all, and you all shall come to life. And you all shall know that I am the WOMB OF LIFE."

⁷ So I prophesied just as I had been commanded and there was a sound as I prophesied and look here! Rattling! And the bones came together, each bone to its bone. ⁸ Then I looked—and look at that!—there were upon them, sinews, and flesh came upon them, and skin covered them up; yet there was no breath-that-is-spirit in them. ⁹ Then God said to me, "Prophesy to the breath-that-is-spirit, prophesy, earth child, and say to the spirit-that-is-breath: Thus says the Highest, the BREATH OF LIFE: From the four winds-of-breath-and-spirit, come spirit-breath and breathe-spirit upon these who have been slain, that they may come to life." ¹⁰ So I prophesied just as God commanded me and she, the breath-that-is-spirit, came into them and they came to life and stood upon their feet, a vast legion.

¹¹ Then God said to me, "Child of earth and Eve, these bones are the whole house of Israel. They are saying, 'Our bones are dried up and our hope is dead; we are utterly cut off.' ¹² Therefore, prophesy and say to them, 'Thus says the Highest, the WELLSPRING OF LIFE: I am going to open your graves and I will raise you all up from your graves, my people, and I will bring you all back to the land of Israel.'¹³ So you all shall know that I am the AUTHOR OF LIFE when I open your graves and raise you all up from your graves my people. ¹⁴ And I shall put my breath-that-is-spirit within you all and you shall come to life, and I shall cause you all to rest on your own earth; then you shall know that I, the AUTHOR OF LIFE, have spoken and will act," says the SOURCE OF LIFE.

Psalm 49:1–2, 5–15

¹ Hear this, all you peoples;
   give ear, all who dwell in the world,
² children of earth, children of Eve,
   rich and poor together.
⁵ Why should I fear in evil days,
   when iniquity at my heels surrounds me?
⁶ [Or] Those who trust in their wealth
   and praise of the abundance of their riches?
⁷ Certainly, it cannot redeem a person,
   or give to God as a ransom.
⁸ For the redemption-price of a soul is costly,
   they come to an end, forever.
⁹ Shall one live eternally
   and never see the Pit?
¹⁰ For when one sees the wise, they die;
   the foolish and ignorant perish together
   and leave to others their wealth.

11 Their graves are their homes for all time,
  their dwelling places from generation to generation,
  though they put their name on lands.
12 Humanity will not recline in grandeur;
  rather they are like the animals that perish.
13 This is the way of the foolish,
  those pleased with their own words. *Selah*
14 Like sheep they are set for Sheol;
  Death shall be their shepherd.
  The upright shall rule over them until the morning,
  and their form shall waste away;
  Sheol shall be their abode.
15 But God will ransom my soul,
  for from the grasp of Sheol she will take me. *Selah*

Ephesians 1:15 Because of this—that I have heard of your faith in Jesus the Messiah, and your love toward all the saints, 16 I do not cease to give thanks for you all as I make mention of you all in my prayers. 17 [I do so] in order that the God of our Redeemer Jesus the Messiah, the Origin of glory, may give you a spirit of wisdom and revelation as you come to know God. 18 [This] so that, with the eyes of your heart enlightened, you all may know what is the hope to which God has called you, what is the glory of God's inheritance among the saints, 19 and what is the surpassing magnificence of God's power for we who believe, according to the working of the power of God's strength. 20 [Power that] God worked in the Messiah when God raised Jesus from the dead and seated him at the right hand of God in the heavenly places, 21 far above all governance and authority and power and dominion and above every name that has been named, not only in this age but also in the one to come.

John 3:1 Now there was a man of the Pharisees—Nicodemus was his name—a leader in the Jewish community. 2 He came to Jesus at night and said to him, "Rabbi, we know that from God you have come as a teacher; for no one can do these signs that you do unless God is with them." 3 Jesus responded and said to him, "Truly, truly, I tell you, without being birthed again—that is being birthed from above, no one can see the majesty of God." 4 Nicodemus said to him, "How can a person be birthed after having grown old? Can a person enter their mother's womb a second time and be birthed?" 5 Jesus answered, "Truly, truly, I tell you, without being birthed of water and spirit no one can enter the majesty of God. 6 What is birthed of the flesh is flesh, and what is birthed of the spirit is spirit. 7 Marvel not that I said to you all, 'You must be birthed again, birthed from above.' 8 The spirit-that-is-wind blows where it wills and you hear the sound of it [the voice of the spirit], but you know not from whence it, she, comes or where it, she, goes. So it is with everyone who is birthed of the Spirit-that-is-like-wind."

PROCLAMATION

Text Notes

In Ezekiel 37:1 and in verse 14, the verb indicating being settled down on the ground after miraculous transport and restored to the previously inhabited land has the primary meaning of "rest," and is in a causative form. "Child of earth [and Eve]" and "earth child" translate *ben adam*, "child (or son) of humanity," indicating Ezekiel's creation and the stuff of creation, *adamah*, the earth, land, soil of verse 14; it also appears in verse 2 of the psalm. In this passage, *ruach* fulfills all three of its primary meanings: spirit, wind, and breath. In this passage, I combine the double and treble entendres with dashes throughout the passage. As *ruach* is feminine and has agency—particularly when understood as "spirit"—I include the feminine pronoun in verse 10. Ezekiel (and to some degree, Jeremiah) uses a rare form for the designing in which the word *adonai* proceeds the Tetragrammaton, which is usually replaced in pronunciation with *adonai*. Rather than read (and later type) *Adonai* ADONAI, the Masoretic Text is marked to be read as *Adonai* ELOHIM, yielding "Lord GOD" in most translations. Following the practice of this work, "Lord" is replaced, and the Tetragrammaton is translated and amplified with descriptive divine titles found in the appendix.

Paul's lengthy sentences have been truncated with the key points from earlier phrases brought forward to later phrases to facilitate clarity. In verse 17, "Origin" replaces "Father."

John 3 is fertile with puns and lush with birthing language that has arguably been overheard, illustrated by the effect of exchanging "born again" for "birthed again." I have labored to craft a translation that includes those interplays. In verse 1, I use "the Jewish community" to render "the Jews" (which has become something of a negative epithet) while keeping Jewish identity central. "Majesty" in verses 3 and 5 represents the totality of who God is as well as "where" God is without portraying God as a too-human monarch with imperial aspirations, which is what king/doms were in the world of the text. Verse 8 is truly puntastic: In the one case, the same word means both "sound" and "voice," and in the other, the same word means both "wind" and "spirit." In both cases, one set of meanings is animate and the other inanimate *in the contemporary interpretive context*. However, in the world of the text, it would have all been seen as animate, divinely so, to some degree. Lastly, while commenting on the wordplay, Raymond Brown (Anchor Bible Commentary, *John*, p. 131) states that the wordplay "cannot be reproduced in English." I demur.

Preaching Prompts

In the season of Lent, we walk more closely with the shadow of death than perhaps at any other time, save when we are knowingly approaching our own death or walking with someone else to theirs. We walk knowing that death is not the end. This ancient knowledge comes to us through many sources, including our scriptures. In the first lesson, God dramatically shows Ezekiel, and us, that not even a desiccated pile of disarticulated bones is firmly in the grasp of death. The power of God's spirit, as pervasive as the wind, enlivens us with each breath. God's breath, God's spirit, and the wind are aspects of a single reality, a single word in Hebrew.

The claim of the first passage (that nothing and no one is ever fully dead to God) will be tested by the empire that will put Jesus to death. Those who walked with Jesus to his death and those who fled from him in his death will also be tested. We who begin the journey of Lent will experience our own testing. For the psalmist, God is the one who rescues from death on this side of the grave. But for those satisfied with their own success and acquisitions, the grave will be their home for all time (v. 11). Death will be their eternal shepherd (v. 14). For some in the world of the text, resurrection is a faint hope, and for others, it is no hope at all. It is against this background that the Ezekiel passage would have been heard as an extraordinary claim, particularly among the ruins of what had once been a self-governing nation reduced to occupation and deportation. The claim of resurrection would remain an astonishing one in the world of the Gospels and in the world of the Epistles.

And in what may be a very familiar Gospel passage, Jesus uses feminine God-language rooted in the grammar of his mother-tongue in which spirit is feminine, to teach that we all must be born of the Spirit as he was—though there will naturally be some differences in our spiritual conception. The journey with Jesus to end through death and resurrection is also a birthing journey, a holy pregnancy.

In preaching these passages, one may wish to reflect that God is not concerned about our birthing or capacity to birth but rather that we are birthed through the Spirit. This gestational framework is one that includes all persons without regard to gender identity and performance, fertility, or parenthood. We are all the Spirit-born children of God should we choose to make that holy passage into new life. To have a holy Lent is to walk with Jesus pondering all these things.

LENT II

Genesis 31:25–27 43–50; Psalm 144:3–4, 12–15;
Romans 8:18–25; Luke 8:40–55

Genesis 31:25 Laban overtook Jacob. Now Jacob had pitched his tent in the hill country, and Laban with his kinsfolk camped in the hill country of Gilead. ²⁶ And Laban said to Jacob, "What have you done? You have robbed my heart and herded off my daughters like captives of the sword. ²⁷ Why did you sneak to run away and rob me and not tell me? I would have sent you away with celebration and singing, with drumming and strumming."

⁴³ Then Laban said to Jacob, "These daughters are my daughters, these children are my children, these flocks are my flocks, and all that you see, it is mine. Now what can I do today about these my daughters, or about their children whom they have birthed? ⁴⁴ Now, come, let us make a covenant, I and you, and let it be a witness between me and you." ⁴⁵ So Jacob took a stone, and set it up as a pillar. ⁴⁶ Then Jacob said to his kin, "Gather stones," and they took stones, and made a *gal*, a heap; and they ate there by the heap. ⁴⁷ Laban called it Jegar-sahadutha, but Jacob called it Gal-Ed (Heap of Witness). ⁴⁸ Laban said, "This heap is a witness between me and you today." Therefore, he called it Gal-Ed, ⁴⁹ and the pillar Mizpah (Watchtower), for he said, "The Holy One watch between me and you, when we are out of sight of the other. ⁵⁰ If you treat my daughters violently, or if you take women in addition to my daughters, though no one else is with us, see, that God is witness between me and you."

Psalm 144:3–4, 12–15

³ Womb of Life, what is humanity that you even know them,
    or the woman-born that you think of them?
⁴ Humanity is like a breath;
    whose days are like a passing shadow.
¹² Our sons in their youth
    are like plants full grown,
    our daughters are like cornerstones,
    cut for the building of a palace.
¹³ Our barns are full,
    from produce of every kind;
    our sheep have increased by thousands,
    many thousands in our surroundings.
¹⁴ Our cattle are heavy,
    there is no breach in the walls, no exile,
    and no cry of distress in our surroundings.
¹⁵ Happy are the people to whom such blessings fall;
    happy are the people whose God is the Womb of Life.

Romans 8:18 I consider that the sufferings of this present time are not worth comparing with the glory about to be revealed to us. [19] For the creation waits with eager longing for the revealing of the daughters and sons of God; [20] for the creation was subjected to futility, not of its own will but by the will of the one who subjected it, in hope [21] that the creation itself will be set free from its bondage to decay and will obtain the freedom of the glory of the daughters and sons of God. [22] We know that the whole creation has been groaning in labor pains until now; [23] and not only the creation, but we ourselves, who have the first fruits of the Spirit, groan inwardly while we wait for adoption, the redemption of our bodies. [24] For in hope we were saved. Now hope that is seen is not hope. For who hopes for what is seen? [25] But if we hope for what we do not see, we wait for it with patience.

Luke 8:40 Now when Jesus returned [from casting demons into a herd of pigs], the crowd of women, children, and men welcomed him, for they were all waiting for him. [41] And hear this! There came a man whose name was Jairus, a leader of the synagogue. And he fell at the feet of Jesus and urged him to come to his house. [42] For he had an only daughter, about twelve years old, and she was dying.

Now as he went, the crowd of women, children, and men nearly crushed Jesus. [43] And there was a woman who had a [vaginal] hemorrhage for twelve years, and though on physicians she had spent her entire life [savings], not one was able to cure her. [44] She came up behind Jesus touching the fringe of his garment and immediately her [vaginal] hemorrhage stopped. [45] Then Jesus asked, "Who touched me?" When all denied it, Peter said, "Sir, the crowds surround you and are pressing in." [46] But Jesus said, "Someone touched me; for I discerned that power had gone out from me." [47] When the woman saw that she was not hidden, trembling she came forward and falling down before Jesus she declared in the presence of all the women and men why she had touched Jesus and how she was immediately healed. [48] Jesus said to her, "Daughter, your faith has saved you, go in peace."

[49] While Jesus was speaking, someone came from the synagogue leader's house saying, "Since your daughter is dead, do not trouble the teacher any longer." [50] When Jesus heard this he replied, "Fear not. Only believe and she will be saved." [51] Now when Jesus came to the house, he did not allow anyone to enter with him except Peter, John, and James, and the child's mother and father. [52] Everyone else was weeping and wailing for her, but Jesus said, "Weep not for she is not dead but sleeping." [53] And they laughed at him, knowing that she was dead. [54] But Jesus took her by the hand and calling out he said, "Child, get up!" [55] And her breath-and-spirit returned and she got up that moment; then Jesus directed them to give her something to eat.

PROCLAMATION

Text Notes

Jegar-sahadutha in Genesis 31:47 is the Aramaic name for Gal-Ed, which also means Heap (of stones) of Testimony. The verb "watch" in verse 49 is from the same root as Mitzpah, *tz-p-h*. "Out of sight" is literally "hidden" from each other in verse 49. In verse 50, the verb *anah* refers to physical affliction and sexual violence; it is a primary indicator of rape, describes Sarah's abuse of Hagar, Egyptian oppression of the Israelites, and the rapes of Dinah, Tamar, and the Levite's low-status wife.

In Psalm 144:3, "woman-born" replaces "children of man."

In Luke 8:42, the verb *sympnigō* indicates pressing so close so as to choke off plant growth such as by weeds and is used euphemistically to describe significant pressure by a crowd closing in, nearly to the point of choking, according to BDAG. In verses 43–44, I specify "vaginal" hemorrhage because the term *hrusis* (= *zav/ah*) is used exclusively for vaginal and penile discharges in the LXX (see Leviticus 15:19, 25–26, 28, 30, 33; 20:18; Deuteronomy 23:10). The singular noun (contra NRSV) indicates a singular continuous flow for the duration of the twelve years. I add "savings" to "life"; the phrase is *she spent all her life*. In verse 44, the "fringe" is the sacred fringe God commands the Israelites to put on the corners of their garments (Numbers 15:38–39; Deuteronomy 22:12); known by the Hebrew name *tzit-tzit*, it is still worn by Jews in certain traditions of Judaism. In verse 45, I use "sir" rather than "master" in keeping with this project's aim to mitigate slave-holding language for Jesus and for God. In verse 48, *sōzō*, "to save," has a primary meaning of saving one's life, meaning their physical life. This is in keeping with the Hebrew Bible, in which salvation is deliverance from death and disease and from oppression and occupation; salvation in the Hebrew Bible and in New Testament passages influenced by the Israelite tradition is primarily communal with occasional individual narratives. When it refers to what contemporary readers may think of as "saving one's soul," it also carries the sense of saving the whole person. It reoccurs in verse 50; however, some translations, such as NRSV, use different words to render it in each use. The "all" of verse 52, rendered here "everyone else," refers to persons from the crowd who accompanied them and the members of the household. While persons of any gender may have wept aloud, the ritual wailing would have been done by female members of the household. In verse 55, *pneuma* means both "breath" and "spirit."

Preaching Prompts

These Lenten readings offer an opportunity to reflect on our valuation of other human persons, individually and collectively, particularly those who are most vulnerable. In these lessons, daughters are the most vulnerable, reflecting their continuous status in Israelites society. Yet in each case, God or someone acting in alignment with God's values ensures their survival and thriving. In the first lesson, a father seeks to protect his daughters from the rarely acknowledged reality of domestic violence in the scriptures and from the interpersonal harm that can arise in a plural or polygamous marriage.

It may surprise some that the well-known Mizpah covenant, "May the Lord watch between me and thee," is in actuality a covenant guaranteeing the protection and well-being of women, Leah and Rachel, from spousal abuse and additional wives and children. This is a useful text to address family dynamics, including violence. It should be noted that the women are not party to the covenant; they are its patriarchal subjects.

The psalm celebrates human, plant, and animal life in full bloom as the very good gifts of God and here, one of very few references to daughters in the psalms or larger tradition. It represents an enlarging of the iris, a pulling back to see all of humanity in proper perspective alongside all of creation. The hierarchies between humans, including those rooted in gender and sexuality, are flattened in cosmic perspective. The Epistle sees the cosmic perspective and raises it to an eschatological one: the adoption and redemption of all human bodies and souls. The use of gendered language here suggests an understanding that our human distinctiveness, including our gender and sexuality, are such core parts of our identity that they are preserved in our eternal, cosmic, eschatological salvation. Put another way, there is no salvation that requires the sacrifice of our gender and sexual identities. Considering these things at length means asking if we treat folks like all the things that make them uniquely human are the very things God seeks to preserve for all eternity.

LENT III

Exodus 16:2–18; Psalm 65:5–13; Acts 27:1, 27–38; Luke 9:12–17

Exodus 16:2 Now the whole congregation of Israelite women and men grumbled against Moses and against Aaron in the wilderness. 3 The Israelite women and men said to them, "If only we had been handed over to die at the hand of the SOURCE OF LIFE in the land of Egypt when we dwelled by the cookpots of meat and ate our fill of bread; for you all have brought us out into this wilderness to kill this whole assembly with hunger!" 4 Then the WELLSPRING OF LIFE said to Moses, "I am going to rain bread from the heavens for you all, and every day the people—women, children, and men—shall go out and glean enough for the needs of the day so I might assess whether they will follow my instruction or not. 5 Now it shall be that on the sixth day when they prepare what they bring in; it will be twice as much as they glean on other days." 6 Thus Moses and Aaron said to all the Israelite women and men: "In the evening you all shall know that it was the GOD WHO SAVES who brought you all out of the land of Egypt. 7 Then, in the morning, you all—women, children, and men alike—shall see the glory of the Fire of Sinai who has heard your grumbling against the Holy One of Old. For what are we [two, Moses and Aaron] that you all should grumble against us?" ⁸ Then Moses said, "When the Gracious One gives you all by evening meat to eat and bread in the morning, to the point of satisfaction, because the God Who Hears has heard the grumbling that you grumble against God, what are we? Your grumbling is not against us but against the Mother of Creation."

⁹ Then Moses said to Aaron, "Say to the whole congregation of the Israelite women and men, 'Draw near to the presence of God Whose Name is Holy for God has heard your grumbling.'" ¹⁰ And it happened as Aaron spoke to the whole congregation of the Israelite women and men that they turned toward the wilderness and the glory of the Radiant God appeared in the cloud. ¹¹ Then the Architect of Heaven spoke to Moses and said, ¹² "I have heard the grumbling of the Israelite women and men; say to them, 'As evening begins you all shall eat meat and in the morning you all shall be satisfied with bread; then you all shall know that I am the Holy One your God.'"

¹³ And it happened that in the evening quails came up and covered the camp, and in the morning there was a layer of dew around the camp. ¹⁴ Now the layer of dew lifted and look at that! On the surface of the wilderness was something thin, flaky, as thin as frost on the ground. ¹⁵ When the Israelite women and men saw it, they said to one another, "[*Mah na* meaning,] What is it?" For they did not know what it was. Moses said to them, "It is the bread that the Holy One of Old has given you all to eat. ¹⁶ This is what the Majesty of the Ages has commanded: 'You all shall glean of it for each mouth to eat, an omer [about two quarts] to a person according to the headcount of persons, each person taking some for those in their own tents.'" ¹⁷ And this did the Israelite women and men, some more, some less. ¹⁸ Yet when they measured against an omer, there was no excess for the one with more, and the one with less had no lack; they gleaned enough for each mouth to eat.

Psalm 65:5–13

¹ To you silence is praise, God in Zion;
and to you vows shall be performed,
² You who answer prayer!
To you shall all flesh come.
³ When deeds of iniquity overwhelm us,
you forgive our transgressions.
⁴ Happy are those whom you choose and bring near
to dwell in your courts.
We shall be satisfied with the goodness of your house,
your holy temple.
⁵ Through wondrous deeds you answer us with deliverance,
O God of our salvation,
hope of all the ends of the earth

    and of the farthest seas.
6 You established the mountains through your might;
    you are girded with strength.
7 The one who silences the roaring of the seas,
    the roaring of their waves,
    the rumble of the peoples.
8 They who live at the farthest reaches are awed by your signs;
    you make the dawnings of morning and evening sing for joy.
9 You attend the earth and water her,
    you enrich her greatly;
    the river of God is full of water;
    you provide the people with grain,
    thus you have established it.
10 Irrigating earth's furrows,
    smoothing her ridges,
    softening her with showers,
    and blessing her growth.
11 You crown the year with your goodness;
    your paths overflow with fatness.
12 The pastures of the wilderness overflow,
    and with joy the hills gird themselves.
13 The meadows are clothed with flocks,
    the valleys arrayed in grain;
    indeed, they shout for joy.

Acts 27:1 Now, when it was adjudged that we were to sail for Italy, they handed over Paul and some other prisoners to a centurion by name of Julius of the Imperial Cohort.

27 And when the fourteenth night had come, we were drifting across Adria [the Adriatic Sea]; about midnight the sailors reckoned they were nearing land. 28 And they took depth soundings and found twenty fathoms [about one hundred and twenty feet deep]; they set out a little farther and again took depth soundings finding fifteen fathoms [about ninety feet deep]. 29 Fearing lest we strike some rugged surfaces, they cast four anchors from the stern and prayed for day to come. 30 But the sailors tried to flee from the ship and lowered the [smaller] boat into the sea on the pretext of putting out anchors from the bow. 31 Paul said to the centurion and the soldiers, "Unless these persons stay in the ship, it will not be possible to save you all." 32 Then the soldiers cut away the ropes of the boat and let it fall.

33 Now as day was beginning to break Paul urged all of them to share some food, saying, "Today is the fourteenth day that you have been waiting, having received no food. 34 Therefore I urge you all to share some food, for it will help your salvation; for not one among you all a single hair from your heads will lose." 35 Paul said this and took bread and giving thanks to God in the presence of all, he broke it and began to eat. 36 Then they were all encouraged and accepted

food for themselves. ³⁷ (We were in all two hundred seventy-six souls in the ship.) ³⁸ When they were satisfied with their provision, they lightened the ship by throwing the grain into the sea.

Luke 9:12 Now the day was beginning to fade and the twelve came to Jesus and said, "Send the crowd away so they can go into the surrounding villages and countryside to lodge and get provisions; for we are here in a desolate wilderness place." ¹³ Yet Jesus said to the twelve, "You all give them something to eat." But the twelve said, "We have no more than five loaves and two fish lest we go buying food for all these people." ¹⁴ For there were about five thousand men. Then Jesus said to his disciples, "Sit them down in groups of about fifty each." ¹⁵ The disciples did so and made them all—women, children, and men—sit down. ¹⁶ And taking the five loaves and the two fish, Jesus looked up to heaven and blessed and broke them, and gave them to the disciples to set before the crowd. ¹⁷ And all—including women and children—ate and were filled. And the remainder was gathered up, twelve baskets of broken pieces.

PROCLAMATION

Text Notes

In Exodus 16:15, I have brought forward the pun on the name and sound of *manna* from verse 31 (which is not a part of the reading). The form that actually occurs in verse 15 is truncated, *man*.

It remains unclear as to whether there were any women prisoners jn the larger complement of those on the ship in Acts 27. NRSV adds "men" to verse 31 where the gender-neutral "these" has no further specificity; I clarify with the equally gender-neutral "person" there. Verse 37 describes the occupants of the ship as "souls," again, gender inclusive. The language around sharing, receiving, and eating food can be translated in a number of ways. The verb *metalabein* in verses 33–44 means "to receive" and "to share" rather than "to take" and better fits with Paul's offering of a community meal with salvific implications. Correspondingly the food (*proselabonto*) in verse 36 is better understood as "received." This salvific meal has deliberate resonances with Eucharist. Here, the meal saves the physical person by saving them from hunger. There is also a sense that the meal is sufficient and no more provisions need to be maintained, similar to the manna story.

The invisibility of women in the Lucan text, including their exclusion from the count of those who received a miraculous feeding is at odds with the frequency of the inclusion of women in the Gospel of Luke. The omission of the prophet Miriam from the wilderness grumbling text is a similar act of erasure. *Eremos* in verse 12 means both "wilderness" and "desolate."

Preaching Prompts

These readings call our attention to the various tables at which we sit to offer, receive, or share meals and the sanctity of table communion apart from the Eucharistic meal. In each of these passages, the responsibility falls on one or more members of the community to feed others and share in the tables that are set. Each person was to gather mana notches for themselves but for "their tent," everyone who lived in their home. However much each individual in the family brought home, it would be enough for everyone. In the psalm, God provides and adorns the natural world with abundant food sources. In the reading from Acts, Paul pulls together a meal that serves as a space in which the fears of the sailors who were considering abandoning ship, and their passengers were calmed. That meal strengthened and restored the bonds of community and they all survived, together.

There is a subtle but significant difference between the cast of characters in the Gospel reading: the twelve male apostles and the larger group of disciples that includes women, especially in Luke. The male apostles see the crowd of women, children, and men as a burden. Jesus gives them an opportunity to serve, but they see no easy way, indeed no way is visible in the material world. There is no consideration that the power of God in and through Jesus can transcend these material limitations. A womanist reading takes note that Jesus turns from the men and their lack of vision and faith and turns to the larger community of his followers, one that includes the women who have funded and followed him among other unknown female disciples. These women evoke the long tradition of black women who do the work of the church, often without title or recognition. It is this group that Jesus calls to organize the people and deliver the miracle. These women along with male disciples who are not among the twelve functioned as the sergeants of this army and got them in formation. These disciples gave from what appeared to be an insufficient source, then discovered sufficiency and abundance in the miracle in their hands.

A preacher might invite a congregation to reflect upon the tables at which they sit and serve and share. Who is present, who is excluded? Who is doing the work, and who is taking the credit?

LENT IV

*Numbers 26:33; 27:1–11; Psalm 56:1–13;
Acts 18:1–3, 18–20, 24–28; Luke 10:38–42*

Numbers 26:33 Now Zelophehad ben Hepher had no sons, for he had daughters and the names of the daughters of Zelophehad were: Mahlah, Noah, Hoglah, Milcah, and Tirzah.

^{27:1} [After the division of the land] the daughters of Zelophehad came forward. Now Zelophehad was the child of Hepher descended from Gilead descended from Machir

descended from Manasseh—of the Manassite clans—descended from Joseph. The names of his daughters were: Mahlah, Noah, Hoglah, Milcah, and Tirzah. ² They [the sisters] stood before Moses and before Eleazar the priest, the leaders, and the whole congregation of women, children, and men at the entrance of the tent of meeting and they said: ³ "Our father died in the wilderness, yet he was not among the assembly of those who assembled themselves together against the MAJESTY OF THE HEAVENS in the company of Korah; for his own sin he died, and he had no sons. ⁴ Why should the name of our father be withdrawn from his clan because he had no son? Give to us a possession among our father's brothers."

⁵ Now Moses brought their case forward before the JUDGE OF ALL THE EARTH. ⁶ And the JUDGE OF ALL FLESH spoke to Moses, saying: ⁷ Since the daughters of Zelophehad are correct in their word, you shall indeed give them a hereditary possession among their father's brothers and pass the possession of their father to them. ⁸ To the women and men of Israel you shall speak, saying, "When a man dies and has no son, then you all shall pass his possession on to his daughter. ⁹ If he has no daughter, then you shall all give his possession to his brothers. ¹⁰ If he has no brothers, then you all shall give his possession to his father's brothers. ¹¹ And if his father has no brothers, then you all shall give his possession to his nearest relative of his clan and he shall possess it. It shall be for the women and men of Israel a statute and ordinance just as the JUST GOD commanded Moses."

Psalm 56:1–13

¹ Be gracious to me, God, for people trample on me;
 all day long fighters crush me.
² My enemies trample on me all day long,
 for many fight against me, Exalted One.
³ On days I fear,
 I, I place my trust in you.
⁴ In God, whose word I praise,
 in God I trust; I am not afraid.
 What can flesh do to me?
⁵ All day long they my words slander;
 against me for evil all their thoughts are.
⁶ They attack, they hide, they watch my steps
 according to their designs on my soul.
⁷ On account of their iniquity free me from them;
 in wrath bring down the peoples, God!
⁸ You yourself have kept count of my wandering;
 put my tears in your bottle. Are they not in your scroll?
⁹ Then my enemies will turn back on the day I call out.
 This I know, that God is for me.
¹⁰ In God, whose word I praise,

in SHE WHO SPEAKS LIFE, whose word I praise:
11 in God I trust; I shall not fear.
What can the woman-born do to me?
12 Upon me are my vows to you God;
I shall offer thank offerings to you.
13 For you have delivered my soul from death—
and were not my feet [kept] from falling?—
that I may walk before God in the light of life.

Acts 18:1 After [speaking at the Areopagus] Paul departed Athens and went to Corinth. 2 And he found a Jew, by name Aquila, a native of Pontus recently come from Italy with his wife Priscilla because Claudius had ordered all Jews to depart Rome; Paul went to them. 3 And because he had the same trade, he stayed with them and they worked together; they were tentmakers by trade.

18 Now Paul, after staying there for quite some time, said farewell to the sisters and brothers and sailed for Syria and with him were Priscilla and Aquila; he cut his hair at Cenchreae for he had taken a vow. 19 When they arrived in Ephesus, Paul left them there, but first he himself went into the synagogue and had a discussion with the other Jews. 20 When they asked him to stay longer, he declined.

24 Now a certain Jewish man, Apollos by name, a native of Alexandria, an eloquent man, well-versed in the scriptures, came to Ephesus. 25 This man had been instructed in the Way of the Messiah and spoke with a fiery spirit and taught accurately the things concerning Jesus, though he knew only the baptism of John. 26 He began to speak boldly in the synagogue, but when Priscilla and Aquila heard him, they took him in and explained the Way [of God] to him more accurately. 27 And when he wished to cross over into Achaia, the sisters and brothers encouraged him and wrote to the disciples to welcome him; upon his arrival he greatly helped those who had through grace come to believe.

Luke 10:38 Now as Jesus and his disciples went on the way, he entered a certain village; a certain woman, by name Martha, welcomed him into her home. 39 She had a sister named Mary who was sitting at the Teacher's feet listening to his word. 40 But Martha was distracted by a great deal of serving; so she came to Jesus and asked, "Teacher, do you not care that my sister has left me to do all the serving by myself? Speak to her so that she might help me." 41 But the Teacher answered her, "Martha, Martha, you are worried and bothered by much. 42 Yet only one thing is necessary; Mary has chosen the better portion, which will not be taken away from her."

PROCLAMATION

Text Notes

In Psalm 56:5 (Heb v. 6), the verb '-*tz-v*, "grieve" or "rebuke" in the Qal occurs in the Piel where it has the sense of "slandering" the *d'var*—"words," "matter," or "thing"—of the psalmist. Alter renders it as "frustrating. In verse 6 (Heb v. 7), "they hope/wait for my life/soul" becomes their "designs for my soul." The opening line of the following verse is fragmentary; I follow Robert Alter in reconstructing the first-person object pronoun. The second line of verse 9 can also be translated as "God is mine." In verse 11 (Heb v. 12),

"woman-born" replaces *adam*, "humanity."

While Acts 18:25 makes reference to "the Way of the Lord [Messiah here]," "the Way" in verse 26 is amended to "the Way of God" in some manuscripts. It is included in brackets as it appears in the dominant Nestle-Aland Greek text (28th revision).

In Luke 10:38, Martha welcomes Jesus to "hers," the object "home" must be inferred. In Luke 10:40, "serving" is *diakonia*, "ministry" that can be the rich hospitality of the culture or its extension, the ministry of service to others and to God through serving others that will eventually become formalized as an office in the church, ordination in most cases. In the same verse, "listening" means "heeding" as well as "hearing." The "word" or "message" of Jesus is his *logos*. Verse 42 exists in different forms in relevant manuscripts; some have Jesus saying "only [a] few things are necessary."

Preaching Prompts

These lessons center women and their word in matters of religious and cultural authority in relation to God's word and Jesus as the Word for Laetare Sunday (the fourth Sunday in Lent when the severity is lessened and pink may be worn). The inheritance saga of the daughters of Zelophehad is one of the most important legal cases in the Torah. One measure of their significance is that they are mentioned in the canon more times than the resurrection account of Jesus (see Numbers 26:33; 27:1–11; 36:1–12; Joshua 17:3–6; 1 Chronicles 7:15). While Moses failed to obey God and give them their land and conditions would be placed on their eventual inheritance, the divine verdict stands, that these women were "right" in their word. God endorsed their verdict. They would return to protest and petition as many times as necessary, and Joshua would eventually give them their land after the death of Moses. For more on their story, see the chapter on them in *Womanist Midrash*.

In Acts, Priscilla and her husband "take in" a junior colleague (in terms of preparation) and supplement his education. They do not shame, censure, or fire him. And he does not reject their teaching or Priscilla's leadership. Their different understandings do not lead to schism. Priscilla is a Jewish woman evicted from Rome with her husband in the Jewish expulsion ordered by Emperor Claudius in Acts 18:2 and is one of the teaching elders or leaders of the early church. (Bernadette Brooten has demonstrated conclusively that women leaders in the ancient synagogue used the title in her book of the same title; as male Christian leaders adopted the language, it is reasonable to presume Christian women did as well.) Priscilla, sometimes rendered Prisca, is listed before her husband, more often than not, indicating to some that she was the senior, more learned disciple (Acts 18:2, 18, 26; Romans 16:3; 1 Corinthians 16:19; 2 Timothy 4:19). Her name certainly precedes in the reeducation of Apollos. Paul describes her and her husband—in that order—as his coworkers in Romans 16:3 and she is listed first as pastor of the house church in 2 Timothy 4:19. (I say "pastor" because there is no dispute that men led the churches in their homes when listed; I reckon her as more senior pastor than copastor.)

Mary and Martha are portrayed as relating to Jesus in different ways that have, unfortunately, traditionally been constructed as binary opposites. Patriarchal exegesis has lauded Mary for her study of the word while, in many cases, denying women access to seminary and ministry studies and ordination, and has critiqued Martha for being too preoccupied with "housework" while arguing for the home as women's primary God-ordained sphere of operation, all at the same time. Jesus's response is often treated as a rebuke when in the text, it is simply a conversational response. The "one" and "many" things are not clear. What is clear is that Martha is doing too much, whether that is cooking and preparing too many dishes or simply too much fussing about Jesus. Why Mary's portion is "better" is equally unclear, though it is easy to say that it is better and best to sit at the feet of Jesus and study the word with him as his disciple. It will be important for the preacher to validate and honor the ministries of service and hospitality that so often fall on women.

LENT V

1 Kings 10:1–10, 13; Psalm 131:1–3;
1 Thessalonians 1:2–10; Luke 11:27–32

1 Kings 10:1 Now the Queen of Sheba heard of the fame of Solomon ascribed to the Name of the MOST HIGH and she came to test him with hard questions. ² And she came to Jerusalem in force, extremely heavy, with camels carrying spices and a very great quantity of gold and precious stones; then she came to Solomon and she told him all that was on her heart. ³ And Solomon responded to her—all her remarks; there was nothing hidden from the king that he did not respond to for her. ⁴ Then the Queen of Sheba saw the whole of the wisdom of Solomon—the house that he had built, ⁵ and the food of his table, and the seating of his slaves, and the stationing of his attendants, and their clothing, and his cupbearers, and his burnt offerings that he offered at the house of the GOD WHO DWELLS ABOVE THE CHERUBIM, and there was no more breath in her.

⁶ So she said to the king, "It was true—the word I heard in my land of your words and of your wisdom. ⁷ Yet I did not trust the words until I came and my own eyes saw and see here! Not even half had been told me; your wisdom and wealth surpass the report that I heard. ⁸ Happy are your women! Happy are your slaves, they who stand before you continually and hear your wisdom! ⁹ May the WISDOM OF THE AGES, your God, be blessed, the one who delights in you so to give you the throne of Israel through the everlasting love of the GOD WHO IS LOVE for Israel; God has made you king to deliver justice and righteousness." ¹⁰ Then she gave to the king one hundred twenty talents of gold, spices, a great quantity, and precious stones; never again did there come such spices in that abundance as what she, the Queen of Sheba, gave to King Solomon.

¹³ And King Solomon gave to the Queen of Sheba her every desire that she requested, as well as what he gave her out of his own hand, Solomon's private holding. Then the Queen of Sheba turned about and went back to her own land with her slaves.

Psalm 131:1–3

¹ WOMB OF LIFE, my heart is not lifted up,
 nor my eyes exalted;
 I do not keep company with things
 great and too wondrous for me.
² Rather, I have soothed and quieted my soul,
 like a weaned child with her mother;
 my soul is like a weaned child within me.
³ Israel, hope in the WELLSPRING OF LIFE
 from now until forever.

1 Thessalonians 1:2 We give thanks to God at all times for you all, mentioning you all in our prayers, laboring, ³ remembering your work of faith and labor of love and perseverance of hope in our Redeemer, Jesus the Messiah, before our God and Creator. ⁴ We know, friends and kin beloved by God, that God has chosen you all. ⁵ Because our gospel was among you all not in word only, but also in power and in the Holy Spirit and in complete certainty, in the same way you all know how exactly we were among you for your sake. ⁶ And you all became imitators of us and of the Redeemer, receiving the word in persecution with the joy of the Holy Spirit. ⁷ Thus you all became an example to all the believers in Macedonia and in Achaia. ⁸ For from you all has sounded forth the word of the Redeemer not only in Macedonia and Achaia; rather, in every place your faith in God has become known, so that we have no need to speak about it. ⁹ For they report about us what kind of welcome we had among you and how you turned to God from idols to serve a living and true God. ¹⁰ And turned to wait for God's Son from heaven, whom God raised from the dead—Jesus, who rescues us from the wrath that is coming.

Luke 11:27 While Jesus was [teaching about unclean spirits], raising her voice, a woman in the crowd and said to him, "Blessed is the womb that gave birth you and the breasts that nursed you!" ²⁸ But Jesus said, "On the contrary, blessed are those who hear the word of God and keep it."

²⁹ Now when the crowds of women, children, and men were increasing, Jesus began to say, "This generation is an evil generation; it seeks a sign and no sign will be given to it except the sign of Jonah. ³⁰ For just as Jonah became a sign to the women, children and men of Nineveh, so the Son of Woman will be to this generation. ³¹ The Queen of the South will rise at the judgment with the men of this generation and condemn them because she came from the ends of the earth to listen to the wisdom of Solomon, and see here! Something greater than Solomon is here! ³² The people of Nineveh will rise up at the judgment with this generation and condemn it, because they repented at the proclamation of Jonah, and see here! Something greater than Jonah is here!

PROCLAMATION

Text Notes

In 1 Kings 10:1, the "hard questions" could also be translated as "difficult riddles." In biblical Hebrew literature, the heart is the center of reasoning, wisdom, and understanding. While others change "heart" to "mind" in verse 2 (see NRSV, CEB, and JPS), I preserve the traditional reading. The "house" that Solomon showed off in verse 4 was more likely his own than the house of God. The temple was sixty by twenty cubits and thirty cubits high (1 Kings 6:2); it took seven years (1 Kings 6:38). In contrast, he spent thirteen years building his primary residence (1 Kings 7:1), a single hall in it was one hundred by fifty cubits, also thirty cubits high (1 Kings 7:2), a second hall was fifty by thirty cubits (1 Kings 7:6) and there were two more halls (1 Kings 7:7). His proper home was "the same construction," and he made a duplicate for the Egyptian princess he married (1 Kings 7:8).

The ancient witnesses are split on whether Solomon's "women" or "men" are "happy (or blessed)" in verse 8; the LXX, Peshitta, and Ethiopic (Mahibere Hawariyat) have "women" and the MT, Targum, and Vulgate have "men"—and not people. There is no extant Dead Sea Scroll with the verse. In translation, NRSV alone, among major translations, has "wives [=women]"; Alter, Fox, and JPS have "men," and the CEB and Inclusive Bible have "people." My choice of "women" reflects my understanding of the context and intent, showing Solomon's magnanimity, particularly given the mention of slaves in the same verse. Astonishment over the treatment of women communicates that more and better than over the treatment of men. Lastly, while the same word is used for both women in general and wives in particular, an argument can be made that if the original/intended reading was *nashim*, women/wives, Solomon's famous collection of intimate partners—primary and secondary wives—was meant. In verse 13, I preserve the idiom "out of the hand of King Solomon" with its explication, "out of his private funds."

The Queen of Sheba has an enduring legacy in the scriptures and religious writings of several religions. Her fame is tied to that of Solomon through her visit and recognition of his wisdom in the biblical texts (1 Kings 10, duplicates in 2 Chronicles 9; Matthew 12:42; Luke 11:31), to conversion from sun worship in the Qur'an (*al-Naml* 27:15ff), to Solomon's philosophy student (Josephus, *Antiquities* 8.6.2ff), to a child who is the progenitor of the Ethiopian monarchy. While unnamed in either Testament, she is Bilqis in the Qur'an and Makeda in the *Kebra Nagast*, the Ethiopian national hagiography. Her nation has been identified with the Sabeans on the Yemeni portion of the Arabian Peninsula to eastern Africa, generically called "Ethiopia" in antiquity. Her wealth may well have surpassed his. Her gift (20 percent of his annual income) of 120 talents gold was roughly equal to 4,200 kilos, or 9,259.42 pounds, of gold. With gold trading at $1830.30 per ounce in 2022, the nearly 150,000 ounces would be worth $271,160,262.81.

1 Thessalonians 1:4 is a powerful statement of belonging, so much so that a reading of "friends and kin" is preferable to "sisters and brothers" in this case.

The Lukan Jesus speaks quite harshly about the current generation (see Luke 7:31; 9:41; 11:29–32, 50–51; 16:8; 17:25; 21:32). Only in this passage does he specify the men of the generation. Luke 7:31 specifies "people" using an inclusive term for humanity; none of the others have any specificity. The reference to the "Queen of the South" in Luke 11:31 (and Matthew 12:42) is widely understood to refer to the Queen of Sheba in the world reading and writing the Christian scriptures and subsequently in early church and contemporary biblical interpretation. The Kebra Nagast explicitly makes the connection, "the Queen of the South of whom [Jesus] spake was the Queen of Ethiopia (Kebra Nagast 21, *Concerning the Queen of the South*).

Preaching Prompts

These readings on the final Sunday of Lent focus on our willingness to receive the word and wisdom from all of the sources that God uses to bring revelation into our lives. The Queen of Sheba had her own wisdom, wealth, knowledge, and majesty. She heard of another set of wisdom stories from a community that differed from hers. She went to inquire but as a peer and not a supplicant. The psalm suggests the most appropriate learning posture—openness to hear and to learn. Similarly, the believing community in the Epistle is praised for their learning posture, one of imitation of the gospel lived and proclaimed in their midst. Jesus condemns "this generation" for not being open to word and wisdom, the gospel in their midst. The Queen of Sheba is, for him, the model of discipleship. And as such, she will serve as his judicial peer holding them accountable. The rhetoric, "this generation," is not literal. Jesus is not rebuking the crowds. His grammar (or that of his biographer) specifies the men of the generation. And as Jesus is beginning to turn toward Jerusalem, it may be best to understand the expression as "this generation of leaders": they who are not open to his word and wisdom.

FEAST OF THE ANNUNCIATION, MARCH 25

Zephaniah 3:14–20; Canticle 15, the Magnificat (Luke 1:46–55);
2 Corinthians 6:16b–18; Luke 1:26–38

Zephaniah 3:14 Sing aloud daughter of Zion; shout, all ye Israel!
  Rejoice, daughter, and exult with all your heart, daughter of Jerusalem!
¹⁵ The JUDGE OF ALL FLESH has taken away the judgments against you,
  and has turned away your enemies, daughter.
  The sovereign of Israel, CREATOR OF THE HEAVENS AND EARTH,
  is in your midst, daughter; no longer shall you fear evil.
¹⁶ On that day it shall be said to Jerusalem:
  Fear not, Zion; do not let your hands grow weak, daughter.
¹⁷ The AGELESS ONE, your God, is in your midst, daughter,
  a warrior who will deliver salvation;
  who will rejoice over you with gladness, daughter,
  God will renew you in love, daughter;
  God will exult over you, daughter, with loud singing.
¹⁸ Those who are grieved on account of the festivals,
  I will remove from you, daughter,
  so, daughter, that you will not bear their reproach.
¹⁹ I will deal with all your oppressors, daughter, at that time.
  And I will save the lame and gather the outcast,
  and I will change their shame into praise
  and renown in all the earth.
²⁰ At that time I will bring you all home, at the time when I gather all of you;
  for I will make you all renowned and praised
  among all the peoples of the earth,
  when I restore your fortunes before all of your eyes,
  says the GOD WHO IS SALVATION.

Canticle 15, the Magnificat, Luke 1:46–55
⁴⁶ "My soul magnifies the Holy One,
⁴⁷ and my spirit rejoices in God my Savior,
⁴⁸ for God has looked with favor on the lowliness of God's own servant.
  Surely, from now on all generations will call me blessed;
⁴⁹ for the Mighty One has done great things for me,
  and holy is God's name.
⁵⁰ God's loving-kindness is for those who fear God

from generation to generation.
51 God has shown the strength of God's own arm;
God has scattered the arrogant in the intent of their hearts.
52 God has brought down the powerful from their thrones,
and lifted up the lowly;
53 God has filled the hungry with good things,
and sent the rich away empty.
54 God has helped God's own child, Israel,
a memorial to God's mercy,
55 just as God said to our mothers and fathers,
to Abraham and Hagar and Sarah, to their descendants forever."

2 Corinthians 6:16 For we are the temple of the living God; as God said:

"I will dwell in them and walk among them,*
and I will be their God,
and they shall be my people."
17 *Therefore, "Come out from them,*
and be separate from them," says the Holy One,
and, "Touch nothing unclean,"
then, "I will take you all in."
18 *and, "I will be your parent,*
and you shall be my daughters and sons,"
says the Almighty Everlasting God.

Luke 1:26 In the sixth month the angel Gabriel was sent by God to a town of Galilee, Nazareth, 27 to a virgin betrothed to a man whose name was Joseph, of the house of David. And the name of the virgin was Mary. 28 And the angel came to Mary and said, "Rejoice, favored one! The Most High God is with you." 29 Now, she was troubled by the angel's words and pondered what sort of greeting this was. 30 Then the angel said to her, "Fear not Mary, for you have found favor with God. 31 And now, you will conceive in your womb and give birth to a son, and you will name him Jesus. 32 He will be great and will be called the Son of the Most High, and the Sovereign God will give him the throne of his ancestor David. 33 He will reign over the house of Jacob forever, and of his sovereignty there will be no end." 34 Then Mary said to the angel, "How can this be, since I have not known a man intimately?" 35 The angel said to her, "The Holy Spirit, She will come upon you, and the power of the Most High will overshadow you; therefore the one born will be holy. He will be called Son of God. 36 And now, Elizabeth your kinswoman has even conceived a son in her old age, and this is the sixth month for she who was called barren. 37 For nothing will be impossible with God." 38 Then Mary said, "Here am I, the woman-slave of God; let it be with me according to your word." Then the angel left her.

---

* All citations, direct quotes, from the first testament are italicized.

PROCLAMATION

Text Notes

Bat Zion (or Jerusalem) can mean both Daughter Zion, the city *or* a daughter of Zion, a woman from the city. In Isaiah 40:9, reading "daughter of" reveals a female prophet crying out to Jerusalem (compare NRSV and JPS translations). Because the addressee is feminine, all of the verbs to her are also feminine; I reproduce "daughter" in places where English masks the frequency of feminine address. Verse 18 is notoriously difficult to translate: see the discussion in my commentary on Zephaniah in the *Wisdom* series.

In Luke 1:55, the inclusive plural *pateras* can mean ancestors, parents, or fathers. Since God's promises were not just to Abraham and God also made promises to Hagar (Genesis 16:10–13; 21:17–18), and for Sarah (through Abraham in Genesis 17:15–16), I have expanded "Abraham and his descendants" to reflect that. Abraham also had children with Keturah; their offspring would also be beneficiaries of the promises made Abraham; however, God does not make a promise directly to her in the scriptures.

In Mary's linguistic and cultural world, in Hebrew and Aramaic, the spirit is feminine; the Syriac text uses a feminine verb for the spirit in Luke 1:35. Also in her world, there was no distinction between servant and slave. Mary is not saying she will wait on God hand and foot in verse38; she is giving God ownership of her body, ownership slaveholders claimed without consent.

Preaching Prompts

In its original context, Daughter Zion was most likely the city. Here I suggest hearing it through the experience of the pregnant Virgin reflecting on her scriptures in light of her experience.

The appointed Epistle is a collection verse fragments strung together, many out of context. The phrases are inexact quotes, whether looking at Hebrew or Greek antecedents, shaped for deployment here. Leviticus 26:11–12 has the same sense as in 2 Corinthians 6:16. Verse 17 of the Epistle links a fragment found in both Ezekiel 20:34 and 20:41 to a line from Isaiah 52:11 calling for a second Exodus from Egypt. Verse 18 takes God's promise to David for Solomon to be his father in 2 Samuel 7:14 and makes it second person plural, "your all" instead of "his," and adds "daughters" to the altered text in Greek.

Angelic lore is largely pseudepigraphal beginning in 2 Esdras. While Gabriel and Michael appear in the Hebrew Bible (Daniel 8:16; 9:21; 10:13, 21; 12:1), they are not identified as angels. However, Raphael is called an angel in Tobit 5:4.

There is some irony in the pains the Gospel takes to connect Jesus to David and the Hebrew Scriptures, and choice of translators to anglicize the names of the holy family and disciples, undermining their Jewish identity. A further irony is that

Jesus's Davidic heritage rests on Joseph's genealogy and the supposition that Mary is from the same tribe as was common but not required. Mary's only relative in the text, Elizabeth is the wife of a priest. Priests married within the priestly line nearly exclusively, making her likely a *bat cohen*, priest's daughter as well. What this means for Mary's heritage and that of Jesus is unclear.

PALM SUNDAY—LITURGY OF THE PALMS

Matthew 21:1–11; Psalm 118:19–29

Matthew 21:1 Now they had come near Jerusalem and reached Bethphage on the Mount of Olives, then Jesus sent two disciples, saying to them, "Go into the village before you, and immediately you will find a donkey tied, and a colt with her; release them and bring them to me. ³ If anyone says anything to you, just say this, 'The Son of Woman needs them.' And they will send them immediately." ⁴ This took place to fulfill what had been spoken through the prophet, saying,

⁵ "Tell the daughter of Zion,

'Look, your sovereign is coming to you,
humble, and mounted on a donkey,
and on a colt, the foal of a donkey.'"

⁶ The disciples went and did just as Jesus had instructed them; ⁷ they brought the donkey and the colt, and put their cloaks on them, and he sat on them. ⁸ A very large crowd spread their cloaks on the road, and others cut branches from the trees and spread them on the road. ⁹ The crowds that were going before him and the one following were shouting, saying:

"*Hosanna to the Son of David!*
Blessed is the one who comes in the name of the Holy One!
Hosanna in the highest!"

¹⁰ When Jesus entered Jerusalem, the whole city was shook, asking, "Who is this?" ¹¹ The crowds were saying, "This is the prophet Jesus from Nazareth in Galilee."

Psalm 118:19–29

¹⁹ Open for me the gates of righteousness,
 that I may enter them
 and give thanks to the LIVING GOD.
²⁰ This is the gate to the HOLY PRESENCE;
 the righteous shall enter through it.
²¹ I thank you that you have answered me
 and you have become my salvation.
²² The stone that the builders rejected

has become the chief cornerstone.
23 This is Our God's doing;
it is marvelous in our eyes.
24 This is the day that the Fount of Creation has made;
let us rejoice and be glad in it.
25 Ah! Holy One, help, save us!
Ah! Holy One, haste, deliver us!
26 Blessed is the one who comes in the name of the Most High God.
We bless you from the house of the Holy One.
27 The Faithful One is God,
and she has given us light.
Bind the festal offering with ropes of branches,
up to the horns of the altar.
28 You are my God, and I will give thanks to you;
you are my God; I will exalt you.
29 Give thanks to the Holy One, for she is good,
for her faithful love endures forever.

PROCLAMATION

Text Notes

The text has Jesus use the title "Lord" for himself in Matthew 21:3. In keeping with the aims of this volume (expansive and explicitly feminine language for God and humanity), I employ a translation of the messianic title Jesus often uses for himself here. (See commentary on Advent 1, Year A.) In verse 5, the Gospel quotes Zechariah 9:9, seeming not to understand the poetic parallelism that describes the same animal in two ways; he appears to sit on both in verse 7. The Gospel adds an introduction to "*the* daughter of Zion," adding the definite article not common in this expression in Greek, begging the question to whom it is addressed. In verse 9, the crowd chants Psalm 118:26, a procession psalm for entering the temple also recited during Passover.

The assonant and alliterative poetry of Psalm 118:25 (the "Hosanna" verse) is difficult to reproduce: *Ana Ya hoshia na; Ana Ya chatzlicha na*. The "hosanna" pronunciation comes from the Greek transliteration of the Hebrew. Verse 27 is unclear in a number of places: "bind the feast with clouds." Since portions of sacrificial animals were eaten, "festal offering" is likely, and "ropes" and "branches" are each one letter away from "clouds." "God's faithful love endures forever" is one of the oldest liturgical refrains in the Hebrew Bible; see the opening and closing of this psalm (118) and Psalms 106:1, 107:1 anad the entirety of Psalm 136.

Preaching Prompts

While this is not traditionally a preaching occasion, one may choose to frame the liturgy with a brief preface or blurb in the leaflet or alternately address it in the subsequent sermon (if the liturgy precedes another service).

The ubiquity of monarchy in the scriptures and the worlds from which they emerge reflect more about the humans who received and recorded and translate and interpret them, than it does about God, who inspired and speaks through them. Monarchs were the most powerful persons in those worlds, and they, with their power and regalia, provided a vocabulary for talking about God. Jesus subverts that to some degree by reinterpreting that title in such a way as to perplex even those who knew him best.

These lessons provide an opportunity to talk about our language and imagery for God in and out of the Bible (and this lectionary) and its impact on persons in terms of class, gender, the performance of gender, and sexual orientation.

PALM SUNDAY—LITURGY OF THE WORD

*Isaiah 49:5–16; Psalm 22:1–11; Galatians 3:23–4:7;
Mark 14:32–15:47 (or Mark 14:32–52)*

Those who prefer to continue the Gospel through the Passion will find the successive verses in the Good Friday readings.

Isaiah 49:5 And now says the AUTHOR OF LIFE,

> who formed me in the womb to be God's slave
> to return Jacob back to God,
> and that Israel might be gathered to God;
> I am honored in the sight of the HOLY ONE OF OLD,
> and my God is my strength.
>
> ⁶ God says,
> "It is too light a thing that you should be my slave
> to raise up the tribes of Jacob [the line of Rebekah],
> and to restore the survivors of Israel [born of Rachel and Leah, and Bilhah and Zilpah]?
> I will give you as a light to the nations,
> for it will be that my salvation reaches to the end of the earth."
> ⁷ Thus says the FAITHFUL ONE,
> the Redeemer of Israel, God's holy one,
> to one despised, abhorred by the nations,
> the slave of rulers,

"Queens and kings shall see and arise,
   princes and princesses, and they too shall prostrate themselves,
   on account of the Fire of Sinai, who is faithful,
   the Holy One of Israel, who has chosen you."
8 Thus says the Mighty God:
   In a favorable time have I answered you,
   on a day of salvation have I helped you;
   I have kept you and given you
   as a covenant to the people,
   to establish the land,
   to apportion the desolate portions;
9 saying to the prisoners, "Go free!"
   to those who are in darkness, "Let yourselves be seen."
   Along the paths they shall pasture,
   and on all the bare heights shall be their pasture.
10 They shall not hunger nor shall they thirst,
   neither shall heat nor sun strike them down,
   for the one who mother-loves them shall lead them,
   and by springs of water shall guide them.
11 And I will turn all my mountains into a pathway,
   and my highways shall be raised up.
12 Look! These shall come from far away,
   and see! These from the north and from the sea to the west,
   and these from the southland of Syene.
13 Sing for joy, you heavens, and exult O earth;
   let mountains break forth into singing!
   For the Tender Loving One has comforted God's people,
   and will mother-love God's suffering ones.
14 But Zion said, "The Everlasting God has forsaken me,
   my Sovereign has forgotten me."
15 Can a woman forget her nursing child,
   or mother-love for the child of her womb?
   Even these may forget,
   yet I, no, I will not forget you.
16 See, I have engraved you on the palms of my hands;
   your walls are continually before me.

Psalm 22:1–11

1 My God, my God, why have you forsaken me?
   Why are you so far from my deliverance, from the words of my groaning?

² My God, I cry by day, and you do not answer;
   and by night, and for me.
³ Yet you are holy,
   enthroned on the praises of Israel.
⁴ In you our mothers and fathers trusted;
   they trusted, and you rescued them.
⁵ To you they cried, and were freed;
   in you they trusted, and they were not put to shame.
⁶ But I am a worm, and not human;
   scorned by humankind, and despised by people.
⁷ All who see me mock me;
   they flap their lips at me, they shake their heads:
⁸ "Commit yourself to the SAVING ONE; let God rescue
   and deliver the one in whom God delights!"
⁹ Yet it was you who drew me from the womb;
   keeping me safe on my mother's breast.
¹⁰ On you was I cast from birth,
   and since my mother's womb you have been my God.
¹¹ Be not far from me,
   for trouble is near
   and there is none to help.

Galatians 3:23 Now before faith came, we were garrisoned and guarded under the law until the faith that was coming should be revealed. ²⁴ Therefore the law was our instructor until Christ came, so that we might be justified by faith. ²⁵ But now that faith has come, we are no longer subject to an instructor, ²⁶ for in Christ Jesus you are all daughters and sons of God through faith. ²⁷ So, as many of you as were baptized into Christ are clothed in Christ. ²⁸ There is no Jew or Greek, there is no slave or free, there is no male and female; for all of you are one in Christ Jesus. ²⁹ And if you belong to Christ, then you are Abraham's [and Sarah's] offspring, heirs according to the promise.

⁴:¹ I say that as long as heirs are minors, they are no better than slaves, though they are the masters of all; ² but they remain under guardians and trustees until the time set by the father. ³ So also for us; while we were minors, we were enslaved by the constitutive elements of the world. ⁴ But when the fullness of time had come, God sent God's own Son, born of a woman, born under the law, ⁵ to redeem those who were under the law, so that we might receive adoption like children. ⁶ And because you are children, God has sent the Spirit of God's own Son into our hearts, crying, "Abba! Father!" ⁷ So you are no longer a slave but a child, and if a child then also an heir, through God.

[Mark 14:32 Jesus and his disciples went to a place called Gethsemane and he said to his disciples, "You all sit here while I pray." ³³ He took with him Peter and James and John and began to be deeply moved and distressed. ³⁴ And said to them, "My soul is deeply grieved, to the point of death; you all stay here, and stay awake." ³⁵ And going a little farther, he threw himself on the ground and prayed that, if possible, the hour might pass from him. ³⁶ He said, "Abba, Father, all things are possible for you; remove this cup from me; yet not what I want, but what you do." ³⁷ Jesus came and found them sleeping; and he said to Peter, "Simon, are you sleeping? Could you not stay awake one hour? ³⁸ Stay awake and pray that you all may not come into the time of trial; the spirit indeed is willing, but the flesh is weak." ³⁹ And again he went away and prayed, saying the same thing. ⁴⁰ And once more he came and found them sleeping, for their eyes were very heavy; and they did not know what to say to him. ⁴¹ Jesus came a third time and said to them, "Are you all sleeping, still, and taking your rest? Enough! The hour has come. Look! The Son of Woman is betrayed into the hands of sinners. ⁴² Get up, let us go. See, my betrayer is at hand."

⁴³ And instantly, while he was still speaking, Judas, one of the twelve, arrived; with him there was a crowd with swords and clubs from the chief priests, the religious scholars, and the elders. ⁴⁴ Now the betrayer had given them a sign, saying, "The one I kiss is he; seize him and lead him away safely." ⁴⁵ Then when Judas came, he went up to Jesus immediately and said, "Rabbi!" and kissed him. ⁴⁶ Then they laid hands on him and took him. ⁴⁷ But one of the bystanders drew his sword and struck the slave of the high priest and cut off his ear. ⁴⁸ Then Jesus said to them, "Is it as for a bandit you all have come out with swords and clubs to seize me?? ⁴⁹ Daily I was with you all in the temple teaching, and you did not seize me. But let the scriptures be fulfilled." ⁵⁰ All of them deserted him and fled. ⁵¹ A certain young man was following Jesus, with just a fine cloth on his naked flesh. They caught hold of him, ⁵² but he forsook the fine cloth and ran off naked.]

⁵³ They took Jesus to the high priest; and they assembled all the chief priests, the elders, and the religious scholars. ⁵⁴ Now Peter followed him from afar into the courtyard of the high priest and was sitting with the attendants, warming himself at the fire. ⁵⁵ Now the chief priests and the whole council sought testimony against Jesus to put him to death but found none. ⁵⁶ For many gave false testimony against him, yet their testimony did not agree. ⁵⁷ Some rose and gave false testimony against him, saying, ⁵⁸ "Well, we heard him say, 'I will destroy this hand-made temple, and in three days I will build another, that is not hand-made.'" ⁵⁹ But even on this point their testimony did not agree. ⁶⁰ Then the high priest stood up before them and said to Jesus, "No response? What are they testifying against you?" ⁶¹ But he was silent and answered nothing. Again, the high priest spoke to him, "Are you the Messiah, the Son of the Blessed One?" ⁶² Jesus said, "I am; and

> *you will see the Son of Woman*
> *seated at the right hand of the Power,*
> and *coming with the clouds of heaven."*

⁶³ Then the high priest tore his clothes and said, "Why do we still need witnesses? ⁶⁴ You all have heard his blasphemy! How does it appear to you?" All of them condemned

him, "Guilty! This is death!" ⁶⁵ Some began to spit on him, to blindfold him, and to strike him, saying to him, "Prophesy!" Then the attendants took him and beat him.

⁶⁶ While Peter was below in the courtyard, one of the high priest's enslaved girls came by. ⁶⁷ When she saw Peter warming himself, she stared at him and said, "You were also with the Nazarene, Jesus." ⁶⁸ But Peter denied it, saying, "I do not know or even understand what you are saying." Then he went out into the front courtyard. Then the cock crowed. ⁶⁹ And the enslaved girl, on seeing him, began to say to the bystanders again that this man is one of them. ⁷⁰ But again he denied it. Then after a little while the bystanders said to Peter again, "Certainly you are one of them, for you are a Galilean." ⁷¹ But he began to curse and swore, "I do not know this person you are talking about." ⁷² And suddenly the cock crowed for the second time. Then Peter remembered the thing Jesus had said to him, "Before the cock crows twice, you will deny me three times." And he threw himself down and sobbed.

¹⁵:¹ As soon as it was morning, the chief priests took a counsel with the elders and religious scholars and the whole council. They bound Jesus, led him away, and handed him over to Pilate. ² Pilate asked him, "Are you the King of the Judeans?" He answered him, saying, "You say so." ³ Then the chief priests accused him of many things. ⁴ But Pilate asked him again, "Have you no reply? See how many charges they bring against you." ⁵ But Jesus made no further reply, thus Pilate was amazed.

⁶ Now at the festival Pilate used to release one prisoner to them, whoever they asked. ⁷ Now there was a man called Barabbas in prison with the rebels who in the rebellion had committed murder. ⁸ So the crowd came and began to ask Pilate to do for them according to his custom. ⁹ Then he responded to them, saying, "Do you all want me to release the King of the Judeans to you?" ¹⁰ For he recognized that it was out of jealousy that the chief priests had handed him over. ¹¹ Then the chief priests stirred up the crowd that instead Barabbas might be released for them. ¹² Pilate again responded to them, "What then do you wish me to do with the one you call the King of the Judeans?" ¹³ They shouted more [than before], "Crucify him!" ¹⁴ Pilate asked them, "Why, for doing what evil?" But they shouted all the more, "Crucify him!" ¹⁵ So Pilate, wanting to satiate the crowd, released Barabbas to them; then he handed Jesus over for flogging and to be crucified.

¹⁶ Then the soldiers led him into the courtyard of the property, which is the military headquarters, and they called together the entire cohort. ¹⁷ And they clothed him in purple, and they put on him thorns woven into a crown. ¹⁸ And they began saluting him, "Hail, King of the Judeans!" ¹⁹ They struck his head with a reed, spat upon him, and knelt in homage to him. ²⁰ After mocking him, they stripped him of the purple and put his clothes on him. Then they led him away to crucify him.

²¹ They compelled a passerby, a certain Simon of Cyrene who was coming from the countryside, to carry his cross; he was the father of Alexander and Rufus. ²² Then they brought Jesus to the Golgotha place (which means Skull Place). ²³ And they offered him myrrh wine, but he did not take it. ²⁴ And they crucified him, and divided his clothes, casting lots among themselves for what each would take.

⁲⁵ It was the third hour [past dawn] when they crucified him. ²⁶ The writing above of the accusation against him read, "The King of the Judeans." ²⁷ And with him they crucified two revolutionaries, one on his right and one on his left.

²⁹ The passersby reviled him, shaking their heads and saying, "Ha! You would destroy the temple and build it in three days—³⁰ save yourself, and come down from the cross!" ³¹ In the same way the chief priests, with the religious scholars, mocked him among themselves and said, "He saved others; himself he is unable to save. ³² The Messiah, the King of Israel! Come down from the cross now that we may see and believe." Those who were crucified with him also demeaned him.

³³ Now when it was the sixth hour [of the day, or noon], darkness came over the whole land until the ninth hour [of the day, about three in the afternoon]. ³⁴ At the ninth hour Jesus cried out with a loud voice, "*Eloi, Eloi, lema sabachthani?*" which means, "My God, my God, why have you forsaken me?" ³⁵ When some of the bystanders heard it, they said, "Listen, he is calling Elijah." ³⁶ And someone ran and filled a sponge with vinegary wine, put it on a stick, and gave it to him to drink, saying, "Wait, let us see whether Elijah will come to take him down." ³⁷ Then Jesus gave a great cry and breathed out a final time. ³⁸ And the curtain of the temple was torn in two, from top to bottom. ³⁹ Now when the centurion, stationed facing him, saw that in this way Jesus breathed out at the end, he said, "Truly this man was God's Son!"

⁴⁰ There were also women watching from a distance; among them were Mary the Magdalene, and Mary the mother of James the younger and of Joses, and Salome. ⁴¹ These women followed him and ministered to him when he was in Galilee, and there were many other women who had come up with him to Jerusalem.

⁴² When evening had come, since it was the day of Preparation—the day before the sabbath—⁴³ Joseph of Arimathea, a respected member of the council, who himself was also waiting for the reign of God, went boldly to Pilate and requested for the body of Jesus. ⁴⁴ Then Pilate wondered that Jesus was now dead, and summoning the centurion asked him whether he had been dead for some time. ⁴⁵ When he learned it from the centurion, he gave the corpse to Joseph. ⁴⁶ Then Joseph bought a fine cloth, and taking him down, wrapped him in the fine cloth, and put him in a tomb that had been hewn out of rock. He then rolled a stone against the door of the tomb. ⁴⁷ Mary the Magdalene and Mary the mother of Joses saw where he was put.

PROCLAMATION

Owing to the length of the Palm Sunday Gospel, the commentary section will be longer than for other readings.

Text Notes

The same word is used in Isaiah 49:5 and verse 7, yet NRSV, JPS, and CEB all translate Israel as God's "servant" but the nation as the "slave of rulers." "Servant" occludes the expectation of complete domination/submission, including the ability to maim, kill, breed, rape, impregnate, and sell the person without consequence.

Hebrew plurals like "monarchs/kings" and "princes" in Isaiah 49:7 are inclusive. I have expanded both to reflect the presence of female royals in and at the head of some nations. "Go free" in verse 9 uses the primary verb of the exodus. Syene, or Sinim, in verse 12 is an Egyptian town with a record of some Israelite settlement.

In Isaiah 49:5 and 15, "womb" is the more generic "belly" used broadly for women and men; it is also found in Psalm 22:9–10 (verse 10 also uses the more common specific "womb). In Isaiah 49:13–15, it is paired with "mother-love" (the verb whose root is that same word), and children, including one at the breast, in verse 15. Translating this as "compassion" (NRSV), "pity" (CEB), or just "love" (JPS) eviscerates the intentionally crafted portrait of God as a mother, accomplished despite the use of masculine forms.

The second phrase in Psalm 22:3 can also be translated as "you are holy, enthroned, the Praise of Israel." In verse 9, the Divine Midwife "extracts" the baby; she does not just "catch" him, perhaps suggesting a difficult birth.

In Galatians 3:23ff, translation choices can present the law in an antagonistic and ultimately anti-Jewish manner as "prison" and "disciplinarian" (see NRSV). However, *ephrouroumetha* in verse 23 means to set a guard or garrison; that is a protective action. And in verse 24, a *paidagōgos* is a teacher; *torah* itself means "teaching" and "revelation" more than "law."

One of the verbs that describes Jesus's emotions in Mark 14:33 is only used in that place, making it difficult to define; suggestions range from "amazed" to "gloomy" to "distressed" to "troubled." In verse 34, Jesus expresses his sorrow using the language of Psalms 42:11 and 43:5 in Greek: "my soul is cast down." Similarly, the description of soldiers gambling for Jesus's clothes matches the wording of Psalm 22:18 in Greek. Judas is concerned that Jesus's arrest be "safely" in verse 44; he is a complex character with mixed motives. The "attendants" in verse 54 can provide a number of services; the word is more "assistant" than "guard," as is commonly translated. The enslaved "girls" in Mark 14:66–69 could be young women. "Girl" is often used to denote their minor legal status. The criminals crucified with Jesus in Mark 15:27 could have been thieves or highway bandits; the root of *lēstēs* is stolen goods. However, the semantic range includes revolutionaries and insurrectionists. This latter understanding may be what is meant, given the mention of imprisoned rebels (using a different word, *stasiastēs*) in verse 7. The vinegar wine in verse 36 draws on Psalm 69:21. The nature of the women's ministry to Jesus in 15:41 should be understood as wholistic: spiritual and material. Many Greek manuscripts use the more explicit *ptōma*, "corpse," rather than *soma*, "body," for Jesus's remains in Mark 15:44.

Verse 28 is missing from most translations as its origin hails from less well-regarded manuscripts.

Preaching Prompts

As Holy Week begins, one may wish to explore God's sorrow over a world that crucifies as well as over a crucified beloved child, a mother's sorrow as well as a father's. In Isaiah 49, God is the divine mother whose love emanates from her womb, most specifically in verses 13–15.

Contemporary discomfort with slave language should not overshadow the degree to which it was normative in the biblical text and its theologies. For the biblical ear, "slave of God" and "slave of Sarah" were equally acceptable and nonremarkable. The linguistic distinction between being a "servant" of God and being held in slavery is entirely artificial to the text and permits slave-holding societies to embrace servitude of God as pertaining to them while holding others in bondage in a fictive distinct category.

In Psalm 22, the most obvious divine feminine image is God as midwife and lactation guide in verse 9. There is also the birthing mother who has no voice and makes no cry. In verse 10, God seems to have become a foster parent for a perhaps abandoned child; the child is thrown (away?) onto God. God can be both midwife and foster mother here. We do not know if the birth mother cannot or will not keep her child. She can be preached in conversation with the reminder that women do abandon children in Isaiah 49, yet without demonization. In keeping with Palm Sunday, she can be read as giving her child over to God, whatever his fate.

Galatians 3:23–24 describes the law as a protective, not punitive, garrison and guard. Though addressing a Gentile Church on whom the Torah (or *torah* broadly) was never binding, Paul uses "we" regarding the law. In a rhetorical flourish, Paul argues that the particularities that characterize individuals and communities no longer exist "in Christ," yet he continues to operate as though those categories continue and are normative. Our adoption and kinship do not require us to leave ourselves or our identities behind.

There are very few women and girls in the Passion narratives. Here in Luke there are girls or women held in slavery by the chief priest. Missing is the wife of Simon of Cyrene, the Cross-Bearer; he is named with reference to his sons, but no mention is made of their mother.

The Passion narratives on Palm Sunday and Good Friday have been used to incite lethal physical violence against Jewish communities by the Church and its ministers. They have also been used to craft violent, anti-Semitic theologies that blame Jews for the death of Jesus, demean and defame Judaism, and deem it failed and its covenants replaced. It is important to acknowledge that history while repudiating it and repenting of it, and affirming God's fidelity to all her covenants and all her peoples. It is essential to be in conversation with our Jewish neighbors and to listen more than speak. I strongly recommend reading the scriptures in conversation with Jewish scholars, for example, with the *Jewish Study Bible* and *Jewish Annotated New Testament*.

MONDAY IN HOLY WEEK

Jeremiah 31:8–13; Psalm 22:19–31; Hebrews 1:1–9; John 12:1–7

Jeremiah 31:8 Look! I am going to bring them from the land of the north,
>and I will gather them from the farthest parts of the earth,
>among them blind and lame, pregnant and birthing, together,
>a great assembly, they shall return here.
>⁹ With weeping they shall come,
>and with consolations I will lead them back,
>I will have them walk by streams of water,
>on a straight path, they shall not stumble on it;
>for I am a parent to Israel,
>and Ephraim is my firstborn.
>¹⁰ Hear the word of the HOLY ONE, you nations,
>and declare it in the islands far off;
>say, "The One who scattered Israel will gather him,
>and will keep him as a shepherd a flock."
>¹¹ For the FAITHFUL ONE has ransomed Jacob [of Rebekah's line]
>and has redeemed him from hands too strong for him.
>¹² They shall come and they shall sing on the heights of Zion,
>and they shall be radiant over the goodness of the GRACIOUS GOD,
>over the grain, and over the new wine, and over the oil,
>and over the young of flock and herd;
>their souls shall become like a watered garden,
>and they shall never languish again.
>¹³ Then shall young women rejoice in dance,
>and young men and elders together.
>I will turn their mourning to joy;
>I will comfort them, and give them joy for sorrow.

Psalm 22:19–31
>¹⁹ SAVING GOD, be not far away!
>My strength, hasten to help me!
>²⁰ Deliver my soul from the sword,
>my life from the clutch of the dog!
>²¹ Save me from the mouth of the lion!
>For on the horns of the wild oxen you have responded to me.
>²² I will tell of your name to my sisters and brothers;
>in the midst of the congregation, I will praise you:

23 You who revere the Fount of Life, praise her!
   all the offspring of Leah and Rachel, Bilhah and Zilpah glorify her.
   Stand in awe of her all you of Rebekah's line.
24 For she did not despise or abhor
   the affliction of the afflicted;
   she did not hide her face from me,
   and when I cried to her, she heard.
25 On your account is my praise in the great congregation;
   my vows I will pay before those who revere her.
26 The poor shall eat and be satisfied;
   those who seek her shall praise the Mother of All.
   May your hearts live forever!
27 All the ends of the earth shall remember
   and turn to the Wellspring of Life;
   and all the families of the nations
   shall worship before her.
28 For sovereignty belongs to the She Who Is Holy,
   and she rules over the nations.
29 They consume and they bow down,
   all the fat ones of the earth before her,
   they bend their knees,
   all who go down to the dust,
   and cannot save their soul.
30 Later descendants will serve her;
   future generations will be told about our God,
31 they will go and proclaim her deliverance
   to a people yet unborn,
   saying that she has done it.

Hebrews 1:1 Many times and in many ways God spoke to our mothers and fathers through the prophets, female and male. ² In these last days God has spoken to us by a Son, whom God appointed heir of all there is, and through whom God created the worlds. ³ The Son is the brilliance of God's glory and reproduction of God's very being, and the Son undergirds all there is by his word of power. When the Son had made purification for sins, he sat down at the right hand of the Majesty on high, ⁴ having become much greater than the angels, as the name he inherited is more excellent than theirs.

⁵ For to which of the angels did God ever say,
   "You are my Child; today I have begotten you"?
   Or this,
   "I will be their Parent, and they will be my Child"?

⁶ Then again, when God brings the firstborn into the world, God says,
"*Let all the angels of God worship him.*"
⁷ On the one hand, of the angels God says,
"*God makes winds into celestial messengers,*
and flames of fire into God's ministers."
⁸ But of the Son God says,
"*Your throne, O God, is forever and ever,*
and the righteous scepter is the scepter of your realm.
⁹ *You have loved righteousness and hated lawlessness;*
therefore God, your God, has anointed you
with the oil of gladness beyond your companions."

John 12:1 Now Jesus, six days before the Passover, came to Bethany where Lazarus was who he raised from the dead. ² There they gave a dinner for him and Martha served while Lazarus was one of those at the table with him. ³ Mary took a pound of a balm made of expensive pure nard, anointed the feet Jesus, and wiped them with her hair. The house was filled with the scent of the perfume. ⁴ But Judas Iscariot, one of his disciples, the one who was about to betray him, said, ⁵ "Why was this balm not sold for three hundred denarii and the money given to the poor?" ⁶ Now he said this not because he cared about the poor, but because he was a thief; he kept the moneybag, and whatever was put into it, he stole. ⁷ Jesus said, "Leave her alone. It was for the day of my burial that she kept it."

PROCLAMATION

Text Notes

In Jeremiah 31:9, arguably, "consolations" became "supplications," the literal reading, when a letter was dropped.

In Psalm 22:23, "the offspring of Jacob" are identified by their mothers/matriarchs, enslaved and free; similarly, "Rebekah's line" stands in for "the offspring of Israel."

In keeping with the aims of this work, foremothers and female prophets are made explicit in Hebrews 1:1. *Megalōsynēs*, "Majesty," in Hebrews 1:3, as a feminine noun, marks a rare use of feminine language to describe God or her attributes in the New Testament.

The following verses quote the earlier scriptures widely and often out of context: Hebrews 1:5 quotes Psalm 2:7, where the anonymous psalmist says God told them they were God's begotten child, probably initially heard with regard to David. The next quote is from 2 Samuel 7:14 (and its duplicate, 1 Chronicles 17:13), where the promise of God to be a parent to a future monarch is to one of David's descendants. Given the difficulty of asserting biological gender for heavenly beings, I use the neuter "child" and "parent" in verse 5. Verse 6 quotes Deuteronomy 32:43 and Psalm 97:7 from Greek, where the original "gods" were replaced by "angels" to correct toward a pure monotheism. Verse 7 quotes Psalm 104:4, playing on the primary meaning of angel, "messenger." Verses 8–9 quote Psalm 45:6–7, where the first verse refers to God, but the second refers to the king whose wedding psalm it is (Ahab, since Jezebel is the only princess of Tyre to marry into Israel).

Preaching Prompts

A second iteration of the woman who anoints Jesus is traditional on Monday of Holy Week, an earlier version having been read on the last Sunday of Lent. Today the woman is Mary, sister of Martha and the resurrected Lazarus in John. The Jeremiah 31 reading offers the hope of consolation for those who mourn, just as Lazarus's resurrected body at the table with Jesus does.

The context of Jeremiah 31 is God's promise to restore Israel after the Babylonian devastation; our reading affirms the faithfulness of God to her people in each generation, building on, not replacing, the earliest reading. In some ways, Jeremiah 31 is an answer to the plea for salvation in Psalm 22. It is important to remember that "salvation" in the Hebrew Scriptures is physical salvation from death or other danger, and normally national or corporate. Paraphrased by Jesus (his recitation does not quite match Hebrew or Greek versions in either Matthew 27:46 or Mark 15:34), Psalm 22 became the Psalm of the Cross, a principal text of Holy Week.

Hebrews 1 calls us back to the fidelity of God who spoke through prophecy but now speaks through her Holy Child. (Some have concluded from this that prophecy came to an end; however, prophets appear scattered throughout the New Testament.) The amount of prooftexting in this short section raises the eyebrows of a biblical scholar yet reminds us how flexible ancient interpreters found the scriptures. That flexibility enabled them to reinterpret them in light of Jesus while still holding their previous understandings. Christians have all too often abandoned contextual readings, seizing upon this type of exegesis, neglecting other biblical models.

The last line of the Gospel points us to the tomb where we needs must linger.

TUESDAY IN HOLY WEEK

Isaiah 49:1–6; Psalm 123; Philippians 3:17–21; Matthew 21:12–17

Isaiah 49:1 Listen to me, you coastlands,
   give heed, you peoples from far away!
   The LIFE-BREATH OF CREATION called me from the womb,
   from the innermost parts of my mother God made my name known.
 ² God made my mouth like a sharp sword,
   in the shadow of God's own hand did God hide me;

God made me a polished arrow,
in God's own quiver did God hide me away.
³ And God said to me, "You are my slave,
Israel, the one in whom I will be glorified."
⁴ But I said, "in vain have I labored,
for nothingness and vanity have I spent my strength;
yet surely my judgment is with the Righteous Judge,
and my recompense with my God."
⁵ And now says the Author of Life,
who formed me in the womb to be God's slave
to return Jacob back to God,
and that Israel might be gathered to God:
I am honored in the sight of the Holy One of Old,
and my God is my strength.
⁶ God says,
"It is too light a thing that you should be my slave
to raise up the tribes of Jacob [the line of Rebekah]
and to restore the survivors of Israel [born of Rachel and Leah, and Bilhah and Zilpah]?
I will give you as a light to the nations,
for it will be that my salvation reaches to the end of the earth."

Psalm 123

¹ To you I lift up my eyes,
the one who is enthroned in the heavens!
² See! It is just as the eyes of the enslaved
are toward the hand of their lord,
as the eyes of an enslaved girl
toward the hand of her mistress,
just so our eyes look to the Mighty One our God,
until God shows us favor.
³ Have mercy upon us, Merciful One, have mercy upon us,
for we have had more than our fill of contempt.
⁴ Our soul has had more than its fill
of the scorn of those who are at ease,
of the contempt of the proud.

Philippians 3:17 Become imitators of me together, sisters and brothers, and observe those who walk according to our example. ¹⁸ For many of them—as I have often told you all, and now I tell you even with tears—walk as enemies of the cross of Christ. ¹⁹ Their end is destruction; their god is the belly; and their glory is in their shame; their minds are set on earthly things. ²⁰ But our citizenship is in heaven, and it is from there that we are expecting a Savior, Jesus Christ, our Sovereign, ²¹ who will transform the body of our humiliation that it may bear the likeness of the body of his glory, through the force that also enables him to make all things subject to himself.

Matthew 21:12 Then Jesus entered the temple and drove out all who were selling and buying in the temple, and the tables of the moneychangers he overturned, as well as the station of those who sold doves. ¹³ He said to them, "It is written,

> *'My house shall be called a house of prayer';*
> *but you all are making it a den of robbers.'*

¹⁴ And they came to him in the temple, those who were blind and disabled, and he cured them. ¹⁵ Now when the chief priests and the religious scholars saw the amazing things that he did, and heard the girls and boys crying out in the temple, "Hosanna to the Son of David," they became angry. ¹⁶ They said to him, "Do you hear what these are saying?" Jesus said to them, "Yes; have you never read,

> *'Out of the mouths of infants and nursing babies*
> *you have prepared praise for yourself'?"*

¹⁷ He left them, went out of the city to Bethany, and spent the night there.

PROCLAMATION

Text Notes

In Isaiah 49:4, the poet-prophet speaking in the first person emphasizes redundantly, "I, I said" what she or the unidentified servant about whom she is prophesying said to God upon being commissioned in God's service. Writing long past the time of Isaiah proper, the gender and identity of the prophet are unknown. (I discuss the possibility of the author being a woman in *Daughters of Miriam: Women Prophets in Ancient Israel*.) The "nothingness" in verse 4 is the "shapelessness" of the earth at its creation, the *tohu* of the poetic phrase, *tohu vavohu*, "formless and shapeless," of the earth before its shaping in Genesis 1:2.

Psalm 123 makes explicit the psalmist's understanding that God is a slave-master, and we, women and men alike, are God's slaves. This understanding pervades the scriptures. Linguistically, the human slave-master, "lord," in verse 2, is the same word as "Lord," most often used to represent God's unpronounceable name formed of the letters YHVH. This volume eschews that language while wrestling with its lingering theology. Philippians 3:20 uses the Greek equivalent for lord, *kyrion*, for Jesus.

In Philippians 3:19, the belly, *koilia*, the marks of one of the carnal obsessions of the "earthly" believer, can refer to innards broadly or to the womb, thereby perhaps to gluttony or lust.

Where the Greek text has "children" in Matthew 21:15, I have specified "girls and boys"; girls have extremely low visibility in the scriptures but would have been present in the temple. There is no reason to presume that only boys acclaimed him, given the plural form allows for the presence of girls.

Preaching Prompts

These texts emphasize the sovereignty of God and of Christ, calling attention to the great gulf between God and humanity in troubling and troublesome language. At the same time, they frame the story of the One who crossed and closed that gulf, looking more human than divine this week. We may be helped by remembering that the Church writes from a position of vulnerability, believing in faith that it won't always be that way. Paul, in particular, is imprisoned. One might wish to think of the crucified Church looking to its own resurrection.

The various servants in latter Isaiah are sometimes the nation, sometimes a coming monarch, sometimes a messiah, and sometimes indeterminate. This passage speaks in messianic terms and was so understood by Christian readers.

As is often the case, the Epistle distinguishes physical, bodily, and earthly from what is spiritual and heavenly. It is worth remembering that there was a widespread belief that Christ's return was imminent, and we would soon have little use for this world. It is our task to interpret this text in light of our continuing reality and the season, Holy Week, in which the physicality of salvation is made manifest.

Matthew 21:13 fuses Isaiah 56:7 and Jeremiah 7:11 into a single citation. Dr. Amy-Jill Levine helpfully reminds us that a "den of robbers" is not a place where there is criminal activity, just as a lion's den is not where lions do their hunting and killing. It is the refuge, or abode, meaning that the moneychangers who were essential to the proper functioning of the temple were not robbing people. She suggests that Jesus's rebuke, like Jeremiah's before him, was that the unrepentant had made the temple a social club rather than a place of prayer; she also notes that the table-turning would have been a rather small demonstration given the scale of the complex (*Entering the Passion of Jesus: A Beginner's Guide to Holy Week*, chapter 2, "The Temple: Risking Righteous Anger").

Individual women are hard to locate in the Gospel reading but would have been among the worshippers, praying and making their own offering; some likely would have been among those Jesus healed. Jesus evokes but does not mention women when citing Psalm 8:2/3 in Greek (verse numbers vary by language): women birthed and nursed the infants who offer praise to God.

WEDNESDAY IN HOLY WEEK

Ezekiel 17:22–24; Psalm 36:5–10; 1 John 2:7–14; Matthew 23:37–39

Ezekiel 17:22 Thus says the Sovereign God:

> I myself will take a sprig of cedar
> from its very top;
> and I will place it;
> from the topmost of its most tender branch
> I will pluck it and I myself will plant it
> on a high and lofty mountain.
> ²³ On the mountain height of Israel
> I will plant it,
> that it may lift up its boughs and bear fruit,
> and become a noble cedar.
> Under it every kind of bird shall live;
> every kind of winged creature shall nest
> in the shade of its branches.
> ²⁴ All the trees of the field shall know
> that I am the Creator of All.
> I bring low the high tree,
> I make high the low tree;
> I dry up the green tree
> and I make the dry tree sprout buds.
> I the Ageless God have spoken;
> I will make it so.

Psalm 36:5–10

> ⁵ Holy One, throughout the very heavens is your faithful love,
> your faithfulness beyond the clouds.
> ⁶ Your righteousness is like the eternal mountains,
> your judgments are like the mighty deep;
> you save humankind and animalkind alike, Faithful One.
> ⁷ How precious is your faithful love, O God!
> All the woman-born take shelter in the shadow of your wings.
> ⁸ They feast on the abundance of your house,
> and you give them drink from the river of your delights.
> ⁹ For with you is the fountain of life;
> in your light we see light.
> ¹⁰ Extend your faithful love to those who know you,
> and your justice to the upright of heart!

1 John 2:7 Beloved, no new commandment do I write you all, but an old commandment that you have had from the beginning; that commandment is the word that you have heard. [8] Yet I am writing you all a new commandment that is true in Christ and in you, because the shadow is passing away and the true light already shines. [9] Whoever says, "I am in the light," while hating a sister or brother, is in shadow still. [10] Whoever loves a sister or brother lives in the light, and in such a person there is no occasion for stumbling. [11] But whoever hates another sister or brother is in shadow, walks in shadow, and does not know where to go, because the shadow dims the eyes.

[12] I am writing to you, little children,
    because your sins are forgiven on account of Christ's name.
[13] I am writing to you, mothers and fathers,
    because you know the one who is from the beginning.
    I am writing to you, young women and men,
    because you have conquered the evil one.
[14] I write to you, children,
    because you know the Creator.
    I write to you, mothers and fathers,
    because you know the one who is from the beginning.
    I write to you, young people,
    because you are strong
    and the word of God abides in you,
    and you have overcome the evil one.

Matthew 23:37 "Jerusalem, Jerusalem, that kills the prophets and stones those who are sent to it! How often have I desired to gather your children together as a hen gathers her chicks under her wings, and you were not willing! [38] See, your house is left to you, desolate. [39] For I tell you all, you will not see me again until you say, 'Blessed is the one who comes in the name of the Holy One.'"

PROCLAMATION

Text Notes

In the psalm, the noun *el*, God, is used as an adjective describing the mountains in verse 6.

Preaching Prompts

Today's lessons revolve around Jesus's journey to Jerusalem, where even on the way to his death, he expressed his longing to mother Jerusalem through its violent inclinations. In these lessons, birds function as both images for a sheltering God and images for a huddled humanity and are themselves creatures of the natural world for whom God also cares.

Ezekiel 17:22–24 is a highly allegorical text that can be read as a description of a messianic figure who has noble (lofty) origins but is tender rather than hardened. The community founded around and beneath sheltering branches of this "tree" is diverse and flourishing. As in other prophetic texts, God brings low what is high and exalts what is low.

The psalm echoes the theme of God's faithfulness to bird and tree, extending it to all animals and all humanity. Here, God is winged, sheltering all life within her wings.

The Epistle exhorts us to replicate the love God has for creation for each other. It also offers a hint that the heaviness and shadow of Holy Week will give way to light.

Jesus's embrace of Jerusalem, its history and hopes, ugly realities, looming threats, sacred space, and all of its people—citizens, immigrants, pilgrims, and occupiers—was all inclusive. There is room for all in his embrace.

MAUNDY THURSDAY

Exodus 15:11–21; Psalm 136:1–16; Hebrews 11:23–28; Matthew 26:17–56

Exodus 15:11 "Who is like you, MIGHTY ONE, among the gods?

> Who is like you, resplendent in holiness,
> revered praiseworthy, working wonders?

¹² You stretched out your right hand,
the earth swallowed them.

¹³ You led, in your faithful love, the people whom you redeemed;
you guided them by your strength to your holy abode.

¹⁴ The peoples heard, they quaked;
pangs like labor seized the inhabitants of Philistia.

¹⁵ Then the chiefs of Edom were dismayed;
the rulers of Moab, trembling seized them;
all the inhabitants of Canaan melted away.

¹⁶ Terror and dread fell upon them
by the might of your arm;
they became still as a stone
until your people, REDEEMING GOD, passed by,
until the people whom you acquired passed by.

¹⁷ You brought them and planted them on the mountain of your own possession,
the place, SHELTERING GOD, you made for your dwelling,
the sanctuary, Most High God, that your hands have established.

¹⁸ The EVERLASTING GOD will reign forever and ever."

¹⁹ The horse of Pharaoh and his chariots and charioteers went into the sea, and the MIGHTY GOD turned the waters of the sea back upon them; but the daughters and sons of Israel walked through the sea on dry ground.

²⁰ Then the prophet Miriam, Aaron's sister, took a hand-drum in her hand, and all the women went out after her with hand-drums and with dancing. ²¹ And Miriam sang to them, women and men:

> "Sing to the INDOMITABLE GOD who has triumphed triumphantly;
> horse and rider God has thrown into the sea."

Psalm 136:1–16

1. Give thanks to the FOUNT OF LIFE, who is good,
   for her faithful love is everlasting.
2. Give thanks to the God of gods,
   for her faithful love is everlasting.
3. Give thanks to the Majesty of Majesties,
   for her faithful love is everlasting;
4. who alone does great wonders,
   for her faithful love is everlasting;
5. who through insight made the heavens,
   for her faithful love is everlasting;
6. to the one who spread out the land upon the waters,
   for her faithful love is everlasting;
7. to the one who made the great lights,
   for her faithful love is everlasting;
8. the sun to govern the day,
   for her faithful love is everlasting;
9. the moon and stars to govern the night,
   for her faithful love is everlasting;
10. who struck Egypt through their firstborn daughters and sons,
    for her faithful love is everlasting;
11. and brought Israel out from among them,
    for her faithful love is everlasting;
12. with a strong hand and an outstretched arm,
    for her faithful love is everlasting;
13. who cut the Red Sea in two,
    for her faithful love is everlasting;
14. and made Israel pass over through the midst of it,
    for her faithful love is everlasting;
15. but churned Pharaoh and his army in the Red Sea,
    for her faithful love is everlasting;

¹⁶ who walked her people through the wilderness,
for her faithful love is everlasting.

Hebrews 11:23 By faith Moses was hidden after his birth by his mother and father for three months, because they saw that the child was beautiful; and they were not afraid of the king's commandment. ²⁴ By faith Moses, after he had grown up, refused to be called a son of Pharaoh's daughter, ²⁵ rather choosing ill-treatment with the people of God than enjoyment of the transitory pleasures of sin. ²⁶ He considered abuse for the sake of the Messiah to be greater wealth than the treasures of Egypt, for he was looking ahead to the reward. ²⁷ By faith he left Egypt, unafraid of the anger of the king; for he persisted as though he saw the unseen. ²⁸ By faith he kept the Passover and the sprinkling of blood, in order that the destroyer of the firstborn would not touch the firstborn daughters and sons of Israel.

Matthew 26:17 On the first day of Unleavened Bread the disciples came to Jesus, saying, "Where do you want us to prepare for you to eat the Passover?" ¹⁸ He said, "Go into the city to a certain person, and say, 'The Teacher says, My time is near; I will keep the Passover at your house with my disciples.'" ¹⁹ So the disciples did just as Jesus instructed them, and they prepared the Passover meal.

²⁰ When it was evening, he reclined at table with the twelve, ²¹ and while they ate, he said, "Truly I tell you, one of you will betray me." ²² And they became deeply grieved and each one began to say to him, "Not me, is it Rabbi?" ²³ He responded and said, "The one who dipped his hand into the bowl with me will betray me. ²⁴ Indeed, the Son of Woman goes away as it is written of him, but woe to the person by whom the Son of Woman is betrayed! It would have been better for that person not to have been born." ²⁵ Judas, who betrayed him, responded and said, "It wasn't me was it, Rabbi?" He replied, "You said it."

²⁶ While they were eating, Jesus took a loaf of bread, and blessing it, he broke it, and gave it to the disciples, saying, "Take, eat; this is my body." ²⁷ Then he took a cup, and giving thanks he gave it to them, saying, "Drink from it, all of you; ²⁸ for this is my blood of the covenant, which is poured out for many for forgiveness of sins. ²⁹ I tell you all, I will not drink again of this fruit of the vine until that day when I drink it new with you all in the realm of my Abba." ³⁰ And when they had sung the hymn, they went out to the Mount of Olives.

³¹ Then Jesus said to them, "You will all become scandalized to the point of desertion because of me this night; for it is written,

'For I will strike the shepherd,
and the sheep of the flock will be scattered.'

³² But after I am raised, I will go ahead of you all to Galilee." ³³ Peter said to him, "Though all become scandalized and desert because of you, I will never desert you." ³⁴ Jesus said to him, "Truly I tell you, this very night, before the cock crows, you will deny me three times." ³⁵ Peter said to him, "Should it be necessary I die with you, I will not deny you." Then likewise said all the disciples.

³⁶ Then Jesus came with his disciples to a place called Gethsemane, and he said to them, "You all sit here while I go pray there." ³⁷ He took Peter and the two sons of Zebedee and began to be grieved and distressed. ³⁸ Then he said to them, "My soul is deeply grieved, to the point of death; you all stay here, and stay awake with me." ³⁹ And going on a little, he fell on the ground and prayed, saying, "My Father, if it is possible, let this cup pass from me; nevertheless not what I want but what you do." ⁴⁰ Then he came to the disciples and found them sleeping; and he said to Peter, "So, you all were not strong enough to stay awake with me one hour? ⁴¹ Stay awake and pray that you all may not come into the test; indeed, the spirit is willing, but the flesh is weak." ⁴² Again, for the second time, Jesus went away and prayed, saying, "My Father, if it is not possible for this to pass lest I drink it, let your will be done." ⁴³ And again he came and found them sleeping, for their eyes were heavy. ⁴⁴ So leaving them again, he went away and prayed for the third time, saying those words again. ⁴⁵ Then he came to the disciples and said to them, "Sleep now and take your rest. See, the hour is at hand, and the Son of Woman is betrayed into the hands of sinners. ⁴⁶ Get up, let us go. Look, my betrayer is at hand."

⁴⁷ While Jesus was still speaking, Judas, one of the twelve, came and with him was a large crowd with swords and clubs from the chief priests and the elders of the people. ⁴⁸ Now the betrayer had given them a sign, saying, "The one I kiss is he; take him." ⁴⁹ At once he came up to Jesus and said, "Shalom, Rabbi!" and kissed him. ⁵⁰ Jesus said to him, "Friend, this is why you have come." Then they came and laid hands on Jesus and took him. ⁵¹ Suddenly, someone with Jesus reached out with his hand, drew his sword, and struck the slave of the high priest, cutting off his ear. ⁵² Then Jesus said to him, "Return your sword to its place; for all who choose the sword will perish by the sword. ⁵³ Do you think I am not able to ask my Father, who will at once send me more than twelve legions of angels? ⁵⁴ How then would the scriptures be fulfilled, which say it must be thus?" ⁵⁵ At that hour Jesus said to the crowds, "Is it as for a bandit you all have come out with swords and clubs to seize me? Daily in the temple I sat teaching, and you did not arrest me. ⁵⁶ But all this has happened, so that the scriptures of the prophets may be fulfilled." Then all the disciples deserted him and fled.

PROCLAMATION

Text Notes

In Exodus 15:13, God's holy "abode" can also be understood as a pasture. The instrument Miriam and the other women play in verse 20 is a hand-drum, traditionally played by women across the ancient Afro-Asiatic world. "Tambourine" is anachronistic; they did not yet exist. In verse 21, Miriam exhorts the entire community or just the men—either can be indicated by the plural verb; however, the women are already following her, according to the previous verse.

In Matthew 26:18, the grammar used for the person who hosts Jesus is masculine; it may be generic for "person," as translated above. In verse 22 and elsewhere, "Rabbi" replaces "Lord" for direct address. In verse 49, I use "shalom" as the greeting, reflecting the culture of Jesus rather than the literary world of the Greek text.

Preaching Prompts

Passover and Holy Week and Easter are linked seasonally, thematically, and theologically. In some languages, the word for Easter is "Pascha," making the connection more explicit. The two seasons are also connected by violence. In the Exodus and Passover stories, Israel, God's beloved, is saved, and God sends their oppressors to their deaths. Painfully, those deaths are celebrated in psalms and songs. In Holy Week, Jesus, God's beloved, is executed by his—still God's beloved—people's oppressors. His death will also be commemorated in songs of praise. Each offers an opportunity to reflect on who we say God is in conversation with the scriptures.

The necessity for Jesus to observe Passover is just one of many reminders that Jesus was a religiously observant Jew who never broke with Judaism. The singular host in Matthew 26:18 seemingly obscures women from the household who would have done or helped with the actual work: cleaning, shopping, meal preparation, cooking, serving, and hosting. Since the more inclusive "disciples" is used rather than presumptively exclusively male "apostles," it is reasonable to expect the presence of women, particularly since these disciples prepared and served the meal, verse 19. Should female and male disciples have been present, it would be likely that children would be present, given that Passover is a family and community meal. (It should be noted that the form of the Passover meal at the time of Jesus, and even in the literary construction of the evangelists, was not a seder, which form developed later.) The mention of "the twelve" in verse 20 does not foreclose the possibility of a larger group at more than one table.

GOOD FRIDAY

Judges 11:29–40; Psalm 22; Hebrews 12:1–4; Luke 22:14–23:56

Judges 11:29 The Spirit of the HOLY ONE, she was upon Jephthah, and he passed through Gilead and Manasseh. He passed on to Mizpah of Gilead, and from Mizpah of Gilead he passed on to the Ammonites. 30 And Jephthah vowed a vow to the HOLY ONE OF OLD, and said, "If you will give the Ammonites into my hand, 31 then it shall be that the one who comes out—whoever comes out—of the doors of my house to meet me, when I return having finished with the Ammonites, shall be the HOLY ONE'S, I will offer them up as a burnt offering." 32 Then Jephthah crossed over to the Ammonites to fight against them and the HOLY ONE gave them into his hand. 33 He smote a mighty smiting on them from Aroer until you come to Minnith, twenty towns, and as far as Abel-keramim. So, the Ammonites were subdued before the people of Israel.

34 Then Jephthah came to his home at Mizpah, and there was his daughter coming out to meet him with drums and with dancing. Only she, an only child; he had no son or daughter apart from her. 35 When he saw her, he tore his clothes, and said, "Ah! My

daughter, you have knocked me down; you have become my trouble! I—I opened my mouth to the HOLY ONE, and I cannot take back my vow." ³⁶ She said to him, "My father, you have opened your mouth to the HOLY ONE, do to me according to what has gone out of your mouth, after that the HOLY ONE has taken vengeance through you against your enemies, against the Ammonites." ³⁷ And she said to her father, "Let be done for me this thing: Release me for two months, and I will go and go down among the hills, and weep for my virginity, I and my women-friends." ³⁸ Then he said, "Go," and sent her away for two months. So, she left, she and her women-friends, and wept over her virginity among the hills. ³⁹ And it was at the end of two months, she returned to her father, who did to her what he vowed in his vow. She had never known a man and she became an observance in Israel. ⁴⁰ Year by year the daughters of Israel would go out to tell the story of the daughter of Jephthah the Gileadite for four days.

Psalm 22

¹ My God, my God, why have you forsaken me?
  Why are you so far from my deliverance, from the words of my groaning?
² My God, I cry by day, and you do not answer;
  and by night, and there is no rest for me.
³ Yet you are holy,
  enthroned on the praises of Israel.
⁴ In you our mothers and fathers trusted;
  they trusted, and you rescued them.
⁵ To you they cried, and were freed;
  in you they trusted, and they were not put to shame.
⁶ But I am a worm, and not human;
  scorned by humankind, and despised by people.
⁷ All who see me mock me;
  they flap their lips at me, they shake their heads:
⁸ "Commit yourself to the SAVING ONE; let God rescue
  and deliver the one in whom God delights!"
⁹ Yet it was you who drew me from the womb;
  keeping me safe on my mother's breast.
¹⁰ On you was I cast from birth,
  and since my mother's womb you have been my God.
¹¹ Be not far from me,
  for trouble is near
  and there is none to help.
¹² Many bulls surround me,
  mighty bulls of Bashan encompass me;
¹³ they open wide their mouths at me,

like a lion, ravaging and roaring.
14. I am poured out like water,
and all my bones are disjointed.
My heart is like wax;
it is melted within my being.
15. My mouth is dried up like a potsherd,
and my tongue cleaves to my jaws;
in the dust of death you lay me down.
16. For dogs are all around me;
a conclave of evildoers encircles me.
Like a lion they ravage my hands and feet.
17. I can count all my bones.
They gloat and stare at me.
18. They divide my clothes among themselves,
and for my clothing they cast lots.
19. SAVING GOD, be not far away!
My strength, hasten to help me!
20. Deliver my soul from the sword,
my life from the clutch of the dog!
21. Save me from the mouth of the lion!
For on the horns of the wild oxen you have responded to me.
22. I will tell of your name to my sisters and brothers;
in the midst of the congregation I will praise you:
23. You who revere the FOUNT OF LIFE, praise her!
All the offspring of Leah and Rachel, Bilhah and Zilpah glorify her.
Stand in awe of her all you of Rebekah's line.
24. For she did not despise or abhor
the affliction of the afflicted;
she did not hide her face from me,
and when I cried to her, she heard.
25. On your account is my praise in the great congregation;
my vows I will pay before those who revere her.
26. The poor shall eat and be satisfied;
those who seek her shall praise the MOTHER OF ALL.
May your hearts live forever!
27. All the ends of the earth shall remember
and turn to the WELLSPRING OF LIFE;
and all the families of the nations
shall worship before her.
28. For sovereignty belongs to the SHE WHO IS HOLY,

and she rules over the nations.
29 They consume and they bow down, all the fat ones of the earth before her,
they bend their knees, all who go down to the dust,
and cannot save their soul.
30 Later descendants will serve her;
future generations will be told about our God,
31 they will go and proclaim her deliverance to a people yet unborn,
saying that she has done it.

Hebrews 12:1 Therefore, since we are surrounded by so great a cloud of witnesses, let us also put aside every weight and entangling sin, and with endurance let us run the race that is set before us, ² looking to Jesus the originator and perfecter of our faith, who for the sake of the joy that was set before him endured the cross, its shame disregarding, and at the right hand of the throne of God has taken his seat.

³ Consider the one who endured such hostility against himself from sinners, so that you all may not grow weary or your souls grow faint. ⁴ Not to this point have you all in your struggles against sin resisted to the point of shedding blood.

Luke 22:14 Now when the hour came, he took his place at the table, and the apostles with him. ¹⁵ Then Jesus said to them, "I have greatly desired to eat this Passover with you all before I suffer. ¹⁶ For I tell you all, I will not eat it until it is fulfilled in the realm of God." ¹⁷ Then Jesus took a cup, giving thanks. He said, "Receive this and divide it among yourselves; ¹⁸ for I tell you all that from now on I will not drink of the fruit of the vine until the reign of God comes." ¹⁹ Then Jesus took a loaf of bread, giving thanks, he broke it and gave it to them, saying, "This is my body, which is given for you all. Do this in remembrance of me." ²⁰ And he did the same with the cup after supper, saying, "This cup that is poured out for you is the new covenant in my blood. ²¹ Look, the hand of the one who betrays me is with me, on the table. ²² For indeed the Son of Woman is going as it has been determined, but woe to the one by whom he is betrayed!" ²³ Then they began to ask among themselves, which one of them was about to do this.

²⁴ There was also an argument among them as to which one of them should be considered the greatest. ²⁵ But Jesus said to them, "The royals of the Gentiles lord it over them, and those who have power over them are called benefactors. ²⁶ But not so with you all, rather the greatest among you must become like the youngest, and the leader like one who serves. ²⁷ For who is greater, the one who is at the table or the one who serves? Is it not the one at the table? Yet I am among you all as one who serves.

²⁸ "You are the ones who have remained with me in my trials, ²⁹ so then I covenant with you all, just as my Father has covenanted with me, a royal inheritance, ³⁰ so that you all may eat and drink at my table in my realm, and you all will sit on thrones governing the twelve tribes of Israel.

³¹ "Simon, Simon, listen! The Adversary has demanded to sift all of you like wheat, ³² but I have prayed for you in order that your faith not fail, and you, when you have turned back, strengthen your brothers." ³³ Then he said to Jesus, "Rabbi, I am ready to go with you to prison and to death!" ³⁴ But Jesus said, "I tell you, Peter, this day the cock will not have crowed three times, before you deny knowing me."

³⁵ Then Jesus said to them, "When I sent you out without a purse, bag, or sandals, did you lack anything?" They said, "Not a thing." ³⁶ He said to them, "But now, the one who has a purse must take it, and likewise a bag. And the one who does not have one must sell his cloak and buy a sword. ³⁷ For I tell you, this scripture must be fulfilled in me, *'And he was counted among the lawless,'* and indeed that which pertains to me is coming to its completion." ³⁸ So they said, "Rabbi, see, here are two swords." He replied to them, "It is sufficient."

³⁹ Then Jesus came out and went, as was his custom, to the Mount of Olives and the disciples followed him. ⁴⁰ When he was at the place, he said to them, "Pray that you not enter into testing." ⁴¹ Then he withdrew from them about a stone's throw on bended knee and prayed, ⁴² "Father, if you are willing, take this cup away from me; yet, not my will but yours be done." ⁴³ [Then an angel from heaven appeared to him and strengthened him. ⁴⁴ In agony he prayed more earnestly, and his sweat became like drops of blood falling down upon the ground.] ⁴⁵ When he rose from prayer, he came to the disciples and found them sleeping from grief. ⁴⁶ And he said to them, "Why are you sleeping? Get up and pray that you not enter into testing."

⁴⁷ While he was speaking, suddenly there was a crowd, and the one called Judas, one of the twelve, was leading them. He approached Jesus to kiss him. ⁴⁸ But Jesus said to him, "Judas, is it with a kiss that you betray the Son of Woman?" ⁴⁹ When those around him saw what was happening, they asked, "Rabbi, should we strike with the sword?" ⁵⁰ Then one of them struck a person enslaved by the high priest and cut off his right ear. ⁵¹ But Jesus responded, saying, "Enough of this!" And he grasped his ear and healed him. ⁵² Then Jesus said to ones who had come for him, the chief priests, the officers assigned to the temple, and the elders, "Have you all come out with swords and clubs as if I were a bandit? ⁵³ When I was with you daily in the temple, you did not lay hands on me. But this is your hour, and the power of darkness!"

⁵⁴ Then they seized him and led him away, bringing him into the house of the high priest. But Peter was following from afar. ⁵⁵ They kindled a fire in the middle of the courtyard and sat down together; Peter sat among them. ⁵⁶ Then a slave-girl, seeing him near the fire, looked intently at him and said, "This one also was with him." ⁵⁷ But he denied it, saying, "Woman, I do not know him." ⁵⁸ After a time someone else, on seeing him, said, "You are one of them too." But Peter said, "Man, I am not!" ⁵⁹ Then about an hour later another one insisted, "On the truth, this one was with him too, for he is a Galilean." ⁶⁰ But Peter said, "Man, I do not know what you are talking about!" Immediately, while he was speaking, the cock crowed. ⁶¹ The Savior turned and looked at Peter. Then Peter remembered the word of the Messiah, how he had said to him, "Before the cock crows today, you will deny me three times." ⁶² And Peter went out and wept bitterly.

⁶³ Now the men who were holding Jesus mocked him and beat him; ⁶⁴ they also blindfolded him and asked him, "Prophesy! Who is it that struck you?" ⁶⁵ They yelled much other abuse at him.

⁶⁶ Then when day came, the elders of the people, chief priests and religious scholars, gathered together and brought him to their council. ⁶⁷ They said, "If you are the Messiah, tell us." Jesus replied to them, "If I tell you, you will not believe, ⁶⁸ and if I ask a question, you will not answer. ⁶⁹ But from now on the Son of Woman will be seated at the right hand of the power of God." ⁷⁰ They all asked, "Are you, then, the Son of God?" He said to them, "You say that I am." ⁷¹ Then they said, "What further testimony do we need; we have heard it ourselves from his own lips!"

²³:¹ Then the assembly rose as a body and brought Jesus before Pilate. ² They began to accuse him, saying, "We found this man leading our nation astray, forbidding paying taxes to the emperor, and saying that he is a messiah, a king." ³ Then Pilate questioned him, saying, "Are you the king of the Judeans?" He answered, "You say so." ⁴ Then Pilate said to the chief priests and the crowds, "I find no cause for legal action against this person." ⁵ But they insisted, saying, "Because he stirs up the people by teaching throughout all Judea, from Galilee to this very place."

⁶ Upon hearing this, Pilate asked if the person was a Galilean. ⁷ Now when he learned that he was under Herod's authority, he sent him to Herod, who himself was in Jerusalem at that time. ⁸ When Herod saw Jesus, he was extremely glad, for he had wanted to see him for a long time, because he had heard about him and hoped to see him perform some sign. ⁹ Herod questioned him to his satisfaction, but Jesus answered him nothing. ¹⁰ The chief priests and the religious scholars stood by, vehemently accusing him. ¹¹ Herod and his soldiers also treated him with contempt and mocked him, and he put a majestic robe on him, and sent him back to Pilate. ¹² That very moment Herod and Pilate became friends with each other; previously they had been each other's enemy.

¹³ Pilate then called together the chief priests, the leaders, and the people, ¹⁴ and said to them, "You brought me this person for leading the people astray. Look now, I have examined him in your presence and have not found this person guilty of your charges against him. ¹⁵ Nor has Herod, for he sent him back to us. Look here, there is nothing deserving death in his case. ¹⁶ Therefore whip and release him."

¹⁸ Then they shouted together, saying, "Away with him! Release for us Barabbas!" ¹⁹ (Who for a rebellion that had taken place in the city, and for murder, had been put in prison.) ²⁰ Again Pilate addressed them, wanting to release Jesus, ²¹ but they kept shouting, saying, "Crucify, crucify him!" ²² A third time he said to them, "Why, what evil has he done? I have found nothing deserving death in him; I will, therefore, have him whipped and release him." ²³ But they insisted with loud shouts that he should be crucified, and their voices prevailed. ²⁴ So Pilate passed sentence to grant their demand. ²⁵ So he released the one in prison for rebellion and murder who they asked for, and he handed Jesus over as they wished.

²⁶ As they led Jesus away, they seized Simon of Cyrene who was coming from the country, and they laid on him the cross to carry behind Jesus. ²⁷ A great number of people followed him, and a group of women who were beating their breasts and wailing for him. ²⁸ But Jesus turned to them and said, "Daughters of Jerusalem, do not weep for me, weep only for yourselves and for your children. ²⁹ Look, the days are surely coming when they will say, 'Blessed are barren women, and wombs that have never given birth, and breasts that have never nourished.' ³⁰ *Then they will begin to say to the mountains, 'Fall on us'; and to the hills, 'Cover us.'* ³¹ For if when the wood is green they do this, when it is dry what will happen?"

³² Now two criminals were also led away to be put to death with him. ³³ And when they came to the place called Skull, there they crucified Jesus with the criminals, one on his right and one on his left. ³⁴ [And then Jesus said, "Father, forgive them; for they know not what they do."] *They divided his clothing by casting lots.* ³⁵ And the people stood there, watching; but the leaders ridiculed him, saying, "Others he saved; let him save himself if he is the Messiah of God, God's chosen one!" ³⁶ The soldiers also mocked him, coming and offering him vinegar wine, ³⁷ and saying, "If you are the King of the Judeans, save yourself!" ³⁸ There was also an inscription above him, "This is the King of the Judeans."

³⁹ One of the criminals who was hanging there derided him, saying, "Are you not the Messiah? Save yourself and us!" ⁴⁰ But the other rebuked him, saying, "Do you not fear God, since you are under the same death sentence? ⁴¹ And we indeed justly, for what we have done merits what we are receiving, but this one has done nothing wrong." ⁴² Then he said, "Jesus, remember me when you come into your realm." ⁴³ Jesus replied to him, "Truly I tell you, today you will be with me in Paradise."

⁴⁴ And it was now about the sixth hour [of the day, or noon], and darkness came over the whole land until the ninth hour [of the day, about three in the afternoon]. ⁴⁵ The sun's light ceased, and the curtain of the temple was torn in the middle. ⁴⁶ Then Jesus, crying with a loud voice, said, "Father, into your hands I commend my spirit." Saying this then, he breathed out a final time. ⁴⁷ Now when the centurion saw what had happened, he praised God, saying, "This man was indeed innocent." ⁴⁸ And all the crowds that had gathered for this spectacle saw what had happened, beating their breasts, they turned back. ⁴⁹ All those who knew him stood far off; the women who had followed him from Galilee were watching these things.

⁵⁰ Now, take note, there was a man named Joseph, a member of the council, a good man and a righteous one. ⁵¹ He had not agreed with the council and their action. He was from the Judean town of Arimathea, and he was waiting for the reign of God. ⁵² This man went to Pilate and requested the body of Jesus. ⁵³ Then he took it down, wrapped it in a linen cloth, and laid it in a tomb hewn from rock where no one had yet lain. ⁵⁴ It was the day of Preparation, and the sabbath was dawning. ⁵⁵ The women followed, the ones who had come with him from Galilee, and they saw the tomb and how his body was placed. ⁵⁶ Then the women returned, and prepared spices and balms.

On the sabbath they rested according to the commandment.

PROCLAMATION

Owing to the length of the Passion Gospel, the commentary section will be longer than for other readings.

Text Notes

In Judges 11:31, the word *shalom* is used to indicate completion; the verb is used similarly in Modern Hebrew, for example, to complete a purchase or pay the check. In verse 37 and following, virginity symbolizes a stage of life; the grief is about not reaching the full measure of womanhood in her culture, marrying, and mothering. In verse 40, the women gather to memorialize the woman sacrificed by her father; the verb is "recount," not as usually translated "lament."

The psalmist locates her heart in her "belly" in verse 14. The verb for the violence done to the psalmist's hands and feet is missing. The LXX and traditional Jewish exegesis (Rashi) supply it.

Throughout this passion account in Luke, "Rabbi" replaces "Lord" so as not to further divinize slave language. For third-person references, Messiah, Christ, and Savior will be used. Also, "enslaved person" rather than "slave" distinguishes between a person and their circumstances. The Eucharistic instruction in Luke 22:17 can be translated as "take" or "receive" (this cup). In the Hebrew Scriptures, to judge is to govern, administer, oversee, rule, and render justice. That full sense is intended in Luke 22:30 rather than passing judgment on Israel. The Adversary, the Satan, occurs in verse 31 with the definite article as in Hebrew, where the term is a title or description; further contemporary notions of Satan are often postbiblical. Verses 43–44 in chapter 22 and verse 34 in chapter 23 are not present in all manuscripts, as indicated by brackets.

In Luke 23:2 and 14, the more common translation "perverting (leading astray here), has an unnecessary sexual connotation in English. Jesus's accusers testify that he says he is *a messiah*; there is no direct object. The term was not unique to Jesus. Hebrew *meshiach* is translated by Greek *christos*; David and Cyrus are each God's messiah, God's christ in the Hebrew and Greek versions of 2 Samuel 23:1 and Isaiah 45:1, which parallel Luke 23:35 where Jesus is disbelieved as the Christ/Messiah of God. The term, otherwise translated "anointed," also applies to monarchs and priests.

The robe with which Jesus was mocked in Luke 23:11 was "bright" or "shiny," suggesting rich embroidery or embellishment. Some less reliable manuscripts include a verse 17, which is generally removed from critical translations: *He had to release one prisoner for them because of the festival.*

Jesus quotes Hosea 10:8, where people ask for the mountains and hills to cover them in Luke 23:30. Verse 34, "Father, forgive them . . ." is missing in many manuscripts. "Into your hands, I commend my spirit" in verse 46 from Psalm 31:5 can also be translated, "Into your hands, I place my life." In verse 49, "those who stood" are a mixed gender as indicated by the text (grammatically, an all-male group is also possible); those who were watching were the women, according to the feminine plural verb, which excludes males. In contrast, the "they" who rested on the sabbath in verse 56 is inclusive.

A final note: the NRSV translation that Joseph of Arimathea, "who, *though* a member of the council," was "good and righteous" in Luke 23:50 excludes the whole of the Sanhedrin from the possibility of being good and righteous normatively. It is more than an uncharitable reading; it is anti-Judaistic and contributes to the anti-Semitic legacy and practices of the Church.

Preaching Prompts

This lectionary pairs the brutal deaths of Jephthah's daughter and Jesus. Each of their deaths is horrific—at one level, unnecessary slaughter—and each death is believed by someone in their respective story to serve a greater good. The disparate portraits and motives of the two fathers in relation to the death of their sole child offer fruitful space to address the crucifixion beyond the limits of atonement theology. Each of these texts requires us to ask who it is we think God is.

Jephthah, taken from his mother, a sex worker, by his father, Gilead, was rejected by his brothers and his father's wife. The troubled boy is not unrelated to the troubled man. He is desperate for affirmation. Note that God had already given Jephthah victory over the Ammonites in Judges 11:32 before he makes a vow to "ensure" his win. Jephthah's god is familiar to many: rigid and unyielding, apparently incapable of forgiving a rash vow, making human sacrifice the only acceptable appeasement. Jephthah doesn't test his theology; he doesn't bargain with God like Abraham. He doesn't offer himself as a recipient of divine rage; he does not fight for the life of his child. His parenthood, like his theology, leaves much to be desired. As is the case in rigid, fundamentalist, patriarchal systems, women's lives hold little value and are expendable. In spite of the lethal limits of the system in which she finds herself constrained, Jephthah's daughter carves out space for herself and other women, illuminating and memorializing the deficiencies of a god like Jephthah's.

The psalmist's God is lightyears away from the tyrant Jephthah worships; God is savior rather than destroyer. The psalmist's God is part nurse, part midwife, trustworthy and praiseworthy. In Matthew and Mark, Jesus turns to this psalm and this God on the cross, making it virtually inseparable from Good Friday. In Luke's Passion, Jesus quotes Psalm 31, which shares the theme of trusting a trustworthy God for salvation.

Hebrews calls us to look to Jesus in the company of the faithful. Luke presents a roster of the faithful where women are more fully present than in other accounts. The spaces where women are missing are also instructive, opportunities for conversations about who is greater and what it meant for the greatest to serve the least, with apparently no women in the room. How different would the Church have looked if that teaching were applied to systemic structural inequities between genders and cultures as a start?

Women are rendered invisible in the crowds that characterize the narrative, visible as enslaved girls, weeping women who accompany Jesus on his death march, and the women who were family, friends, followers, and disciples—some in more than one category—standing watch until the end. In spite of the gruesome horror, Jesus's female companions and followers, family and friends, watched and did not turn away, according to Luke 23:49; the text cannot make the same claim of the male apostles and disciples. These women were faithful in and beyond the horror that seemed to mark the end of their shared journey.

HOLY SATURDAY

Job 14:1–14; Psalm 31; Philippians 2:1–8; Matthew 27:57–66

Job 14:1 "Woman-born,
humankind is short of days and full of turmoil.
² They sprout like a flower and wither,
flee like a shadow and do not endure.
³ Are your eyes, then, open to such a one as this?
Do you bring me into judgment with you?
⁴ Who can make a clean thing out of an unclean thing?
No one.
⁵ If their days are fixed,
the number of their months is in your keeping,
it is because you have set their boundaries that they cannot pass.
⁶ Look away from them, and they sit at ease,
until they complete, like laborers, their days.
⁷ For there is hope for a tree,
if it is cut down, that it will be renewed,
and that its branches will not fail.
⁸ Its root grows old in the earth,
and its trunk dies in the dust.
⁹ At the scent of water it will bud
and put forth branches like a sapling.
¹⁰ Mortals die, and are carried away;
the woman-born perish, and where are they?
¹¹ As waters dissipate from a sea,
and a river dries up and dissipates,
¹² so a person lies down and does not rise again;

until the heavens are no more,
they will not awake or be stirred from their sleep.
13 Grant that you would hide me in Sheol,
that you would cover me until your wrath is past,
that you would set for me a boundary, and remember me.
14 If a person dies, will they live again?
All the days of my service I would wait
until my change come.

Psalm 31

1 In you, WOMB OF LIFE, I take refuge;
let me not ever be put to shame;
in your righteousness rescue me.
2 Incline your ear to me;
quickly deliver me.
Be for me a rock of refuge,
a stronghold to save me.
3 For you are my rock and my stronghold;
for your name's sake lead me and guide me.
4 Free me from the net that is hidden for me,
for you are my refuge.
5 Into your hand I commit my spirit;
you have redeemed me, ARK OF SAFETY, God of truth.
6 I hate those who attend to worthless vanity,
but in the MOTHER OF ALL I place my trust.
7 I will exult and I will rejoice in your faithful love,
because you have seen my affliction;
you have studied my soul's sorrows.
8 Yet you have not handed me over to the hand of the enemy;
you have set my feet in a broad place.
9 Be gracious to me, MOTHER OF MERCY, for I am in distress;
my eyes waste away with angry tears,
my soul and body too.
10 For my life is spent in sorrow,
and my years in sighing;
because of my iniquity my strength fails,
and my bones waste away.
11 Because of my enemies I am a disgrace to all,
and to my neighbors, more,
an object of dread to those who know me;
those who see me in the street flee from me.

¹² I have been forgotten from the heart like one who is dead;
    I have become like a ruined vessel.
¹³ Because I hear the whispering of many,
    terror surrounds in their scheming together against me,
    as they plot to take my life.
¹⁴ Yet I, in you I trust, FAITHFUL GOD;
    I declare, "You are my God."
¹⁵ My times are in your hand;
    deliver me from the hand of my enemies and those who hound me.
¹⁶ Let your face shine upon your slave;
    save me in your faithful love.
¹⁷ GRACIOUS GOD, let me not be put to shame,
    for I call upon you;
    let the wicked be put to shame;
    let them go silent to Sheol.
¹⁸ Let lying lips be stilled
    the ones that speak against the righteous,
    arrogant with pride and contempt.
¹⁹ How great is your goodness
    that you have secured for those who fear you,
    and that you do for those who take refuge in you,
    before all the woman-born.
²⁰ In the shelter of your presence you shelter them
    from human plots;
    you hide them safe under your shelter
    from contentious tongues.
²¹ Blessed be the MOTHER OF CREATION,
    who is marvelous in her faithful love to me,
    a city under siege.
²² Now I, I had said in my alarm,
    "I am cut off from your sight."
    However, you heard my supplications
    when I cried to you for help.
²³ Love GOD WHOSE NAME IS HOLY, all you her godly ones.
    The FAITHFUL GOD preserves the faithful,
    and repays with interest the one who acts out of pride.
²⁴ Take courage, and she shall strengthen your hearts,
    all you who wait for the MOTHER OF ALL.

Philippians 2:1 If then there is any encouragement in Christ, any consolation from love, any communion in the Spirit, any tenderness and compassion, ² make my joy complete. Be wise in the same way, having the same love, united and sharing the same wisdom. ³ Do nothing from self-interest, but in humility regard others as better than yourselves. [4] Each of you, look not to your own interests, but rather to the interests of others. [5] Let the same wisdom be in you all that was in Christ Jesus,

> [6] who, though he was in the form of God,
> did not regard equality with God
> as something to be seized,
> [7] but emptied himself,
> taking the form of a slave,
> being born in human likeness;
> then being found in human form,
> [8] he humbled himself
> and became obedient to the point of death,
> even death on a cross.

Matthew 27:57 When it was evening, a rich person came from Arimathea, Joseph, who was also a disciple of Jesus. [58] He went to Pilate and requested the body of Jesus; then Pilate commanded it to be given to him. [59] So Joseph took the body and wrapped it in clean linen, [60] and laid it in his new tomb, which he had hewn in rock. Then he rolled a great stone to the door of the tomb and departed. [61] Mary Magdalene and the other Mary were there, sitting before the tomb.

[62] Now, the next day, which was after the day of Preparation, the chief priests and the Pharisees gathered before Pilate. [63] They said, "Lord, we remember what that deceiver said while he was still alive, 'After three days I will rise.' [64] Command, therefore, the tomb be secured until the third day; otherwise his disciples may go and steal him, and tell the people, 'He has been raised from the dead,' and the last deception would be worse than the first." [65] Pilate said to them, "You may have a squad; go, secure it as you can." [66] So they went with the guard and secured the tomb, sealing the stone.

PROCLAMATION

Text Notes

Job 14 begins its reflection on mortality using inclusive language, "those born of women," and "humanity" in verse 1, then shifts to masculine language, "(male) warrior" in verses 10 and 14, and "man" in verse 12. I apply inclusive language to the other human references in the passage. Job's address shifts from second to third person in verses 6 and 13. Verse 13 begins, "Who will grant. . . ." In his book-length legal complaint, Job looks (rhetorically at least) for someone to compel God to do justly by him. That is part of the theological scandal of the book.

In verse 4 of the psalm, "free me" is the "let my people go" verb of the exodus. In verse 9, there is only one "eye" and tears are lacking; "body" is "belly/womb."

Somewhat contradictorily, "to go silently to Sheol" can also be "to go weeping to Sheol." "Shelter" in nominal and verbal forms as a poetic device. "Godly ones" in verse 23 are often translated anachronistically as "saints," importing Christian language and theology into the Hebrew Scriptures.

There is considerable disagreement over the meaning of *eritheian* in Philippians 2:3, translated here as "self-interest"; some other possibilities are "strife," "contentiousness," "selfishness," or "selfish ambition." According to its earlier usage in Aristotle, it may mean "a self-seeking pursuit" for political office in that case. (See the corresponding entry in the *A Greek-English Lexicon of the New Testament and Other Early Christian Literature, BDAG*.)

The use of "Lord" for Pilate serves as a reminder the title was not unique to Jesus, nor a particularly religious one, but one of hierarchy, signifying Pilate's authority as the face of the Roman occupation. Translations like NRSV, which preserve it for Jesus but change it for other characters, are intentionally misleading.

Preaching Prompts

Holy Saturday may be the most liminal space in the Christian liturgical cycle. Passion has become pathos. The death of Jesus stupefies, but the breaking dawn has not dispelled the waking dream. Yet the liturgical remembrance is part of a thousands-year-old cycle, and we know what the next dawn brings. We struggle not to anticipate that dawn. These lessons underscore our finitude, our mortality and that of all living things, and the mortality of Jesus, Son of Woman, Son of God, Child of Earth.

Job's reflection on his own mortality comes in the midst of his address to God in chapters 12–14, responding to Zophar's chapter 11 rebuke, blaming Job for the evil that has befallen him. In this lesson, Job's ruminations on his inevitable death are accompanied by the reminder that death is part of the cycle of life in nature. Without knowing the hope that Christians hold dear, Job expects a "no" to the question of whether a person who has died will live again. He and the psalmist expect all the dead to go to Sheol (Job 14:13; Psalm 22:17). The psalmist commits her fragile life (v. 5) and finite times (vev. 14–15) into God's hands, fully aware of her own mortality. The psalm also includes the remembrance of God's fidelity (vv. 7, 19–21, 23) and assurance that God hears the cry of her faithful (v. 22).

As a Holy Saturday text, Philippians 2 presents a Jesus as empty of divinity as his body in the tomb was empty of life. Here Jesus humbles himself to experience the finitude of the human experience, mortality, and one of its most common and most horrific occurrences: a violent death at human hands.

We hold all of these things in our hearts as we wrestle with implications, sitting, watching, and waiting with Miriam, Mary of Migdala, and another woman who also bears the name of Israel's first prophet. They knew not for what they waited. Though we know, we keep vigil with them.

EASTER—THE GREAT VIGIL

At least two of the following Lessons are read, of which one is always the Lesson from Exodus. After each Lesson, the psalm or canticle listed, or some other suitable psalm, canticle, or hymn, is sung.

A God-Crafted Creation: Genesis 1:1–2, 26–27; 2:1–4

Genesis 1:1 When beginning he, God, created the heavens and the earth, ² the earth was shapeless and formless and bleakness covered the face of the deep, while the Spirit of God, she, fluttered over the face of the waters.

²⁶ And God said, "Let us make humankind in our image, according to our likeness; and let them rule the fish of the sea, and the birds of the heavens, and the animals, and the whole earth, and over every creeping creature that creeps upon the earth."

²⁷ So God created humankind in God's own image,
in God's own image, God created them;
female and male, God created them.

²:¹ And the heavens and the earth were complete, along with all their multitude. ² Then God finished on the seventh day the work that God had done, and rested on the seventh day from all the work that they had done. ³ So God blessed the seventh day and sanctified it, because on it God rested from all the work that God had done in creation.

⁴ These are the generations of the heavens and the earth when they were created.

Canticle of the Three Young Men: Daniel (LXX) 3:52–60

⁵² "Let the earth bless the Creator of All;
let her sing hymns to God and highly exalt God forever.
⁵³ Bless the Creator of All, mountains and hills;
sing hymns to God and highly exalt God forever.
⁵⁴ Bless the Creator of All, all that grows in the ground;
sing hymns to God and highly exalt God forever.
⁵⁵ Bless the Creator of All, seas and rivers;
sing hymns to God and highly exalt God forever.
⁵⁶ Bless the Creator of All, you springs;
sing hymns to God and highly exalt God forever.
⁵⁷ Bless the Creator of All, you sea monsters and all that swim in the waters;
sing hymns to God and highly exalt God forever.
⁵⁸ Bless the Creator of All, all birds of the air;
sing hymns to God and highly exalt God forever.
⁵⁹ Bless the Creator of All, all wild animals and cattle;
sing hymns to God and highly exalt God forever.

⁶⁰ Bless the Creator of All, all people on earth;
   sing hymns to God and highly exalt God forever."

The Salvation of Hagar and Ishmael: Genesis 21:2, 8–21

² Sarah conceived and gave birth to a son for Abraham in his old age, at the set time of which God had spoken to him.

⁸ The child grew, and was weaned, and Abraham made a great feast on the day of Isaac's weaning. ⁹ Then Sarah saw the son of Hagar the Egyptian woman, whom she had given birth to for Abraham, playing. ¹⁰ So she said to Abraham, "Drive out this slave woman with her son; for the son of this slave woman shall not inherit with my son, with Isaac." ¹¹ The situation was evil in Abraham's eyes on account of his son. ¹² And God said to Abraham, "See it not as evil in your eyes on account of the boy and on account of your slave woman. In all that Sarah says to you, obey her voice, for it is through Isaac that offspring shall be named for you. ¹³ Yet even the son of the slave woman I will make a nation also, because he is your offspring." ¹⁴ So Abraham rose early in the morning, and took bread and a skin of water, and gave it to Hagar. He placed it on her shoulder, along with the child, and sent her away. Then she walked away and wandered in the wilderness of Beer-Sheba.

¹⁵ When the water in the skin was gone, she thrust the child under one of the bushes. ¹⁶ Then she went and sat herself down before him some way off, about the distance of a bowshot; for she said, "Let me not see the death of the child." So, she sat before him and she lifted up her voice and she wept. ¹⁷ And God heard the voice of the boy, and the messenger of God called to Hagar from the heavens, and said to her, "What troubles you, Hagar? Fear not; for God has heard the voice of the boy where he is. ¹⁸ Rise, lift the boy and hold him with your hand, for a great nation of him I will make." ¹⁹ Then God opened her eyes and she saw a well of water. She went, and filled the skin with water, and let the boy drink.

²⁰ God was with the boy, and he grew up; he settled in the wilderness, and became an archer. ²¹ He settled in the wilderness of Paran, and his mother acquired a wife for him from the land of Egypt.

Psalm 27:5–7, 10–14

⁵ She will shield me in her shelter
   when the day is evil;
   she will cover me under the cover of her tent;
   she will raise me high on a rock.
⁶ Now my head is raised up
   above my enemies surrounding me,
   and I will offer in her tent
   sacrifices with shouts of joy;
   I will sing and make melody to the GOD WHO SAVES.

⁷ Hear my cry, Faithful One, when I cry aloud,
   be gracious to me and answer me!
¹⁰ If my mother and father forsake me,
   the Compassionate God will gather me in.
¹¹ Teach me, Righteous One, your way,
   and lead me on a smooth path
   because of my enemies.
¹² Do not give me over to the throats of my foes,
   for lying witnesses rise against me,
   and they breathe violence.
¹³ If I but believe, I shall see the goodness of She Who is Faithful
   in the land of the living.
¹⁴ Wait for the Living God;
   be strong, and let your heart take courage;
   wait for God Whose Name is Holy!

From Slavery to Freedom: Exodus 14:26–29; 15:20–21

¹⁴:²⁶ Now the Holy One said to Moses, "Stretch out your hand over the sea, so that the water may come back upon the Egyptians, upon their chariots and charioteers." ²⁷ So Moses stretched out his hand over the sea and the sea turned back; by the break of dawn it was back to its strength, and the Egyptians fled at its approach. Then the Living God shook the Egyptians in the midst of the sea. ²⁸ The waters returned and covered the chariots and the charioteers, the whole army of Pharaoh that came after them into the sea; not a single one of them remained. ²⁹ And the women, children, and men of Israel walked on dry ground through the sea, the waters a wall for them on their right and on their left.

¹⁵:²⁰ Then the prophet Miriam, Aaron's sister, took a drum in her hand; and all the women went out after her with drums and with dancing. ²¹ And Miriam sang to them:

"Sing to the God Who Saves, for God has triumphed triumphantly;
horse and rider God has thrown into the sea."

Song of Miriam and Moses: Exodus 15:1–3, 11, 13, 17–18

¹ Moses and the women and men of Israel sang this song to the Holy One of Old:

"I will sing to the God Who Saves, for God has triumphed triumphantly;
horse and rider God has thrown into the sea.
² The Mighty God is my strength and my might,
   God has become my salvation.
   This is my God, whom I will praise,
   my mother's God and my father's God, whom I will exalt.
³ The Dread God is a warrior;
   Too Holy to be Pronounced is God's name.

11 "Who is like you, Most High, among the gods?
   Who is like you, majestic in holiness,
   awesome in splendor, working wonders?
13 In your faithful love you led the people whom you redeemed;
   you guided them by your strength to your holy habitation.
17 You brought them in and planted them on the mountain that is your own possession,
   the place, Faithful God, that you made your dwelling place,
   the sanctuary, Sovereign One, that your hands have established.
18 God who is Majesty will reign forever and ever."

Rahab's Salvation: Joshua 2:1–7, 12–14; 6:15–17, 23

2:1 And Joshua son of Nun sent two men, spies, secretly from Shittim, saying, "Go, surveil the land, surveil Jericho." So, they went and entered the house of a prostitute—her name was Rahab—and they lay down there. 2 Now the king of Jericho was told, "Look now, men have come here tonight from the Israelites to search out the land." 3 Then the king of Jericho sent to Rahab, "Bring out the men, the ones who came to you, who came to your house, for they have come to search out the whole of the land." 4 Now the woman had taken the two men and hid them. Then she said, "True, the men came to me, but I did not know from where they came. 5 And it was when the gate was to close at dark that the men went out. I do not know where the men went. Hurry, chase after them, for you can reach them." 6 However, she had brought them up to the roof and hidden them in the stalks of flax that she had laid out for herself on the roof. 7 So the men chased after them along the path of the Jordan up to the fords. The gate was shut as soon as the pursuers had gone out.

12 [Rahab said,] "Now I bid you all swear to me by the Faithful God—for I have done faithfully by you all—that you also will do faithfully by my father's household. Give me a trustworthy sign. 13 Now, spare my mother and my father, my sisters and my brothers, and all who belong to them, and deliver our lives from death." 14 The men said to her, "Our life for yours, even unto death! If you do not tell this our business, then when the Faithful God gives to us the land we will deal faithfully and honestly with you."

6:15 And it happened on the seventh day that they rose early, at the break of dawn, and circled the city in the same way seven times. Only on that day that they circled the city seven times. 16 And it was the seventh time, when the priests blew the ram's horns, Joshua said to the people, "Shout! For the Faithful One has given you the city. 17 The city and all that is in it shall be devoted to the Holy One. Only Rahab the prostitute, she shall live and all who are with her in her house because she hid the messengers we sent."

23 So the youths who were the spies went in and brought Rahab out, along with her mother, her father, her sisters and brothers, and all who belonged to her—all her kinfolk they brought out—and set them outside the camp of Israel.

Canticle: Wisdom 5:1–5; 6:6–7

^{5:1} The righteous will stand with great confidence
in the presence of those who have oppressed them
and those who make light of their labors.
² When the unrighteous see, they will be shaken with a terrible fear,
and they will be amazed at the unexpected salvation.
³ They will speak amongst themselves, repenting,
and out of distress of spirit they will groan, and say,
⁴ "These are persons whom we once held in derision
and made the meaning of insult—we were foolish.
We reckoned their lives as madness
and their end without honor.
⁵ Why have they been numbered among the daughters and sons of God?
And why is their lot among the holy ones?"
^{6:6} For the least may be pardoned in mercy,
but the mighty will be mightily tested.
⁷ For the Sovereign of all will not draw back from anyone,
or show respect to greatness;
because small and great alike God made,
and God takes thought for all alike.

Deborah Saves the People: Judges 4:1–10, 23

¹ And again the men and women of Israel did what was evil in the sight of the HOLY ONE OF SINAI, for Ehud [the Judge] was dead. ² So the HOLY ONE sold them into the hand of King Jabin of Canaan, who reigned in Hazor; the commander of his army was Sisera, who lived in Harosheth-ha-goiim. ³ Then the women and men of Israel cried out to GOD WHO HEARS; for Jabin had nine hundred chariots of iron, and had oppressed the Israelites with ruthlessness for twenty years.

⁴ Deborah, a woman, a female prophet, a fiery woman, she was judging Israel at that time. ⁵ She used to sit under the palm of Deborah between Ramah and Bethel in the hill country of Ephraim; and the women and men of Israel came up to her for judgment. ⁶ She sent and called for Barak ben Abinoam from Kedesh in Naphtali, and said to him, "Did not the MOST HIGH, the God of Israel, command you? Go! March on Mount Tabor, and take ten thousand men from the tribe of Naphtali and the tribe of Zebulun. ⁷ I will march toward you to draw to you by the Wadi Kishon Sisera the commander of Jabin's army, with his chariots and his troops; and I will give him into your hand." ⁸ Then Barak said to her, "If you will go with me, then I will go; but if you will not go with me, I will not go." ⁹ And she said, "I will surely go with you; however, there will be no glory for you on the path you are taking, for the MIGHTY GOD will sell Sisera into the hand of a woman." Then

Deborah got up and went with Barak to Kedesh. ¹⁰ Barak summoned Zebulun and Naphtali to Kedesh; and ten thousand men went up with him; and Deborah went up with him.

²³ And on that day, God subdued King Jabin of Canaan before the women and men of Israel.

Canticle of Deborah: Judges 5:1, 4–7, 12, 24, 31

¹ Then Deborah and Barak ben Abinoam sang on that day, saying:

⁴ "MIGHTY ONE, when you went out from Seir,
  when you marched from the field of Edom,
  the earth and the heavens dripped,
  even the clouds dripped water.
⁵ The mountains melted before the MOST HIGH, the One of Sinai,
  before the ONE GOD, the God of Israel.
⁶ "In the days of Shamgar son of Anath,
  in the days of Jael, caravans ceased
  and travelers traversed the byways.
⁷ The mighty grew fat in Israel,
  they grew fat on plunder,
  until you arose, Deborah,
  you arose as a mother in Israel."
¹² "Awake, awake, Deborah!
  Awake, awake, utter a song!
  Arise, Barak, capture your captives,
  ben Abinoam."
²⁴ "Most blessed of women be Jael,
  the wife of Heber the Kenite,
  of tent-women most blessed."
³¹ "So perish all your enemies, HOLY ONE OF OLD!
  But those who love God will be like the sun rising in its might."

And the land was pacified for forty years.

Jehosheba Saves the King of Judah: 2 Kings 11:1–4, 10–12

¹ Now Athaliah, Ahaziah's mother, saw that her son was dead, she stood up and destroyed all the royal offspring. ² Then Jehosheba, daughter of King Joram, sister of Ahaziah, took Joash, Ahaziah's son, and she stole him away from among the daughters and sons of the king who were being killed; she put him and his nurse in a bedroom. Thus, she hid him from Athaliah, and he was not put to death. ³ [The prince] remained with Ahaziah six years, hidden in the house of the EVER-LIVING GOD, while Athaliah reigned over the land.

⁴ But in the seventh year Jehoiada [the High Priest and Josheba's husband] sent for the captains of the Carites and of the bodyguards and had them come to him in the house of

the Holy One. He made a covenant with them and had them swear it in the house of the Holy One of Old; then he showed them the son of the king.

¹⁰ The priest [Jehoiada] gave to the captains of the hundreds the spears and shields that had been King David's, which were in the house of the Living God. ¹¹ Then the guards stood, each with his weapons in his hand, from the south of the temple to the north of the temple, next to the altar and the temple, around the king on every side. ¹² Then he brought out the son of the king, put the crown on him, and gave Joash the testimony [of royalty]. They made him king and anointed him; they clapped their hands and shouted, "Long live the king!"

Psalm 9:1–2, 7–11, 13–14

¹ I will give thanks to the God Who Saves with my whole heart;
   I will tell of all your wonderful deeds.
² I will rejoice and exult in you;
   I will sing praise to your name, Most High.
⁷ God who is Majesty sits enthroned forever,
   she has established her throne for judgment.
⁸ She judges the world in righteousness;
   she judges the peoples with equity.
⁹ She Who is Faithful is a stronghold for the oppressed,
   a stronghold in times of trouble.
¹⁰ They trust you, they who know your name,
   for you do not forsake those who seek you Redeeming God.
¹¹ Sing praises to the Holy One enthroned in Zion.
   Declare her deeds among the peoples.
¹³ Be gracious to me, Gracious One.
   See what I suffer from those who hate me.
   You lift me up from the gates of death,
¹⁴ so that I may recount all your praises,
   and in the gates of Daughter Zion,
   rejoice in your salvation.

Judith Saves Her People: Judith 8:9–10, 32–34; 13:3–14, 17–18

⁸:⁹ Now Judith heard the wicked words of the people against the ruler because they were disheartened from lack of water, and when she heard all the words that Uzziah said to them, and how he swore to them to surrender the town to the Assyrians after five days. ¹⁰ So she sent her slave-girl, who was set over all she possessed, to summon Uzziah and Chabris and Charmis, the elders of her town.

³² Then Judith said to them, "Hear me and I will do a thing that will go down from generation to generation of our daughters and sons. ³³ You all shall stand at the gate this night and I shall go out, I along with my slave-girl, and within the days which you have promised to

hand over the town to our enemies, the Holy One will visit Israel through my hand. [34] None of you all should investigate my task; for I will not tell you until I have completed my work."

[13:3] Now Judith had told her slave-girl to stand outside the bedchamber and to wait for her to come out, as she did other days; for she said she would go out for her prayer. She spoke to Bagoas these same words. [4] So everyone went out beyond sight, and no one was left in the bedchamber, either small or great. Then Judith, standing beside his bed, said in her heart, "Holy God of all power, look with care in this hour on the work of my hands for the exaltation of Jerusalem. [5] Now is the time to help your heritage and to carry out my intention to destroy the enemies who have risen up against us."

[6] She came to the bedpost at Holofernes's head, and took down his sword from there. [7] Then she came toward his bed, caught the hair of his head, and said, "Give me strength today, Holy God of Israel!" [8] And she struck his neck twice with all her might, and cut off his head. [9] Then she rolled his body off the bed and snatched the canopy from the post. A little later she went out and gave Holofernes's head to her slave-girl, [10] who placed it in her food bag.

Then the two women went out together, according to their custom at the time for prayer. They passed through the encampment, circled the valley, and went up the mountain to Bethulia, and came to its gates. [11] From a distance Judith called out to the guards at the gates, "Open! Open the gate! God, our God, is with us, working deeds of power in Israel and might against our enemies, as God has done today!"

[12] And it happened when the men of her town heard her voice, they rushed to come down to the gate of the city and summoned the elders of the city. [13] They all ran together, from small to great, for it was extraordinary to them that she returned. They opened the gate and welcomed the women. Then they lit a fire to provide light, and gathered around the women. [14] Then Judith said to them with a loud voice, "Hallelujah! Hallelujah! Praise God, who did not withdraw mercy from the house of Israel, but has broken our enemies by my hand this night!"

[17] All the people were completely astounded. They bowed down and worshiped God, and said with one accord, "Blessed are you our God, who has this day humiliated the enemies of your people." [18] Then Uzziah said to Judith, "O daughter, you are blessed by the Most High God above all other women on earth, and blessed be the Holy God, who created the heavens and the earth, who has guided you to cut off the head of the leader of our enemies."

The Song of Judith: Judith 16:1–6, 13

[1] Judith said:
Begin praise for my God with drums,
sing to my Sovereign with cymbals.
Craft a psalm and a praise for God;
exalt God and call upon God's name.
[2] For the Holy One is a God who crushes wars,

> whose encampments are in the midst of the people,
> who delivered me from the hands of my pursuers.
> ³ Assyria came down from the mountains of the north;
> it came with multitudes of its warriors,
> the same multitude blocked up the waterway,
> and their cavalry covered the hills.
> ⁴ Assyria boasted that it would burn up my territory,
> and kill my young men with the sword,
> and throw my infants to the ground,
> and give my children away as spoils of war,
> and despoil my virgins.
> ⁵ But the Almighty God dismissed them
> with a feminine hand.
> ⁶ For their mighty one did not fall by the hands of the young men,
> nor did the sons of the Titans strike him down,
> nor did tall giants lay him out;
> but Judith daughter of Merari
> with the beauty of her person undid him.
> ¹³ I will sing to my God a new song:
> Holy One, you are great and glorious,
> wonderful in strength, invincible.

Epistle: Acts 16:13–15

¹³ On the day of the sabbath we went out the gate by the river, where we thought there was a place of prayer; and we sat down and spoke to the women who gathered there. ¹⁴ Now a certain woman named Lydia, a merchant of purple cloth from the city of Thyatira, a worshiper of God, was listening to us. The Messiah opened her heart to listen eagerly to what was said by Paul. ¹⁵ As she was baptized along with her household, she urged us, saying, "If you have judged me to be faithful to Christ, come and stay at my home." And she persuaded us.

Gospel: Matthew 28:1–10

¹ After the sabbath, as the first day of the week was dawning, Mary Magdalene and the other Mary went to see the tomb. ² And look! There was a great earthquake, for a messenger of God, descending from heaven, came and rolled away the stone and sat upon it. ³ Its appearance was like lightning, and its clothing white as snow. ⁴ For fear of the messenger, the guards shook and were as though dead. ⁵ But the messenger responded to the women and said, "Fear not; I know that you all are looking for Jesus who was crucified. ⁶ He is not here; for he has been raised, just as he said. Come, see the place where he lay. ⁷ Then go quickly and tell his disciples, 'He has been raised from the dead, and see, he is on to Galilee ahead of you; there you all will see him.' This is my message for you." ⁸ So the women left the tomb

quickly with fear and great joy and ran to tell his disciples the news. ⁹ Then, all of a sudden, Jesus met them and said, "Shalom!" And they came to him, took hold of his feet, and bowed down worshipping him. ¹⁰ Then Jesus said to them, "Fear not; go and tell my sisters and brothers to go to Galilee; there they will see me."

PROCLAMATION

Text Notes

In the very first lines of Genesis, and therefore of the Bible, Jewish or Christian, both masculine and feminine verbs are used for God, masculine for God, feminine for the spirit. Ultimately God's human creation will reflect their creator as female and male. The translation follows that early pattern and uses pronouns of both genders throughout the passage. In Genesis 2:2, I also use "they" for God, a reminder that God transcends the binary language in which God is disclosed and that some of those created in the image of God are nonbinary.

In Genesis 21:9, the nature of Ishmael's play (or mocking) is not explained. The NRSV and RSV add "with Isaac," which is not in the text, leading to the demonization of Ishmael as a child. Some commentators go so far as to accuse him of sexually abusing Isaac based on this fiction. In verse 11, Abraham finds the situation "extremely evil," though the word encodes a range of negativity. Hagar's motion in putting her child under the tree is explosive: "throw" or "cast." The idiomatic expression in verse 17, "What is with you?" sounds harsher to English-speaking ears than the traditional, "What troubles you?"

In Psalm 27:11, "teach" is the verbal form of *torah,* which is more properly "teaching" or "revelation" than law. In verse 12, "throats" translates *nephesh*, "soul." The usage is rare but occurs in Job 24:12, Jeremiah 4:10, and Habakkuk 2:5. In verse 24, the number of grammatically masculine subjects leaves open another possible translation, familiar from the King James Version: "Be of good courage and God will strengthen your heart."

The Canticle of the Three Young Men comes from the Greek version of Daniel in the Septuagint. A larger selection of verses occurs in the Song of the Three Young Men used as a canticle in the Book of Common Prayer. In many Protestant Bibles like the NRSV, translations of Greek portions of Daniel and Esther are published in a separate section with the Deuterocanonical/Apocryphal books. In Catholic Bibles like the Inclusive Bible, the Greek-based portions are woven in, resulting in an alternate set of verse numbers. This passage is verses 74–82 in the *New English Translation of the Septuagint* (NETS). The NETS translation was influential in my own here.

In Exodus 15:2, I add "my mother's God." While Moses will have to ask who God is and what is the divine Name, Moses's mother, Yocheved, Jochebed, bears the

Name in the first syllable of her name and may be the oldest name in the Hebrew Bible, including a portion of the Name. In verse 3, God is thoroughly anthropomorphized as "a man of war."

Like Miriam's Song, Judges 5 is one of the oldest works in the Hebrew Bible, replete with translation challenges. In Judges 4:4, Deborah is a woman of *lappidoth*. While many have contrived a husband, the word is the adjective "fiery" or "flaming" with a feminine ending. Further, unlike every male character in the book, *lappidoth* does not have any family information line for Barak, son of Abinoam. The feminine singular verb in 5:1 indicates Deborah led the song, and Barak followed her lead. An earlier version of the translation of Judges 4–5 and detailed translation notes can be found in *Daughters of Miriam: Women Prophets in Ancient Israel*.

Some details of 2 Kings 11 are filled in with the more detailed account in 2 Chronicles 23.

The sense of the story in Judith is that she dines with the enemy general, maintaining her virtue, got him drunk, and assassinated him. In the critical scene, the tent where Holofernes sleeps is confusingly described as hers in 13:3. Previously, 12:1 and following indicate Judith is staying in his dining tent. In 13:14, I use the traditional "Hallelujah" for the Jewish (woman whose name means just that, a Jewish woman).

In Matthew 28, I have translated the divine messenger in neuter terms, since grammatical gender may not be biologically significant—if the category even applies—to a divine messenger.

Preaching Prompts

While these texts may not be preached on Easter, commentary is offered for those who will choose one for the early service on Easter day. Those preparing for non-lectionary sermons may find the lesson/canticle pairings fruitful. For example, Psalm 27 takes on new meaning when heard from the perspective of Hagar and Ishmael.

In the Exodus account, the God who saves Israelite lives takes Egyptian lives. The scriptures celebrate the liberation and often the deaths of the Egyptians, though later texts will acknowledge that the peoples of Egypt and Israel's other adversaries are also God's. The Exodus Canticle is understood by some scholars to have been Miriam's initially, perhaps just the contents of Exodus 15:21. The longer song in Exodus 15:1–18 then derives from the shorter.

Note that in Joshua 2, the spies do not surveil the land or Jericho. They head straight for a brothel and "lay down." That expression is used for sex and for sleeping. "Spend the night" unnecessarily shifts the reader away from the plain understanding of why men go to a brothel. Joshua 6:23 calls them "youth" or "boys," which may contribute to their decision. This text provides an opportunity to talk about sex work and its criminalization and the (often upstanding) men who buy sex. Tying in Jesus's friendships with sex workers may help frame this text in an Easter sermon.

Note that Rahab's father's household in 2:12 is different from her household in 2:1. She seeks the salvation of her entire family, whether they live with her or not, perhaps, no matter what they think about her line of work. In verse 13, "spare" is less than a command and more than a request. She saves all who are in the house with her in verse 17, the ark of safety she offers may well encompass people who are not related to her. Rahab and her family are delivered using the primary verb of the exodus in Joshua 6:17–18.

Selections from Wisdom chapters 5 and 6 pair with the Rahab story, reminding the reader and hearer that God saves and redeems who God wills, including and particularly those who are thought to be sinful and beyond God's reach and care.

Athaliah is the only woman in the Bible to rule Israel or Judah on her own; functionally, she was a king, as neither Israel nor Judah had queens, a title not used by royal wives. Separately, the queen-mothers of Judah were the mothers of the ruling king in Judah and did serve in an official capacity.

While some number of the women who followed Jesus were present at his resurrection in Matthew 28:10, there were certainly more who, like all of his male followers, were not.

EASTER DAY—EARLY SERVICE

The early Easter service traditionally uses lessons from the Great Vigil of Easter. Choose a first lesson from the Vigil and use the psalm, Epistle, and Gospel readings from the Vigil.

EASTER DAY—PRINCIPAL SERVICE

Isaiah 49:1–13; Psalm 18:2–11, 16–19; Hebrews 11:1–2, 23–24, 28–39; Matthew 28:1–10 or John 20:1–10 (11–18)

Isaiah 49:1 Listen you coastlands to me,
   And pay heed, you peoples from afar!
   The CREATOR OF ALL called me from the womb,
   from my mother's belly God made my name known.
² God made my mouth like a sharpened sword,
   and in the shadow of God's own hand, hid me;
   God made me like a polished arrow,
   in God's own quiver, hid me.
³ And God said to me, "You are my slave,

Israel, in you I am glorified."
4 But I, I said, "In vain have I labored,
I have spent my strength for nothingness and vanity;
surely my judgment is with the FAITHFUL ONE,
and my wages with my God."
5 And now says the AUTHOR OF LIFE,
who formed me in the womb to be God's slave,
to return Jacob back to God,
and that Israel might be gathered to God;
I am honored in the sight of the HOLY ONE OF OLD,
and my God is my strength.
6 God says,
"It is too light a thing that you should be my slave
to raise up the tribes of Jacob [the line of Rebekah],
and to restore the survivors of Israel [born of Rachel and Leah, and Bilhah and Zilpah]?
I will give you as a light to the nations,
for it will be that my salvation reaches to the end of the earth."
7 Thus says the FAITHFUL ONE,
the Redeemer of Israel, God's holy one,
to one despised, abhorred by the nations,
the slave of rulers,
"Queens and kings shall see and arise,
princes and princesses, and they too shall prostrate themselves,
on account of the FIRE OF SINAI, who is faithful,
the Holy One of Israel, who has chosen you."
8 Thus says the MIGHTY GOD:
In a favorable time I have answered you,
on a day of salvation I have helped you;
I have kept you and given you
as a covenant to the people,
to establish the land,
to apportion the desolate portions;
9 saying to the prisoners, "Go free!"
to those who are in darkness, "Let yourselves be seen."
Along the paths they shall pasture,
and on all the bare heights shall be their pasture.
10 They shall not hunger nor shall they thirst,
neither shall heat nor sun strike them down,
for the one who mother-loves them shall lead them,

  and by springs of water shall guide them.
11 And I will turn all my mountains into a pathway,
  and my highways shall be raised up.
12 Look! These shall come from far away,
  and see! These from the north and from the sea to the west,
  and these from the southland of Syene.
13 Sing for joy, you heavens, and exult O earth;
  let mountains break forth into singing!
  For the TENDER LOVING ONE has comforted God's people,
  and will mother-love God's suffering ones.

Psalm 18:2–11, 16–19

2 The ROCK WHO GAVE US BIRTH is my rock,
  and my fortress, and my deliverer,
  my God, my rock in whom I take refuge,
  my shield, and the horn of my salvation, my stronghold.
3 I call upon the HOLY ONE, may she be praised,
  and from my enemies I shall be saved.
4 The snares of death encompassed me;
  the rivers of wickedness assailed me.
5 The snares of Sheol encircled me;
  the snares of death confronted me.
6 In my distress I called upon SHE WHO HEARS;
  to my God I cried for help.
  From her temple she heard my voice,
  and my cry came before her, to her ears.
7 Then the earth shuddered and quaked;
  the foundations also of the mountains trembled
  and were shaken because of her anger.
8 Smoke went up from her nostrils,
  and consuming fire from her mouth;
  burning coals blazed forth from her.
9 She spread out the heavens, and descended;
  thick darkness was under her feet.
10 She mounted up on a cherub, and flew;
  she soared upon the wings of the wind.
11 She made darkness her veil around her,
  her canopy dark waters and thick clouds.
16 She reached down from on high, she took me;
  she drew me out of the multitude of water.

17 She delivered me from my strong enemy,
and from those who hate me;
for they were too mighty for me.
18 They confronted me in the day of my calamity;
yet the SHELTERING GOD was my support.
19 She brought me out into a broad place;
she delivered me, because she delights in me.

Hebrews 11:1 Now faith is the essence of things hoped for, the conviction of that which is not seen. ² By faith, indeed, were our ancestors approved.

²³ By faith Moses was hidden after his birth by his mother and father for three months, because they saw that the child was beautiful; and they were not afraid of the king's commandment. ²⁴ By faith Moses, after he had grown up, refused to be called a son of Pharaoh's daughter.

²⁸ By faith he kept the Passover and the sprinkling of blood, in order that the destroyer of the firstborn would not touch the firstborn daughters and sons of Israel.

²⁹ By faith they passed through the Red Sea as though on dry land, but when the Egyptians chose to try, they were drowned. ³⁰ By faith the walls of Jericho fell when encircled for seven days. ³¹ By faith Rahab the prostitute did not perish with those who did not believe, because she had received the spies in peace.

³² And what more should I say? For time would fail me to tell of Gideon, Barak, Samson, Jephthah, of David and Samuel and the prophets, female and male, ³³ who through faith conquered realms, administered justice, obtained promises, stopped the mouths of lions, ³⁴ quenched raging fire, escaped the edge of the sword, were made strong out of weakness, became mighty in war, felled foreign armies. ³⁵ Women through resurrection received their dead. Other women and men were tortured, refusing to receive a release, in order to obtain a better resurrection. ³⁶ Yet other women and men received a trial of mocking and whipping, and even chains and imprisonment. ³⁷ They were stoned, they were sawed in two, they were slaughtered by sword; they went about in animal-skins, in sheepskin and goatskin, impoverished, oppressed, tormented. ³⁸ The world was not worthy of them. They wandered in deserts and mountains, and in caves and holes in the ground.

³⁹ And all these, commended for their faith, did not receive what was promised.

Matthew 28:1–10 *is available with commentary in the readings for the Great Vigil of Easter. John* ²⁰ *is the customary alternative. The reading from the Gospel of John may be read in longer or shorter form.*

John 20:1 Now it was the first day of the week, Mary Magdalene came, early on while it was still dark, to the tomb and saw the stone removed from the tomb. ² So she ran and went to Simon Peter and to the other disciple, the one whom Jesus loved, and said to them, "They have taken the Messiah out of the tomb, and we do not know where they have laid him."

³ Then Peter and the other disciple came and went to the tomb. ⁴ The two were running together, but the other disciple ran ahead of Peter and reached the tomb first. ⁵ And bending down to see, saw the linen wrappings lying there, but he did not enter. ⁶ Then Simon Peter came, following him, and went into the tomb, and he saw the linen wrappings lying there ⁷ and the facecloth that had been on Jesus's head not lying with the linen wrappings but rolled up separately in another place. ⁸ Then the other disciple, who reached the tomb first, went in and saw and believed. ⁹ Indeed they did not understand the scripture, that it was necessary for Jesus to rise from the dead. ¹⁰ Then the disciples returned once more to their homes.

[¹¹ Now Mary stood outside, facing the tomb, weeping. As she wept, she bent down to see in the tomb. ¹² Then she saw two angels in white sitting, one at the head and the other at the feet, where the body of Jesus had been lying. ¹³ They said to her, "Woman, why do you weep?" She said to them, "Because they have taken my Savior, and I do not know where they have laid him." ¹⁴ Having said this, she turned around and saw Jesus standing, but she did not know that it was Jesus. ¹⁵ Jesus said to her, "Woman, why do you weep? For whom do you look?" Thinking that he was the gardener, she said to him, "Sir, if you have carried him away, tell me where you have laid him, and I will take him away." ¹⁶ Jesus said to her, "Mary." She turned and said to him in Aramaic, "Rabbouni!" (which means Teacher). ¹⁷ Jesus said to her, "Do not hold me, because I have not yet ascended to the Father. Rather, go to my brothers and say to them, 'I am ascending to my Father and your Father, to my God and your God.'" ¹⁸ Mary Magdalene went and announced to the disciples, "I have seen the Savior;" and she told them that he had said these things to her.]

PROCLAMATION

Text Notes

Given there is no concrete present tense in biblical Hebrew, it can be difficult to determine whether an imperfect verb should be translated into present or future tense. In Isaiah 49:3, the question of whether God *is* glorified in Israel or *will be* is open. I have chosen the present to suggest that even in their brokenness, or perhaps because of it, God is glorified in her faithful relationship with an often unfaithful partner. A portion of Isaiah 49 read today overlaps with the one read on Psalm Sunday. See textual and preaching commentary there for further notes.

In Psalm 18:2, I draw the divine name from Deuteronomy 32:18, "You neglected the Rock that gave birth to you; you forgot the God who writhed in birth-labor for you."

The Greek word *hypostasis* means the "essence of a thing," as in the relationship between Jesus and God articulated with this same word earlier in Hebrews 1:2–3. In Hebrews 11:1, faith is the essence of that which is hoped for. In 11:2, "to be approved" is the sense of the verb to "be martyred" or "bear witness" when it is the passive voice. The citizens of Jericho in Hebrews 11:31 can be translated as either they who "were disobedient" or "did not believe." Each is problematic in the context of the earlier story. If disobedient, when? To what message? If unbelieving, then to what?

Note that the celestial messengers speak with one voice in John 20:13. In verse 15, Mary addresses Jesus with the honorific given to any man of status or used to show respect, "master" or "lord," also used for those who held slaves. It also signifies Jesus's own authority and sovereignty. Her demand that this unknown person tell her where Jesus has been taken is expressed in the imperative, as a command. Exclamation point or period? Does Jesus exclaim her name or call it softly or plainly in verse 16? I imagine the latter.

Hebrew and Aramaic are recognized as distinct languages now; they were not always so understood; the terms are used interchangeably in the scriptures.

Preaching Prompts

The anonymity of the Servant Songs in Isaiah has led to them being easily interpreted through the story of Jesus. As an Easter reading, the text reminds us of the importance of the life Jesus lived, not just the death he died, a life that was shaped and molded by scriptures like Isaiah 49.

The psalmist is delivered from certain death in her time by being saved from her enemies and their traps. Yet that is not the limit of the power of the God who harnesses the clouds as her chariot. Psalm 18 also serves as a response to Psalm 22 in the earlier plaintive liturgies of Holy Week and Good Friday; the pleas for deliverance and trust in God are answered by the fact of deliverance. God is able to deliver. God is faithful to deliver. Even to and through death.

The Epistle to the Hebrews forms a bridge to the Gospel. In this Epistle penned to Jewish, and therefore Hebrew, people, the author links that faith to the faith of their people (and collaborators) across time. Yet the list of heroes in Hebrews 11 that recounts that faith reads like a patriarchal revisionist history. For example, Barak replaces Deborah, and Jephthah, who murdered his own daughter, is included in 11:32. (However, since Deborah ruled and delivered in the period mentioned, and other women prophets followed her, and the plural "prophets" includes both genders, I have specified "prophets, female and male.") Ironically, it will be women's faithfulness to Jesus at the cross and tomb that will lead to the first proclamations of his resurrection. As a second lesson, the last line of this reading points forward to a promise realized in that resurrection and its proclamation.

With all of the alleluias, it is hard to remember that Easter morning begins in sorrow. Grieving and dumbfounded, women make their way to the tomb, where their friend, teacher, and savior lies. They are not singing alleluia. In John's Gospel, their motivation has been erased; they have been reduced to Mary Magdalene and one "we" in verse 2. They do not enter the tomb, counter to other accounts. They fetch men who go first, then Mary follows them. The male disciples leave, and once again, Jesus is attended only by women, now just Mary. He reveals himself to her and sends her as his messenger bearing his word.

She announces, *aggellousa*, the good news that Jesus has appeared to her and has a message for the men who were not present. That "announcement" is related to the words for messengers, human or divine ones, sometimes called angels, and their messages; they share a common root. Interpreters have struggled with what to make of Jesus telling Mary not to touch or hold or hold on to him in John 20:17. Some wince at what they hear as harsh language, as when he asks his mother, "Woman, what concern is that to you and to me?" in John 2:4. I wonder if it is that we do not hear "woman" charitably as a form of address. What may be missed are the parallels to Thomas: Mary sees, hears, speaks with, and touches her savior. Having seen his death, what other than the word of the risen Christ could compel her to let go?

EASTER DAY—EVENING SERVICE

Isaiah 25:6–9; Psalm 118:14–26; 2 Timothy 2:8–13;
Luke 24:13–35 (or 24:13–27)

Isaiah 25:6 The COMMANDER of heaven's legions will make for all peoples on this mountain,

    a feast of rich food, a feast of well-aged wines,
    of rich food prepared with marrow, of refined well-aged wines.
7 And God will destroy on this mountain
    the shroud that shrouds all peoples,
    the veil that veils all nations.
8 God will swallow up death forever.
    Then the SOVEREIGN GOD will wipe away tears from every face,
    and will sweep aside the shame of God's people from the whole earth,
    for GOD WHOSE NAME IS HOLY has spoken.
9 It will be said on that day,
    Look! This is our God; in whom we hope, and who saved us.
    This is the CREATOR OF ALL in whom we hope;
    let us be glad and rejoice in God's salvation.

Psalm 118:14–26

14 The MIGHTY GOD is my strength and my might
    and has become my salvation.
15 The sound of song and of salvation is in the tents of the righteous:
    "The right hand of the MOST HIGH is mighty;
16 the right hand of the MIGHTY GOD is exalted;

> the right hand of the Most High is mighty."
> 17 I shall not die, but I shall live,
> and recount the deeds of the Ancient Of Days.
> 18 The Merciful God has punished me severely,
> but to death did not hand me over.
> 19 Open to me the gates of righteousness,
> that I may enter through them
> and give thanks to the Fount Of Justice.
> 20 This is the gate of the Living God;
> the righteous shall enter through it.
> 21 I thank you for you have answered me
> and have become my salvation.
> 22 The stone the builders rejected
> has become the chief cornerstone.
> 23 This is the Mighty God's doing;
> it is marvelous in our eyes.
> 24 This is the day that the Creator Of All has made;
> let us rejoice and be glad in it.
> 25 Save us, we pray, Saving One!
> Generous One, we pray, grant us prosperity!
> 26 Blessed is the one who comes in the name of God Who Is Holy.
> We bless you from the house of the Ever-Living God.

2 Timothy 2:8 Remember Jesus Christ, raised from the dead, from the line of David [and Bathsheba]; that is my gospel, ⁹ for which I suffer hardship, even to chains, like a criminal. But the word of God is not chained. ¹⁰ Because of this, therefore I endure everything for the sake of the elect, in order that they may also obtain salvation in Christ Jesus with eternal glory. ¹¹ This is a trustworthy saying:

> For if we die together, we will also live together;
> 12 if we endure, we will also reign together;
> if we deny [Christ], he will also deny us;
> 13 if we are faithless, faithful he remains,
> for he cannot deny himself.

Luke 24:13 Now see, two of them on that very day [the first day of the week] were going to a village that was seven miles from Jerusalem; its name was Emmaus. ¹⁴ And they talked with each other about all the things that had happened. ¹⁵ And it happened while they were talking and questioning that Jesus himself came near and accompanied them. ¹⁶ Yet their eyes were kept from recognizing him. ¹⁷ And Jesus said to them, "What is this conversation you are having with each other while you journey?" They stood in place, sorrowful. ¹⁸ Then one of them, whose name was Cleopas, replied to him, saying, "Are you the only foreigner in Jerusalem who does not know the things that have happened there these days?" [19] Jesus asked them, "What kind of things?" They replied, "About Jesus the Nazarene, who was a man, a prophet mighty in deed and word before God and all the people. [20] Also how our chief priests and leaders surrendered him to be sentenced to death and crucified him. [21] But we had hoped that he was the one to soon redeem Israel. Now besides all this, instead, it is now the third day since these things have taken place. [22] Then again, certain women of our community astounded us. They were at the tomb this morning. [23] And when they did not find the body, they came back and told us they had seen a vision of angels who said Jesus was alive. [24] Then some of those who were with us went to the tomb and found it just as the women had said, but they did not see him." [25] Then Jesus said to them, "Oh, foolish souls, and how slow of heart to believe all that the prophets have spoken! [26] Was it not necessary that the Messiah should suffer these things to enter into his glory?" [27] And starting from Moses and from all the prophets, Jesus interpreted to them the things about himself in all the scriptures.

[28] When they came near the village to which they were going, Jesus walked ahead as if he were going on. [29] So they urged him strongly, saying, "Stay with us, because it is almost evening and the day is nearly over." Then he went in to stay with them. [30] When Jesus was at the table with them, he took bread, blessed and broke it, and gave it to them. [31] And their eyes were opened, and they recognized him. And he vanished from before them. [32] They said to each other, "Were not our hearts burning within us while he was talking to us on the way, while he was opening up the scriptures to us?" [33] Now that same hour they rose up and returned to Jerusalem and found the eleven and others with them gathered together. [34] They were saying, "Really! The Savior has risen, and has appeared to Simon!" [35] Then they told what had happened on the way, and how Jesus had been made known to them in the breaking of the bread.

PROCLAMATION

Text Notes

There are regular differences in how biblical passages are broken into verses between translations. In Isaiah 25, the last line of what is verse 7 in some Christian Bibles like NRSV begins verse 8 in Hebrew and in Jewish Bibles and other Christian Bibles, like CEB. I follow the Hebrew and JPS here. In verse 9, the tense of God's salvation can be understood as past or present. God's record of faithfulness makes her trustworthy; pushing these texts into a future time diminishes that past faithfulness.

Psalm 118 is a literary work of art in Hebrew with a lattice of repeating elements that circle from the last line to the beginning. In verse 25, which yields "hosanna," an alternate pronunciation for *hoshia-na* in the Psalm.

Many translations of 2 Timothy 2:11–13 add "with him" throughout for poetic balance; the object and preposition are not present. Verse 12 requires an object for the verb; I have supplied "Christ" from verse 10.

In Luke 24:25, Jesus says, "Oh foolish X . . ." There is no noun present; the adjective includes object information, masculine or inclusive plural. Common translations are "foolish men," "ones," or "people."

Preaching Prompts

On this Principal Feast of the Resurrection, the Church proclaims that death is not the end. This notion appears intermittently in the Hebrew Bible: Elisha raises a widow's son from death in 2 Kings 4, and Daniel 12:1–2 proclaims an unambiguous resurrection. Frequently cited, Job 19:26 is ambiguous and well-known. In Ezekiel 37, the dry bones represent the resurrection of the nation of Israel; see verse 11. Against this background, Isaiah 25 proclaims that the day is coming when God will destroy death forever, swallowing it up. Belief in resurrection will become normative for most traditions of Judaism, including that of Jesus, for Christians, as well as for Muslims.

Psalm 118 is a festival hymn in the form of a temple liturgy. It is part of the Great *Hallel* (Praise) recited during the major festivals: Passover, Pentecost (*Shavuoth*), and Booths (*Sukkot*). Many understand the Hallel to be the "hymn" that Jesus and the disciples sang after the Last Supper, particularly when it is formed as a Passover meal (though likely not a seder). In these readings, Psalm 118 echoes the theme of salvation in Isaiah 25. In verse 17, the line "I shall not die but live" likely refers to deliverance from death rather than resurrection. Together these collected readings present a God who delivers on both sides of death. While the psalm emphasizes deliverance from death, 2 Timothy offers an ancient hymn for the believer confident in resurrection after death.

It's hard to know what to make of Jesus calling the disciples foolish in Luke 24:25. It sounds like a rebuke but may have been said in humor with a twinkle, the way a text, tweet, or e-mail may sound harsher than intended.

The Road to Emmaus stories are Easter evening stories. The traveling disciples have had all day to grapple with incomprehensible claims of resurrection from sister disciples. Notably, they don't doubt the women; rather, they find the whole saga—trial, crucifixion, and resurrection claims—simply astounding. This is an important reminder that the terrible images of the crucifixion and the trauma it generated don't simply vanish with proclamation of the good news. The disciples are traumatized and on an emotional rollercoaster.

Jesus, the Bread of Life, confected in the womb of the Blessed Virgin, makes himself known in the breaking of bread. Jesus, who is bread, offers bread, and Jesus, who is the Word, interprets the word. When Jesus interprets the scriptures—in

Luke 24:27, Torah and Prophets, and in Luke 24:44, Torah, Prophets, and Psalms—the text does not say he shows where the scriptures "predict" him. Reducing the relationship of Jesus with the Hebrew Bible to prediction and fulfillment presents a skewed view of prophecy, scripture more broadly, and Jesus. Rather, I understand him to teach the scriptures that are foundational to him, his identity, his teaching, and his ministry, after which he patterned himself, which scriptures Christians subsequently read through Jesus.

One of the travelers is male; the other is not described. Grammatically, they could have been a woman and man or two men. There were women, children, and men in the village where they stopped absent from the text, as are their hosts. The only women's voices are the echoing proclamations that Christ is risen from the dead.

MONDAY IN EASTER WEEK

1 Peter 1:3–9; Psalm 16:8–11; John 20:19–23

Note: Easter Week services do not traditionally include a Hebrew Bible reading. In the traditional pattern, the first lesson is a New Testament lesson followed by the psalm and Gospel.

1 Peter 1:3 Blessed be the God and Father of our Redeemer Jesus Christ who in great mercy has engendered a new birth for us into a living hope, through the resurrection of Jesus Christ from the dead, ⁴ into an inheritance that is incorruptible, undefiled, and unfading, kept in the heavens for you all, ⁵ who in the power of God are kept through faith for a salvation ready to be revealed in the end time. ⁶ In this you rejoice even when necessary for you to suffer various trials, ⁷ in order that the examination of your faith, more precious than gold, which though perishable is tested by fire, may be found yielding praise and glory and honor when Jesus Christ is revealed. ⁸ You have not seen him, yet you love him. You do not see him now, yet you believe in him and rejoice with a joy glorious and beyond words. ⁹ You are receiving the completion of your faith, the salvation of your souls.

Psalm 16:8–11

⁸ I keep the FAITHFUL ONE before me always;
   because she is at my right hand, I shall not be moved.
⁹ Therefore my heart rejoices, and my inner being delights;
   even my body resides in safety.
¹⁰ For you will not abandon my soul to Sheol,
   or let your faithful one see the Pit.
¹¹ You show me the way of life.
   There is fullness of joy in your presence;
   delights fill your right hand forevermore.

John 20:19 When it was evening on that day, the first of the week, and the doors of the house where the disciples were closed for fear of the Judeans, Jesus came and stood in their midst and said to them, "Peace be with you all." [20] And having said this, Jesus showed them his hands and his side, then the disciples rejoiced when they saw the Messiah. [21] Jesus said to them again, "Peace be with you all, just as the God of Peace has sent me, so I send you all." [22] When Jesus had said this, he breathed on them and said to them, "Receive the Holy Spirit; [23] if you forgive the sins of any, they are forgiven them; if you retain the sins of any, they are retained."

PROCLAMATION

Text Notes

The reading from 1 Peter has rather long, unwieldy sentences that make for challenging reading, particularly aloud.

In Psalm 16, Sheol, the abode of the dead in the Israelite worldview, was variously described as a place of great gloom, deep below the surface of the (flat) earth. It is an equitable destination for great and small, righteous and wicked. Presumed to be inescapable except by the rarest of miracles, deliverance from Sheol refers to escape from death and its clutches *before* death. The "Pit" is an occasional synonym for Sheol and the grave.

In the Gospel of John, the disciples in the house are as Jewish as their fellow residents of Judea, as Jewish as Jesus. It would be centuries before there was clear separation between Jews and Christians. Scriptural language pitting Jesus, his disciples, and the early Christians against "the Jews" is one of the more challenging aspects of our faith.

Preaching Prompts

These Easter Week first Lesson readings explore some of the Church's earliest reflections on resurrection. All of the psalms focus on God's deliverance from death and its abode in the Israelite worldview, Sheol. The Gospel readings center the stories from immediately after the resurrection.

The Epistle addresses believers who, like us, have not seen Jesus yet believe. The active voice in the Epistle emphasizes that the readers and hearers, and we, are being kept by God and that they and we are receiving the salvation of our souls.

Rather than a fixed point at which we "were" saved, we live into our salvation in faith.

The second-person addresses of the Epistle and psalm—the first to the reader, the second to God—do not include gendered language. There are, of course, women among the believers to whom the Epistle is written and women who would have prayed, and perhaps composed, the psalmist's prayer. We are left to imagine them.

The women are necessarily absent from the Gospel, having proclaimed the good news of Jesus's resurrection to male disciples who still don't quite get it, let alone its implications for a fearless life. They, Mary Magdalene and other women, suggested by the "we" in John 20:2, are arguably still telling the news. What to make of the gift of the Holy Spirit breathed onto those disciples hiding in the house? It matters that the power and authority to forgive and retain sins is connected to the receipt of the Holy Spirit, grammatically and theologically. The text appears to be organizing, if not setting up, a hierarchy in the community. This early statement of the nascent community's priorities shows them continuing Jesus's radical work, declaring the forgiveness of sins.

TUESDAY IN EASTER WEEK

1 Corinthians 15:3–7; Psalm 18:1–6; Luke 24:36–43

1 Corinthians 15:3 For I handed on to you all as primary what I, in turn, had received, that Christ died for our sins in accordance with the scriptures. ⁴ And that he was buried, and that he was raised on the third day in accordance with the scriptures. ⁵ And that he was seen by Cephas, then the twelve. ⁶ Then he was seen by more than five hundred sisters and brothers together, many of whom remain, though some have died. ⁷ Then he was seen by James, then all the apostles.

Psalm 18:1–6

¹ I love you, MIGHTY ONE, my strength.
² The ROCK WHO GAVE US BIRTH is my rock,
  and my fortress, and my deliverer,
  my God, my rock in whom I take refuge,
  my shield, and the horn of my salvation, my stronghold.
³ I call upon the HOLY ONE, may she be praised,
  and from my enemies I shall be saved.
⁴ The snares of death encompassed me;
  the rivers of wickedness assailed me.
⁵ The snares of Sheol encircled me;
  the snares of death confronted me.
⁶ In my distress I called upon SHE WHO HEARS;
  to my God I cried for help.
  From her temple she heard my voice,
  and my cry came before her, to her ears.

Luke 24:36 While they [two of Jesus's disciples] were talking about this [his resurrection], he himself stood between them and said to them, "Peace be with you." ³⁷ Now they were frightened and became terrified, and thought they were seeing a spirit. ³⁸ Jesus said to them,

"Why are you troubled, because of thoughts rising in your hearts? [39] Look at my hands and my feet; that it is I. Touch me and see; for a spirit does not have flesh and bones as you see I have." [40] And saying this, Jesus showed them his hands and his feet. [41] Yet still disbelieving and in their joy and wondering, he said to them, "Have you any food here?" [42] They gave him a piece of broiled fish, [43] and he took it in their presence and ate.

PROCLAMATION

Text Notes

One of the ways in which the translation of the scriptures is often anti-Judaistic is the intentional changing of Jewish names in the New Testament to Gentile forms. "James" in 1 Corinthians 15:7 is a case in point. His name is Jacob, *Iakob* in Greek, yet translators use "Jacob" for the Hebrew Bible patriarch occurring in the New Testament while treating the Hebrew names of people in the Jesus story differently. Changing *Mariam* (Greek Miriam) to Mary is another example of what is a standard practice. These changes obscure and, in some cases, erase the primary Jewish identity of the family and followers of Jesus.

The occasion of Psalm 18 is David's escape from Saul; that introduction takes up the first verse in Hebrew. The psalm proper begins with "He said," often included with the introductory verse. David's "love" in what is now verse 1, as Christian translations number the psalms, is *racham*, mother-love, love that is rooted in the womb, *rechem*, and otherwise used only by God to express her love. From David, we should perhaps read it as gesturing toward a reciprocal love that originates deep within.

Verse 3 of the psalm has the passive "be praised" without supporting grammar. Other translators have added, "*worthy to* be praised." Some translations render verse 3 in the future (see NRSV and KJV). However, the introduction makes clear David is reflecting on his past deliverance. The imperfect here is more present, i.e., because of God's faithfulness, whenever I call on God as before, I shall be saved.

The Gospel uses the same word for "spirit" (as in the Holy Spirit) for spirit of the dead, or what we might hear as "ghost" in Luke 24:37 and in verse 39.

Preaching Prompts

Given that the Epistles predate the Gospels, the brief telling of the good news of Jesus's resurrection triumph over the grave is one of the first recorded articulations of the Gospel. It lacks all of the narrative detail and the women evangelists collectively or by name. Not only is Mary Magdalene missing, but there is no mention of Mary, the mother of Jesus, or the beloved disciple. It lacks the angels and reports only Peter (called Cephas) and the twelve as initial witnesses. The text does go on to position Paul as in the chain of apostles.

The mention of James receiving his own post-resurrection appearance is significant. Long understood to be the brother of Jesus, the appearance has been interpreted as confirming James as leader of the emerging church. While the Epistle is invested in hierarchy (hence the lack of women) and continuity, Jesus also takes time to appear to family in the person of his beloved brother. The appearances to the more than five hundred in the plural form that can be inclusive, mixed—with only one male required, or all-male suggest Jesus going to his beloveds to comfort and assure them after his death.

Jesus's evening journey with the pair, or perhaps couple, of disciples on the road to Emmaus reads like an expansion of the note in 1 Corinthians 15 about Jesus's appearances to so many. Even with the scolding of beloved teacher and friend, the account reads as comforting and affectionate. As with the five hundred, only one of these disciples must be male grammatically; I chose to read the other as female, likely a spouse.

WEDNESDAY IN EASTER WEEK

1 Corinthians 15:12–20; Psalm 30:1–5; Luke 24:44–53

1 Corinthians 15:12 Now if Christ is preached as raised from the dead, how can some of you say there is no resurrection of the dead? [13] For if there is no resurrection of the dead, then Christ has not been raised; [14] and if Christ has not been raised, then our preaching has been in vain along with your faith. [15] Then we are even found to be false witnesses of God, because we bore witness of God that God raised Christ—whom God did not raise if the dead are not raised. [16] For if the dead are not raised, then Christ has not been raised. [17] And if Christ has not been raised, your faith is useless and you are yet in your sins. [18] And therefore those who have died in Christ have been destroyed. [19] If for this life we have only hoped in Christ, we are of all people most pitiable. [20] But now indeed Christ has been raised from the dead, the first fruits of those who have died.

Psalm 30:1–5

[1] I will exalt you, ARK OF SAFETY, because you have pulled me up
and have not let my enemies rejoice over me.
[2] HEALING ONE, my God, I cried to you for help,
and you healed me.
[3] EVER-LIVING GOD, you brought my soul up from Sheol;
you preserved my life from descent to the Pit.
[4] Sing praises to the FAITHFUL GOD, you her faithful;
give thanks remembering her holiness.
[5] For her fury is a moment, her favor a lifetime.
Weeping may pass the night, yet in the morning, joy.

Luke 24:44 Jesus said to [the two disciples], "These are my words that I spoke to you while I was still with you all, because everything must be fulfilled in the teaching of Moses, the prophets, and the psalms written about me." [45] Then he opened their minds to understand the scriptures. [46] Then he said to them, "So it is written, the Messiah is to suffer and to rise from the dead the third day, [47] and repentance and forgiveness of sins is to be preached in his name to all nations, beginning from Jerusalem. [48] You are witnesses of these things. [49] Now look! I am sending you the promise of my Father. You all stay in the city until you have been clothed with power from on high."

[50] Then Jesus led them out as far as Bethany, and lifting his hands, he blessed them. [51] While he was blessing them, Jesus retreated from them and was carried up into heaven. [52] And they worshiped him, and returned to Jerusalem with great joy; [53] and they were in the temple every day blessing God.

PROCLAMATION

Text Notes

Both of the readings from 1 Corinthians 15 and Luke 24 continue from the previous day, even though not contiguous.

Preaching Prompts

People have grappled with the Jesus story from the very beginning. Even in a world in which miracles were accepted uncritically, some of the claims about Jesus were astounding—a word that occurs often in the Gospels. As now, there were those for whom a literal resurrection was difficult to believe. Paul's rebuttal draws a straight line from the resurrection to the forgiveness of our sins and our salvation.

The wonder and incredulity of the disciples on the Emmaus road contrasts with doctrinal disputers in Corinth. The disciples are overjoyed and accept the miracle, though they do not seem to understand it. Jesus calls them back to the Jewish scriptures, somewhat fewer than would eventually be canonized: Torah, Prophets, and only psalms from the third traditional division, Writings. (In the Hebrew Bible, the Prophets include Joshua, Judges, Samuel, Kings, Isaiah, Jeremiah, Ezekiel, and the Minor Prophets. The Writings include everything else not in the Torah; Daniel is not a prophet in Jewish tradition.) In other passages, the scriptures consist of the Torah (Law) and Prophets, suggesting the Writings were still in formation (see Matthew 22:40; Luke 16:16; Acts 13:15; Romans 3:21).

Physical salvation is the theme of the psalm as it is all of Easter Week. Deliverance, salvation, and resurrection are available to all without regard for gender or its performance. However, the scriptures and their writers will try to make these stories make sense in the world they knew, with all of its hierarchies in place for the most part.

THURSDAY IN EASTER WEEK

1 Corinthians 15:35–44; Psalm 49:5–15; John 21:4–14

1 Corinthians 15:35 Now then, someone will ask, "How are the dead raised? In what kind of body do they come?" 36 Fool! What you plant is not brought to life unless it dies. 37 Now, about what you plant, you do not plant the body that will be but a bare seed, for example, wheat or of some other grain. 38 Yet God gives it a body as God wills, and to each kind of seed its own body. 39 Not all flesh is the same flesh; rather there is one flesh for human beings, another for animals, another for birds, and another for fish. 40 Yet there are heavenly bodies and earthly bodies, while the glory of the heavenly is one kind, and that of the earthly is another. 41 There is one glory of the sun and another glory of the moon, yet another glory of the stars, each star even differs in glory.

42 So it is with the resurrection of the dead. What is planted is perishable; what is raised is imperishable. 43 It is planted in dishonor; it is raised in glory. It is sown in weakness; it is raised in power. 44 It is planted a physical body; it is raised a spiritual body. If there is a physical body; there is also a spiritual body.

Psalm 49:5–15

5 Why should I fear in evil days,
   when iniquity at my heels surrounds me?
6 Those who trust in their wealth
   and praise of the abundance of their riches?
7 Certainly, it cannot redeem a person,
   or can one give [it] to God as their ransom.
8 For the redemption-price of a soul is costly,
   they come to an end, forever.
9 Shall one live eternally
   and never see the Pit?
10 For when one sees the wise, they die;
   the foolish and ignorant perish together
   and leave to others their wealth.
11 Their graves are their homes for all time,
   their dwelling places from generation to generation,
   though they put their name on lands.
12 Humanity will not recline in grandeur;
   rather they are like the animals that perish.
13 This is the way of the foolish,
   those pleased with their own words. *Selah*
14 Like sheep they are set for Sheol;
   Death shall be their shepherd.

> The upright shall rule over them until the morning,
> and their form shall waste away;
> Sheol shall be their abode.
> ¹⁵ But God will ransom my soul,
> for from the grasp of Sheol she will take me. *Selah*

John 21:4 Now when morning came, Jesus stood on the beach; but the disciples did not know that it was Jesus. ⁵ Jesus said to them, "Children, do you have any fish prepared?" They answered him, "No." ⁶ Then he said to them, "Cast the net to the right side of the boat, and you will find some." So, they cast it, and they were not able to drag it in because of the abundance of fish. ⁷ That disciple whom Jesus loved said to Peter, "It is the Messiah!" When Simon Peter heard that it was the Messiah, he put on some clothes, for he was naked, and threw himself into the sea. ⁸ But the other disciples came in the boat, dragging the net full of fish, for they were not far from the land, only two hundred cubits [about a hundred yards] off.

⁹ As soon as they turned back to land, they saw a fire there, with fish laid over it, and bread. ¹⁰ Jesus said to them, "Bring some of the fish that you have just caught." ¹¹ So Simon Peter went up and dragged the net to land, full of large fish—one hundred fifty-three—and with so many the net was not torn. ¹² Jesus said to them, "Come and eat." Now none of the disciples dared to ask him, "Who are you?" because they knew it was the Messiah. ¹³ Jesus came and took the bread and gave it to them, and did the same with the fish. ¹⁴ Now this was the third time that Jesus appeared to the disciples after he was raised from the dead.

PROCLAMATION

Text Notes

There are a couple of phrases in the psalm, in verses 7 and 13, that are difficult to translate. I have drawn from the translations of the Jewish Publication Society and Robert Alter, *The Hebrew Bible: A Translation with Commentary*.

Preaching Prompts

Resurrection is the foundation of the Gospel Easter story and even when proclaimed as a certainty, holds a full share of mystery. It seems unreasonable to expect folk to have no questions or to mock them or call them names (i.e., "fool" in 1 Corinthians 15:36) for asking. The Gospel story, resurrection included, is strong enough to bear the weight of our questions, and God, unlike the apostle, is eternally patient with them.

The psalmist trusts in God for her deliverance, recognizing that wealth is of no avail and there is no price that can be placed on a human life.

John 21 offers a potential narrative response to the questioners mocked in the Epistle. What kind of body do the resurrected have? In this story, one that is solid and tangible, capable of mundane tasks like cooking. One that was recognizable to those who had known the formerly dead. While not putting an end to questions about the resurrection, John 21 demonstrates that the resurrected Jesus has the same demeanor and shows the same care for his disciples that he did in his previous life.

While some forms of fishing were likely performed by women or men, the dragnet fishing indicated by the text, along with Peter's casual nudity, suggests only male disciples were present. This is in keeping with the theme that the male disciples needed to be convinced.

FRIDAY IN EASTER WEEK

Romans 6:5–11; Psalm 86:8–13; Mark 16:9–15, 19–20

Romans 6:5 For if we have been united in a death like Christ's, we will certainly be so within the resurrection. ⁶ This we know, that our old self was crucified with him so that the body of sin might be destroyed, and we might no longer be enslaved to sin. ⁷ The woman or man who has died is freed from sin. ⁸ But if we have died with Christ, we believe that we shall also live with him. ⁹ We know that Christ, being raised from the dead, will never die; death no longer has dominion over him. ¹⁰ For dying, he died once to sin, in living, he lives to God. ¹¹ So also should you consider yourselves dead to sin and alive to God in Christ Jesus.

Psalm 86:8–13

⁸ There is none like you among the gods, MOST HIGH,
  and there are no works like yours.
⁹ All the nations that you made shall come,
  and they shall bow down before you Sovereign One,
  and they shall glorify your name.
¹⁰ For you are great and work wonders;
  you are God, you alone.
¹¹ Teach me, HOLY ONE, your way,
  that I may walk in your truth;
  let my heart be undivided to revere your name.
¹² I give thanks to you, Sovereign One my God, with my whole heart,
  and I shall glorify your name forever.
¹³ For great is your faithful love toward me;
  you have delivered my soul from the depths of Sheol.

Mark 16:9 Now after he rose early on the first day of the week, Jesus appeared first to Mary Magdalene from whom he had cast out seven demons. ¹⁰ She went out and she told the ones mourning and weeping who had been with him. ¹¹ But when they heard that he lives and was seen by her, they did not believe. ¹² After this Jesus was made known in another form to two of [the disciples] as they were walking into the countryside. ¹³ And they went back and told the rest, but they did not believe them. [14] Now later on, while they were sitting at table, Jesus appeared to the eleven themselves and he rebuked their lack of faith and stubbornness, because they did not believe those [the women] who saw Jesus after he had risen. [15] Then Jesus said to them, "Go into all the world and proclaim the good news to all creation."

[19] And then Jesus the Messiah, after he had spoken to them, was taken up into heaven and sat down at the right hand of God. [20] And they went out proclaiming the good news everywhere, the Messiah worked with them and confirmed the message by the signs that followed.

PROCLAMATION

Text Notes

Mark's Gospel has a variety of endings that shock many Bible readers who think the scriptures were unchanged from inception. They are missing from the oldest most reliable manuscripts, Sinaticus and Vaticanus, and from more than a hundred Syriac, Coptic, and Armenian manuscripts; in many of the manuscripts in which they are found, they are set off with notations equivalent to an asterisk denoting lack of originality. There is near-universal acceptance that verses 1–8 are original. Some scholars further subdivide the remaining verses. The Church (across denominations) treats them as authoritative to varying degrees, and they do appear in an abridged form in the lectionary of the Episcopal Church.

In Mark 16:12, the description of Jesus appearing in "another form" to two disciples "walking in the countryside" closely resembles the Emmaus Road story in Luke 24. In verse 14, Jesus "reprimands" or "rebukes" the (presumably male) disciples for not believing "those" who proclaimed his resurrection. I have specified "the women" here; they were "those" who were not believed, Mary Magdalene, another Mary, and Salome in Mark 16:1.

Preaching Prompts

Whether in spite of or because of being part of the addendum to Mark, 16:14 includes a strong rebuke by Jesus for those who did not believe the gospel of his resurrection from the dead preached by women, perhaps because it was preached by women. It still speaks to those who discount the words and ministries of women. The disciples are sent to preach to all creation, and Jesus won't let them be treated like the women: he will work with them, verse 20, providing signs to confirm the message. For the women and the few male disciples, his appearances were the sign. And for some, women and men, surely the women's witness was sufficient. It would have been enough for children. The signs and ascension in verse 19 point to a new reality: Jesus will not continue to appear as he had. And at some point, the signs will come to an end as well. All that will remain will be the proclamation of the gospel by women and men and the faith of those who choose to believe.

SATURDAY IN EASTER WEEK

Acts 13:29–38; Psalm 116:1–9; Matthew 28:8–10, 16–20

Acts 13:29 Now when they had finished doing everything written about him, they took him down from the tree and laid him in a tomb. ³⁰ But God raised him from the dead. ³¹ He appeared for many days to those [women and men] who traveled with him from Galilee to Jerusalem, and they are now his witnesses to the people. ³² And we proclaim the good news to you that what God promised to our mothers and fathers ³³ God has fulfilled for us, their children, by raising Jesus; as also it is written in the second psalm,

> "*You are my Son; today I have begotten you.*"

³⁴ Because God raised him from the dead, never to return to corruption, God spoke thusly,

> "*I will give you the holy promises of David.*"

³⁵ Therefore David has also said in another psalm,

> "*You will not let your holy one experience corruption.*"

³⁶ For indeed David, after he had served the purpose of God in his own generation, died, and was placed beside his mothers and fathers, and experienced corruption; ³⁷ yet the one whom God raised up saw no corruption. ³⁸ Let it be known to you, therefore, my sisters and brothers, that through this man forgiveness of sins is proclaimed to you.

Psalm 116:1–9

¹ I love the GOD WHO HEARS,
 for God has heard my voice and my supplications.
² For she opens her ear to me,
 whatever day I call.
³ The snares of death encompassed me;
 the torments of Sheol took hold of me,
 I found distress and sorrow.
⁴ Then I called on the name of the HOLY ONE OF OLD:
 "HOLY ONE, please, save my life!"
⁵ Gracious is the FOUNT OF JUSTICE, and righteous;
 our God loves [like a mother].
⁶ The FAITHFUL ONE protects the simple;
 I was brought low and she saved me.
⁷ Return, O my soul, to your rest,
 for the GRACIOUS ONE has dealt generously with you.
⁸ For you have delivered my soul from death,
 my eyes from tears,

my feet from stumbling.
9 I shall walk before the AUTHOR OF LIFE
in the lands of the living.

Matthew 28:8 So the women left the tomb quickly with fear and great joy and ran to tell his disciples the news. ⁹ Then all of a sudden Jesus met them and said, "Shalom!" And they came to him, took hold of his feet, and bowed down worshipping him. ¹⁰ Then Jesus said to them, "Fear not; go and tell my sisters and brothers to go to Galilee; there they will see me."

¹⁶ Now the eleven disciples went to Galilee, to the mountain to which Jesus sent them. ¹⁷ And when they saw him, they bowed down worshipping him; but some doubted. ¹⁸ Then Jesus came and said to them, saying, "All authority in heaven and on earth has been given to me. ¹⁹ Go therefore and make disciples of all nations, baptizing them in the name of the Father and of the Son and of the Holy Spirit, ²⁰ and teaching them to obey everything that I have commanded you. Now look, I am with you always, to the end of the age."

PROCLAMATION
Text Notes
In Acts 13:33–35, Paul cites Psalm 2:7, Isaiah 55:3, and Psalm 16:10 from the LXX (note the psalms are known to be numbered while chapter and verse numbers would not be added for centuries). Paul is in synagogue addressing "Men of Israel, and others who fear God." Women were not excluded from synagogue and would have also been present. "God-fearers" was often language for Gentile worshippers. Paul's language, "men" and "brothers," excludes women and renders them invisible in this passage. Are women to understand themselves included, or is Paul specifically addressing men exclusively, figuring they'll pass the good news on to the women in their lives? I read his language as customarily androcentric and patriarchal, as is the bulk of scripture, and make women visible as appropriate.

In Matthew 28:8, the word translated as "authority" also means "power." In verse 10, Jesus tells the women to tell his "siblings" to go to meet him in Galilee. That certainly includes the eleven male disciples but is not necessarily limited to them. At some point, the eleven receive other more specific instructions to go to a particular mountain indicated by verse 16.

Preaching Prompts
In Acts 13, Paul tells the Gospel story, adding his own proof-texting exegesis of the Hebrew Scriptures to "prove" that Jesus, who was nothing like the warrior messiah many expected, and some scriptures predicted, was nevertheless the fulfillment of the scriptures. Paul is demonstrating the flexibility of the scriptures for reinterpretation

in every age; rereading them in light of Jesus yields tantalizing and suggestive readings, which now, with full knowledge of the Jesus story, seem specifically predictive. These are particularly Christian ways of reading the Hebrew Bible. It is important to remember that Jewish readings, even of passages considered messianic, do not always focus on a single individual. Sometimes the entire nation is the messianic figure, sometimes an individual or specific ruler, and sometimes an unknown individual.

In Psalm 116:5, God's love is articulated with the word whose root is "womb," often unhelpfully translated as "merciful" or "compassion."

The Gospel reading combines the resurrection appearances to the women, Mary Magdalene and the "other" Mary, and to the eleven remaining disciples. The women believe immediately and run with joy to tell the news. They are also afraid, perhaps of what this might mean, potentially more violence. The male disciples also bowed down before Jesus, but they do not yet believe. The story of the church will soon become their story as they proclaim the resurrection they first doubted. It might be worthwhile to imagine the evangelism of the women, how the women and men they proclaimed the good news to also became part of the new and expanding church.

SECOND SUNDAY OF EASTER

Acts 1:3–8, 12–14 (or Judith 8:1–17); Psalm 6:1–10;
Romans 8:31–39; Luke 18:18–30

The Sundays of Easter traditionally have a choice of readings from the Hebrew Bible and Acts for the first lesson. This volume will offer readings from Judith as the alternate to selections from Acts.

Acts 1:3 Jesus presented himself to them, living, after his suffering through many convincing proofs, by appearing to them forty days and speaking about the reign of God. [4] And staying with them, Jesus commanded them not to leave Jerusalem, rather to wait there for the promise of the Faithful One: "What you heard from me. [5] For John baptized with water, but you will be baptized with the Holy Spirit not many days from this one." [6] When they [the disciples] came together, they asked Jesus, "Rabbi, is this the time when you will restore sovereignty to Israel?" [7] He replied, "It is not for you to know the times or seasons that the Creator has set through divine authority. [8] But you will receive power when the Holy Spirit comes upon you, and you will be my witnesses in Jerusalem, in all Judea and Samaria, and to the end of the earth."

[12] Then they returned to Jerusalem from the mount called Olivet, which is near Jerusalem, a sabbath day's journey away. [13] And when they entered the city, they went upstairs to the room where they were staying: Peter, and John, and James, and Andrew, Philip and Thomas, Bartholomew and Matthew, James son of Alphaeus, and Simon the Zealot, and

Judas son of James. ¹⁴ All these were persevering in prayer together with women, including Mary the mother of Jesus, as well as his [sisters and] brothers.

Judith 8:1 Now Judith heard in those days [that Nebuchadnezzar's army approached]. She was the daughter of Merari son of Ox son of Joseph son of Oziel son of Elkiah son of Ananias son of Gideon son of Raphain son of Ahitub son of Elijah son of Hilkiah son of Eliab son of Nathanael son of Salamiel son of Sarasadai son of Israel. ² And her husband Manasseh was of her tribe and ancestry; now he died during the days of the barley harvest. ³ For while he was overseeing the binding of the sheaves in the field, burning heat came upon him and he fell upon his bed and died in Bethulia, his city. And they buried him with his ancestors in the field between Dothan and Balamon. ⁴ And Judith lived in her house, being widowed three years and four months. ⁵ And she had made herself a tent upon the roof of her house and placed sackcloth around her waist and upon her were the garments of her widowhood. ⁶ Now she fasted all the days of her widowhood except for the day before the Sabbath and the Sabbath itself, the day before the new moon, the day of the new moon, and the feasts and rejoicings of the house of Israel. ⁷ And she was beautiful in appearance and very lovely of face. Her husband Manasseh left her gold and silver, female and male servants, cattle and fields, and she remained over them. ⁸ And there was no one who brought an evil word against her, for she revered God very much.

⁹ Now Judith heard the evil words of the people against the ruler because they were fainthearted from the lack of water. Judith also heard all the words that Uzziah said to them, swearing to hand over the city to the Assyrians in five days. ¹⁰ And sending her favorite slave-woman, the one who was set over all she possessed, summoned Uzziah, Chabris, and Charmis, the elders of her city. ¹¹ And they came to her and she said to them:

"Listen now to me, rulers of the inhabitants of Bethulia, for it is not right, your word you have spoken to the people this day. And you all have placed this oath, which you all have spoken between God and you. And you all said you will surrender the city to our enemies in the next few days if the Holy One does not turn and help you all. ¹² So then who are you, you all who have tested God on this very day, and placed yourselves greater than God in the midst of those born of women? ¹³ And now God Almighty you question; none of you will learn anything, ever. ¹⁴ The depths of the human heart you cannot plumb, and the volume of their thoughts you cannot comprehend. And how much more God, the One who made all this, will you search out and know God's mind and comprehend God's thoughts? By no means kindred; do not anger the Holy One our God.

¹⁵ "For if God is not willing in the next five days to help us, God has the power to shelter us or to destroy us at any time God wishes before the faces of our enemies. ¹⁶ As for you, do not attempt to bind the counsel of the Holy One our God. Not like those born of women is God to be threatened nor like any child of human parents who waver. ¹⁷ Therefore, while we wait for God's salvation, let us call upon God for help and if it pleases God, God will hear our voice."

Psalm 6:1–10

¹ Compassionate One, do not, in your wrath, rebuke me,
and do not, in your rage, reprove me.
² Have mercy on me, Faithful One, for I am fragile;
Gracious God, heal me, for my very bones are terrified.
³ My soul also is beyond terrified,
while you, Holy One, how long?
⁴ Turn, Healing One, save my soul;
deliver me for the sake of your faithful love.
⁵ For in death there is no remembrance of you.
In Sheol who can praise you?
⁶ I am weary with my sighing;
every night I flood my bed;
with my tears, my couch, I deluge.
⁷ My vision narrows from anger;
worn down because of all my foes.
⁸ Turn from me, all you workers of iniquity,
for the God who is Majesty hears the sound of my weeping.
⁹ The Glorious One has heard my petition;
the God Who Dwells Above the Cherubim accepts my prayer.
¹⁰ All my enemies shall be put to shame and thrown into a very great panic;
they shall turn back and be put to shame in a moment.

Romans 8:31 What then shall we say about these things? If God is for us, who is against us? ³² God is the one who did not spare the very Child of God, but rather for all of us, handed the Messiah over. Will not God—with Christ—also give us everything else? ³³ Who then will bring any charge against the elect of God? God is the one who justifies. ³⁴ Who will condemn? It is Christ Jesus, the one who died, moreover the one who was raised and who is at the right hand of God, who intercedes for us. ³⁵ Who will separate us from the love of Christ? Will affliction, or distress, or persecution, or famine, or nakedness, or peril, or sword? ³⁶ As it is written,

> *"For your sake we are being killed all day long;*
> *we are accounted as sheep to be slaughtered."*

³⁷ No, in all these things we are completely victorious through the one who loved us. ³⁸ For I am convinced that neither death, nor life, nor angels, nor powers-that-be, nor things that are, nor things that will be, nor powers, ³⁹ nor height, nor depth, nor anything else in all creation, will be able to separate us from the love of God in Christ Jesus our Redeemer.

Luke 18:18 Now a certain ruler asked Jesus, "Good Teacher, what must I do to inherit eternal life?" ¹⁹ And Jesus said to the ruler, "Why do you call me good? No one is good but God alone. ²⁰ The commandments you know:

> *You shall not commit adultery;*
> *You shall not murder;*
> *You shall not steal;*
> *You shall not bear false witness;*
> *Honor your mother and father."*

²¹ Now the ruler replied, "All these have I kept from youth." ²² Yet when Jesus heard this, he said to the ruler, "Still one thing is lacking. Sell all that you own and distribute it to the poor and you will have treasure in the heavens; then come, follow me." ²³ But hearing this the ruler became sad being extremely wealthy. ²⁴ Then looking at the ruler [being full of sorrow] Jesus said, "How hard it is for those who have riches to enter the majesty of God! ²⁵ Indeed, it is easier for a camel to go through the eye of a needle than for someone who is wealthy to enter the majesty of God."

²⁶ Now the women and men who heard it said, "Then who can be saved?" ²⁷ But Jesus said, "What is impossible for the woman-born is possible for God." ²⁸ Then Peter said, "Look here! We have left our homes and followed you." ²⁹ And Jesus said to them, "Truly I tell you, there is no one who has left house or wife or kinfolk or parents or children, for the sake of the majesty of God, ³⁰ who will not get back very much more in this age and in the age to come, eternal life."

PROCLAMATION

Text Notes

Acts 1 begins by summarizing Jesus's ministry in Luke through instructions given to the apostles in verses 1–3. In the following verses, the "they" and "them" seem to refer to a larger group than the disciples, which becomes clear by verse 14, setting the stage for Pentecost in chapter 2. As in Luke, "disciples" should be presumed to be gender-inclusive unless there is specific limiting language, even though individual and named women appear much more infrequently in Acts than in Luke. In Acts 1:12, "a sabbath's day journey" indicates the amount of walking one could do on Sabbath; across time, the distance has ranged from one-third to two-thirds of a mile with variables such as whether one is pasturing animals and whether one is still in a city (determined by how far apart are the houses). It is certainly possible that the sisters of Jesus were present with his male siblings in verse 14; the grammar allows for inclusion.

In Judith 8:8, "revere" articulates her experience of God. In both Hebrew and Greek, the relevant vocabulary encompasses both reverence and the more common translation, "fear." "Reverence" more fully articulates the nature of God-human relationships in and out of the scriptures. The *habra* in verse 10 is an enslaved person with special status.

Romans 8:36 quotes Psalm 44:22. The familiar martial language "more than conquerors" found in NRSV and KJV is not required by the text of verse 37; the primary meaning is victorious to the point of a rout. Given the harm of militarized Christianity, I follow the Peshitta and CEB in preserving "victorious" for *hupernikomen*. Rulers and their domains, *archai*, the latter the "principalities" of the Peshitta and KJV, are encompassed in the "powers-that-be" of verse 38.

Luke 18:20 quotes a section of the Ten Commandments that is common to both iterations, Exodus 20:12–16 and Deuteronomy 5:16–20. The language about Jesus being "full of sorrow" in verse 23 does not appear in all manuscripts. Verse 29 addresses the abandonment of 1) wives—but not husbands, 2) parents (using a gender-inclusive term), and 3) kinfolk (using a term that can mean siblings, male siblings, or close relatives) for the sake of the gospel. The women who followed Jesus either had husbands in tow or were apparently not worried about leaving their spouses behind.

Preaching Prompts

Property, possessions, and patrimony, oh my! We are physical beings in a material world (thank you, Madonna) with material concerns. Neither our materiality nor our material needs are bad or wrong, but when they become our sole priority, our souls are imperiled. In the first lesson, the disciples of Jesus are still looking for the majesty of God in the wrong place. They are focused on restoring the ancient majesty of the nation-state of Israel rather than what it means that with the life, death, and resurrection of Jesus, the majesty of God has come to these material bodies. While Jesus was concerned about what occupation does to human persons, he was not invested in the political disposition of the land of Israel. That focus does not suggest that we should be disinterested in the fate of nations, especially those under occupation; rather, our focus is to be on the persons harmed by occupation and those who commit atrocities in the name of a nation-state or political vision.

The land that became known as "Israel" was inhabited Canaanite land claimed by Israel in the name of their God, who has become our God. Even as religious readers, it is incumbent upon us to acknowledge that a divine claim justifying occupation is a story that must be interrogated ethically, including and most importantly, from the perspective of the occupied people. The essay "Canaanites, Cowboys, and Indians" by Robert Allen Warrior is a great help in this regard. (The 1989 essay has been republished in a number of venues, including *Native and Christian: Indigenous Voices on Religious Identity in the United States and Canada* [New York: Routledge, 1996]). However, as an Israelite scriptural anthology, the scriptures focus exclusively on the injustices experienced by Israel when it was subject to enslavement, occupation, and colonization by a roster of nation-states and empires, including Egypt, Assyria, Babylonia, Greece, Persia, and Rome.

The story of Judith is set against the tyranny of the Assyrian Empire. Judith has an abundance of material possessions and a legendary patrimony but is a model of piety even in the most dangerous and desperate times. Her outrage that her leaders had promised to hand over the land of her ancestors was not rooted in a desire to hold onto her land and possessions but rather the audacity of her city leaders to put temporal limits on God to deliver them within five days or else. In this way, Judith became both a model of piety and an example of a wealthy person who could indeed get a camel through the eye of a rhetorical needle.

The psalm could well be one that Judith prayed (should the timelines have aligned). But Judith has her own psalm (Judith, ch. 16; unlike the vast majority of other biblical women, Judith has a torrent of words preserved in the canon). The psalmist has no regard for possessions, property, or patrimony. They are concerned for their fragile mortal life. And in that concern, turn to the Author of Life. The psalm is, as the whole of the scriptures, occupation literature with enemies of one sort or another at hand.

In the Epistle, the nascent church is under Roman occupation. In this reading, material possessions are far from mind because survival, individual and collective, is at stake. As in the psalm and in the theology of Judith, God is the only recourse for liberation and salvation, which, in the theology of the First Testament world, are the same thing.

In the Gospel, Jesus rejects consumerism, if not capitalism, with something that looks a whole lot like socialism. And at the same time he acknowledges the importance of the items and persons we treasure, the very real losses incumbent upon following him. In this teaching, the vision of heaven he presents is one in which those losses will be restored. All of these lessons call us to identify our values and assess what it is and who it is we treasure.

THIRD SUNDAY OF EASTER

Acts 8:1–12 (or Judith 9:1–14); Psalm 74:1–12;
Ephesians 6:10–18; Luke 12:49–53

Acts 8:1 Now Saul approved of [the mob of men] killing Stephen. There began that day a great persecution against the church in Jerusalem; everyone was scattered throughout the countryside of Judea and Samaria except the apostles. ² Devout men buried Stephen and they made a great lamentation over him. ³ But Saul was razing the church from house to house, going in and dragging off women and men; he handed them over to prison. ⁴ Now the women and men who were indeed scattered went around proclaiming the word.

⁵ So Philip went down to the city of Samaria proclaiming the Messiah to them. ⁶ Now the crowds of women and men as one paid heed to what was said by Philip, hearing and

seeing the signs that he did. ⁷ For those who had unclean spirits were crying out with great shrieks and they came out of many who were possessed, and many others who were paralyzed or lame were healed. ⁸ So there was great joy in that city.

⁹ Now a certain man named Simon had previously—in the city—been practicing magic and he amazed the people of Samaria, saying that he was someone great. ¹⁰ Everyone from the least to the greatest paid heed to him, saying, "This is the power of God that is called Great." ¹¹ Now they paid him heed because for a long time with his magic he had amazed them. ¹² And when they believed Philip proclaiming the good news about the reign of God and the name of Jesus Christ, they were baptized, both women and men.

Judith 9:1 Now Judith fell on her face, put ashes on her head, and stripped off the sackcloth she was wearing, and just as was being offered, in the house of God in Jerusalem, the evening incense, Judith cried out to the Most High with a loud voice and said:

² Holy God of my ancestor Simeon, to whom you gave in hand a sword for revenge on those foreigners who forced open a virgin's womb for defilement and stripped naked her thigh for shame and desecrated her womb into a disgrace. . . . For you said, "It shall not be done!" Yet they did it. ³ In return you gave up their rulers for slaughter and their bed—which was ashamed of their deceitfulness, was itself deceived—for blood, and you struck down slaves with sovereigns and sovereigns on their seats. ⁴ You gave up their wives for booty and their daughters to captivity and all their booty to be divided among your beloved sons who were zealous with zeal for you and found detestable the pollution of their blood and called on you, the One Who Helps. O God, my God, hear me also, a widow!

⁵ You indeed have done the former things and those to come; those now at hand and those yet to come you conceived. ⁶ And the things you devised presented themselves and said, 'Look! Here we are!' For all your ways stand ready and your judgment is done through foreknowledge.

⁷ Look! For the Assyrians greatly multiplied in power, exalted themselves through horse and rider, boasting in the might of their foot soldiers and trusting in shield and spear, and bow and sling, and do not know you are the Holy One who crushes wars. ⁸ Holy is your Name. Smite their strength with your power and shatter their might in your wrath; for they intend to desecrate your sanctuary and to pollute the tabernacle, the resting place of your glorious Name, and to strike off with iron the horns of your altar. ⁹ Look at their insolence and send your wrath upon their heads. Give my widow's hand strength for what I have conceived. ¹⁰ Strike down the slave through the deceit of my lips and even the ruler, the ruler with his attendant; crush their uprising with a feminine hand.

¹¹ For your might is not in numbers, nor your sovereignty in the strong; but you are the God of those held of no account, helper of the lowly, protector of the vulnerable, defender of those who have despaired, savior of those without hope. ¹² Yea! Yea! God of my ancestor, God of the heritage of Israel, Sovereign of the heavens and earth, Creator of the waters,

Majesty of all your creation, hearken to my prayer! [13] Grant that my word and deceitfulness yield trauma wounds and whipping stripes on those who, against your covenant and against your sacred house and against Mount Zion and against the house your children possess, have devised cruelty. [14] And as for the whole of your nation and every tribe, grant them the knowledge to know that you are God, the God of all power and might, and that there is no one who protects the people of Israel other than you!"

Psalm 74:1–12

1. Why God, do you reject for all time;
   your rage smoke against the sheep of your pasture?
2. Remember your congregation you acquired before time,
   that you redeemed to be the tribe of your heritage;
   Mount Zion, where you came to dwell upon it.
3. Lift up your steps to the perpetual ruins;
   every kind of evil has the enemy done in the sanctuary.
4. Your foes have roared within your meeting-place;
   they set their emblems there.
5. It was perceived like when they go up
   upon a tangle of trees with axes.
6. And then its carved work altogether,
   with hatchets and hammers, they smote it.
7. They set your sanctuary on fire;
   they brought it to the ground,
   defiling the dwelling place of your Name.
8. They said within their hearts, "We will crush them";
   they burned all the meeting-places of God in the land.
9. Our emblems we no longer see;
   there is no longer any prophet [woman or man],
   and there is no one among us who knows how long.
10. How long, God, is the adversary to taunt?
    Is the enemy to defame your name for all time?
11. Why do you hold back your hand;
    your right hand, unavailable, in your bosom?
12. Yet God my Sovereign is from before time,
    working salvation in the midst of the earth.

Ephesians 6:10 From this point on, be strengthened in the Messiah and in the power of Christ's strength. [11] Put on the whole armor of God, so that you may be able to stand against the scheming of the devil. [12] For our struggle is not against enemies of blood and flesh, but against the rulers, against the authorities, against the cosmic powers of this present darkness, against the spiritual forces of evil in the heavenly places. [13] Therefore take up the whole armor of God, so that you may be able to resist on that day of evil, and having prepared in every way, to stand firm. ¹⁴ Stand therefore with the belt of truth wrapped around your waist and put on the breastplate of righteousness. ¹⁵ Put on your feet preparation to proclaim the gospel of peace. ¹⁶ In everything, take the shield of faith with which you will be able to quench all the flaming arrows of the evil one. ¹⁷ And take the helmet of salvation and the sword of the Spirit, which is the word of God. ¹⁸ With every prayer and supplication, at all times, pray in the Spirit. And for this, keep awake at all times persevering in supplication for all the saints.

Luke 12:49 "I have come to cast fire upon the earth and I would that it were already blazing! ⁵⁰ Now, I have a baptism with which to be baptized and how much pressure is closing in until it is completed! ⁵¹ Do you all think that I have come to bring peace to the earth? No, I tell you, (it is) the contrary, division! ⁵² From now on five in one home will be divided, three against two and two against three. ⁵³ They will be divided:

> father against son
> and *son against father*,
> mother against daughter
> and *daughter against mother*,
> mother-in-law against her daughter-in-law
> and *daughter-in-law against mother-in-law*."

PROCLAMATION
Text Notes

Acts 7:2 indicates that only men were the addressees of Stephen's discourse, where they are identified as "brothers and fathers." Given the setting of the scene before "the council (the Sanhedrin)" in 6:12 and the testimony of "witnesses" in 6:13—a category exclusive of women at that time—it does not seem appropriate to infer women as active participants. Additionally, Acts 8:2 limits those who buried Stephen to men.

Judith's highly emotional prayer in chapter 9 is a series of long phrases that do not always culminate in complete sentences. The invocation of Simeon in verse 2 harkens back to the rape of Dinah bat Leah in Genesis 34:1–31: In Genesis 34:25, Simeon ben Leah (Judith's ancestor according to her genealogy in 8:1), and Levi ben Leah killed all of the men and older boys of Shechem in retribution for their prince raping their sister Dinah, after tricking them into covenanting with God by circumcision and attacking them when they were unmanned. Simeon and Levi are the "beloved" sons of Judith 9:2. In this case, the inclusive translation "children" in NRSV, NRSVue, and CEB is misleading; the *sons* of Jacob qua Israel retaliate. In Judith's recitation of her family's ancestral story in her prayer, she refers to Levi and Simeon at a minimum, and all of her brothers potentially, committing retributive rapes for the sake of Dinah's despoiled honor, asserting God hands over women (and girls?) for that purpose. (See Carey A. Moore, *Judith*, Anchor Bible Commentary, p. 191.) Thus, Judith's telling of her family history, as written and edited by an unknown—likely male—hand, preserved *lex talionis* elements omitted in the equally heavily edited Genesis account.

In Judith 9:3, my translation, "slaves with sovereigns and sovereigns on their seats," preserves the alliteration of the underlying text; however, the "seats" are actually "thrones." A preacher might say, "Paupers and princes and princes upon their perches." Judith uses the same verb, "desecrate," to describe the violation of women's bodies and the violation of God's sanctuary in verses 2 and 8. I have translated Judith's reference to the "God of [her] *patros*" as her "ancestor" rather than "father" since she invokes her ancestor Simeon in the beginning of her prayer, though it can mean either. In verse 13, Greek *trauma* and *molopa* both mean "wound"; I have supplied lexical context from the semantic range to differentiate them. The "whipping stripes" are the same as in Isaiah 53:5, "By his stripes we are healed."

God's "rage" in Psalm 74:1 is the divine "nose" complete with snorting smoke. The image of God as a bull runs deep among the peoples of ancient Israel and their surrounding nations. There is some perplexing grammar in the psalm. In verse 3, God is directed to "exalt" her steps. In verse 5, "being made known like/as going" was rendered as "it was perceived like when they go up." Similarly, God's right hand is "finished" or "completed," leading to a translation of "unavailable."

In Luke 12:50, the verb *sunecho* has a broad semantic range, including stress and pressure that surrounds and closes in causing distress; the verb lacks an object in the verse. Verse 53 cites and expands Micah 7:6.

Preaching Prompts

"In the midst of life we are in death" (Book of Common Prayer, p. 492). In this Easter season, when we celebrate the triumphs of life over death, these readings full of conflict, including horrific acts of violence, might seem to be out of place. Yet in the aftermath of the glorious resurrection of Jesus, the world remained and remains crucified and crucifying even as it is redeemed and being redeemed. The Acts lesson illustrates the bloody birth of the Church from waves of martyrdom adding to the bloodshed of continuing crucifixions. The alternative lesson in Judith presents a woman and a city under siege as part of a more than thousand-year continuing cycle of violence—in narrative time—painfully aware of the faith to which women were particularly vulnerable in war, rape. Her theology of retributive violence, like Saul's theology of violence in the name of and on behalf of God, are both theologies of death, and both continue to permeate the post-resurrection world in different ways. The psalmist, likely writing in the immediate aftermath of the destruction of the temple and concomitant violence against women and men and their children, cries out for God to respond to the horror she has seen with a "strong right hand," signifying an equally violent response. Ephesians draws on martial accoutrement to prepare the question to proclaim the gospel and resist the forces of evil that remain in the world in spite of the triumph of Easter. And in the Gospel, Jesus is *not* the One of Peace of our long acquaintance. Here, he prophesies the conflict that will follow his sojourn on earth, as so aptly illustrated in the Acts lesson. What are we to say to these things?

FOURTH SUNDAY OF EASTER

Acts 12:6–17 (or Judith 10:1–8); Psalm 69:1–3, 13–17, 30–34;
Philemon 1:1–2, 7–16; Luke 13:10–17

Acts 12:6 Now when Simon Peter was about to be handed over to Herod, on that night he was sleeping between two soldiers, bound with two chains with guards in front of the door securing over the prison. ⁷ And suddenly an angel of the Most High stood over Peter! And a light shone in the cell and the angel struck Simon's side and awaken him and said to him, "Get up quickly!" Then the chains fell from his hands. ⁸ And the angel said to him, "Get dressed and put on your sandals." And he did. Next the angel again said to him, "Put on your clothes and follow me." ⁹ So Simon went out and followed the angel and did not know that what the angel had done was real; he thought he was seeing a vision. ¹⁰ Then they passed the first guard, then the second; they came to the iron gate which all on its own opened to them. And they went out and passed one street and suddenly the angel left him. ¹¹ Then Peter came to himself, saying, "Now I know that the Most High really sent their angel and delivered me from the hand of Herod the king, and from what the people of Judea were expecting." ¹² Realizing this, he went to the house of Mary, the mother of John called Mark, where a sufficiently large number [of believers, sisters and brothers] were assembled there and praying. ¹³ Now he knocked at the door of the courtyard and an enslaved young woman named Rhoda came to reply to him. ¹⁴ And recognizing Peter's voice, in her joy, she did not open the gate; rather, she ran back and announced that Peter was standing at the gate of the courtyard. ¹⁵ Now they said to her, "You are insane!" But she firmly maintained that it was so. Then they said to her, "It is his angel." ¹⁶ Now Peter continued knocking at the gate and opening [the gate] they saw him and were amazed. ¹⁷ Then signaling to them with his hand to be still, he described to them in detail how the Most High brought him out from the prison. And he said to them, "Tell these things to James and to the sisters and brothers." And he left and went to another place.

Judith 10:1 And it came to pass, that Judith ceased crying out to the God of Israel and completed all these words. ² And she rose from falling prostrate and summoned her favorite slave-woman and went down into the house where she stayed on Sabbath days and on her feast days. ³ Then Judith removed the sackcloth which she had put on and stripped off the garments of her widowhood, and she bathed her body with water and anointed herself with thick ointment, and combed the hairs of her head and placed a headdress upon it and put on the garments of her gladness which she had clothed herself in the days of the life of her husband Manasseh. ⁴ Then she chose sandals for her feet and put on anklets and bracelets and rings and earrings and the whole constellation of her ornaments, and she adorned herself for enticing the eyes of men, all who would see her. ⁵ And she gave her favored slave-woman a leather bag of wine and a jar of oil and she filled a bag with barley meal and fig cake and fine bread, and she wrapped all of her vessels and placed them upon her [slave-woman].

⁶ So they went out to the gate of the city of Bethulia and they came upon Uzziah and the elders of the city, Chabris and Charmis. ⁷ When they saw her and her face was transformed and her attire altered, they marveled at her beauty, greatly and repeatedly, and said to her: ⁸ "May the God of our mothers and fathers grant you be the means of grace and may you accomplish your mission, for the pride of the daughters and sons of Israel and the exaltation of Jerusalem."

Psalm 69:1–3, 13–17, 30–34

¹ Save me, God,
for the waters have come to my throat.
² I sink in deep mire,
there is no foothold;
I come into deep waters,
and the flood overwhelms me.
³ I am weary with my crying;
my throat is parched.
My eyes fail,
waiting for my God.
¹³ Yet I make my prayer to you, the Wisdom of the Ages.
At a favorable time,
God, in the wealth of your faithful love, answer me,
with your certain salvation.
¹⁴ Rescue me from the mire,
and let me not be sunk;
let me be delivered from my enemies
and from the deep waters.
¹⁵ Let not the flood waters overwhelm me,
let not the Deep swallow me up;
let not the Pit close its mouth over me.
¹⁶ Answer me, Gracious God, for your faithful love is good;
according to the wealth of your maternal love, turn to me.
¹⁷ Do not hide your face from your slave,
for I am in distress; hurry to answer me.
³⁰ I will praise the name of God with song;
I will magnify her with thanksgiving.

³¹ This will please the CREATOR OF ALL more than an ox
or a bull with horns and hoofs.
³² Let the oppressed see it and be glad;
you who seek God, let your hearts flourish.
³³ For the FAITHFUL GOD hears the needy,
and those who belong to her and are imprisoned,
she does not despise.
³⁴ Let the heavens and earth praise her,
the seas and everything that moves in them.

Philemon 1 Paul, a prisoner of Jesus the Messiah and Timothy our brother:

To Philemon our beloved and our coworker, ² and to Apphia our sister, to Archippus our comrade in arms, and to the church in your house:

⁷ Much joy and encouragement have I from your love, because the beating hearts of the saints have been refreshed through you, my brother. ⁸ Therefore, I have great freedom in the Messiah to command you in what is proper. ⁹ For the sake of love would I rather petition; this I, Paul, do as an elder and now also as a prisoner of Jesus the Messiah. ¹⁰ I am appealing to you for my child whom I birthed during my imprisonment, Onesimus. ¹¹ Formerly to you he was useless, but now, to you and to me he is useful. ¹² I am sending him to you, he who is my own heartbeat. ¹³ I wanted to hold him with me in your place so that he might serve me during my imprisonment for the gospel. ¹⁴ However, without your consent I would do nothing so that your good work would not be forced rather, voluntary. ¹⁵ Perhaps for this reason he removed himself from you for some time that for all time you would then have him. ¹⁶ No longer as a slave but more than a slave—a brother beloved—especially to me but even more to you, both in the flesh and in the Redeemer.

Luke 13:10 Now Jesus was teaching in one of the synagogues on the Sabbath. ¹¹ And suddenly there was a woman who had a spirit of infirmity that for eighteen years had crippled her; she was bent over and was not able to stand up completely. ¹² Now when Jesus saw her, he called out and said, "Woman, you are set free from your infirmity." ¹³ Then he laid his hands on her and immediately she stood up straight and began glorifying God. ¹⁴ But the leader of the synagogue, being indignant because it was on the Sabbath that Jesus had cured, said to the crowd of women, men and children, "There are six days on which one ought work; so come on those and be healed and not on the Sabbath day." ¹⁵ But the Messiah answered him and said, "Hypocrites! Each of you, do you not on the Sabbath untie your ox or donkey from the manger and lead it to drink? ¹⁶ And ought not this woman, a daughter of Abraham [and Sarah] whom Satan bound—Look!—for eighteen long years, ought she not be set free from this bondage on the Sabbath day?" ¹⁷ When Jesus said this, all those who opposed him were put to shame and the entire crowd rejoiced at all the glorious things being done by him.

PROCLAMATION

Text Notes

Acts 12:12 describes the praying assembly as *hikanos*, "a sufficient number," without specifying a specific sufficient number of *who* or *what*. (There is no indication of what a sufficient number of praying persons would be). I have supplied options for articulating the praying congregation; the presence of female disciples should be presumed.

Note that the house is Mary's, with no mention of a husband. While widowhood might be presumed, it is also the case that women could own property outright. By whatever means, home ownership marks Mary as wealthy; she uses her wealth, including her home, to support the burgeoning Jesus movement. She is also a slave owner; owning human beings as chattel was not yet considered to be at odds with following Jesus. This fact should not be glossed over in exegesis or preaching. Neither should the literary use of Rhoda as the butt of the theological joke in the chapter, as well-argued by Margaret Aymer in the *Women's Bible Commentary* (Louisville: Westminster John Knox Press, 2012), 543–544.

The chapter also grants insights into the angelology of the period; they apparently believed—at least for the moment—that a person's angel resembled them. Now, what is meant by "angel" is unclear. In the Common English Bible, it is "guardian angel" (though it is unclear why a person's guardian angel would resemble them). The public domain translation of the Peshitta by James Murdock uses "ghost," which might be the appropriate alternate understanding.

Judith's *mitra* headdress in 10:3 reflects Greek social and cultural expectations for women during the Hellenistic period, evoked by the "headband" in the CEB. The word itself is used for a variety of headdresses, from those of Israelite priests to Persian monarchs; the generic "headdress" is preferable to the "tiara" of both editions of the NRSV. The narrator is almost at a loss for Judith's beauty in verse 7; they "marveled at her beauty, greatly and repeatedly." In verse 8, *pateron* can be parents or fathers; I have chosen the most inclusive option, specifying "mothers" and, similarly, "daughters" in the same verse. Following the NETS, the blessing upon Judith in verse 8 is that she be *for* grace rather than the traditional "grant her grace." Note: Some translations append the first words of verse 9 to the end of verse 8.

The Deep and the Pit In Psalm 69:15 are legendary sites associated with death, in some ways parallel to Sheol. In verse 16, God's maternal love is love that emanates from and shares the same root as the womb.

In Philemon 1:1, the language of "sibling" is reserved for leaders in the church, Brother Timothy and Sister Apphia—but not the addressee, Philemon—rather than for the community of believers as in other discourses. The "beating hearts" of verse 7 refer to the inward parts, womb, and other internal organs such as the bowels and signify a locus for emotion; see also the "heartbeat" of verse 12. Additionally, the language of "heartbeat" is used by some black women to refer to children they have birthed, and Paul will use birthing and begetting language and refer to Onesimus as his "child" in verse 10. Paul's parentage of Onesimus is articulated with *egennesa*, to biologically parent or become a parental figure or, possibly, in this case—bring someone into Christ through baptism. Womanist New Testament scholars use the language of birthing here: Mitzi Smith in the *Women's Bible Commentary,* 3rd ed. (Louisville: Westminster/John Knox, 2012), 606, and Angela Parker in her essay, "You Cannot Pay Back What You Have Never Owned: A Conversation on Reparations and Paul's Letter to Philemon" in *Reparations and the Theological Disciplines: Prophetic Voices for Remembrance, Reckoning, and Repair.* Edited by Michael Barram, Drew G. I. Hart, Gimbiya Kettering, and Michael J. Rhodes. (Lexington Books: Lanham, 2023). 91-106.

In identifying himself as an "elder," Paul is evoking both his age and his status; the "old man" of NRSV, NRSVue, and CEB does not capture the full sense. In verse 11, the utility of Onesimus should be understood to include his sexual utility. Indeed, the language of "usefulness," a pun on his name, might more easily be recognized as sexual according to Alicia J. Batten in the *Wisdom Commentary* volume on Philemon (Collegeville, MN: Liturgical Press), p. 246; see also Joseph Marchal, "The Usefulness of an Onesimus: The Sexual Use of Slaves and Paul's Letter to Philemon," *JBL* 130 (2011): 749–770. There is no small irony that Paul wants Onesimus to serve him instead of his master/owner; the service is articulated with the *diakone*, familiar to many from "diaconal" service. There is no suggestion of freeing Onesimus to his own choices. In verse 15, the passive verb can mean that Onesimus was (rhetorically) removed from Philemon or that he removed himself.

Preaching Prompts

This fourth Sunday of Easter, the blooms from Easter Sunday are drooping and fading. The hallelujahs continue as we focus on the transformation wrought by the resurrection of Jesus. But we are also in a world that continues to oppress and occupy people based on their core identity and one that continues to lynch radicals and revolutionaries who threaten their power and its currency, fear. In each of these readings, someone confronts or is confronted by a bastion of power, and there is an opportunity for liberation of self or other. In each, the response of characters who represent the community of God's beloved respond to that power differently, inviting us to consider our response and whether we, as the church, are truly in the business of liberation. The psalm could be prayed by Judith or Peter or Onesimus, or the woman living with a crippling condition. It is a petition to the God who saves and delivers.

In the first lesson, Peter is in bondage comprised of literal chains and a physical prison. They prove no match to the power of the God who is the author of freedom. In the same lesson, Rhoda is held in the bondage of slavery. She is held in the bondage of slavery by Mary, who might be considered a pastor in the new-born post-resurrection Jesus movement, perhaps the head of the Church that meets in her home. Rhoda's testimony is not believed. She is woman and enslaved, two categories of human persons who will continue to be held in different kinds of societal, cultural, and legal bondage with very real physical consequences, including violence and death. Rhoda is mocked; though she is proved right first, she is made the butt of a joke. Peter is free, but Rhoda remains enslaved in a Christian household. The lack of a repudiation of human trafficking in enslavement by Jesus remains an aching wound for some.

In the alternate first lesson, Judith's people are under occupation. She is free, a wealthy widow with sufficient beauty to weaponize. She will use gender expectations to her advantage; her ability to do so is largely because of her class status and because of the privilege that comes along with beauty. Though she is known for her piety, once she dresses herself in keeping with the beauty norms of her society, the male characters see and engage her differently. In her continuing story, she will turn the male gaze against her would-be seducer (at best, but the threat of rape is always present). Even with wealth and beauty and the freedom to travel, she is still a vulnerable member of an oppressed class. Gender-based assumptions and expectations remain a kind of bondage.

Onesimus and Rhoda were persons who were valued for their "usefulness" and, as demonstrated in the letter to Philemon, were treated as objects, bought and traded and retained for personal use. Paul wrote not for the liberty of Onesimus but that he be made available to him, free in name only. *Nota Bene*: Onesimus occurs in the readings for the following Sunday.

The miracle in the Gospel reading is about more than the power of Jesus to deliver, save, heal, redeem, and liberate. It is also about societal attitudes that cultivate indifference to some of the kinds of bondage under which people live. We see that with enslavement and the treatment of women throughout the canons of scripture. It is Eastertide, and though the stone has been rolled away, we are not yet all free. So many of the examples in this lesson turn on gender assumptions and expectations; it would be useful to talk about the person who lives under oppression in our midst because of their gender identity and appearance, some of whom remain in mortal peril.

FIFTH SUNDAY OF EASTER

*Acts 16:13–22, 40 (or Judith 13:1–16); Psalm 102:17–21, 25–28;
Colossians 4:10–17; Luke 15:1–10*

Acts 16:13 On the day of the sabbath we went out the gate by the river, where we thought there was a place of prayer; and we sat down and spoke to the women who gathered there. [14] Now a certain woman named Lydia, a merchant of purple cloth from the city of Thyatira, a worshiper of God, was listening to us. The Messiah opened her heart to listen eagerly to what was said by Paul. [15] As she was baptized along with her household, she urged us, saying, "If you have judged me to be faithful to Christ, come and stay at my home." And she persuaded us.

[16] One day, as we were going to the place of prayer, we met an enslaved girl who had a spirit of divination and brought her masters a great deal of money by fortune-telling. [17] While she followed after Paul and us, she cried out, "These persons are slaves of the Most High God, who proclaim to you a way of salvation." [18] This she did for many days. But it bothered Paul, who turned and said to the spirit, "I order you in the name of Jesus Christ to come out of her." And it came out that hour.

[19] Now when her masters saw that their hope of financial gain was gone, they seized Paul and Silas and into the marketplace they dragged them before the authorities. [20] When they had brought them before the magistrates, they said, "These persons are disturbing our city; they are Judeans [21] and are preaching traditions that are not right for us to follow as Romans." [22] The crowd joined against them and the magistrates had them stripped of their clothing and ordered them to be beaten with batons.

[40] Now when they came out from the prison, they entered the house of Lydia and when they saw and encouraged the sisters and brothers there, they left.

Judith 13:1 Now when evening came, the king's slaves hastened to leave. And Bagoas secured the tent from the outside and shut out those present from the presence of his lord and they went to their beds, for they were all weary from the drinking that was going on for so long. [2] Judith was alone in the tent, but Holofernes collapsed upon his bed because of the pouring out of [so much] wine. [3] Then Judith had told her slave-girl to stand outside the bedchamber and to wait for her to come out, as she did other days; for she said she would go out for her prayer. She spoke to Bagoas these same words. [4] So everyone went out beyond sight, and no one was left in the bedchamber, either small or great. Then Judith, standing beside his bed, said in her heart, "Holy God of all power, look with care in this hour on the work of my hands for the exaltation of Jerusalem. [5] Now is the time to help your heritage and to carry out my intention to destroy the enemies who have risen up against us."

[6] And she came to the bedpost at Holofernes's head and took down his sword from there. [7] Then she came toward his bed, caught the hair of his head, and said, "Give me strength today, Holy God of Israel!" [8] And she struck his neck twice with all her might, and

cut off his head. ⁹ Then she rolled his body off the bed and snatched the canopy from the post. A little later she went out and gave Holofernes's head to her slave-girl, ¹⁰ who placed it in her food bag. Then the two women went out together, according to their custom at the time for prayer. And they passed through the encampment, circled the valley, and went up the mountain to Bethulia, and came to its gates. ¹¹ Then, from a distance, Judith called out to the guards at the gates, "Open! Open the gate! God, our God, is with us, working deeds of power in Israel and might against our enemies, as God has done today!"

¹² And it happened when the men of her town heard her voice, they rushed to come down to the gate of the city and summoned the elders of the city. ¹³ And they all ran together, from small to great, for it was extraordinary to them that she returned. And they opened the gate and welcomed the women and they lit a fire to provide light and gathered around the women. ¹⁴ Then Judith said to them with a loud voice, "Hallelujah! Hallelujah! Praise God, who did not withdraw mercy from the house of Israel, but has broken our enemies by my hand this night!"

¹⁵ Then, taking the head from the bag, showing it, she said to them, "See here! The head of Holofernes, the head general of the Assyrian army, and see now! The canopy on which he was lying in his drunkenness, and the Most High struck him down with a feminine hand. ¹⁶ And as the Eternal One lives, who kept me on my way in which I went, what deceived him was my face—to his utter ruin—and that he committed no sin with me, to defile or shame me."

Psalm 102:17–21, 25–28

¹⁷ God regards the prayer of the destitute,
and she does not despise their prayer.
¹⁸ Let this be engraved for a generation to come,
so that a people yet unborn may praise the WISDOM OF THE AGES:
¹⁹ that she looked down from her holy height,
from heaven the CREATOR OF ALL beheld the earth,
²⁰ to hear the groaning of the prisoner,
to set free those who were condemned to die;
²¹ so that the Name of the HOLY GOD may be recounted in Zion,
and her praise in Jerusalem.
²⁵ In the time before time you laid the foundation of the earth,
and the heavens are the work of your hands.
²⁶ They shall perish, yet you shall abide,
and all of them will all wear out like a garment.
like clothing you change them and they pass away.
²⁷ Yet you are the One and your years will not end.
²⁸ The daughters and sons of your slaves shall be settled,
and their offspring shall be established in your presence.

Colossians 4:10 Aristarchus my fellow prisoner greets you all, so too Mark the cousin of Barnabas, about whom you have received instructions; if he comes to you, welcome him. [11] And Jesus who is called Justus [greets you]. These of the circumcised are my only coworkers for the realm of God, and they have been a comfort to me. [12] Epaphras, who is one of you, a slave of the Messiah Jesus, greets you all. He is always fighting for you all in his prayers, so that you may stand mature and fully assured in everything that is the will of God. [13] For I testify for him that he has [done] much hard labor for you all and for those in Laodicea and in Hierapolis. [14] Luke, the beloved physician, and Demas greet you. [15] Give my greetings to the sisters and brothers in Laodicea, and to Nympha and the church in her house. [16] And when this has been read among you all, make it so that it is read in the Laodicean church; and you all read the one from Laodicea. [17] And say to Archippus, "See that the ministry you have received in the Messiah, that you fulfill it."

Luke 15:1 Now it happened that all the tax collectors and sinners were coming near to listen to Jesus. [2] And the Pharisees and the biblical scholars were grumbling and saying, "This one welcomes sinners and dines with them." [3] Then Jesus spoke to them telling this parable, saying: [4] "Which mother's child among you having a hundred sheep and losing one of them does not leave the ninety-nine in the wilderness and go after the one that is lost until you find it? [5] And finding it, lay it on your shoulders and rejoice? [6] And when you come back to your home, you call together your friends and neighbors, saying to them, 'Rejoice with me because I have found my lost sheep.' [7] I say to you all, in the same way, there will be more joy in heaven over one sinner who repents than over ninety-nine righteous somebodies who have no need for repentance. [8] Or, what woman having ten silver drachma coins [worth ten days wages], if she loses one of them does not light a lamp, sweep the house, and search until she finds it? [9] Then finding it, she calls together her friends and neighbors, saying, 'Rejoice with me because for I have found the coin that I lost.' [10] In the same way I tell you, there is joy in the presence of the angels of God over one sinner who repents."

PROCLAMATION

Text Notes

Where grammatically and rhetorically possible, I translate the language of "slavery" to reflect what was done to persons—being enslaved—rather than identify them by their state (as in Acts 16:16) and preserve "slave" in the text when that would have been what was said and meant in context. The divining spirit is called a "python," a reference to the python guarding the Delphi Oracle which then became a euphemism for all sorts of vocal performances, including divination and ventriloquism. The word translated as "fortune-telling" can also be translated as "divination" or "prophecy."

In Acts 16:22, Paul and Silas are publicly stripped to humiliate them as well as facilitate their flogging. Forcible stripping is a personal violation and sexually violent; imagine the crowd catcalling and hooting, mocking whatever of their anatomy was revealed.

"Engrave" in verse 18 of the psalm reflects the dual meanings of the root, "to write" and "to cut."

The presence of "Nympha and the church in her house," attested in what is the oldest, most authoritative manuscript that includes the passage, raised questions for early curators of the scriptures, which were not resolved by the change of her name to a male form in later manuscripts, including the *Textus Receptus* used for the KJV where she has been masculinized. The purported masculine form, *Nymphas*, does not exist in the historical or literary record, while Nympha occurs some sixty times. (See Ross Kraemer's entry in *Women in Scripture: A Dictionary of Named and Unnamed Women in the Hebrew Bible, the Apocryphal/Deuterocanonical Books, and the New Testament*.) That Colossians also calls for submissive women/wives has led to further speculation, including that Nympha was a widow (see the *Wisdom Commentary* on Colossians by Cynthia Briggs Kittredge and Claire Miller Colombo).

Throughout this project, as in Luke 15:2, I use "biblical scholars" to designate the "scribes" of the rabbinic period, as the term "scribe" communicates a narrow understanding of these Torah scholars. In the double parable on losing and finding, I use the second person "you" rather than the third person found in the text. In verse 4, "mother's child" translates *anthropos*, "human/person."

Preaching Prompts

"Injustice anywhere is a threat to justice everywhere. We are caught in an inescapable network of mutuality, tied in a single garment of destiny. Whatever affects one directly, affects all indirectly."

—The Rev. Dr. Martin Luther King Jr., "Letter from a Birmingham Jail."

This week's readings demonstrate the imperfect liberation of the Jesus movement in antiquity and call us to examine our own imperfect liberation. As Dr. King taught us, we are not truly free if someone else is in bondage, under oppression, or in peril. The continuance of persons being held in bondage illustrates the ease of (tacitly) accepting societal structures in stratifications even while proclaiming a death-defying risen savior and liberator. Peter's bondage was unacceptable, and he was set free by a divine hand. Rhoda's bondage is background—we are not supposed to consider it as we celebrate Peter's freedom. A homiletic exercise might be to ask who is writing the stories we live and what and who are relegated to the background to be accepted with no further thought.

In the episode from Judith, there are enslaved persons held in bondage by the king, seen and unseen in the narrative. Judith is a wealthy woman who holds persons in bondage as well; indeed, enslaved persons were counted as well, along with livestock, crops, and land. Judith has a favored slave woman she trusted to manage her affairs. She is instrumental in Judith's plan to liberate her people, with no credit or praise. Judith and her people will be free, but the persons Judith holds in bondage will remain enslaved.

In the Epistle, the expanding Church is under harsh persecution, and Paul is imprisoned with other disciples. In this passage, the language of enslavement is theologized and used to describe one's relationship with God across the testaments. Free members of the community are greeted by name, including Nympha, a homeowner in whose home the Church meets for worship. In no case is a second person identified as the head of a house church when a congregation gathers in a person's home. As the Church in our world has moved to put an end to enslavement—including that which continues around the world and comparable exploitative practices here at home—the Church often fails to reproduce and maintain the women's leadership documented in our earliest texts.

In the Gospel, Jesus tells the same parable in two different ways: In the first, often more familiar parable of the lost sheep, the God figure is a male shepherd (though women and girls were also shepherds). In the second, the parable of the lost coin—often separated from the preceding parable as in RCL—a woman homeowner is the God figure. Just as enslavement should not be overlooked in other texts or as the social and cultural background of the scriptures, neither should the diversity of God's language present in the scriptures. Jesus uses feminine imagery for God here. (The cover of Year W of *A Women's Lectionary for the Whole Church*, illustrated by Pauline Williamson, portrays this parable.)

The psalm offers a portrait of a God who liberates those held in bondage without regard to class, caste, or stratification by the lived experience, theology, and hope of the psalmist. Each of the readings allows us to reconstruct the theological imagination (and its limitations) of our spiritual ancestors and the God of faith and experience. The task of the theologian and homiletician is to reconcile these different portraits of God with the one in whom we believe, and if we proclaim faith in the one who liberates from all bonds as easily as from death, then we have work to do extending and ensuring that liberation for all.

SIXTH SUNDAY OF EASTER

Acts 17:1–4, 10–12 (or Judith 15:8–13); Psalm 9:1–14, 18–20;
Titus 3:1–8; Luke 18:1–8

Acts 17:1 Paul and Silas had traveled through Amphipolis and Apollonia. They came to Thessalonica, where there was a Jewish synagogue. ² As was his custom, Paul went and on three sabbaths presented to them from the scriptures, ³ explaining and demonstrating it was necessary for the Messiah to suffer and to rise from the dead: "This is the Messiah, Jesus who I proclaim to you all." ⁴ Now, some of [those Jews] were persuaded and joined Paul and Silas, as did a great many of the devout Greeks and not a few of the prominent women.

¹⁰ Then, the sisters and brothers immediately that night sent Paul and Silas away to Beroea; when they arrived, they went to the Jewish synagogue. ¹¹ These [persons] were more high-born and open-minded than in Thessalonica; they received the word with great eagerness. Daily they examined the scriptures to see if these things were so. ¹² Thus many of them therefore believed, including highly respected Greek women and not just a few [Jewish] men.

Judith 15:8 Now Joakim the high priest and the council of the people of Israel residing in Jerusalem came in order to see the good things which the Most High had done for Israel and to see Judith and wish her well. ⁹ Now when they came to her, they blessed her, all with one accord and they said to her, "You are the exaltation of Jerusalem; you are the great pride of Israel; you are the great boast of our people. ¹⁰ You have done all these things by your hand; you have done good for Israel and God is well pleased over them. Be blessed before Shaddai [the Nurturing God], for all time." And all the people said: "May it be so." ¹¹ Then all the women, children, and men plundered the camp for thirty days and they gave Judith the tent of Holofernes and all the silverplate and the couches and the basins and all his furniture and she took them and placed them upon her mule, and she hitched her wagons and harnessed them upon them.

¹² And all the women of Israel gathered together so as to see her and they blessed her and some of them performed a dance for her, and she took olive branches wrapped in ivy in her hands and she gave them to the women who were with her. ¹³ And the women crowned themselves with olive [wreaths], she and those with her and she went before all the people in the dance leading all the women and every man of Israel armed, following along with wreaths and they were singing hymns aloud.

Psalm 9:1–14, 18–20

¹ I will give thanks to the GOD WHO SAVES with my whole heart;
I will tell of all your wonderful deeds.
² I will rejoice and I will exult in you;
I will sing praise to your Name, Most High.
³ When my enemies turned back,
they stumbled and perished before you.
⁴ For you have done justly for me;
you sit on the throne judging righteously.
⁵ You have rebuked the nations, you have destroyed the wicked;
you have erased their name for all time.
⁶ The enemy—they are finished—perpetual ruins;
[their] cities you have uprooted;
you have destroyed any remembrance of them.
⁷ GOD WHO IS MAJESTY sits enthroned forever,
she has established her throne for judgment.

⁸ She judges the world in righteousness;
    she judges the peoples with equity.
⁹ SHE WHO IS FAITHFUL is a stronghold for the oppressed,
    a stronghold in times of trouble.
¹⁰ They trust you, they who know your name,
    for you do not forsake those who seek you REDEEMING GOD.
¹¹ Sing praises to the HOLY ONE enthroned in Zion.
    Declare her deeds among the peoples.
¹³ Be gracious to me, GRACIOUS ONE.
    See what I suffer from those who hate me.
    You lift me up from the gates of death,
¹⁴ so that I may recount all your praises,
    and in the gates of Daughter Zion,
    rejoice in your salvation.
¹⁸ For the needy shall not always be forgotten,
    nor the hope of those oppressed by poverty perish for all time.
¹⁹ Rise up JUDGE OF ALL THE EARTH!
    Let not mortal-kind prevail;
    let the nations be judged before you.
²⁰ Put them in fear DREAD GOD;
    let the nations know that they are mortal. *Selah*

Titus 3:1 Now remind the sisters and brothers with regard to rulers and persons in authority, to be submissive, to be obedient; for every good work, to be ready: ² To blaspheme no person; to be gentle, showing every courtesy to all persons. ³ For we were once foolish, disobedient, enslaved to all kinds of passions and pleasures, in malice and envy living our lives, and we were hateful, hating one another. ⁴ When the graciousness and loving kindness of God our Savior appeared, ⁵ God saved us through the water of rebirth and renewal by the Holy Spirit, not because of any works of righteousness that we had done, but according to God's mercy. ⁶ This Spirit God poured out on us abundantly through Jesus Christ our Savior, ⁷ so that, having been justified by God's grace, we might become heirs according to the hope of life eternal.

Luke 18:1 Jesus told the disciples a parable about the need to pray continually and not be discouraged. ² He said, "There was a judge in a certain city who neither feared God nor respected people. ³ There was a widow in that city and she came to him continually and saying, 'Grant me justice against my accuser.' ⁴ And he was not willing for some time; but later he said to himself, 'Though I do not fear God or no respect anyone else, ⁵ yet because this widow persists in troubling me, I will grant her justice, so that she may not ultimately come to violence against me.'" ⁶ And the Messiah said, "Listen to what the unjust judge says. ⁷ And will not God grant justice to the elect of God who cry to God day and night? Will God forbear in helping them? ⁸ I tell you all, God will quickly grant justice to them. And yet, when the Son of Woman comes, will he find faith on the earth?"

PROCLAMATION

Text Notes

In the world of the text, a "synagogue" is a generic gathering place; it was not yet an (a nearly) exclusively a place of Jewish worship, hence the need to specify "Jewish" in the text.

"To have words" in Acts 17:2 can mean anything from discussing to disputing; here it is "at" them rather than "with" them, yielding "presented to them." In verse 11, the same word means both "high-born" and the characteristic of being open-minded deriving from that status or accompanying education. While many translations present the women and men as equally high in standing, the adjective is feminine plural and thus refers only to the women; likewise, "Greek" is feminine plural. The men are neither Greek nor of high status. This text is one of very few places where women precede men in the order of their mention.

The "well-wishing "of Judith in 15:8 is more properly "to speak peace to her." Verse 9 refers to the Israelite people as a "race." Given the complexity of the term in modernity, including completely different sets of meanings than in antiquity, I use "people" as does NRSVue; NRSV and CEB use the more political "nation." The Hebrew text of Judith to which I have access includes one in rabbinic study format (with no contemporary citation information) and the more well-attested Grintz translation and reconstruction; both have *ha'am*, people. Verse 10 uses the divine title *pantokrator*, which regularly translates *Shaddai*, "the Breasted God" (which I render as "the Nurturing God" here and "the Nursing God" elsewhere; see my translation of Job 33:4 in the children's book *Dear Mama God* by Daneen Akers, illust., Gilliam Gamble [Watchfire Media, 2023]). See also Job 5:17; 11:7; 27:13; 32:8; 34:10 (and multiple others in Job); a *shad* is a breast. The Hebrew manuscripts of Judith I consulted are divided: the rabbinic one simply has the unspoken Divine Name YHWH; the Grintz has YHWH *Tzaba'oth* (Sabbaoth, familiar as "Lord of Hosts" angelic military formations), see Jehoshua M. Grintz, *The Book of Judith: A Reconstruction of the Original Hebrew Text with Introduction, Commentary, Appendices, and Indices*, in Hebrew with English Summary (Jerusalem: Bialik Institute, 1957). In Judith 15:13, the men sing "with their mouth," rendered "aloud."

There are a number of difficult to translate phrases in the psalm; verse 6 is simply a collection of words.

I have preserved the literal "blaspheme" in Titus 3:2 to illustrate the severity of the charge.

The "justice" the widow seeks in verse 3 of the Gospel, *ekdikēson*, includes the notion of vengeance; her adversary—one possible translation of *antidikou*—can also be understood as a plaintiff or accuser who has brought legal charges against her. In Luke 18:5, the corrupt judge uses a bit of dramatic hyperbole with the verb *hypōpiazō*, meaning "to blacken the eye." While most translations treat the expression as euphemistic for "wearing [him] out," the BDAG *Greek-English Lexicon of the New Testament and Other Early Christian Literature* lists as its first meaning: "to blacken an eye, give a black eye, strike in the face . . . of a woman who is driven to desperation and who the judge in the story thinks might in the end express herself physically. . . . Hyperbole is stock-in-trade of popular storytelling. Some prefer to understand [*hypōpiazō*] in this pass[age] in [this] sense." In 1 Corinthians 9:27, Paul describes "punishing" (or "pummeling") his body using the same verb.

Preaching Prompts

In these lessons, God shows up as a transforming and liberating power, changing external circumstances and internal realities. In the first lesson from Acts, God shows up in the scriptures changing hearts, minds, and worldviews. The scriptures are the First Testament in *either* Hebrew or Greek, with differing numbers of books, given the longer Greek canon. In the alternate lesson from Judith, God shows up in the bloody hands of Judith, who could easily be added to the ranks of Israel's saviors in the book of Judges. God is also present in the women's liturgy, rare and without peer in the Hebrew scriptures. The psalm is a plea for God to show up in an act of individual deliverance; it could have been the prayer of either Judith or the widow in Luke. In the Epistle, God shows up in spite of our past, independent of any good or spiritual work we might do, though we are called to do them. In the Gospel, God shows up in the actions of an unwilling, stubborn, unjust vessel because a woman persisted in seeking justice. As the Speaker of the House, Mitch McConnell said of Elizabeth Warren, "Nevertheless, she persisted."

The contexts for each of these readings are complex and sometimes contradictory to the liberation being articulated and demonstrated, modeling the way in which we seek words of liberation from a text in which not all are free. Paul and Silas interpret the scriptures of their culture through the hermeneutic lens of the Jesus story. It is a new way of reading and one which leads toward liberation. But it is not the only way to read the First Testament (or any other). We are not all so honest about or so aware of how we read and interpret scriptures and how that contributes to or curtails liberation.

The Judith story is an extension of the salvation epic narrative tradition of the Hebrew Scriptures. In that tradition, liberation and salvation are not individual events; rather, they are corporate. That worldview will shape the emerging text church. However, hierarchies will remain—enslavement of human persons, class stratification, and gender disparity; the Epistle purporting to be correspondence between Paul and Titus includes some of these. In the *Women's Bible Commentary*, Johanna Dewey describes these widely disputed "Pauline" dispatches as "represent[ing] perhaps the most total capitulation of Christianity to the patriarchal (hierarchical and male-dominated) social structure of the Roman Empire to be found in the New Testament." ([Louisville: Westminster/John Knox Press, 2012], 595). The Epistle calls for obedience and submission to persons in authority with no exceptions, maintaining that hierarchy. The Gospel celebrates the faith and perseverance of a woman who refuses to accept an unjust verdict; she does not submit. Her liberation is in resistance.

FEAST OF THE ASCENSION

Acts 1:1–11; Psalm 24; Revelation 3:20–22; Luke 24:46–53

Acts 1:1 In the first writing, I worked on, Theophilus, everything Jesus did and taught from the beginning [2] until the day he instructed the apostles whom he had chosen through the Holy Spirit and was taken up to heaven. [3] Jesus presented himself to them, living, after his suffering through many convincing proofs, by appearing to them forty days and speaking about the reign of God. [4] And staying with them, Jesus commanded them not to leave Jerusalem, rather to wait there for the promise of the Faithful God, "What you heard from me. [5] For John baptized with water, but you will be baptized with the Holy Spirit not many days from this one."

[6] When they [the disciples] came together, they asked Jesus, "Rabbi, is this the time when you will restore sovereignty to Israel?" [7] He replied, "It is not for you to know the times or seasons that the Sovereign God has set through divine authority. [8] But you will receive power when the Holy Spirit comes upon you, and you will be my witnesses in Jerusalem, in all Judea and Samaria, and to the end of the earth."

[9] And saying this as they were watching, Jesus was taken up, and a cloud took him out of their sight. [10] While they were gazing up toward heaven as Jesus was going, suddenly two in white robes stood by them. [11] They said, "Galileans, why are you standing looking up into heaven? This Jesus, who has been taken up from you into heaven, will come in the way as you saw him go into heaven."

Psalm 24

[1] To the CREATOR OF ALL belongs the earth and all that fills her,
    the world, and those who dwell in her.
[2] For God upon the seas has founded her,
    and on the rivers has established her.
[3] Who shall ascend the hill of the HOLY ONE?
    And who shall stand in God's holy place?
[4] The woman or man who has clean hands and pure hearts,
    who does not lift up their [hands] to what is false,
    and does not swear deceitfully on their souls.

⁵ [Instead] they will lift up a blessing from the Faithful God,
   and what is right from the God of their salvation.
⁶ Such is the generation of those who seek God,
   who seek the face of the God of Rebekah. *Selah*
⁷ Lift up your heads, you gates!
   and be lifted up, you everlasting doors!
   that the One of glory may come in.
⁸ Who is the One of glory?
   The Fire of Sinai, strong and mighty,
   the God who is Majesty, mighty in battle.
⁹ Lift up your heads, you gates!
   and be lifted up, you everlasting doors!
   that the One of glory may come in.
¹⁰ Who is this One of glory?
   The Commander of heaven's legions,
   God is the One of glory. *Selah*

Revelation 3:20 "Look! I stand at the door and knock. If you hear my voice and open the door, I will come in to you and dine with you, and you with me. ²¹ To the one who conquers, I will give a place with me on my throne, just as I myself conquered and sat down with my Abba on God's throne. ²² Let anyone who has an ear listen to what the Spirit is saying to the churches."

Luke 24:46 Then Jesus said to them, "So it is written, the Messiah is to suffer and to rise from the dead, on the third day, ⁴⁷ and repentance and forgiveness of sins is to be preached in his name to all nations, beginning from Jerusalem. ⁴⁸ You are witnesses of these things. ⁴⁹ Now look! I am sending you the promise of my Abba. You all stay in the city until you have been clothed with power from on high." ⁵⁰ Then Jesus led them out as far as Bethany, and lifting his hands, he blessed them. ⁵¹ While he was blessing them, Jesus retreated from them and was carried up into heaven. ⁵² And they bowed down and worshiped him, and returned to Jerusalem with great joy; ⁵³ and they were in the temple every day blessing God.

PROCLAMATION

Text Notes

The divine beings in Acts 1:10 are described as "men" using the human term. Curiously, there are no female divine beings, messengers, angels, etc., in the canon. It is not clear whether women are present at the Ascension, obscured by masculine grammar. If they are not present, it is worth asking why not when women have been the birthing wombs, companion witnesses, participants in, and preachers of the entire Christ story. It is tempting to say the women were out in the world proclaiming the gospel while the men still needed one more sign. Yet, there were women with these very men (who are identified as the remaining apostles by name in Acts 1:13). If they were not with them at the Ascension, how did they learn of the meeting-place? Since they seemed to have arrived at the same time, they could not have been very far. The texts and the cultures of the biblical world collude to minimize and erase women.

In Psalm 24:1–2, I have retained the feminine grammatical gender of the earth since it fits well with the contemporary notion of earth as mother. In verse 6, "the God of Rebekah" replaces "the God of Jacob."

Preaching Prompts

Chronologically, the Gospel for the Feast of the Ascension goes before the first reading from Acts. It may be useful to reread the Acts account of the Ascension *after* the Gospel, perhaps at the beginning of the sermon (if tacking it on to the Gospel seems like liturgical heresy). The Gospel points to the Ascension in Acts 1, and Acts 1 points to Pentecost, coming soon in the next chapter.

In the Ascension, the glory of the Resurrection ratchets up another level. The risen Christ appears to followers—addressed as "men" but possibly inclusive—and prepares the burgeoning church for the baptism of the Holy Spirit. The psalm makes clear that God is the One of glory, and only the pure-hearted can stand in her presence. The multiple Ascension accounts highlight the divinity of the post-Ascension Christ. Revelation 3 reminds us that the divine, risen, and ascended Christ is not so far away that he cannot come to us. He can and will still meet us at the table. For the Church, that meeting is primarily in the Eucharist. Christ also comes to us in communion with one another. That communion, whether at the Eucharist or beyond, is communal, not hierarchal, though the scriptures and their authors will continue to assert ancient hierarchies, particularly along class and gender lines.

SEVENTH SUNDAY OF EASTER

Acts 17:22–18:4 (or Judith 16:18–25); Psalm 149:1–6; Romans 16:1–16; Luke 13:18–30

Acts 17:22 Now Paul stood in the center of the Areopagus and said, "Athenians, I see in everything how devout you are. ²³ For passing through and regarding objects of your worship, I found an altar with the inscription, 'To an unknown god.' What, therefore, you all worship as unknown, this is what I proclaim to you: ²⁴ The God who made the world and everything in it, the one who is Sovereign of heaven and earth, does not live in temples made by human hands. ²⁵ Neither is God served by human hands because of needing anything, since God gives to all life and breath and all things. ²⁶ From one person God made all nations, all persons—women, men, and children—to inhabit the face of the earth and God ordered seasons and the boundaries of their habitation, ²⁷ that they would search for God and perhaps reach for God and find God, yet indeed God is not far from any one of us. ²⁸ For 'In God we live and move and have our being'; just as some among your poets have said, 'For we too are the offspring God.'

²⁹ "Since we are the offspring God, we ought not to think that the divine is like gold, or silver, or stone, an image formed by the craft and creativity of women and men. ³⁰ At one time God overlooked ignorance; now God commands all women and men everywhere to repent. ³¹ For God has fixed a day on which God intends to judge the world in righteousness through a person whom God has appointed, giving assurance to all by raising him from the dead." ³² They heard of the resurrection of the dead. Some scoffed, yet others said, "We will hear you again about this." ³³ Thus Paul left from their midst. ³⁴ Now some joined him, believing, including Dionysius the Areopagite and a woman named Damaris, as well as others with them.

¹⁸:¹ After this Paul departed from Athens and went to Corinth. ² There he found a Jewish man named Aquila, a native of Pontus, who had recently come from Italy along with his wife Priscilla because Claudius had commanded every Jewish woman, child, and man to leave Rome; Paul went to see them. ³ Now, because he was of the same trade, Paul stayed with them and they worked together; they were tentmakers by trade. ⁴ Every sabbath he would make arguments in the synagogue and would try to persuade Jewish and Greek women and men.

Judith 16:18 When they came into Jerusalem, they worshipped God and when the people were purified, they offered up their whole burnt offerings and their voluntary offerings and the gifts. ¹⁹ Then Judith dedicated all the trappings of Holofernes, all that the people had given her along with the canopy which she herself had taken from his bedroom; she gave [them] to God as a consecrated offering. ²⁰ And the people continued celebrating in Jerusalem in front of the holy precincts for three months, and Judith remained there with them.

²¹ After those days each returned to their inheritance and Judith departed for Bethulia and remained there on her property, and in her time she was renowned in all the land. ²² And many desired her yet, no man knew her all the days of her life from the day Manasseh her husband died and was added to his people. ²³ And as for Judith, [her renown] continued, increasing in greatness; and she grew old in the house of her husband—one hundred and five years. Also, she released her favored slave-woman and set her free. Thus, Judith died in Bethulia and they buried her in the cave of her husband, Manasseh. ²⁴ And the house of Israel mourned Judith seven days; also she had divided what she had to all the near-kin of Manasseh her husband and the nearest of her people before she died. ²⁵ And there was not again one person who terrified the women, children, and men of Israel in the days of Judith or after her death, for a long time.

Psalm 149:1–6

¹ Praise the AGELESS GOD!
   Sing to the BREATH OF LIFE a new song,
   her praise in the congregation of the faithful.

² Let Israel be glad in her Maker;
let the children of Zion rejoice in their Sovereign.
³ Let them praise her Name with dance;
with drum and sing praise to her.
⁴ For the Ever-Present God delights in her people;
she adorns those afflicted through poverty with liberation.
⁵ Let the faithful exult in glory;
let them sing for joy on their couches.
⁶ Let exalted praises of God be in their throats
and two-edged swords in their hands.

Romans 16:1 I commend to you all our sister Phoebe, a deacon of the church in Cenchreae, ² so that you all may receive her in Christ as is worthy of the saints, and stand by her in whatever thing she may need of you, for she has been a benefactress of many, and of myself as well.

³ Greet Prisca and Aquila, my coworkers in Christ Jesus, ⁴ and who for my life risked their necks, to whom not only I give thanks, but also all the churches of the Gentiles, ⁵ and the church in their house. Greet Epaenetus my beloved, who was the first fruit in Asia for Christ. ⁶ Greet Mary, who has worked much among you all. ⁷ Greet Andronicus and Junia, my kin and my fellow prisoners; they are eminent among the apostles, and they were in Christ before I was. ⁸ Greet Ampliatus, my beloved in Christ. ⁹ Greet Urbanus, our coworker in Christ, and Stachys my beloved. ¹⁰ Greet Apelles, who is proven in Christ. Greet those who belong to Aristobulus. ¹¹ Greet Herodion, my kinsman. Greet those who belong of Narcissus in Christ. ¹² Greet Tryphaena and Tryphosa who toil in Christ. Greet the beloved Persis who has worked much in Christ. ¹³ Greet Rufus, chosen in Christ, and greet his mother who is also mine. ¹⁴ Greet Asyncritus, Phlegon, Hermes, Patrobas, Hermas, and the sisters and brothers [or friends and kin] who are with them. ¹⁵ Greet Philologus and Julia, Nereus and his sister, and Olympas, and all the saints with them. ¹⁶ Greet one another with a holy kiss. All the churches of Christ greet you.

Luke 13:18 Jesus said now then, "What is the Majesty of God like? And to what should I compare it? ¹⁹ It is like a mustard seed that a person took and sowed in their garden, and it grew and became a tree, and the birds of the heavens made nests in its branches." ²⁰ And Jesus said again: "To what should I compare the Mystery of God? ²¹ It is like yeast that a woman took and folded in with three measures of flour until all was leavened."

²² And Jesus went through towns and villages, teaching, making his way to Jerusalem. ²³ Now, someone asked him, "Rabbi, is it only a few who will be saved?" Jesus said to all of them: ²⁴ "Struggle to enter through the narrow door; for many, I tell you, will seek to enter and will not be able. ²⁵ Once the owner of the house has gotten up and shut the door and you stand outside and begin to knock at the door, saying, 'Honored One, open to us,' then the homeowner will say to you all, 'I do not know any of you or where you have come from.'

²⁶ And you all will begin to say, 'We ate with you and we drank with you and in our streets you taught.' ²⁷ But the homeowner will say, 'I do not know any of you or where you have come from. Get away from me, all you workers of iniquity!' ²⁸ There will be weeping and gnashing of teeth when you see [Hagar, Sarah, Keturah, and] Abraham and [Rebekah and] Isaac, and [Leah, Rachel, Bilhah, and] Jacob and all the women and men who were prophets in the Movement of God, and you yourselves thrown out. ²⁹ Then people will come from east and west, from north and south, and will eat in the Magnificence of God. ³⁰ Indeed, some are last who will be first, and some are first who will be last."

PROCLAMATION

Text Notes

Throughout this project, I use expansive language to describe the space where God is, often preserving some sense of the royal language but resisting the social-political structure of a "kingdom" in heaven or in earth. Across these volumes, readers will find more familiar translation choices such as "the reign of God" or "the realm of God." In the later volumes, I have deployed majesty, moving further away from a physical space mirroring the petty kingdoms and empires-in-waiting of earth. In today's Gospel reading, I have pushed even further, using a series of M words: Majesty, Mystery, Movement, and Magnificence (in vv. 18–19, 28–29). As always, readers and preachers are welcome to make their own choices, particularly those most appropriate for their context.

The marketplaces of ideas in which Paul spoke were open to women and men, and he drew believers from all, though, as is common in Acts, his language often only addressed men. Here, Paul limits his address to men, "You men of Athens . . ." using the gendered term rather than the inclusive term for humanity in 17:22. In verse 34, the text says that "men" joined becoming believers, including Dionysius (a male name) and "a woman named Damaris" (and others). I understand that "men" to be inclusive in meaning though not in form, like "mankind," and that there were other women among the new believers in Athens other than Damaris.

Priscilla is a Jewish woman evicted from Rome with her husband in the Jewish expulsion ordered by Emperor Claudius in Acts 18:2 and is one of the teaching elders or leaders of the early church. (Bernadette Brooten has demonstrated conclusively that women leaders in the ancient synagogue used the title in her book of the same title; as male Christian leaders adopted the language, it is reasonable to presume Christian women did as well.) Priscilla, sometimes rendered Prisca, is listed before her husband more often than not, indicating to some that she was the senior, more learned disciple (Acts 18:2, 18, 26; Romans 16:3; 1 Corinthians 16:19; 2 Timothy 4:19). Her name certainly precedes in the reeducation of Apollos. Paul describes her and her husband—in that order—as his coworkers in Romans 16:3

and she is listed first as pastor of the house church in 2 Timothy 4:19. (I say "pastor" because there is no dispute that men led the churches in their homes when listed; I reckon her as more senior pastor than copastor.)

The voluntary offerings of Judith 16:18 are "*anathema*" in Greek and "*cherem*" in Hebrew; they are both cursed and consecrated. Judith 16:23 is a series of words with very little connective tissue; I have endeavored to add as little as possible to make it readable.

The inclusion of all the matriarchs as an option for the reader presents the theological challenge which, in part, gave birth to this project. The devotional reader and the preacher will have to determine in what way "weeping and gnashing of teeth" is different (if at all) when the souls in the parable include the great mothers of scripture along with the fathers.

Preaching Prompts

Eastertide is winding down, but what comes next will be hardly quiescent. This week's lessons lead us to Jerusalem, the center of worship and home of the living God on earth, and point to the home of God beyond space and time, an abode that transcends concepts like kingdom, dominion, reign, and realm, and even a farmer's growing mustard tree or a woman's rising dough. Our imaginations are insufficient, yet we are called to imagine with God and put our hearts and hands to work in that shared vision.

In Acts, Paul points to a God who does not require the temples lovingly crafted by the hands of women and men yet does not disdain or disparage them. Paul and the early followers of the Jesus movement would continue to worship in Jerusalem, whose temple was imagined in some way to reflect the cosmos around God without claiming any kind of literalist replication of the heavenly expanse.

Yet Jerusalem will remain as a place of unparalleled holiness. A place where Jews, including those who follow Jesus, will return season after season for holidays (as we shall see next week) or for moments of individual or corporate celebration and devotion, as Judith illustrates from days long gone by.

Paul and the women and men who were his coworkers, as exemplified in Romans 16, understood their call to build a church to be a call to build a community and not an edifice. They understood that just as the space that God inhabits could not be contained in words or a single set of images, the community of God centered on the life, teachings, and resurrection of Jesus would not be able to be contained in a single nation, let alone a building. These early apostles, disciples, coworkers, and collaborators also demonstrate that the work of the gospel cannot be contained in or limited to one kind of person: women and men, enslaved and free, Jews from Judea at home and abroad, Greeks and other Gentiles from all over the world will leaven the dough of the movement, mystery, and majesty of God in this world.

PENTECOST VIGIL (OR EARLY SERVICE)

Joel 2:27–32 (or Exodus 19:1–19); Psalm 139:7–14;
Acts 2:1–18; John 4:7–26

Joel 2:27 You all shall know that I am in the midst of Israel,
and that I, the Holy One of Sinai, am your God and there is no other.
And my people shall not be put to shame ever again.
²⁸ And it shall be after that,
I will pour out my Spirit on all flesh;
and your daughters and your sons shall prophesy,
your elders shall dream dreams,
and your youths shall see visions.
²⁹ Even on the enslaved women and men,
in those days, will I pour out my Spirit.

³⁰ I will place portents in the heavens and on the earth, blood and fire and pillars of smoke. ³¹ The sun shall be turned to darkness, and the moon to blood, before the great and terrible day of the Dread God comes. ³² Then it shall be that everyone who calls on the name of the Faithful God shall be saved; for in Mount Zion and in Jerusalem there shall be those who escape, as the Holy One of Old has said, and among the survivors, those whom the God Who Saves calls.

Exodus 19:1 On the third new moon after the women, children, and men of Israel had gone out of the land of Egypt, on that day, they entered the wilderness of Sinai. ² They had journeyed from Rephidim, entered the wilderness of Sinai, and camped in the wilderness; Israel camped there in front of the mountain. ³ Then Moses went up to God and the Holy One of Old called to him from the mountain, saying, "Thus you shall say to the house of Jacob, and tell the women, children, and men of Israel: ⁴ You all have seen what I did to the Egyptians, that I raised you all up on the wings of eagles and brought you all to myself. ⁵ Now, if you all obey my voice and keep my covenant, you all shall be my treasure from among all peoples, for the whole earth is mine. ⁶ And you all shall be for me a sovereignty of priests and a holy nation. These are the words that you shall speak to the women, children, and men of Israel."

⁷ So Moses came and called the elders of the people and placed before them all these words that the Holy One had commanded him. ⁸ Then the people, women and men, all answered together: "Everything that the Holy One has spoken we will do." And Moses conveyed the words of the people to the Holy One of Sinai. ⁹ Then the Holy One said to Moses, "I will come to you in an impenetrable cloud, so that the people can hear when I speak with you and also trust you always." When Moses had told the words of the people to the Holy One, ¹⁰ the Holy God said to Moses: "Go to the people and have

them consecrate themselves today and tomorrow. Have them wash their clothes, [11] and be prepared for the third day, because on the third day the MOST HIGH will come down upon Mount Sinai in the sight of all the people. [12] You shall set a boundary around the people, saying, 'Take heed not to go up the mountain or to touch the edge of it yourselves; anyone who touches the mountain shall surely be put to death. [13] No hand shall touch them, rather they shall be stoned or shot with arrows; whether animal or human, they shall not live.' When the ram's horn sounds a long blast, they may go up on the mountain." [14] So Moses went down from the mountain to the people. He consecrated the people, and they washed their clothes. [15] And Moses said to the people, "Prepare for the third day; do not go near a woman."

[16] And it was on the third day as morning came there was thunder and lightning, as well as a cloud heavy upon the mountain, and a blast of a trumpet so loud that all the people who were in the camp trembled. [17] Then Moses brought the people out of the camp to meet God. They stationed themselves at the base of the mountain. [18] Now Mount Sinai was in smoke, because the HOLY ONE OF OLD had descended upon it in fire; the smoke ascended like the smoke of a kiln, while the whole mountain shook violently. [19] And it was that as the sound of the trumpet grew stronger and stronger, Moses would speak and God would answer him in thunder.

Psalm 139:7–14

[7] Where can I go from your spirit?
Or where from your presence can I flee?
[8] If I ascend to the heavens, there you are;
if I recline in Sheol, see, it is you!
[9] If I take up dawn's wings,
if I settle at the farthest reaches of the sea,
[10] even there your hand shall lead me,
and your right hand shall hold me fast.
[11] If I say, "Surely darkness shall cover me,
and night will become light behind me,"
[12] even darkness is not dark to you;
night is as daylight,
for dark is the same as light.
[13] For it was you who crafted my inward parts;
you wove me together in my mother's womb.
[14] I praise you, for I am awesomely and marvelously made.
Wonderous are your works;
that my soul knows full well.

Acts 2:1 When the day of Pentecost had come, they were all together in the same place. [2] And there came suddenly from heaven a sound like the sweeping of a mighty wind, and it filled the entire house where they were sitting. ³ Then there appeared among them divided tongues, as of fire, and one rested on each of them. ⁴ And all of them were filled with the Holy Spirit and they began to speak in other tongues just as the Spirit gave them to speak.

⁵ Now there were dwelling in Jerusalem devout Jews from every nation under heaven. ⁶ Now at this sound the crowd gathered and was confused because each heard them speaking in the native language of each. ⁷ Amazed and astounded, they asked, "Are not all these who are speaking Galileans? ⁸ And how do we hear, each in our own native language? ⁹ Parthians and Medes and Elamites, and those who live in Mesopotamia, Judea and Cappadocia, Pontus and Asia, ¹⁰ Phrygia and Pamphylia, Egypt and the parts of Libya adjacent to Cyrene, and visitors from Rome, both Jews and proselytes, ¹¹ Cretans and Arabs, we hear them speaking in our own tongues about God's deeds of power." ¹² All were amazed and questioning to one another saying, "What does this mean?" ¹³ But others mocking said, "They are filled with new wine."

¹⁴ But Peter, standing with the eleven, raised his voice and addressed them, "Judeans and all who live in Jerusalem, let this be known to you all, and attend to my speech. ¹⁵ For these persons are not drunk as you suppose, it is only the third hour [nine o'clock] in the morning. ¹⁶ No, this is what was spoken through the prophet Joel:

> ¹⁷ 'In the last days it will be, God declares,
> that I will pour out my Spirit upon all flesh,
> and your daughters and your sons shall prophesy,
> and your young men shall see visions,
> and your elders shall dream dreams.
> ¹⁸ Even upon my slaves, both women and men,
> in those days I will pour out my Spirit;
> and they shall prophesy.'"

John 4:7 A Samaritan woman came to draw water. Jesus said to her, "Give me a drink." ⁸ Now his disciples had gone to the city to buy food. ⁹ The Samaritan woman said to him, "How are you, a Judean, asking a drink of me, a woman of Samaria?" (Judeans do not share things in common with Samaritans.) ¹⁰ Jesus answered and said to her, "If you knew the gift of God and who is the one telling to you, 'Give me a drink,' you would have asked him, and he would have given you living water." ¹¹ The woman said to him, "Sir, you have no bucket, and the well is deep. From where do you get that living water? ¹² Are you greater than our ancestor Jacob, the one who gave us the well, and with his daughters and sons and his flocks drank from it?" ¹³ Jesus answered and said to her, "Everyone who drinks of this water will thirst again. ¹⁴ But the one who drinks of the water that I will give will never thirst. The water that I will give will become in them a fount of water springing up into eternal life." ¹⁵ The woman said to him, "Sir, give me this water, that I may never thirst or keep coming here to draw water."

16 Jesus said to her, "Go, call your husband, and come [back] to this place." 17 The woman answered and said to him, "I have no husband." Jesus said to her, "You said rightly, 'I have no husband.' 18 For five husbands have you had, and now the one you have is not your husband. What you have said is true!" 19 The woman said to him, "Sir, I see that you are a prophet. 20 Our mothers and fathers worshiped on this mountain, yet you say in Jerusalem is the place where people must worship." 21 Jesus said to her, "Believe me, woman, the hour is coming when neither on this mountain nor in Jerusalem will you worship the Sovereign God. 22 You all worship what you do not know; we worship what we know, for salvation is from the Judeans. 23 But the hour is coming, and now is, when the true worshipers will worship the Sovereign God in spirit and truth, for these are the worshippers the Sovereign God seeks. 24 God is spirit, and those who worship God must worship in spirit and truth." 25 The woman said to Jesus, "I know that Messiah is coming" (the one who is called Christ). "When he comes, he will proclaim all things to us." 26 Jesus said to her, "I am, the one who is speaking to you."

PROCLAMATION
Text Notes

Verse numbers in Christian Bibles diverge from those (now) in Hebrew and Jewish Bibles. What is Joel 2:28 in Christian texts is 3:1 in Jewish texts such as the JPS *Tanakh* and Hebrew Masoretic Text, as well as other ancient texts including the LXX and Peshitta. "Elders" in verse 28 is an inclusive plural that grammatically includes women; it can represent chronological age or status. The "elders of Israel" served as an administrative layer (Numbers 16:25; Deuteronomy 27:1, 31:9; Joshua 7:6, 8:10; 1 Samuel 4:3). They are only spoken of as a group, so it is unclear if there were any women among them. In Joel, "elders" is paired with "youth," indicating it should be read chronologically, and therefore, I argue, inclusively.

In Exodus 19:10 and 14, "consecrate" or "sanctify" has a reflexive sense; one does it to oneself, primarily through water: bathing and washing one's clothing. Scholars from the rabbinic period (Rashi, Ramban, Ibn Ezra, and Nahmanides) understood Moses's sanctification of the people to be a charge to them to sanctify themselves, hence "warn them to stay pure" in the JPS. The use of the masculine pronoun "him" for both a person who transgresses the boundary of the mountain and the mountain itself means that in verse 13, the referent of "no hand shall touch him/it" is unclear.

In Psalm 139:14, "marvelous" and wondrous" are the same word. I alternate them for alliteration to give a sense of the poetry.

The author limits the multinational Jews in Jerusalem to "devout men" in Acts 1:5, as though there were no women or none of the women were devout. The androcentric language discounts women who were living in the city and women who did make the journey. Yet Deuteronomy 16:11 specifies celebrating the festival with daughters and sons and women and men who are enslaved in the household (no mention of wives). Similarly, Peter addresses "men of Judea" but also "all who live in Jerusalem" in 1:14; I treat both as inclusive.

In John 4:26, Jesus says, *ego eimi*, "I am," echoing God's self-identification in Exodus 3:14 or, in some other translations, "I am [he]"—the masculine pronoun is missing.

Preaching Prompts

Pentecost, the fiftieth day, marks the end of the Festival of Weeks, *Shavuoth* (from the Hebrew for "weeks"), originally named the festival of "Harvest" (see Exodus 23:16; Leviticus 23:15–16). The seven weeks follow from Passover, and the festivals are entwined. By the time of the New Testament, it was also understood as the anniversary of the revelation of the Torah on Mount Sinai in Exodus 19. These traditions underlie the outpouring of the Holy Spirit on that same day. The Christian observance is inexorably linked to its ancestral Jewish heritage.

Because of its citation in Acts 2, the primary Pentecost narrative, Joel 2 is regarded as fulfilled in the event in Christian interpretation. In Joel, repeated in Acts, "everyone who calls upon the name of the Holy One shall be saved" (or "rescued") means two very different things in each of those contexts. In the Hebrew Bible, salvation, rescue, and deliverance are normally corporate (with few exceptions) and relate to physical safety from threats of violence, war, occupation, and even natural and ecological disasters (as is the case in Joel). In the New Testament, the Church has replaced the nation as the frame of reference; to call upon the name, now of Jesus, is to profess faith in him. It is important to tell the Christian story without erasing or rewriting the story of God's faithfulness to Jewish people or their Israelite ancestors.

Exodus 19 is the story of God's covenant with Israel ratified on Sinai with God present in veiled majesty. The language is, by turns, inclusive and exclusive, inviting reflection on who we understand to be part of and to represent the people of God. The traditional language for Israel, "the sons" or "children of Israel," is both androcentric and inclusive. In verse 8, the people "all" answer, meaning women and men; children would not be subject to a legal agreement like the covenant. ("Children" in the commandments refers to adult children in relation to their parents.) "People" is inclusive and yet is sometimes used as though men are the only ones who count; in verse 15, Moses tells the "people" not to approach women, presumably for sex. In this construction, women are not "people." Perhaps more disturbing, Moses *adds* this line to God's instructions and receives no rebuke. (Compare God's directive in verses 10–13 with those of Moses.) Notwithstanding the attempts of Moses and his writers, God appears to all the women, children, and men of Israel. Though earlier in Exodus, the people see God regularly in the alternating pillars of cloud and fire, God's appearance in verse 15 is perhaps closer than the front of their vanguard and much more dramatic with the addition of thunder and lightning and the sound of God's voice.

Who experiences the touch of the Holy Spirit in Acts 2? Who are the "they"? If they are the upper room community, then they are Mary, the mother of Jesus, and other unnamed women along with the eleven remaining apostles (Acts 1:13–14), plus a newly elected apostle (who will immediately disappear), verses 23–26. "They" may also refer to the larger group of one hundred and twenty in the following verse. An intriguing possibility reads the two together: Mary and an undisclosed number of women together with the twelve apostles constituted the one hundred and twenty. This might explain why Peter chooses Joel to explain the phenomenon because of its explicit inclusivity.

The *Samarians* were the inhabitants of the northern monarchy of Israel who ultimately fell to Assyria and were largely deported. The land was repopulated with other conquered peoples, and their descendants became known as *Samaritans* (see 2 Kings 17:24–34). Judeans held them in low esteem because of their mixed heritage, to which they attributed the differences between their worship traditions. Notably, the Samaritan Pentateuch is the entirety of their Bible; nothing else is canonical, which remains the case for Samaritan Jews in the present. (Ἰουδαίοις should be understood as "Judean" in opposition to Samaritan, as both communities are Jewish.) The dispute about the mountain in John 4:20–22 is rooted in one of the many differences between the Samaritan and Judean Torahs: Whether the mountain in Deuteronomy 27:4 on which Joshua (8:30) later built an altar is Ebal (Judeans) or Gerazim (Samaritans). As a result, the Samaritan temple was built on Mt. Gerizim, the "this mountain" of John 4:22. Palestinian Samaritan Jews continued to worship on the mountain, the temple long destroyed by the Romans in 70 CE.

In John 4:12, the woman mentions Jacob and his children (or sons), which I have made explicitly inclusive given that Jacob had an unknown number of daughters, including one named Dinah, among his thirty-three children (see Genesis 37:35, 46:15).

PENTECOST PRINCIPAL SERVICE

Acts 2:1–18 (or Isaiah 44:1–8); Psalm 104:1–4, 10–15, 27–30; Romans 8:14–27; John 14:8–17

Acts 2:1 When the day of Pentecost had come, they were all together in the same place. ² And there came suddenly from heaven a sound like the sweeping of a mighty wind, and it filled the entire house where they were sitting. ³ Then there appeared among them divided tongues, as of fire, and one rested on each of them. ⁴ And all of them were filled with the Holy Spirit and they began to speak in other tongues just as the Spirit gave them to speak.

⁵ Now there were dwelling in Jerusalem devout Jews from every nation under heaven. ⁶ Now at this sound the crowd gathered and was confused because each heard them speaking in the native language of each. ⁷ Amazed and astounded, they asked, "Are not all these who are speaking Galileans? ⁸ And how do we hear, each in our own native language? ⁹ Parthians and Medes and Elamites, and those who live in Mesopotamia, Judea and Cappadocia, Pontus and Asia, ¹⁰ Phrygia and Pamphylia, Egypt and the parts of Libya adjacent to Cyrene, and visitors from Rome, both Jews and proselytes, ¹¹ Cretans and Arabs, we hear them speaking in our own tongues about God's deeds of power." ¹² All were amazed and questioning to one another saying, "What does this mean?" ¹³ But others mocking said, "They are filled with new wine."

¹⁴ But Peter, standing with the eleven, raised his voice and addressed them, "Judeans and all who live in Jerusalem, let this be known to you all, and attend to my speech: ¹⁵ For these persons are not drunk as you suppose; it is only the third hour [nine o'clock] in the morning. ¹⁶ No, this is what was spoken through the prophet Joel:

> ¹⁷ 'In the last days it will be, God declares,
> that I will pour out my Spirit upon all flesh,
> and your daughters and your sons shall prophesy,
> and your young men shall see visions,
> and your elders shall dream dreams.
> ¹⁸ Even upon my slaves, both women and men,
> in those days I will pour out my Spirit;
> and they shall prophesy.'"

Isaiah 44:1 Hear now, Jacob [Rebekah's child], my slave,
> Israel whom I have chosen!
> ² Thus says the Wellspring of Life who made you,
> who shaped you in the womb and will help you:
> Fear not, Jacob [Rebekah's son], my slave,
> Jeshurun whom I have chosen.
> ³ For I will pour water upon thirsty soil,
> and streams upon the dry ground;
> I will pour my spirit upon your descendants,
> and my blessing on your offspring.
> ⁴ They shall spring up in green [places],
> like willows by flowing waters.
> ⁵ This one will say, "I am God's,"
> that one will name the name of Jacob,
> another will write on their hand, "This belongs to God,"
> and adopt the name of Israel.
> ⁶ Thus says the Ageless God, the Sovereign of Israel,
> and Israel's Redeemer, the Commander of heaven's legions:

I am the first and I am the last;
  apart from me there is no god.
7 Who is like me? Let them proclaim it,
  let them declare it and set it out before me.
  Who like me from old has laid out things which are coming?
  Let them declare to us what will come.
8 Fear not and be not afraid;
  have I not from old told you and declared it?
  You all are my witnesses!
  Is there any god besides me?
  There is no rock; I know not one.

Psalm 104:1–4, 10–15, 27–30

1 Bless the FOUNT OF LIFE, O my soul.
  MOTHER OF ALL, my God, you are very great.
  You don honor and majesty,
2 Wrapped in light as a garment,
  you stretch out the heavens like a tent-curtain.
3 She who lays on the waters the beams of her upper chambers,
  she who makes the clouds her chariot,
  she is the one who rides on the wings of the wind.
4 She is the one who makes the winds her celestial messengers,
  fire and flame her ministers.
10 She is the one who makes springs gush forth in the torrents;
  they flow between the hills.
11 They give drink to every wild animal;
  the wild donkeys slake their thirst.
12 By the torrents the birds of the heavens dwell;
  among the branches they give voice.
13 She is the one who waters the mountains from her high chambers;
  the earth is satisfied with the fruit of your work.
14 She is the one who makes grass to grow for the cattle,
  and vegetation for human labor,
  to bring forth food from the earth,
15 and wine to make the human heart rejoice,
  with oil to make the face shine,
  and bread to sustain the human heart.
27 All of these hope in you
  to provide their food in due season.
28 You give it to them, they glean it;
  you open your hand, they are well satisfied.

²⁹ You hide your face, they are dismayed;
  when you collect their breath, they die
  and to their dust they return.
³⁰ You send forth your spirit, they are created;
  and you renew the face of the earth.

Romans 8:14 Now as many as are led by the Spirit of God are daughters and sons of God. ¹⁵ For you all did not receive a spirit of slavery to fall again into fear, but you have received a spirit of adoption through which we cry, "Abba! Father!" ¹⁶ It is that same Spirit who bears witness with our spirit that we are daughters and sons of God. ¹⁷ And if daughters and sons, then heirs, heirs of God and heirs with Christ, if it is true that we suffer with Christ so that we may also be glorified with Christ.

¹⁸ I consider that the sufferings of this present time are not worth comparing with the glory about to be revealed to us. ¹⁹ For the creation waits with eager longing for the revealing of the daughters and sons of God; ²⁰ for the creation was subjected to futility, not of its own will but by the will of the one who subjected it, in hope ²¹ that the creation itself will be set free from its bondage to decay and will obtain the freedom of the glory of the daughters and sons of God. ²² We know that the whole creation has been groaning in labor pains until now; ²³ and not only the creation, but we ourselves, who have the first fruits of the Spirit, groan inwardly while we wait for adoption, the redemption of our bodies. ²⁴ For in hope we were saved. Now hope that is seen is not hope. For who hopes for what is seen? ²⁵ But if we hope for what we do not see, we wait for it with patience.

²⁶ Likewise the Spirit helps us in our weakness; for we do not know how to pray as is necessary, but that very Spirit intercedes with sighs too deep for words. ²⁷ And God, who searches the heart, knows what is the mindset of the Spirit, because the Spirit intercedes for the saints according to the will of God.

John 14:8 Philip said to Jesus, "Rabbi, show us the Father, and we will be content." ⁹ Jesus said to him, "Have I been with all of you all this time, Philip, and you still do not know me? The one who has seen me has seen the Father. How can you say, 'Show us the Father'? ¹⁰ Do you not believe that I am in the Father and the Father is in me? The words that I speak to you I do not speak on my own; but the Father who dwells in me does the works of God. ¹¹ Believe me that I am in the Father and the Father is in me; but if not, then believe because of the works themselves. ¹² Very truly, I tell you all, the one who believes in me will also do the works I do and even will do greater works than these, because I am going to the Father. ¹³ And whatever you all ask in my name I will do, so that the Father may be glorified in the Son. ¹⁴ If you all ask me anything in my name, I will do it.

¹⁵ "If you love me, you will keep my commandments. ¹⁶ And I will ask the Father, and God will give you another Advocate, to be with you forever. ¹⁷ This is the Spirit of truth, whom the world cannot receive, because it neither sees nor knows the Spirit. You know her, because she abides with you, and she will be in you.

PROCLAMATION

Text Notes

See the discussion of the Acts 2 text in the readings for the Pentecost Vigil/Early Service.

Jeshurun, in Isaiah 44:2, is something of a pet name for Israel from Deuteronomy (see vv. 32:15; 33:5, 26). In verse 4, there is a missing noun to describe the site of flourishing; I have supplied "places."

Psalm 104 switches between second and third person, as is common in the genre. Verses 14–15 use the word that means both bread and food in general in both senses.

In the Hebrew Bible, the Spirit of God (and more broadly) is grammatically feminine. This is not easily visible when reading in English. Translators have historically avoided grammatical constructions that would require a pronoun for the Spirit in the First Testament. Rather, they repeat "the spirit" as the perpetual subject. I have adopted that practice for the translation of John 14:17.

In Greek, in the Septuagint, and in Christian scriptures, the word for "spirit" is neuter, meaning that in the breadth of the scriptures, the spirit is anything and everything but masculine. The deliberate choice to render the spirit in masculine terms in Latin texts such as the Vulgate reflects theological commitments apart from the grammar of the texts. If we were to hear Jesus speak John 14:17 in Aramaic, we would most likely hear the feminine pronouns represented by the translation above.

Preaching Prompts

The outpouring of the Holy Spirit on Pentecost marks the dawn of the Church, but it is not the dawn of the Holy Spirit; she births creation, hovering over her newly hatched brood in Genesis and breathes through the scriptures, celebrated in the final verse of the psalm. Here in Isaiah 44, she is God's promise for coming generations. The God of wind and flame in Psalm 104:4 is the same God, the same Spirit who is the wind and breath of the Pentecostal fire.

Isaiah 44 is significant for its strident monotheism in a largely henotheistic tradition. Henotheism is the worship of one god above others while not denying the existence of the others, i.e., "God of gods," and "choose this day whom you will serve," etc. But in Isaiah 44:8, God says she has never even heard of another god in the rhetoric of her poet-prophet. This is a bold, audacious claim, for the author is not ignorant of the world around her, nor is the God for whom she speaks. Rather, it is both creation and affirmation of a worldview, as is the Pentecost moment.

The psalm is rich with the majesty of creation. And in Romans 8:20 and 22, that same creation waits, longing for us, humanity, to live into the fullness of our glory as the children and God. That same mighty fire-swirling spirit pays for us to live up to and into our full potential like the rest of creation, even when we do not know the words to pray. Indeed, language as we understand it is insufficient; the spirit intercedes and advocates through sounds and sighs beyond our capacity to interpret. The Gospel promises that Advocate, Comforter, and Intercessor will be with us forever.

TRINITY SUNDAY

Hosea 11:1–4; Psalm 130:5–8; 131:1–3; 2 Peter 1:16–18; Matthew 28:16–20

Hosea 11:1 When Israel was a child, I loved them,
    and out of Egypt I called my child.
² They, the Baals, called to them,
    they went out to the Baals;
    they sacrificed and to idols,
    they offered incense.
³ Yet it was I who walked toddling Ephraim,
    taking them by their arms;
    yet they did not know that I healed them.
⁴ I led them with human ties,
    with bonds of love.
    I was to them like those
    who lift babies to their cheeks.
    I bent down to them and fed them.

Psalm 130:5–8; 131:1–3;

⁵ I wait for the WOMB OF CREATION, my soul waits,
    and in her word I hope.
⁶ My soul keeps watch for the Creator,
    more than those who watch for the morning,
    more than those who watch for the morning.
⁷ Israel, hope in the MOTHER OF CREATION!
    For with the CREATOR OF ALL there is faithful love,
    and with her is abundant redemption.
⁸ It is she who will redeem Israel
    from all their iniquities.
¹³¹:¹ WOMB OF LIFE, my heart is not lifted up,
    nor my eyes exalted;
    I do not keep company with things
    great and too wondrous for me.

² Rather, I have soothed and quieted my soul,
   like a weaned child with her mother;
   my soul is like a weaned child within me.
³ Israel, hope in the WELLSPRING OF LIFE
   from now until forever.

2 Peter 1:16 For we did not follow sophisticated mythologies when we made known to you all the power and coming of our Redeemer Jesus Christ, rather we had been eyewitnesses of his majesty. ¹⁷ For Christ from God the Sovereign received honor and glory, a voice came to him from the Majestic Glory, saying, "This is my Son, my Beloved, with whom I am well pleased." ¹⁸ And we ourselves heard this voice that came from heaven, while we were with him on the holy mountain.

Matthew 28:16 Now the eleven disciples went to Galilee, to the mountain to which Jesus sent them. ¹⁷ And when they saw him, they bowed down worshipping him; but some doubted. ¹⁸ Then Jesus came and said to them saying, "All authority in heaven and on earth has been given to me. ¹⁹ Go therefore and make disciples of all nations, baptizing them in the name of the Father and of the Son and of the Holy Spirit, ²⁰ and teaching them to obey everything that I have commanded you. Now look, I am with you always, to the end of the age."

PROCLAMATION
Text Notes

In the first line of Hosea 11, "boy," a very ambiguous term, ranges from prepubescent to young adult and can also represent minor or junior status among adults. The passage moves between conceptions of Israel as a singular collective "boy" to a notion of individuals, "them," in the first two verses. In verse 3, "toddling" renders a verb made out of the word for foot, consistent with the child learning to walk and still being nursed in verse 4. Human "ties" in verse 4 is a pun on ropes and cords and the bonds of human relationships.

In Psalm 130:8, Israel is a singular entity, and their sin is also collective and singular here.

Preaching Prompts

The three-fold way in which God has been traditionally named is male in form (Father and Son) and function (the postbiblical construction of the Holy Spirit as male). This rubric, which seeks to articulate the essential nature and identity of God to be used in worship and prayer, liturgy and preaching, allows men and boys to hear themselves and their pronouns identified with God along with the exclusion and invisibility of women and girls and nonbinary persons. This exclusion is formative for men and boys in casting gender hierarchy from which they benefit in divine terms. For those who do not hear their pronouns invoke their creation as *imago dei* in the language of the Church, trinitarian language and the observance of the Trinity remain a sanctified proclamation of male divinity. For this reason, this project offers more ways to name God drawn from the scriptures.

While the overwhelming majority of God-language is masculine, there remains a significant collection of feminine imagery for and descriptions of God. The description of the soul as a weaned child in Psalm 131:2 invokes an image of God as the mother upon whose breast it rests.

The Epistle writer uses rare language for God, Majestic Glory, in 2 Peter 1:17. (Hebrews uses "the Majesty," on high in 1:3 and in heaven in 8:1.) The Epistle also comes with a healthy caution for those caught up in the Church's often heated, occasionally violent debates over the Trinity, its Persons, and their relationships, hierarchy, and origins. In disputes about "sophisticated" myths or mythologies—and, I add, theologies, philosophies, and church doctrines—the writer turns to their witness of the faith, what they saw and heard. In turn, they pass their testimony down to us.

Matthew 28:19 is the place where what has become the primary Trinitarian formula occurs. (Galatians 4:6 has the same elements but presented discursively: "And because you are children, God has sent the Spirit of God's Son into our hearts, crying, 'Abba! Father!'") While the traditional language will always have a place in the liturgical lexicon, Trinity Sunday offers an opportunity to craft language that draws more widely on the biblical texts and traditions.

Some of mine include:

Sovereign, Savior, and Shelter;
Author, Word, and Translator;
Parent, Partner, and Friend;
Majesty, Mercy, and Mystery;
Creator, Christ, and Compassion;
Potter, Vessel, and Holy Fire;
Life, Liberation, and Love.

SEASON AFTER PENTECOST

The Season after Pentecost runs nearly thirty weeks, and in this extended season in Year C, the lectionary moves through the prophetic books in loose, very loose, chronological order. (It is not possible to put the prophetic books, let alone the larger canon in chrono order.) In the broad structure, the readings are placed in successive political eras and domination, followed by Babylonian occupation and exile, with the hope for return in the Persian period concluding. Daniel, though not a prophet in the prophetic corpus of the Hebrew Bible, has traditionally been understood as a prophet by Christian interpreters reflected by its terminal place in the Septuagint, in which Susannah opens

Daniel (likewise Baruch, a prophet in rabbinic literature, follows Jeremiah). I include it here and place it as a late text but retain the Christian canonical close of the First Testament with Malachi.

Not all books are represented due to a lack of appropriate material. Texts describing violence against women have not been included; however, they will be addressed when they are relevant to included passages. The Gospel readings return to the wealth of Lukan material that surrounds Jesus's journey to Jerusalem and move through John.

PROPER 1 (CLOSEST TO MAY 11)

Jonah 3:1–10; Psalm 85:1–13; 1 Peter 3:8–12; Luke 16:19–31

Jonah 3:1 The word of the Ark of Safety was to Jonah a second time, saying, ² "Get up, go to Nineveh, that great city, and proclaim to her the proclamation that I speak to you." ³ And Jonah set out and went to Nineveh, according to the word of the All-Seeing God. Now Nineveh was a city large enough for gods, a three days' walk across. ⁴ Then Jonah began to go into the city, a day's walk. And he proclaimed, "Forty days more and Nineveh shall be overthrown!" ⁵ And the people of Nineveh believed God and they proclaimed a fast and every person put on sackcloth, from great to small.

⁶ Now the word reached the king of Nineveh and he rose from his throne and pulled his cloak off himself and covered himself with sackcloth and sat among ashes. ⁷ Then he spoke and had it cried out in Nineveh, "By the decree of the king and his nobles say: Whether humankind or animalkind—herd or flock—none shall taste anything; they shall not feed nor shall they drink water. ⁸ They shall be covered with sackcloth, humankind and animalkind, and they shall cry out to God with might, and each person shall turn from their evil ways and from the violence that is in their hands. ⁹ Who knows? God may turn and forebear and turn from [divine] fury that we might not perish." ¹⁰ Now God saw their doings, that they turned from their evil ways, and God forbore the evil that God said would come upon them and did not do it.

Psalm 85:1–13

¹ Faithful God, you have shown favor to your land;
 you turned around the captivity of Rebekah's line.
² You lifted the iniquity of your people;
 you forgave all their sin. *Selah*
³ You withdrew all your wrath;
 you turned away from the fury of your rage.
⁴ Turn us around again, God of our salvation,
 and destroy your anger toward us.

⁵ Will you be angry with us forever?
  Will you extend your wrath from generation to generation?
⁶ Will you not turn us about again that we might live,
  so that your people may rejoice in you?
⁷ Show us your faithful love, LIVING GOD,
  and grant us your salvation.
⁸ Let me hear what God the SAVING ONE will speak,
  for she will speak peace to her people, to her faithful ones,
  let them not turn back to folly.
⁹ Surely her salvation is at hand for those who revere her,
  that her glory may dwell in our land.
¹⁰ Faithful love and truth will meet;
  righteousness and peace will kiss each other.
¹¹ Truth from the ground will spring up,
  and righteousness from the heavens will look down.
¹² The GRACIOUS GOD will give what is good,
  and our land will yield her produce.
¹³ Righteousness will go before her,
  and will make a path for her steps.

1 Peter 3:8 Now the conclusion of the matter is that you all should have unity of spirit, sympathy, love for one another, be tenderhearted and humble. ⁹ Do not repay evil for evil or abusive language for [more] abusive language; but on the contrary, with a blessing. It is for this that you all were called, that all of you might inherit a blessing. ¹⁰ For:

> *Those who desire to love life*
> *and to see good days—*
> *let them keep their tongues from evil*
> *and their lips from speaking deceit.*
> ¹¹ *Let them turn away from evil and do good;*
> *let them seek peace and pursue it.*
> ¹² *For the eyes of the Most High are on the righteous,*
> *and God's ears are open to their prayer.*
> *But the face of the Holy One is against those who do evil.*

Luke 16:19 [Jesus said to the women and men who were his disciples], "There was a certain rich man and he dressed in purple and fine linen and celebrated sumptuously every day. ²⁰ Now there was a certain poor man named Lazarus cast at his gate covered with sores. ²¹ And he longed to be fed with what fell from the table of the rich man; but instead, the dogs would come and lick his sores. ²² Then it happened that the poor man died and he was carried away by the angels to be enfolded in the embrace of Abraham. And then the rich man died and was buried. ²³ Now while in Hades where he was in torment, he raised up his eyes and saw Abraham far off with Lazarus enfolded in his embrace. ²⁴ And he called out, 'Father Abraham, have mercy on me and send Lazarus so that he might dip the tip of his finger in water and cool my tongue; for I am in agony in these flames.' ²⁵ But Abraham said, 'Child, remember that you received your good in your life and Lazarus similarly, evil; but now he is here comforted, while you are in agony. ²⁶ Besides all this, between us and all of you a great chasm has been established so that those who want to cross over from here to you all are unable, and no one can pass from there to us.' ²⁷ So the rich man said, 'Then, father, I ask of you to send him to the house of my father. ²⁸ For I have five siblings—that he may warn them in order that they will not also come into this place of torment.' ²⁹ And Abraham replied, 'They have Moses and the prophets—female and male; they should listen to them.' ³⁰ But he said, 'No, father Abraham rather, if someone from the dead goes to them, they will repent.' ³¹ He said to him, 'If they do not listen to Moses and the women and men who prophesied, then neither if someone rises from the dead will they be convinced.'"

PROCLAMATION

Text Notes

Unlike more common translations, the divine word does not "come" to prophts, it encounters then signified by the verb *hahah*, "to be," "to become" or, "to happen." In Jonah 3:3, Nineveh is described as "a great city, for *elohim*, for gods." While traditionally, the city is described as "an exceedingly large city" (see NRSV, NRSVue, JPS, and "enormous" in CEB), I prefer to retain the folkloric elements. The "people" of verses 5 and 8 are "men," i.e., male humans. However, verse 8 uses inclusive language for humanity. This sets up a paradigm in which male persons were being held accountable for the depredations of Assyria, represented by Nineveh. Yet, as is common in biblical literature, all persons—especially women and children—suffer the consequences of the actions of their leaders. This may also be simply an artifact of androcentric language.

The "evil" ways of humanity in verse 8 find their match in the "evil" God plans to visit upon the city; this is in keeping with some biblical theology in which God brings good and evil, weal and woe. Translations that substitute "calamity" or "disaster" aim to protect God's reputation by reforming the text rather than wrestling with it.

The Hebrew MT text presents two different forms of "captivity" in Psalm 85:1 supported by the LXX; NRSV, JPS, and Alter revise to "fortunes." "The line of Rebekah" replaces "Jacob" in verse 1. In verse 8, NRSV abandons the MT for the LXX; there is no reason to do so. I preserve the Hebrew reading along with JPS and Alter.

The author of 1 Peter quotes Psalm 34:12–16 in verses 10–12 of chapter 3.

In Luke, women are explicitly identified as following and supporting Jesus. Luke 16 is an address to the disciples of Jesus (Luke 16:1), that would necessarily include the women who followed him period. In Luke 16:20, the poor man is "cast" or "thrown" at the gate by an unknown hand. He should be read as having been abandoned rather than having chosen that spot himself. In verse 22, *kolpos*, translated here as "embrace," can mean "bosom/breast/chest" or "womb," perhaps raising the possibility of a trans reading here. As it can also mean "a fold (of clothing)," I have included that sense as well. In verses 29 and 31, I have indicated the presence of female and male prophets.

Preaching Prompts

In this season of the expansion of the Jesus movement, the language of growth signified by the color green is often articulated with regard to the Church as an entity. However, I should rather think of the growth of the persons called to walk in the Way rather than what will become an institutional church allied with empire. The call to repent, quite often accompanied by dire existential threats, is a foundational step in the spiritual growth of persons across the canons of scripture.

I regard the book of Jonah as an elaborate sermon illustration. The foundational texts are Exodus 34:6–7 and Numbers 14:18–19, articulating the characteristics of God as compassionate and merciful, perpetually faithful love, being slow to anger but not letting the guilty off scot-free. Jonah will recite these characteristics somewhat sarcastically when he is outraged that these foreigners who have caused such deep pain in Israel—breaking the monarchy into pieces from which it will never recover and decimating ten of the ancestral tribal houses through exile and brutal occupation—that they should receive the grace of forgiveness immediately upon public acts of repentance and contrition (Jonah 4:1–2).

There is a through line between Jonah and the song in which the God who does good also does evil, punitively when it is assessed that it is the right/righteous punishment for the sins of an individual or, most disturbing, the collective of a city, nation, or people. This is an opportunity to preach about those who are excluded from the halls of power because of systems of government, gerrymandered voting districts, and historical and institutional bias against women and queer and trans folk but who are overrepresented in the negative outcomes that result from government policies that either ignore their needs or actively persecute them. One might also discuss the different kinds of power that individuals hold outside of senior levels and institutional structures and the moral responsibility to use that power and agency for the benefit of others.

Neither the Epistle nor the Gospel disavows this punitive understanding of God. Indeed, it is the basis for the concept of hell, or Hades, as it is represented in the parable about Lazarus and the rich man. The Epistle is contractual and algebraic: do good, and you will get good and will not have to worry about evil befalling you. Unfortunately, this is not the way the world works. There is a need for redress here.

The Gospel makes the point that there will come a point when the work you have done will speak for you, to paraphrase a traditional Black Church saying. The imagery in Jesus's parable of Father Abraham receiving and comforting the downtrodden of the world in his bosom (or womb!) is striking and dramatic and raises all sorts of questions: Will others of the ancestral mothers and fathers receive their physical or spiritual descendants? What is the origin of this understanding of the afterlife?

Though lengthy, I find it worthwhile to quote Josephus who discusses this concept with clarity (*Discourse to the Greeks Concerning Hades*, paragraph 3):

> For there is one descent into this region, at whose gate we believe there stands an archangel with an host; which gate when those pass through that are conducted down by the angels appointed over souls, they do not go the same way; but the just are guided to the right hand, and are led with hymns, sung by the angels appointed over that place, unto a region of light, in which the just have dwelt from the beginning of the world; not constrained by necessity, but ever enjoying the prospect of the good things they see, and rejoice in the expectation of those new enjoyments which will be peculiar to every one of them, and esteeming those things beyond what we have here; with whom there is no place of toil, no burning heat, no piercing cold, nor are any briers there; but the countenance of the just, which they see, always smiles [at] them, while they wait for that rest and eternal new life in heaven, which is to succeed this region. This place we call The Bosom of Abraham.

While the Gospel seems to limit that no one will believe and repent—which means to change their ways and not just their rhetoric—it has been preserved by ancestors who did just that and call us to do so with vividly descriptive stories like this parable and Jonah. They are food and fuel to fuel our growth.

PROPER 2 (CLOSEST TO MAY 18)

Amos 2:6–13; Psalm 105:1–15; Ephesians 2:11–22; Luke 13:22–30

Amos 2:6 Thus says the JUDGE OF ALL THE EARTH:
For three transgressions of Israel,
and for four, I will not take it back
for the selling—for silver!—the righteous soul,
and a needy person—just for a pair of sandals!
⁷ Those who grind into the dust of the earth the heads of the poor
and shove the oppressed off the road;

a man and his father go to the same young girl,
thereby profaning my holy Name.
⁸ And on garments taken as collateral,
they stretch themselves out beside every altar;
and wine [bought with their] fines
they drink in the house of their god.
⁹ And yet I destroyed the Amorite from before them,
whose height was like the height of cedars,
and who was strong as oaks;
I destroyed their fruit from above,
and their roots from beneath.
¹⁰ And I, I brought you all up out of the land of Egypt;
I led you all forty years in the wilderness,
to possess the land of the Amorite.
¹¹ I also raised up from among your children [women and men to be] prophets
and from among your young people, Nazirites.
Is this not so people of Israel?

            A declaration of the LIVING GOD.

¹² But you lot made the Nazirites drink wine,
and the prophets, you all commanded [them],
saying, "Do not prophesy, any of you."
¹³ Look here, I will hold all of you back,
just as a cart is held back when it is full of sheaves.

Psalm 105:1–15

¹ Give thanks to the CREATOR OF ALL, call upon God's Name,
make known God's deeds among the peoples.
² Sing to God, sing praises to God;
Speak on all her wonders.
³ Praise her holy Name;
let the hearts of those who seek the FOUNT OF LIFE rejoice.
⁴ Seek the MIGHTY ONE and her strength;
seek her face always.
⁵ Remember the wonders she has made,
her miracles and the judgments of her mouth:
⁶ [You] descendants of God's servant Abraham [of Hagar and of Sarah],
children of Jacob [of Rachel, Leah, Bilhah, and Zilpah], her chosen ones.
⁷ She is the RIGHTEOUS ONE our God;
throughout in all the earth are her judgments [found].
⁸ She bears in mind—at all times!—her covenant,
the word she commanded for a thousand generations—

⁹ which she inscribed with Abraham [and Hagar and Sarah],
   her oath to Isaac [Sarah's son].
¹⁰ So she established it for Jacob [born of Rebekah] as a statute,
   for Israel as an everlasting covenant.
¹¹ Saying, "To you will I give the land of Canaan
   as your promised inheritance."
¹² When they were few in number,
   just a few and strangers in it,
¹³ and wandering from nation to nation,
   from one sovereign land to another people,
¹⁴ she did not allow a single mother's child to oppress them;
   and she rebuked royalty for their sake:
¹⁵ "Touch not my anointed ones,
   and my prophets, women and men, you shall not harm."

Ephesians 2:11 Now then, remember at one time all of you Gentiles according to [human] flesh called "uncircumcised" by those who are called "circumcised" because of the flesh [changed by] human hands, ¹² you all were at that time without Christ, being alienated from the citizenship of Israel, and strangers to the covenants of promise, having no hope and without God in the world. ¹³ Yet now in Christ Jesus all of you who once were at a great distance have been transformed into being near by the blood of Christ. ¹⁴ For Christ is our peace; in his flesh he has made all into one and has broken down the dividing wall, that is, the hostility between us. ¹⁵ Jesus has abolished the law with its commandments and ordinances, that he might create in himself a single new humanity in place of [Gentile and Jewish believers], thus making peace, ¹⁶ and that he might reconcile all to God in one body through the cross, putting to death hostility through *it [*or through him]. ¹⁷ So Jesus came and proclaimed peace to you all who were far off and peace to those who were near. ¹⁸ For through Jesus all of us have access in one Spirit to the Creator of All. ¹⁹ So then you all are no longer strangers and aliens, but you all are citizens with the saints and members of the household of God, ²⁰ built upon the foundation of the women and men who were apostles and prophets, with Christ Jesus himself as the cornerstone. ²¹ In Christ the whole structure is joined together and grows into a holy temple in the Messiah; ²² in whom you also are built together spiritually into a dwelling place for God.

Luke 13:22 Now Jesus passed through town and village, teaching and making his way to Jerusalem. ²³ Someone asked him, "Anointed One, will only a few be saved?" He said to them, ²⁴ "Struggle to enter through the narrow door; for many, I say to you all, will try to enter and will not be able. ²⁵ After the time the owner of the house has gotten up and shut the door, then you all begin to stand outside and to knock at the door, saying, 'Anointed One, open to us,' and the Anointed One will say to you, 'I do not know you all [or] from where you have come.' ²⁶ Then you all will begin to say, 'We ate and drank with you and you taught in our streets.' ²⁷ And the Anointed One will say, 'I do not know you all [or] from where you have come. *Get away from me, all you* *workers of wickedness!*' ²⁸ There will be weeping and gnashing of teeth when you all see Abraham and Isaac and Jacob and all the prophets [from Miriam and Moses to Huldah and Habakkuk and Anna and Amos] in the majesty of God, and you, thrown out. ²⁹ Then women, children and men will come from east and west, from north and south and will sit down [at the table] in the realm of God. ³⁰ Look here, those who are last will be first and those who are first will be last."

PROCLAMATION

Text Notes

The expression "three . . . and four . . ." is an Israelite cultural aphorism and appears in poetic passages. It is a favorite of Amos, used repeatedly throughout the first chapter and continuing into the second. It also appears in Proverbs 30:15–29. One might compare it to the English language aphorisms "Fool me once, fool me twice" or "Do X one more time. . . ." In Amos 2:7, the "young girl," *na'arah*, is either a juvenile or a woman in a subordinate position, such as a servant. The "wine of fines" is widely understood to be wine purchased with unjust fines levied upon the poor. Verse 11 uses a term for the future prophets that could be translated either as "children" or "sons." It limits Nazarites to young men explicitly; however, women could be Nazarites. The initial instructions in Numbers 6:1–21 treat women and men equally; however, a later revision (Numbers 30:3–9) allows husbands and fathers to know the vows of women broadly (raising the possibility that women made more than one kind of vow).

"Anointed ones" in verse 15 of the psalm, like the "prophets" who follow them, can be collectives that include both genders based on grammar. However, in practice, those who are anointed in the Hebrew Bible are the priesthood and monarchs' inauguration or their rule, of whom there was only one woman during the period covered by the Hebrew Bible, Athaliah.

Ephesians 2:13 uses the verb that means to "become or be born" to describe the process of becoming more like Christ making it more of a "becoming" than a "bringing near" (as in NRSV). I have used the language of "transformation." The Epistle addresses Gentile believers and discusses the relationship between Jewish and Gentile Christians. Most translations refer to "both groups" in verses 14, 16, and 18; however, the adjective also means "all," used here, which both makes more sense without the earlier verses and communicate the intent of the verse beyond its original context. Ironically, Ephesians 2:15 encodes the "hostility" of verse 14 between the two cultures and conflicts with the words of Jesus in Matthew 5:17–18: "Do not think that I have come to abolish the law or the prophets; I have come not to abolish but to fulfill. For truly I tell you, until heaven and earth pass away, not one letter, not one stroke of a letter, will pass from the law until all is accomplished."

The final phrase of verse 16 can be translated as either "through it" or "through him," that is, through Jesus. In verse 18, "Creator of All" serves as the divine title in lieu of "Father." The translation of verse 20 makes clear that women and men served as both prophets (in both testaments) and apostles.

In Luke 13:22 and in verse 25, the questioner and Jesus in his parable use the same title *kurios*, "lord," which I have rendered "Anointed One," given the celestial setting in the parable. Luke 13:27 quotes Psalm 6:9 nearly exactly from the Septuagint—which has "workers of lawlessness." The Masoretic Text has workers of wickedness. The quote is a blend of the two.

Preaching Prompts

These readings focus on belonging to community and the covenants that bind as well as their limitations. These sacred communities each have prophetic voices, persons through whom God communicates the values of the community; one enduring community value is respect for those persons and their voices as they operate gifts that from the time before Israel I have been found among all people without regard to gender. (I am writing this in the aftermath of the expulsion of congregations with women leaders by the Southern Baptist Convention.) The inclusion of all the matriarchs, including the enslaved women Bilhah and Zilpah, in verse 6 of the psalm will require some thoughtful work by the preacher as to whether or not they really are "God's chosen ones."

Violation of the vulnerable, financial exploitation of the poor, and sexual exploitation of women and girls, perhaps as survival sex, in Amos 2:6–7, breaks the communal covenant and incurs the infamous wrath of God. Amos 2:12 also addresses the dismantling of religious "orders," to use contemporary language for the Nazarites and prophets. While the Nazirites were not a religious order as we understand communities of contemplative nuns and monks today, they were, like them, visibly and socially identifiable as persons who dedicated themselves to God in a special individual manner. The breaking of their vows and silencing of the prophets represents an attempt to eradicate witnesses for God in the community and, thereby, the expectations and requirements of God.

In Amos, God reminds the people what she has done for them, bringing them out of enslavement in Egypt and delivering them to and—delivering to them—the land of Canaan. The psalm echoes this claim and records divine concern for the silencing—rhetorical and physical—of the prophets and other consecrated persons. One would hope that the responsible preacher would wrestle with this scriptural claim that inhabited lands could be repossessed and reassigned by divine fiat or claims of divine fiat, and how that language was utilized in the colonization of Africa, the Caribbean, and the colonization, genocide, and attempted this possession of the double American continent.

The Epistle sees a throughline from the community of ancient Israel descended from Sara and Abraham to the community formed around the life and teachings of their descendants Jesus, born of Mary, from the line of Bathsheba and David. Bloodlines and the previous signs of belonging will no longer be the measure of inclusion.

In the Gospel, the criteria for inclusion and belonging to community is the choices one has made similar to the reading from Amos. But the world is at a crossroads and the open door of the community will close for some, such as those described in Amos while it remains open for those from far beyond the initial sacred community. The radical inclusion will be a turning of the tables so that those who were first, and great and wealthy and insiders and privileged, will find themselves at the back of the line—if they have made it in, and there is the possibility that they too will sit around the welcome table.

PROPER 3 (CLOSEST TO MAY 25)

Hosea 1:1–10; Psalm 8:1–10; 1 Peter 2:1–15; Luke 18:15–17

Hosea 1:1 The word of the INSCRUTABLE GOD that was to Hosea ben Beeri in the days of Kings Uzziah, Jotham, Ahaz, and Hezekiah of Judah, and in the days of King Jeroboam ben Joash of Israel: ² When the GOD WHO IS MYSTERY first spoke through Hosea, the FAITHFUL GOD said to Hosea, "Go, take for yourself a whoring woman (as a wife) and children of whoring for, the land itself whores with reckless abandon by forsaking the AUTHOR OF LIFE." ³ So he went and took Gomer bat Diblaim and she conceived and gave birth to a son for him.

⁴ Then the JUDGE OF ALL THE EARTH said to him, "Call his name Jezreel, for a little while longer and I will visit punishment for the blood of Jezreel upon the house of Jehu, and I will put an end to the monarchy of the house of Israel. ⁵ And it shall be that on that day I will break the bow of Israel in the valley of Jezreel."

⁶ Then she conceived again and gave birth to a daughter. Then the INSCRUTABLE GOD said to him, "Call her name Lo-ruhamah—Not Mother-Loved, for no longer will I mother-love the house of Israel or forgive them. ⁷ Yet I will mother-love the house of Judah, and I shall save them by the MIGHTY ONE their God however I will not save them by bow, or by sword, or by war, or by horses, or by riders."

⁸ Then Gomer weaned Lo-ruhamah, and she conceived and gave birth to a son. ⁹ And the CREATOR OF ALL said, "Call his name Lo-ammi for you all are not my people and I am not yours."

¹⁰ Yet it shall be that the number of the women, children, and men of Israel shall be like the sand of the sea, which can neither be measured nor numbered, and in the place where it was said to them, "You all are not my people," it shall be said to them, "Children of the living God."

Psalm 8:1–10

¹ WOMB OF LIFE, our Sovereign,
    how exalted is your Name in all the earth!
² Out of the mouths of infants and children
    your majesty is praised above the heavens.

³ You have set up a stronghold against your adversaries,
   to quell the enemy and the avenger.
⁴ When I consider your heavens, the work of your fingers,
   the moon and the stars you have set in their courses,
⁵ What are we that you should be mindful of us?
   those born of women that you should seek us out?
⁶ You have made us a little lower than God;
   you adorn us with glory and honor;
⁷ You give us mastery over the works of your hands;
   you put all things under our feet:
⁸ All sheep and oxen,
   even the wild beasts of the field,
⁹ The birds of the air, the fish of the sea,
   and whatsoever walks in the paths of the sea.
¹⁰ Womb of Life, our Sovereign,
   how exalted is your Name in all the earth!

1 Peter 2:1 Rid yourselves of all malice, and all deceit, hypocrisy, envy, and all slander. ² Like newborn infants, long for the pure spiritual milk, so that by it you may grow into salvation—³ if indeed you have *tasted that the Holy One is good*.

⁴ Come to Jesus, a living stone, although rejected by humanity yet chosen and precious to God. ⁵ And are yourselves, like living stones, being built into a spiritual house to be a holy priesthood, to offer spiritual sacrifices acceptable to God through Jesus Christ.

Luke 18:15 Now women and men were bringing even babies to Jesus in order that he might touch them; but, when the disciples saw it, they sternly ordered them not to do so. ¹⁶ Then Jesus called for them and said, "Let the children come to me and do not hinder them, for it is to such as these that the majesty of God belongs. ¹⁷ Truly I tell you, whoever does not receive the majesty of God as a child will never enter it."

PROCLAMATION

Text Notes

In Hosea 1:2, the "whoring woman" is a woman of "prostitution/sex work, adultery, infidelity, fornication," etc. The language of "whoredom" is rarely literal in the Hebrew Bible; that is, the women who are called whores are not necessarily sex workers. The term was as much a "slut shaming" term" in the ancient world as it is in the contemporary one. Indeed, its most common usage is to accuse Israel of sexual infidelity against God—with blinders around the implication that Israel's "marriage" to God would then also be sexual.

The expression "to take (a woman)" always indicates what is generally called marriage in the Hebrew Bible, including marriages by force, captivity, enslavement, and other forms of rape-based conjugal unions. In Hosea 1:2, God says, "take a woman and children," not *have* children. This has led many to question whether Gomer already had children, i.e., out of wedlock, and therefore a whore by reputation but not by profession. The nature of the entire episode is unclear as the language slides between the human characters and Israel itself as a character over the first three chapters, suggesting to no small number of scholars that this is a parable.

"Jezreel" of Hosea 1:4–5 is a geographical location in northern Israel situated in the tribe of Issachar. It is significant as the home of Ahinoam, the mother of David's first child (see 2 Samuel 2:2 and 3:2), and infamous as the location of the vineyard Jezebel seized for her husband, Ahab, and finally, as the location of Jezebel's death and gruesome postmortem mastication by dogs largely orchestrated by Jehu. Jezreel also serves as something of a pet name for Israel. The lengthy account of what I refer to as "the Jezebel narrative" runs from 1 Kings 21 to 2 Kings 9 where Jezebel is granted an honorable burial as "the daughter of kings" (2 Kings 9:34). Even though no less worthy than Elisha himself anointed Jehu king at the orders of Elijah, tradition faults Jehu for the bloodbath.

In Hosea 1:6–7, the verb *racham*, to "mother-love" (elsewhere translated as to have "compassion" or even, "pity") has its roots in the word for "womb," *rechem*, hence the preference for translations that make the maternal connection clear. In verse 8, *ammi* means "my people" with the negative being signified by the particle "lo." The well-known line, "you are not my people and I am not your God" relies on the insertion of the missing word "God" at the end of the sentence. As the verse is comprehensible without the addition, I maintain the Hebrew reading.

Psalm 8:5 uses *ben adam*, literally "child/son of humanity" for humanity. Most often, the expression indicates mortality and frailty, see God's repeated address to Ezekiel in chapters 2–5, etc., and Jesus invoking his own mortality in Mark 8:31. More rarely, the expression refers to a divine being, as in Daniel 7:13 (Aramaic). Jesus also uses it in this way; see Luke 21:27. In Psalm 8:6, humanity is created a little lower than God in Hebrew.

First Peter 2:3 cites Psalm 34:8.

Luke 18:15 states that "they" brought infants to Jesus. Grammatically, "they" is inclusive. It is most likely that women brought their infants to Jesus, but it is not impossible that some men did as well; therefore, I have expanded the verb to be as inclusive as possible. In many cases, this project uses majesty to articulate the rain and realm of God and the limitless mystery they enfold rather than a term with roots in a particular political polity prone to violence, invasion, and colonization.

Preaching Prompts

While much preaching understandably focuses on the figure of Gomer and her representation of the people of Israel in a troubling marital metaphor, I invite preachers to consider the children in this family or parable as they are presented. (For a rich treatment of marriage and other divine–human metaphors in the Hebrew Bible, I heartily commend *Battered Love: Marriage, Sex, and Violence in the Hebrew Prophets* by the Rev. Dr. Renita J. Weems [Philadelphia: Fortress Press, 1995]). In a sermon on this chapter, "When Gomer Looks More like God," prompted by Dr. Mark Brummitt, I focus on Gomer nursing her daughter, who stands for God's emotional withdrawal from Israel (https://www.wilgafney.com/2018/09/24/when-gomer-looks-more-like-god/). If God can be seen anywhere in the text through Womanist eyes, it is not the patriarchal male who excoriates his partner for a sexual past—of which he was already aware—when entering the union and then abandons children to fend for themselves out of anger with their mother. However, a whole lot of theology fashions a God in this image. But Gomer is the one cradling the child abandoned by her father to her breast, providing the very mother-love this literary representation of God withholds. (Note the poly-gender depiction of God as husband and father and as the source of mother-love to be withheld.) Womanism asks where are those who are most vulnerable in this text: Gomer's children. Womanism teaches that is where God can be found.

These readings invite attention to the way children and their representations figure as actual or potential locations for divine presence and relationship. Gomer's children are rejected by patriarchal religious sensibilities, but she continues to provide sustenance, nurture, and love. In Psalm 8, infants and children form a terrestrial counterpoint to the celestial choir. In 1 Peter 2:1, new believers are portrayed as infants at their Mother's breast and urged to long for that holy sustenance and not rush themselves off of the breast of God lest they be weaned too soon.

The notion of a nursing nurturing God extends back across the testaments to the name of God, Shaddai, the Breasted God with *shad*, "breast," as its presumed lexical root. Shaddai is invoked in contexts where God is promising or providing fertility, such as Genesis 28:3 and 35:11. Genesis 49:25 offers a blessing from "the God of your father, who shall help you; and by Shaddai, who shall bless you with blessings of the heavens above, blessings of the deep that lies below, blessings of breasts (*shadim*) and womb." (*Shadim* is the plural of *shad*.) There is a possibility that the Akkadian cognate "mountain" is also breast imagery with the mountains as breasts (and snow cap as nipple) that nourish the world through their lifegiving water in the desert realm.

In the Gospel, as minors, children are overlooked as participants in the way of love Jesus has brought to the Earth. Mothers and perhaps other parents and caretakers bring children to Jesus for a blessing because, whatever else he is, he is widely understood to be a holy man. In his arms, infants and children become more than parable props. They are witnesses to the unfolding majesty of God. We who are no longer children must adjust ourselves to their posture, position, and perception to have any hope of being received into that majesty.

Today's sermon might as well be entitled, "What about the children?" The ways in which we as a society fail to honor children as the embodiment of God's unfolding in the world are nearly without number. In this broad American context it is those children who are somehow deemed as "other," who are the most vulnerable: migrant children, native children, black children, poor children, trans children. We need a few more Gomers expanding the capacity of the divine embrace alongside Jesus.

PROPER 4 (CLOSEST TO JUNE 1)

Hosea 2:1, 14–20; Psalm 104:1–4, 10–15, 27–30;
Ephesians 1:3–14; Luke 12:22–28

Hosea 2:1 [People of Israel]: Speak to your brother-kin as Ammi (My People), and to your sister-kin as Ruhamah, Mother's Beloved.

¹⁴ Now then, look! I will now seduce her (your mother),
   and I will lead her through the wilderness,
   and I shall speak to her heart.
¹⁵ From there I will give her her vineyards,
   and make the Achor Valley (the Valley of Trouble) a passage of hope.
   And there she shall respond as in the days of her young womanhood,
   and as in the day when she came up out of the land of Egypt.
¹⁶ And it shall be on that day—

                    A declaration of the FAITHFUL GOD,
   —you (wife) will call me, "My husband,"
   and you shall not call me, "My Lord and Master, My Baal" ever again.
¹⁷ For I shall remove the names of the Baals from her mouth,
   and their names shall be remembered no more.
¹⁸ Then shall I inscribe for them a covenant on that day with the beasts of the field, the
   birds of the air, and the creeping things of the ground, and the bow, the sword, and
   war shall I sever from the land; then I shall lay you down in safety.
¹⁹ And I shall betrothe you to me for all time;
   And I shall betrothe you to me in righteousness and in justice,
   in lovingkindness and in mother-love.
²⁰ And I shall betrothe you to me in faithfulness;
   and you shall know the GOD WHO IS LOVE.

Psalm 104:1–4, 10–15, 27–30

1. Bless the FOUNT OF LIFE, O my soul.
   MOTHER OF ALL, my God, you are very great.
   You don honor and majesty,
2. Wrapped in light as a garment,
   you stretch out the heavens like a tent-curtain.
3. She who lays on the waters the beams of her upper chambers,
   she who makes the clouds her chariot,
   she is the one who rides on the wings of the wind.
4. She is the one who makes the winds her celestial messengers,
   fire and flame her ministers.
10. She is the one who makes springs gush forth in the torrents;
    they flow between the hills.
11. They give drink to every wild animal;
    the wild donkeys slake their thirst.
12. By the torrents the birds of the heavens dwell;
    among the branches they give voice.
13. She is the one who waters the mountains from her high chambers;
    the earth is satisfied with the fruit of your work.
14. She is the one who makes grass to grow for the cattle,
    and vegetation for human labor,
    to bring forth food from the earth,
15. and wine to make the human heart rejoice,
    with oil to make the face shine,
    and bread to sustain the human heart.
27. All of these hope in you
    to provide their food in due season.
28. You give it to them, they glean it;
    you open your hand, they are well satisfied.
29. You hide your face, they are dismayed;
    when you collect their breath, they die
    and to their dust they return.
30. You send forth your spirit, they are created;
    and you renew the face of the earth.

Ephesians 1:3 Blessed be the God and Abba of our Redeemer Jesus the Messiah, who has blessed us with every spiritual blessing in the heavens in the Messiah. ⁴ Just as in choosing us in the Messiah before the foundation of the world to be holy and blameless before God in love, ⁵ God destined us for adoption as their children through Jesus Christ, according to the good pleasure of God's will, ⁶ to the praise of God's glorious grace freely bestowed on us in the Beloved. ⁷ In

Christ we have redemption through his blood, the forgiveness of our trespasses, according to the riches of God's grace. [8] Grace which God has abundantly poured upon us along with all wisdom and understanding. [9] God has made known to us the mystery of God's will according to God's good pleasure that God set forth in Christ. [10] A plan in the fullness of time to gather up all things in Christ, things in the heavens and things on earth, all into Christ. [11] In Christ there is also an inheritance from before time according to the purpose of the one who does all things according to God's counsel and will. [12] This so that we might live for the praise of God's glory, we who first trusted in Christ. [13] In Christ you also heard the word of truth, the gospel of your salvation and believed, and were marked with the seal of the promised Holy Spirit. [14] She is the deposit of our inheritance toward redemption as God's own possession to the praise of God's glory.

Luke 12:22 Jesus said to his disciples [before the multitude of women, children, and men], "Here now I tell you all, worry not about your life, what you will eat, or about your body, what you will wear. [23] For life is more than food, and the body than clothing. [24] Consider the ravens that neither sow nor reap; they have neither vault nor barn and yet, God feeds them. Of how much more value are all of you than the birds! [25] And can any of you by worrying add length [or height] to your life? [26] If then you are not able to do such a small thing, why do you worry about the rest? [27] Consider the lilies, how they grow: they neither toil nor spin; yet I tell you all, even Solomon in all his glory was not clothed like one of these. [28] Now if the grass of the field, which is here today and tomorrow into the furnace is thrown, God clothes, how much more will God clothe you, O you of little faith!

PROCLAMATION

Text Notes

The text of Hosea is numbered differently in the Septuagint (LXX) and Christian Bibles than in Hebrew (and Jewish Bibles in other languages). This is not uncommon and a curse sporadically throughout the First Testament. This project follows the LXX and subsequent Christian tradition. Thus, what is chapter 2:1 here is chapter 2:3 in Hebrew and Jewish tradition.

Hosea 2:1 begins with a plural imperative. The previous addressees in the earlier chapter were Hosea and Israel. Therefore, I have identified "the people of Israel" as the recipient to help the reader. The names of Gomer's children from chapter 1 become emblematic of the people; the language for "sisters" and "brothers" is expensive here, meaning all of one's kin of the same gender identity as a way of circumscribing the entire nation in binary gendered terms. The children's names have been inverted from "Not My People" to "My People" and from "Not Mother-Loved" to "Mother's Beloved."

The reading moves from the first verse to verse 14 (v. 16 in Hebrew) intentionally to avoid the intervening verses in which God batters his spouse, i.e., strips her naked and leaves her to die of thirst in the wilderness, verse 3 (Heb. v. 5). In a domestic violence cycle, verses 14 and the following represent the honeymoon period after an episode of violence. In moving from verse 1 to verse 14, this lectionary creates a new telling of the story without that cycle of violence.

In the "seduction" of Hose 2:14, the text uses a verb for God with a sexual connotation: seducing a virgin in Exodus 22:16 and seduced by a woman who is not his wife in Job 31:9, along with God's most infamous seduction in Jeremiah 20:7 in which the prophet accuses God of seducing him and overpowering him using the shared vocabulary of rape in the Hebrew Bible. (Again, I commend the reader to *Battered Love: Marriage, Sex, and Violence in the Hebrew Prophets* by the Rev. Dr. Renita J. Weems [Philadelphia: Fortress Press, 1995]).

In the "renewal of vows" in verses 19–20 (Heb. vv. 21–23), the feminine language, "I will take you for my wife," which shows up in NRSV, NRSVue, and CEB is not present. The verb is one of betrothal without specifying the gender of the intended explicitly.

Psalm 104 switches between second and third person, as is common in the genre. Verses 14–15 use the word that means both bread and food in general in both senses.

The presence of a larger Ruth for this teaching is established in Luke 12:1. In verse 25, *helikia* means a stretch of time or height and has been translated both ways.

Preaching Prompts

Today's readings press the question of for whom does God care and how. In Hosea 1, God's covenant relationship with Israel is symbolized by a marital covenant, but a hierarchical one in which a spouse can be battered and children abandoned. A bottom-up reading sees that there are enduring relational bonds that are disregarded by the dominant religious reading.

In today's lesson from Hosea 2, there is a recommitment ceremony between God and Israel that is so expansive it includes all of nature. These combined portraits of God are very human and indicative of a deeply troubled and troubling relationship. However, there is grace in a portrait of God—however indebted to a toxic patriarchal masculinity—who turns from their previous violent way and is willing to start over in a love characterized by justice and righteousness, fidelity, and tender love. The preacher will have to navigate the treacherous waters of domestic and family violence. Yet there is also an opportunity to address problematic models of, and sources for, theology, particularly patriarchal ones, including in the text.

From Hosea to the psalm to the Gospel, these texts also articulate a divine ecology featuring repeated references to the birds of heaven and the flora and fauna of earth. It is worth asking why, in such a wholesome description of God's care for the world, women like Gomer and the everyday Israelite women whom she represents in part, receive so much less than crumbs from under the divine table so often. Here,

I think of the line from Macy Gray: "your crumbs of lovin' no longer get me by . . ." (*Still*, Sony BMG Music, 2000).

All of these readings also offer a theology of divine providence, that God provides all we need. This is also a difficult theology because we are aware of so many who are in need. It is useful to remember that the communities that received, canonized, and circulated these texts also lived with need and saw it in their communities. Their "little" and growing faith was in a God larger than and contrary to their circumstances: God of the not yet and "soon come" (the latter a black folk expression with roots in the theology of enslaved persons).

In its providential theology, the Gospel appeals to natural theology: look at the world around you, its harmony, abundance, and balance. This may be heard as a whole to actively preserve, maintain, and restore the balance of the natural world so that it will remain capable of feeding and clothing its host populations. The lack of balance in human relationships, particularly along gender lines and class lines, might also be read as inhibiting our ability to experience the fullness of what God provides. And the grasping greed and wastefulness of humanity, particularly in more developed societies, reneges on the promise of God for abundant provision to those who are most vulnerable.

Lastly, it may be a reflection on the social, cultural, and political vulnerability of the emerging Jesus movement that the Epistle frames the richness and beneficence of God in purely spiritual terms.

PROPER 5 (CLOSEST TO JUNE 8)

Micah 2:6–12; Psalm 80:1–7; 1 Thessalonians 5:12–24; Luke 4:40–43

Micah 2:6 "Stop preaching!" They themselves preach!
"Do not preach of such things;
disgrace will not turn upon us."
7 Does this need to be said, House of Jacob [Heritage of Rebekah]?
Is the spirit of the Gracious One limited?
Are these God's works?
Do not my words do good
to one who walks rightly?
8 Formerly they rose up against my people as an enemy;
publicly you all strip the robe from the peaceful,
from those who pass by trusting
who have turned away from war.
9 The women of my people,
you drive out from the homes they delight in;

from their babies,
you take away my majesty for all time.
10 All of you, get up and go! For this is not a place for rest,
because of impurity that destroys with sickening devastation.
11 A person who went about with a throat full of empty lies [said]:
"I will preach to you of wine and strong drink."
That one would be the preacher for this people!
12 Yet I will surely gather all of you, Jacob [Rebekah's heritage],
I will gather the survivors of Israel;
I will set them together like sheep in a fold,
like a flock in its pasture;
it will resound with people.

Psalm 80:1–7

1 Shepherd of Israel, pray, hearken,
you who lead the line of Rebekah like a flock.
You, enthroned upon the cherubim, pray, shine forth.
2 Before Ephraim and Benjamin and Manasseh,
stir up your might and come to save us!
3 God restore us and let your face shine,
that we may be saved.
4 Sovereign of heaven's vanguard,
how long will you fume at the prayers of your people?
5 You have fed them tears for bread,
and you have given them tears to drink thrice over.
6 You make us the scorn of our neighbors;
our enemies laugh among themselves.
7 God of heaven's vanguard restore us and let your face shine,
that we may be saved.

1 Thessalonians 5:12 We appeal to you all, sisters and brothers, to acknowledge those who labor with you all, and lead you all in Christ, and admonish you all. 13 Esteem them more than before in love because of their work. Be at peace among yourselves. 14 Now we urge you, kindred, to admonish the undisciplined, encourage the discouraged, support the weak, be patient with all. 15 See that none of you repays evil for evil, rather always seek to do good to one another and to all. 16 Rejoice always. 17 Pray without ceasing. 18 In all things give thanks, for this is the will of God in Christ Jesus for you all. 19 Quench not the Spirit. 20 Despise not the words of women or men who prophesy, 21 rather examine everything. To what is good, hold fast. 22 Avoid every appearance of evil.

23 May the very God of peace sanctify you all wholly, and may your spirit and soul and body be kept blameless at the coming of our Redeemer Jesus Christ. 24 The one who calls you is faithful and will do this.

Luke 4:40 [After healing Peter's mother-in-law] as the sun was setting, everyone, as many as had sick persons—women, children, and men, with various diseases—brought them to Jesus and he laid his hands on each of them and cured them. ⁴¹ And also, demons came out of many, shouting and saying, "You are the Son of God!" But Jesus rebuked them and would not permit them to speak, because they knew that he was the Messiah.

⁴² At the dawning of the day Jesus departed and went into a deserted place. And the crowds of women, children and men were looking for him and when they reached him, they wanted to hold him so he would not leave them. ⁴³ Then Jesus said to them, "To other cities must I also proclaim the good news of the majesty of God; for I was sent for this purpose." ⁴⁴ So Jesus continued proclaiming the message in the synagogues of Judea.

PROCLAMATION

Text Notes

In Micah 2:7, the expression about God's spirit being "limited" or "shortened" refers to limitations on God's patience. In verse 8, the often untranslated particle can mean "formally" or "in front [of]." Here, I translate it as "publicly." I include an option to name the lineage of Jacob as the lineage of his mother, Rebekah, in verses 7 and 12 of the first reading.

In the psalm, "the line of Rebekah" replaces "Joseph" in verse 1. The root of "thrice over" in verse 5 shares its form with the number three; see Alter's "triple measure" following the Targum and "three times over" in the CEB.

"Women and men who prophesy" expands "prophet" in 1 Thessalonians 5:20, reflecting the activity of prophets of both genders in both testaments, i.e., Miriam, Deborah, Huldah, Noadiah, Anna, the four virgin daughters of Phillip in Acts 21:9, and the Corinthian women prophets in 1 Corinthians 11:5. (For more on these and others, see my *Daughters of Miriam: Women Prophets in Ancient Israel*.)

Preaching Prompts

Sometimes, the good news is bad news, hard news, or unwelcome news. In the first reading, Micah is acting out the people's rejection of a prophetic message, perhaps his own. The psalmist laments that instead of bread from heaven, God has only supplied tears and more tears in verse 5. The Epistle is a word of admonishment rather than a word of encouragement. In the Gospel, Jesus silences the proclamation of the gospel because it is too soon to tell the full truth about himself. (I note with interest that neither the text nor Jesus silences the exorcised demons because they are unfit to proclaim the gospel of his identity as the holy Child of God; rather, the text is insistent that it was not the time for his identity as the Messiah to be revealed. So then, if Jesus has no word of rebuke for literal or literary "demons" for proclaiming the gospel, some folk treat women worse than Jesus treated demons.)

Sometimes the word from heaven is not what we want or want to hear. The people's rejection of Micah's preaching that led to his mocking retort that the only preacher they wanted to listen to was one proclaiming "wine and strong drink" (Micah 2:12), was in response to a proclamation of disaster to come. At the beginning of the chapter, the prophet preaches against those who coveted and seized houses and lands from their neighbors, verse 2. Through Micah, God expresses outrage that the dispossession of families leaves women homeless, and in the world of the text, as in ours, maternal homelessness leads to disastrous outcomes for their children, verse 12. The prophetic proclamation forth-telling that followed his truth-telling was that the economy of injustice they have fueled will turn and consume them when the foreign nations that covet their lands invade and seize them, (in verse 5, just before this reading). Micah reports the people told him to shut up and stop preaching, verse 6, in the same way, some celebrities are told to shut up and sit down, or in the case of LeBron James, to "shut up and dribble." (On February 16, 2018, television personality Laura Ingraham told LeBron James to "shut up and dribble" in response to his articulated political opinions.)

As in Micah 2, the sorrows of the psalmist and her community were experienced as divine retribution. In response, they cried out to God to be restored to God's good grace, the shining of God's face, that they might be saved (Psalm 80:3). Their prayer is passionate, and as my friend, Pastor Carla Jones Brown, might say, "rambunctious." They are summoning God to get herself together and get in the fight for their deliverance in the first two verses. This is a prayer tradition black folk have taken to heart, calling God to account and reminding God of her promises. In verse 4, the psalmist essentially tells God that God has been angry long enough; it is posed as a rhetorical question out of respect but a womanist maternal hermeneutic reading of that line, such as that employed by the Rev. Dr. Valerie Bridgeman, understands it is no more a question then when your mother asked if you are planning to do the dishes.

In 1 Thessalonians, the apostle writes with a word of discipline. And whoever wants a moral lecture? The Epistle selection is a list of "dos" and "do nots" in softening language. In my sanctified imagination, I imagine that the good news of a long-awaited word from the shepherd was quickly experienced by some, if not many, as the bad news blues. Buried in the message in 1 Thessalonians 5:20 is an exhortation "not to despise the words of prophets." That includes prophets of both genders. We know that they were women prophets and then they said Jesus movement that they continued prophesying for the first few centuries of the Early Church era and that they were silenced by increasingly patriarchal hierarchies that did not heat the apostle's injunction. That is bad news for the Church.

In Luke 4:40–43, the good news that is made manifest in the person of Jesus Christ is teased out from the good news that is the proclamation of his message. That Jesus wants to leave this community is sorrowful, perhaps heartbreaking news. Imagine with me that they have welcomed and fed and sheltered him. In addition to asking for and receiving his healing touch, they have embraced him and placed their babies in his lap and told him their sorrows and joys and talked long into the night. And now this miracle-made-flesh is leaving. What will they do without him in their midst? That is the question for the Church in an era in which Jesus has also physically left us. Today, Jesus is doing his work in the world in a way in which we cannot hold onto him. And while the text is clear that Jesus continues to proclaim his gospel, it does not say what this community does. Do they, woman, man, and child, proclaim the gospel they have seen and heard to neighbors and strangers? How was the community changed for the better as a result of the members of the community being in good health? What will our communities look like if our neighbors have good food, clean water and air, access to healthcare and no longer live under threat of lead poisoning and environmental asthma and maternal morbidity and mortality? Wouldn't that be good news? Unfortunately, the church has tended to limit "the good news" to the words of Jesus or words about Jesus. But everything about him was good news; his work in the world was good news and we are called to that work though our methods will have to differ greatly.

PROPER 6 (CLOSEST TO JUNE 15)

Micah 4:1–10; Psalm 22:22–25; Revelation 15:2–4; Luke 14:1, 12–24

Micah 4:1 And it shall be in the days to come,
  the mountain of the house of the GLORIOUS ONE
  shall be established on the highest of the mountains,
  and it shall be raised up above the hills;
  and they, the peoples, shall stream to it,
² And many nations shall come and say:
  Come! Let us go up to the mountain of the RADIANT ONE,
  to the house of the God of Jacob [the pride of Rebekah];
  that God may teach us God's own ways
  and that we might walk in God's paths."
  For out of Zion shall go forth teaching,
  and the word of the HOLY ONE OF SINAI from Jerusalem.
³ God shall judge between many peoples,
  and shall render verdicts for mighty nations afar off;
  and they shall beat their swords into plowshares,
  and their spears into pruning hooks.
  Nation shall not lift up sword against nation,
  neither shall they learn war any more.
⁴ And each one shall settle under their own vines and under their own fig trees,
  and none shall make them tremble with fear;

for the mouth of the Commander of heaven's legions has spoken.
⁵ For all the peoples walk,
 each in the name of their god;
 but we will walk in the Name of the Holy One our God
 forever and ever.
⁶ In that day—
 a declaration of the Shepherding God:
 I will gather the lame
 and those who have been driven away, I shall collect
 along with those whom I have afflicted.
⁷ And I shall make the lame the remnant,
 and those who were cast off, a strong nation;
 and the Majestic One will reign over them in Mount Zion
 now and for all time.
⁸ And you, watchtower of the flock,
 hill of Daughter Zion, to you it shall come;
 the former dominion shall return,
 the sovereignty of Daughter Jerusalem.
⁹ Now why do you shout so loud, [Daughter]?
 Is there no sovereign within you?
 Has your counselor perished,
 that pangs like a woman in labor have seized you?
¹⁰ Twist and shout, Daughter Zion,
 like a birthing-woman;
 for you shall go forth from the city
 and encamp in the field.
 You shall go to Babylon;
 there you shall be delivered.
 There the Saving God shall redeem you
 from the hand of your enemies.

Psalm 22:22–25

²² I will tell of your name to my sisters and brothers;
 in the midst of the congregation, I will praise you:
²³ You who revere the Fount of Life, praise her!
 all the offspring of Leah and Rachel, Bilhah and Zilpah glorify her.
 Stand in awe of her all you of Rebekah's line.
²⁴ For she did not despise or abhor
 the affliction of the afflicted;

she did not hide her face from me,
and when I cried to her, she heard.
25 On your account is my praise in the great congregation;
my vows I will pay before those who revere her.

Revelation 15:2 Now I saw something like a sea of glass mixed with fire and those who had conquered the beast and its image and the number of its name were standing beside the sea of glass with harps of God. ³ And they sing the song of Moses, the slave of God, and the song of the Lamb:

"Great and marvelous are your works,
Holy God Almighty!
Just and true are your ways,
Sovereign of the nations!
⁴ Who will not fear the Most High
and glorify your name?
For you alone are holy.
All nations will come
and worship before you,
for your righteous acts have been revealed."

Luke 14:1 Now it happened that Jesus was to go to the home of one of the leaders of the Pharisees one Sabbath to eat a meal and they were watching him closely.

¹² And Jesus said to the one who invited him, "When you put on a luncheon or a dinner, do not invite your friends, your sisters and brothers, your near-kin, or rich neighbors so they will do so in return and you would be repaid. ¹³ Rather, when you give a banquet, invite the poor, the crippled, the lame, and the blind. ¹⁴ And you will be blessed because they do not have it to repay you; for you will be repaid in the resurrection of the righteous."

¹⁵ Now one of those reclining at table hearing this said to Jesus, "Blessed are those who will feast at God's welcome table!" ¹⁶ And Jesus replied:

"Now a certain person put on a large dinner and invited many women and men. ¹⁷ And the host sent their slave at the time for the dinner to tell those who were invited, 'Come! For now all is ready.' ¹⁸ And one by one they all began to decline. The first told the host, 'I bought land and have need to go and see it. I beg you to excuse me.' ¹⁹ And another said, 'I bought five yoke-teams of oxen and I am going to examine them. I beg you to excuse me.' ²⁰ Yet another said, 'I have married my bride, this is why I cannot come.' ²¹ And returning, the slave reported these things to the master. Then the owner of the house became angry and said to the slave, 'Go at once to the streets and back roads of the city and bring the poor, the crippled, the blind, and the lame.' ²² And the slave said, 'Master, so it has been done as you commanded and there is still room.' ²³ The master said to the slave, 'Go to the highways and byways and make people come so that my house will be filled. ²⁴ For I say to you all, not one of those who were invited will taste my dinner.'"

PROCLAMATION

Text Notes

The "swords and plowshares" verses in Isaiah 2:4 and Micah 4:3 originate so closely in time that it cannot be determined which proceeds, also the case for the book of Micah and the first forty chapters of Isaiah (First Isaiah). Take note that Joel 3:10 inverts the verse—or perhaps Isaiah/ Micah inverts Joel; it is impossible to date Joel with certainty.

Hebrew grammar makes clear that the addressee in Micah 1:9 is a feminine subject, Jerusalem, described previously as "Daughter Zion," and in the following lines as both "Daughter Zion" and "Daughter Jerusalem."

In Psalm 22:23, "the offspring of Jacob" are identified by their mothers/matriarchs, enslaved and free; similarly, "Rebekah's line" stands in for "the offspring of Israel."

The "Song of Moses" referenced in Revelation 15:3 is Deuteronomy 32.

In Luke 14:15, "welcome table," from the spiritual language tradition of those enslaved in the American South, evokes the majesty and gracious welcome of God not always communicated by a martial political term such as "kingdom."

Preaching Prompts

The scriptures move between God's special concern for her particular people, Israel and an all-encompassing care and concern for the whole of the cosmos, including its flora and fauna, and all the nations of the world. Micah offers a vision of the all-inclusive, all-access welcome table of God, a theme amplified by the reading from Revelation 15. "Peoples" and "nations" signify Gentile, non-Israelite nations and peoples who are welcome to the mount of God. Verse 5 offers the rare acknowledgment of people who worship a different God without threat or condemnation. Those readings focus on the gathered and worshiping congregation as a whole.

Psalm 22, perhaps best known for its portrayal of a suffering soul immortalized by Jesus's recitation of parts of it during his crucifixion, provides the perspective of an individual within the congregation determined to give voice to their own praise and worship. The parable of the supper invitation in Luke 14 provides an opportunity for each person to reserve her seat at the welcome table of God while illustrating how easy it is to miss out on that opportunity. And while there is an emphasis on those foolish guests who missed their once-in-eternity opportunity, one might suggest that after the first round of guests were seated, there could have been round after round of invitations, for the actual welcome table of God will not exceed its seating capacity.

A preacher might explore who gets invited first and why, historically and currently, and who has been relegated to the "if we have room" category. One might consider the limitation of "table" language. Expressions such as "making room at the table" often include a not-so-subtle claim of ownership of the table: it is mine/ours and we will make room for you, reinforcing that your only access is through us. Womanists have observed that first-generation feminists sought a seat at the tables of power, quickly acclimating to the culture of those tables and reproducing the exclusionary practices of those tables "in skirts and heels." Might we beg the indulgence of God to construct another instrument of welcome, and what might that be?

PROPER 7 (CLOSEST TO JUNE 22)
Isaiah 8:1–8; Psalm 34:11–22; 1 John 3:1–3; Luke 9:38–48

Isaiah 8:1 Now the INSCRUTABLE GOD said to me:
"Take for yourself a large tablet and write on it with a common tool, 'For Maher Shalal Hash Baz (meaning: Swiftly Savaged, Rapidly Ravaged).' ² Then I will swear in for myself faithful witnesses—the priest Uriah and Zechariah ben Jeberechiah." ³ So I went to the prophetess and she conceived and she gave birth to a child. Then the FOUNT OF WISDOM said to me:
"Name the child Maher Shalal Hash Baz. ⁴ For before the child knows how to call 'My mother' or 'My father,' the wealth of Damascus and the spoil of Samaria will be carried off by the ruler of Assyria."
⁵ Then again the CREATOR OF ALL spoke to me, yet further:
⁶ "For because this people has refused the waters of Shiloah that flow gently and swoon at Rezin [ruler of the Arameans] and on account of [Israel's king, Pekah] the son of Remaliah—⁷ therefore, the Holy One is bringing up over them the many mighty waters of the [Euphrates] River, the ruler of Assyria and all his glory. And it shall rise above all its channels and overflow all its banks. ⁸ And passing through Judah flooding and pouring over, it shall flow up to the neck and its wingspan shall fill the width of your land, O Immanuel."

Psalm 34:11–22

¹¹ Come, children, listen to me;
    I will teach you the reverence of SHE WHO IS MAJESTY.
¹² Who is the woman or man that desires life,
    and would love long days to enjoy good?
¹³ Keep your tongue from evil,
    and your lips from speaking deceit.
¹⁴ Turn from evil, and do good;
    seek peace, and pursue it.
¹⁵ The eyes of the ALL-SEEING GOD are upon the righteous,

and her ears are open to their cry.
16. The face of the Righteous One is against those who do evil,
to cut off from the earth their memory.
17. The righteous cry out and the Compassionate One hears,
and from all their troubles delivers them.
18. The Loving God is near to the brokenhearted,
and those who are crushed in spirit she saves.
19. The evils [that plague] the righteous are many,
but the Saving God delivers them from them all.
20. She preserves all their bones;
not one of them will be broken.
21. Evil brings death to the wicked,
and those who hate the righteous will be found guilty.
22. The Merciful One redeems the life of her servants;
and none will be found guilty of all who take refuge in her.

1 John 3:1 See what kind of love has our Maker given to us, that we should be called children of God; and we are. The reason the world does not know us is that it did not know God. 2 Beloved, now are we God's children and it has not yet been revealed what we will be. We do know that when God is revealed, we shall be like God, for we shall see God just as God is. 3 And everyone who has this hope in God purifies themselves, just as God is pure.

Luke 9:38 Now suddenly a person from the crowd shouted, "Teacher, I beg you to examine my child; this is my only child. 39 And see here, a spirit seizes the child and immediately, there is shrieking and it shakes the child with foaming [at the mouth], and it will scarcely leave the child, torturing the child. 40 Now I begged your disciples to cast it out, but they were not able." 41 Then Jesus responded saying, "You faithless and twisted generation, how much longer must I be with you and put up with you all? Bring your child here." 42 While the child was coming, the demon threw the child to the ground in convulsions. But Jesus rebuked the unclean spirit, healed the boy, and returned the child to the parent. 43 And all were amazed at the greatness of God. While everyone marveled at everything Jesus was doing, Jesus said to his disciples:
44 "Let sink into your ears these words: Indeed, the Son of Woman is going to be betrayed into woman-born hands." 45 But they did not understand this word and its meaning was concealed from them so that they could not perceive it; and they feared to ask him about this word.
46 Now there arose a debate among them, which one of them was the greatest. 47 But Jesus knowing the debate in their hearts, took a little child and put the child next to him. 48 And Jesus said to them, "Whoever welcomes this child in my name welcomes me and whoever welcomes me welcomes the one who sent me; for the least among of you all is the greatest."

PROCLAMATION

Text Notes

Isaiah 8 is a bit of inside baseball meaning; the intended hearing and reading audience was understood to be intimately familiar with the characters and topography referenced by diminutives. To facilitate the reader with less familiarity, I have supplied the full name and minimal descriptions for the reader's aid. In verse 1, the "tablet" is a "fresh page" in the Septuagint (LXX). The writing (or engraving given tablet) implement is the rather awkward "engraving tool of (a) man/humanity." It has been variously understood as a common, i.e., common man's, tool or as signifying common writing. I suggest there is a bit of a double entendre there, given Isaiah will not put pen to paper or engraving stylus to tablet but will rather use the tool of his manhood to impregnate another prophet. In 8:3, the female prophet is articulated as a prophet (masc. sing.) without the feminine suffix in the Great Isaiah Scroll (1QIsa^a) of the Dead Sea Scrolls collection, making a number of interpretations possible, including the lack of distinction between prophets based on gender.

The "waters of Shiloah" in Isaiah 8:6 will become known as "the Pool of Siloam" in the Christian era.

Psalm 34:19 begins, "Many [are the] evils of the righteous."

In this Lukan parable in Greek, the parent is a man and the child is also male. For the sake of this project, I am using gender-neutral language which, while generic for humanity, is also grammatically correct language in that a father is a parent and a son is a child. In Luke 9:39, it is not possible to distinguish the spirit from the child to determine who was shrieking, as Greek uses the same verbal form for female, male, and neuter subjects. In the following actions it is clear that the spirit performs them upon the child. In Luke 9:45, "they did not understand" is more properly, "they were [and remained] ignorant."

Preaching Prompts

In the Isaiah passage, the monarchies have been decimated and divided. Judah is centered as the continuing people of God and Israel, the remnant of the northern monarchy, and is allied with the Aramaeans, on the verge of invading Judah. So Israel here is "enemy" and not the central perspectival subject. The notion of a nation or people divided and on the verge of civil war will be familiar to the readers of this work in the period leading up to and beyond the 2024 U.S. election. The prophet's critique is that the people are so focused on the angry voices and threatening violence that they have lost sight of the peaceful waters that nourish them and by inference the one who provides the water. Their fear will be self-fulfilling and their land will be inundated, not with waters that bring the desert to life but with an uncontrollable flood of violence. The turning point and the signs along the way are generated by the mysterious female prophet in this passage and whoever—if not she—is the mother of the child Immanuel in the previous chapter. Choosing violence means choosing to be "swiftly savaged and rapidly ravaged," the name of her child in this chapter, Maher Shalal Hash Baz. The name of this child perpetually warns of the consequence while his other brother promises, God is with us. The name of their eldest brother in Isaiah 7:3, Shear-jashub, assures that whatever happens a remnant will survive and return. As no other mother is identified for Isaiah's children, she is likely the mother of them all. It is important to note that there is no indication that they were married. (Lastly, film aficionados may be interested to know that the actor currently known as Mahershala Ali was previously named Maher Shalal Hash Baz before his reversion to Islam.)

In many passages, the use of children and their growth to measure the passage of time (Isaiah 7:15–16; 8:4) brings to the forefront those who are most vulnerable and provides a throughline for these readings. Children represent survival and a survivable future. At the same time, instructions and injunctions to children are given to adults by teachers, elders, their parents, and the previous generation. Minor children are rarely the subject of address for ethical obligations because they have not yet reached the age of responsibility. In these lessons, children are the evidence of salvation, communal salvation. The names of each of Isaiah's children testify to the survival of Israel in the form of Judah, its last surviving enclave. (The name "Israel" is used both for the northern monarchy at war with Judah and the surviving remnant of Judah representing all that is left of the original monarchy and earlier twelve-tribe confederacy.) In Psalm 34, the "children" are the nation and their corporate salvation depends on them choosing the ways of life. In the Epistle, salvation through Jesus bestows upon the believer the status of a child of God, but it is not a personal benefit; the plural language here is significant. In the Gospel, it is not clear if the afflicted child is a juvenile or an adult. There is a tendency in Western culture, or at least American culture, to romanticize children but parents can be equally devoted to an adult child with a life-limiting condition. In addition to the culturally familiar love a parent has for a child and the significance of a surviving child for a person's future lineage and that's the remembrance of them through the perpetuation of their name, the child in the Gospel is also a signifier of how the Gospel of Jesus inverts social categories and hierarchy. It does so with the categories of age and social standing. And while the Jesus of the Gospel does so with regard to gender, the Epistles will struggle with that but neither body of literature will address slavery as more than a rhetorical or literary device. Yet children with all they represent—innocence, curiosity, future potential, the reign, realm, and majesty of God—remain barometers for the degree of safety our society affords and our care for all of them (or failure to do so) as a measure for how we live out the gospel.

PROPER 8 (CLOSEST TO JUNE 29)

Jeremiah 9:17–22; Psalm 126:1–6; Revelation 21:1–7; Luke 23:26–31

Jeremiah 9:17 Thus says the SOVEREIGN OF THE VANGUARD OF HEAVEN:
Reason within yourselves, and call for the keening women
and they shall come;
send for the wise, skilled women
and they shall come.
¹⁸ Let them quickly raise a wailing over us,
so that our eyes may run down with tears,
and our eyelids flow with water.
¹⁹ For a sound of wailing is heard from Zion:
"How we are ruined! We are utterly shamed,
because we have left the land,
because they have cast down our dwellings."
²⁰ Hear now women, the word of SHE WHO THUNDERS,
and let your ears receive the word of God's mouth;
teach to your daughters a wailing,
each woman her neighbor-woman a keening:
²¹ "Death has come up into our windows,
it has entered our palaces,
to cut off the children from the streets
and the young women and young men from the squares."
²² Thus says the DREAD GOD:
"The corpses of the woman-born shall fall
like dung upon the open field,
like sheaves behind the reaper,
and no one shall gather them."

Psalm 126:1–6

¹ *A song of ascending (for pilgrimages)*
When SHE WHO SPEAKS LIFE reversed the captivity of Zion,
we were as dreamers.
² Then was our mouth filled with laughter,
and our tongue with shouts of joy;
then did they say among the nations,
"The GOD WHOSE NAME IS HOLY
has done great things for them."
³ Great things has GOD WHOSE NAME IS HOLY done for us,
and we rejoiced.

⁴ Reverse, REDEEMING GOD, our captivity
   like the watercourses in the Negeb.
⁵ Those who sow in tears
   with shouts of joy shall reap.
⁶ Those who walk around and weep,
   carrying the seed-bag,
   shall come back with shouts of joy,
   carrying their sheaves.

Revelation 21:1 I saw a new heaven and a new earth, for the first heaven and the first earth had passed away, and the sea was no more. ² And I saw the holy city, the new Jerusalem, descending heaven from God, prepared as a bride adorned for her beloved. ³ And I heard a loud voice from the throne saying,

"Look! The home of God is among the woman-born.
God will dwell with them as their God;
they will be God's peoples,
and selfsame God will be with them.
⁴ God will wipe every tear from their eyes.
Death will be no more;
grief and weeping and pain will be no more,
for the first things have passed away."

⁵ And the One who seated upon the throne said, "Look! I am making all things new." The One also said, "Write, for these words are trustworthy and true." ⁶ Then the One said to me, "It is done! I am the Alpha and the Omega, the beginning and the end. I will give to the thirsty from the spring of the water of life freely. ⁷ Those who overcome will inherit these things, and I will be their God and they will be my daughters and sons.

Luke 23:26 As they led Jesus away, they seized Simon of Cyrene who was coming from the country, and they laid on him the cross to carry behind Jesus. ²⁷ A great number of people followed him, and a group of women who were beating their breasts and wailing for him. ²⁸ But Jesus turned to them and said, "Daughters of Jerusalem, do not weep for me, weep only for yourselves and for your children. ²⁹ Look, the days are surely coming when they will say, 'Blessed are barren women, and wombs that have never given birth, and breasts that have never nourished.' ³⁰ *Then they will begin to say to the mountains, 'Fall on us'; and to the hills, 'Cover us.'* ³¹ For if when the wood is green they do this, when it is dry what will happen?"

PROCLAMATION

Text Notes

Shivat-Zion in Psalm 126:1 has traditionally been translated as "the captivity of Zion" (LXX, Vulgate, Wycliffe, Douay, Bishops, Geneva, KJV); more recent translations have determined the root to be a homophone meaning the "previous circumstances (=fortunes) of Zion" (RSV, NRSV, NRSVue, JPS, CEB, Alter). However, the conflicting, competing interpretations are much older among the Dead Sea Scrolls; both possibilities are represented; manuscript 4QPsalms[e] has "captives," and 11QPsalms[a] has "fortunes." While both make sense contextually, I find "captivity" preferable. The same issue occurs in verse 4.

In Revelation 21:26, those who bring glory are unidentified; the subject is included in the verb, inclusive plural. When cities or nations offered tribute in hospitality or conquest, representatives from each section of the populace often participated. The choice of "women, children, and men" rather than the "people" of the NRSV or "they" in the CEB make the population of heaven visible.

In Luke 23:30, Jesus quotes Hosea 10:8, where people ask for the mountains and hills to cover them.

Preaching Prompts

Jeremiah is a lengthy book, often eclipsed in the shadow of Isaiah with its messianic connections to the longer Jesus story and overshadowed by the extraordinary visions in Ezekiel. The next several weeks will pass through Jeremiah. The chapters will not be in numerical order because the book is not in chronological order, and a chronology of its contents is virtually impossible to establish.

The lessons for this week present seasons of sorrow in the life of the people of Israel, Jesus, and God's redeemed. Attendant upon each season is that it is temporary, and that for one reason or another sorrow will return—with the exception of the Revelation text, which marks the end of all sorrow. There can be an assumption that such seasons of sorrow interrupt the flow of our lives and our spiritual journey when, rather, they are an integral part of it. At the same time, the circumstances that lead to profound sorrow are not God-ordained and when they involve interpersonal, social, cultural, or international violence, they are not God's will. God does not require our torture to accomplish divine ends.

In the Jeremiah lesson, weeping is healing, didactic, and prophetic. The guild of professional mourners, a women's profession, facilitates the mourning of the community over their current state during the Babylonian oppression. They model the import of acknowledging individual and communal sorrow to begin the process of healing. In this specific situation, the women do not draw from cultural limits or generate spontaneous limits. God gives them the words for their element using a prophetic form. The "mothers" teach the limit to their "daughters," their own daughters and the name of the apprentice category. It is important to note that the reading intentionally stays with the moment of sorrow and the community does not move on. There is no happy ending. The transformation of mourning and sorrow can take as much time as international realignment. In terms of preaching such a passage, it is important to resist those homiletic models that insist on imposing a "good news" ending on a bad news text.

The psalm portrays the cycles of sorrow and its transformation that mark a human life through the story of Israel's national life. With the remembrance of a previous sorrowful occasion for mourning that was not merely transformed but reversed. That experience becomes a bedrock of faith upon which the intercessor prays for God to do the same thing again because the psalmist knows what God can do and trusts her to do it.

The Gospel presages the most dramatic moment of transformation. Yet, as with the first lesson, the temptation to rush to the end of the story should be resisted. These gathered lessons around lament are designed to facilitate preaching and teaching about the importance of lament, particularly in church settings in which the primary story is triumphalist. In the Gospel, Jesus tells the women who are weeping for him that things are going to get worse and that is sobering because the days about which he prophesied may not have yet come, though some would surely argue that we are living in them now.

The reading from Revelation, representing the culmination of all our stories and our shared stories, is necessarily triumphalist. It serves as the ultimate promise that weeping does not endure forever.

PROPER 9 (CLOSEST TO JULY 6)

Jeremiah 29:1–14; Psalm 33:8–22; James 5:7–11; Luke 21:29–36

Jeremiah 29:1 These are the words of the letter that the prophet Jeremiah sent from Jerusalem to the remainder of the elders among the exiles, and to the priests, the prophets, and all the people, the women, children, and men whom Nebuchadnezzar had taken into exile from Jerusalem to Babylon. ² This was after the departure of King Jeconiah, and the Queen Mother, the court officials, the leaders of Judah and Jerusalem, the artisans, and the smiths from Jerusalem. ³ It was by the hand of Elasah ben of Shaphan and Gemariah ben of Hilkiah, whom King Zedekiah of Judah sent to Babylon to King Nebuchadnezzar of Babylon saying:

⁴ Thus says the COMMANDER of heaven's legions, the God of Israel, to all the exiles whom I have sent into exile from Jerusalem to Babylon:

⁵ Build houses and settle in them; plant gardens and eat their fruit. ⁶ Take women as wives and father sons and daughters; take women as wives for your sons and your daughters,

give to men, husbands, that they may give birth to daughters and sons. Multiply there and do not decrease. ⁷ And seek the well-being of the city where I have sent you all into exile and pray to the God Who Hears on its behalf for, in its well-being will be well-being for all of you.

⁸ For thus says the Commander of heaven's vanguard, the God of Israel:

Let not the prophets and the diviners who are in your midst deceive you, and do not listen to the dreams that you dream. ⁹ For it is a lie they prophesy to you in my Name; I did not send them,

an utterance of the All-Knowing God.

¹⁰ For thus says the Faithful One: When seventy years are fulfilled for Babylon I shall attend you all and I shall establish for you my good word, and return you all to this place. ¹¹ For surely I know the plans I have planned for you all—

an utterance of the Ancient Of Days—

Plans for your well-being and not for evil, to give you all a future and hope. ¹² Then when you all call upon me and you come and you all pray to me, I shall hear you. ¹³ And when you all seek me, you shall find me; if you all seek me with your whole heart. ¹⁴ I will be found by you all,

an utterance of the Gracious God.

And I shall reverse your captivity and gather you all from all the nations and all the places where I have driven you,

an utterance of the Shepherding God.

And I shall return you all to the place from which I banished you into exile.

Psalm 33:8–22

⁸ Let all the earth revere She Who is Wisdom;
let all who dwell in the world stand in awe of her.
⁹ For she spoke, and it came to pass;
she commanded, and it stood fast;
she commanded, and it stood firm.
¹⁰ The Mighty One shatters the counsel of the nations;
she disallows the designs of the peoples.
¹¹ The counsel of the Wisdom of the Ages stands forever;
the designs of her heart to all generations.
¹² Blessed is the nation for whom the Holy One of Old is their God;
the people whom she has chosen as her heritage.
¹³ From the heavens the Most High looks down;

she sees all the woman-born.
14 From her eternal throne she gazes upon
all the inhabitants of the earth.
15 She who fashions their hearts alike
is the one who discerns all their doings.
18 Look! The eye of the FAITHFUL ONE is on those who revere her,
on those who hope in her faithful love,
19 to deliver their soul from death,
and to keep them alive in famine.
20 Our soul waits for SHE WHO SAVES;
she is our help and shield.
21 In her is our heart glad,
because we trust in her holy Name.
22 Let your faithful love, COMPASSIONATE GOD, be upon us,
for it is you in whom we trust.

James 5:7 Be patient, therefore, kindred, until the coming of the Redeemer. Look! The farmer waits for the precious fruit of the earth, being patient with it until it receives the early and the late rains. ⁸ You all must also be patient; strengthen your hearts, for the coming of the Redeemer is drawing near. ⁹ Do not grumble against one another beloved, so that you may not be judged. Look! The Judge is standing at the doors! ¹⁰ As an example of suffering and patience, beloved, take the women and men, the prophets who spoke in the name of the Holy One. ¹¹ See here, we bless those who showed endurance. Of the endurance of Job you have heard; and you all have seen the end goal of the Holy One, that the Holy One is compassionate and merciful.

Luke 21:29 And Jesus told a parable [to the people at the temple when the widow put in her two coins]: "Look at the fig tree and all the trees. ³⁰ When they sprout leaves you yourselves see and know that summer is already near. ³¹ In the same way, when you all see these things taking place, you know that the reign of God is near. ³² Truly I say to all of you, this generation will not pass away until all things have taken place. ³³ Heaven and earth will pass away, but my words will not pass away.
³⁴ Be alert to yourselves so that your hearts are not weighed down with self-indulgence and drunkenness and the cares of this life, and that day catch you suddenly. ³⁵ Like a trap! For it will come upon all who live upon the face of the whole earth. ³⁶ Stay awake at all times, praying so that you all might have the strength to escape all these things that will take place, and to stand before the Son of Woman."

PROCLAMATION

Text Notes

Note that the Queen Mother in Jeremiah 29:2 is not only the mother of the monarch but also a court official herself, often the right-hand advisor to the monarch. (For more, see *Womanist Midrash: A Reintroduction to the Women of the Torah and of the Throne*.) Verse 6 has "take women . . . and give to men . . ."; the biblical languages do not have distinct words for women and wives and husbands and men. To "take a woman" means to form what we contemporarily call a marriage though the equivalent word is almost never used in the Hebrew Bible. As in Psalm 126 in Proper 7, I have retained the older translation "captivity," in verse 14.

In Psalm 33:14, God's "eternal throne" is "the fixed place [where] God sits." In verse 15, human hearts are *yachad*, "together" or "as one"—the cardinal number is the root word.

The setting and context for the Gospel selection come from the beginning of the chapter, verse 2. "Son of Woman" in Luke 21:36 reflects one of the grammatical possibilities of *huios to anthroupou* and an acknowledgment of the human parentage of Jesus.

Preaching Prompts

"How long, O God" is the frequent cry of many a psalmist. It can be imagined to have been the cry of the Israelites in slavery, under every occupation and through every deportation and exile. It has been the cry of black folks through slavery and every white lash, after every moment of progress from reconstruction to the civil rights movement to the election of Barack Obama to the minuscule games of the Black Lives Matter movement. At the heart of that cry is frustration with the timetable of the divine response. This week's readings are situated in moments that call for patience we may not have or do not wish to develop.

The reading from Jeremiah is set in the immediate aftermath of the Babylonian devastation of Judah marking the fall of the last independent enclave of Israel, and the theological horror of the ravishment of the temple in which the God who spoke creation into existence and parted the waters and thundered a covenant from the height of Sinai. In the ancient world, the fall of a temple signified the fall of the god. Perhaps to their disappointment, Jeremiah did not promise immediate divine vengeance, retribution, and liberation. Instead, he pastorally prepared them for life in exile under the rule of their conquerors. This is something that most Americans have not experienced. It is one of the realities that differentiates African Americans from many Africans; enslaved Africans trafficked to the Americas and Caribbean lived under the domination of their enslavers but on foreign soil. Africans conquered and colonized by European nations lived under the barbarism of their conquerors on their beloved soil, watching their centuries-old institutions be dismantled or perverted. And as always, the physical and sexual abuse of women and children and sometimes men. In this situation, Jeremiah says make a life and make a life for your children and grandchildren; keep having babies. Do not let the despair that "this is no world for children" win. And astonishingly, pray for the city in which you are being held captive because the reality is that bad news trickles down. This hard word comes with an assurance that God hears prayer and has plans for them for they are good and will one day reverse their captivity.

The psalm provides reasons to hope in God and trust that she will deliver her people using examples that span centuries and generations, reinforcing the hard truth that there will be some who will die before they or their people experience the promised liberation.

In the Epistle, James commends the renowned patience of Job. Job is a character whose stories likely predate the Hebrew Bible, like those of Daniel that go back to the Canaanite city of Ugarit. (For example, Ezekiel mentions Noah, Daniel, and Job as legendary contemporaries.) That oft-cited patience comes not from the canonical book in which Job demands an accounting from God using legal terminology invoking the notion of a lawsuit. Rather, it comes from the pseudepigraphal post-biblical book written in his name.

And in the Gospel, Jesus teaches believers to read the signs, which is a strategy to give the people waiting on his return a vehicle for hope. Yet there is an immediacy in the words of Jesus that was not born out in the generation who heard his words or in the one who recorded his words. Every generation has (or has had some who) believed these are the times that must surely mark an end to the crucifying world in which we live and its transformation, resurrection, or rebirth into that majestic time and space in which God's love, mercy, and justice will reign supreme. Jesus calls us to a life of readiness. With the patience of Job and the pastoral council of James and Jeremiah, we are to stay ready as long as it takes, trusting in the promises of God because we have seen her mighty acts as celebrated in the psalm.

Black folk in the United States have a saying, "When the nation catches a cold, we catch pneumonia." Our well-being is tied up in the well-being of the nation that oppresses us. Can we hold on to the promises of God through generations of state-sponsored violence? Those preachers who do not come from communities that live this reality will have to situate themselves and their congregations with regard to this multigenerational story. What does it mean to hope in God from their position versus that of those whose experience is central to this story?

PROPER 10 (CLOSEST TO JULY 13)

Jeremiah 31:2–6, 8–11, 13–17; Psalm 118:14–26;
James 5:1–6; Luke 13:31–35

Jeremiah 31:2 Thus says the Fire of Sinai:
>They found grace in the wilderness,
>the people—the women, children, and men, survivors of the sword;
>Israel seeking rest.
>³ From afar the Rock Who Birthed Us appeared to me:
>With an everlasting love have I loved you, daughter;
>that is why I have continued my faithfulness to you.
>⁴ Again shall I build you, daughter, and daughter,
>you shall be built, Virgin Israel!
>Again, daughter, you shall be adorned with your hand-drums,
>and go forth in the dance of those who revel.
>⁵ Again, daughter, you shall plant vineyards
>on the mountains of Samaria;
>the planters shall plant,
>and they shall consume.
>⁶ For there shall be a day when sentinels shall proclaim
>in the hill country of Ephraim:
>'Come, let us go up to Zion,
>to the Glorious One our God.'
>⁸ Look! I am going to bring them from the land of the North,
>and I shall gather them from the farthest parts of the earth,
>among them blind and lame,
>pregnant women and birthing women, all together,
>a great assembly, they shall return here.
>⁹ With weeping will they come,
>and through supplications shall I lead them back;
>I will have them walk by streams of water,
>on a straight path, they shall not stumble on it;
>for I am a parent to Israel,
>and Ephraim is my firstborn."
>¹⁰ Hear the word of the Holy One, you nations,
>and declare it in the islands far off;
>say, "The One who scattered Israel shall gather him,
>and shall keep him as a shepherd a flock."
>¹¹ For the Faithful One has ransomed Jacob [of Rebekah's line]

and has redeemed him from hands too strong for him.
¹³ Then shall young women rejoice in dance,
and young men and elders together.
I shall turn their mourning to joy;
I shall comfort them, and give them joy for sorrow.
¹⁴ I shall satisfy the very souls of the priests with fatness,
and my people, with my goodness shall be satisfied,"

an utterance* of the GOD WHO PROVIDES.

¹⁵ Thus says the HOLY ONE OF OLD:
A voice in Ramah is heard,
wailing, bitter weeping;
Rachel is weeping for her children,
she refuses to be comforted for her children,
because they are no more.
¹⁶ Thus says the MOTHER OF WISDOM:
Daughter, hold back your voice from weeping,
and daughter, your eyes from tears;
for there is a reward for your work, daughter.

An utterance of SHE WHO IS WISDOM:

They shall come back from the land of the enemy.
¹⁷ There is hope for your future.

an utterance of the WOMB OF CREATION:

Your children shall return to their country.

Psalm 118:14–26

¹⁴ The MIGHTY GOD is my strength and my might
and has become my salvation.
¹⁵ The sound of song and of salvation is in the tents of the righteous:
"The right hand of the MOST HIGH is mighty;
¹⁶ the right hand of the MIGHTY GOD is exalted;
the right hand of the MOST HIGH is mighty."
¹⁷ I shall not die, but I shall live,
and recount the deeds of the ANCIENT OF DAYS.
¹⁸ The MERCIFUL GOD has punished me severely,
but to death did not hand me over.
¹⁹ Open to me the gates of righteousness,
that I may enter through them

---

* The divine epithet, "an utterance of YHWH (God's most sacred Name)" is the first person divine equivalent of the third person prophetic formula, "thus says YHWH." It is God emphasizing that it is God speaking. It is also a literary device found frequently in Jeremiah.

and give thanks to the Fount of Justice.
²⁰ This is the gate of the Living God;
the righteous shall enter through it.
²¹ I thank you for you have answered me
and have become my salvation.
²² The stone the builders rejected
has become the chief cornerstone.
²³ This is the Mighty God's doing;
it is marvelous in our eyes.
²⁴ This is the day that the Creator of All has made;
let us rejoice and be glad in it.
²⁵ Save us, we pray, Saving One!
Generous One, we pray, grant us prosperity!
²⁶ Blessed is the one who comes in the name of God Who is Holy.
We bless you from the house of the Ever-Living God.

James 5:1 Come now, wealthy people, weep, wail for the miseries that are coming to you all. ² Your riches are rotting and your clothes are moth-eaten. ³ Your gold and silver have decayed and their decay shall be a witness against you, and it shall eat your flesh like fire. You all have laid up treasure for the last days. ⁴ Listen! The wages of the workers who reaped your fields—which you all defrauded them out of—cry out and the cries of the farm workers have reached the ears of the Commander of heaven's legions. ⁵ You all have lived on the earth in self-indulgence and in luxury; you all have gorged your hearts in a day of slaughter. ⁶ You all have condemned, murdered, the righteous one. Does not God resist you?

Luke 13:31 At the same time [Jesus taught that only a few will be saved] some Pharisees came and said to him, "Go! And depart from here, for Herod wants to kill you!" ³² And Jesus said to them, "You all go and tell that fox for me, 'Listen, I am casting out demons and providing healing today and tomorrow, and on the third day I will be finished. ³³ Yet today, tomorrow, and the one that is coming, I must go, because it is impossible for a prophet to be killed outside of Jerusalem.' ³⁴ Jerusalem, Jerusalem, the city that kills the prophets and stones those who are sent to her! How often have I desired to gather your children together as a hen gathers her brood under her wings, and you were not willing! ³⁵ See here! Your house is left to you. And I tell you, you will not see me until the time comes when you say, 'Blessed is the one who comes in the name of the Holy One.'"

PROCLAMATION

Text Notes

In Jeremiah 31:3, the first person is clear: God appeared "to me"; however, a number of translations amend it to "to him" unnecessarily following LXX where this passage is found in chapter 38 (see NRSV and NRSVue; CEB, "them"). In verses 3–6 and 16, "daughter" signals to the English reader that the prophetic discourse is addressed to a grammatically feminine character, Daughter Zion in this case. North in verse 8 can mean the direction, the now defunct Northern monarchy—perhaps referring to refugees, or the mystical North signifying the uttermost reaches.

The assonant and alliterative poetry of Psalm 118:25 (the "Hosanna") verse, is difficult to reproduce: *Ana Ya hoshia na; Ana Ya chatzlicha na*. The "hosanna" pronunciation comes from the Greek transliteration of the Hebrew.

James 5:3 uses "rust" to describe the tarnishing of gold and silver; "decay" fits better without ascribing rust to metals that do not, in fact, rust. (There is a similar issue in Matthew 6:19, where a separate noun describes the process of consumption by rust or blight or eating food.) I follow the translation of Luke Timothy Johnson for the question form of that latter phrase of verse 6 (see his Anchor Bible Commentary on James). The subject, "God," is elicited from the masculine singular verb and the presence of God earlier in the passage.

In Luke 13:31, the context comes from earlier in the chapter, 13:22.

Preaching Prompts

The somber tone of last week's readings is not consistent with those for this week. Life is not a serial TV show in which the problems of the world are worked out in forty-five minutes and the next week's episode presents a whole new story. Rather, the promise of return and restoration is being kept at a slow pace, and God reminds her people that it is underway, pointing to marks of progress along their journey. Reiterated. The promise is reiterated. But the figure of Rachel appears—literarily, not a spectral apparition—as the figurative mother of the people in Israel because she was the most beloved wife of the person Israel. ("Israel" refers to the following northern monarchy, the person Israel, the collective people of Israel, and the surviving remainder of Judah as the remnant of Israel. Jeremiah shifts between these usages, sometimes in the same passage.) The "Rachel weeping" unit is often severed from the proceed in verses. It is retained here as a reminder that an honest response to the word and work of God on its grand and glorious scope is to acknowledge and lament the unimaginable losses Israel endured as a subjugated people. In so doing, we make space for those who have not seen liberation to do the same, understanding that expressions of grief are not denials or rejection of God's promise.

The Epistle might be heard as a response to Rachel. As she weeps over her children who have been taken from this world: immigrants trying to find safety for their children, murdered by coyote traffickers or succumbing to illnesses while in the custody of indifferent or actively hostile US agencies, the slaughter of sex workers and trans women by men who count on no one caring, and the victims of white supremacist and antisemitic violence, including those across the ages murdered and martyred by Christians—as Rachel weeps for all of these her children, James speaks of a God who sees the plutocrats whose crimes have left many a mother in tears. In pronouncing the "opposition" of the righteous one against them, James is signaling their demons and the end of their reign of terror.

The psalm is a journeying psalm. This pilgrimage hymn provides theological accompaniment for the journey to Jerusalem and its temple, reflecting on God's promise kept over the longer journey set with sorrow and struggle. The song does the work that liturgy should, calling the people together to reflect on their shared history and journey with God, providing encouragement to take the next step of the journey.

The story of Jesus is that of a man who transcended humanity but subjected himself to the full experience of a mortal life subject to death and all the wickedness humanity could conceive, not just the triumphant transformational visit of his journey, but his entire journey is libertive for us. He makes space for Rachel and her grief even as he prepares to destroy its cause, death itself. These lessons can serve as a call for churches and individuals that live with privilege to sit with the injury grief and pain of those communities that are not just vulnerable, but are under active threat by laws, economic policies, and continuing violence from hate groups. Those who continue to weep for the losses that continue to accrue are around us and sometimes in our midst.

For those who will preach the Gospel text, there is an important acknowledgment: the Pharisees are not the anti-Jesus opponents antisemitic readings of them have often made them out to be. Here, the Pharisees are trying to save Jesus's life. They are peers and colleagues, and there are scholars who consider that Jesus may have been a Pharisee himself.

PROPER 11 (CLOSEST TO JULY 20)

Baruch 2:11–15, 19–23; Psalm 18:2–11, 16–17;
2 Thessalonians 2:1–8; Luke 12:4–7

Baruch 2:11 Holy One, God of Israel, who brought out your people from the land of Egypt by a mighty hand and with signs and with wonders and with great power and with an outstretched arm and you made for yourself a Name that until this day [endures]: ¹² We have sinned; we have been ungodly; we have done wrong, Holy One our God, against all of your commandments. ¹³ Let your anger turn away from us, for we are left few in number, among the nations where you have scattered us. ¹⁴ Harken, Holy One, to our prayer and petition and deliver us; and as to those who carried us off, for your sake, grant us favor before their face ¹⁵ so that all the earth may know that you are the Holy One our God; that your Name has been called upon Israel [and Sarah, Rebekah, Rachel, Leah, Zilpah, Bilpah] and upon their offspring.

¹⁹ For it is not because of any righteous acts of our mothers and fathers or our queen mothers and their sons that we throw ourselves down for mercy, we, we before you, Holy One, our God. ²⁰ For you have brought your anger and wrath against us, just as you spoke by the hand of your women servants and men servants, the prophets, saying:

²¹ Thus did the Holy One say: Bend your shoulder and serve the king of Babylon, and dwell in the land which I gave to your mothers and fathers. ²² And if you all do not obey the voice of the Holy One to work for the king of Babylon, ²³ I will make to fail from the towns of Judah and from outside of Jerusalem a voice of merriment and a voice of delight, a voice of bridegroom and a voice of bride, and all the land will become untrodden by inhabitants.

Psalm 18:2–11, 16–17

² The Rock Who Gave Us Birth is my rock,
  and my fortress, and my deliverer,
  my God, my rock in whom I take refuge,
  my shield, and the horn of my salvation, my stronghold.
³ I call upon the Holy One, may she be praised,
  and from my enemies I shall be saved.
⁴ The snares of death encompassed me;
  the rivers of wickedness assailed me.
⁵ The snares of Sheol encircled me;
  the snares of death confronted me.
⁶ In my distress I called upon She Who Hears;
  to my God I cried for help.
  From her temple she heard my voice,
  and my cry came before her, to her ears.
⁷ Then the earth shuddered and quaked;
  the foundations also of the mountains trembled
  and were shaken because of her anger.
⁸ Smoke went up from her nostrils,
  and consuming fire from her mouth;
  burning coals blazed forth from her.
⁹ She spread out the heavens, and descended;
  thick darkness was under her feet.
¹⁰ She mounted up on a cherub, and flew;
  she soared upon the wings of the wind.

> ¹¹ She made darkness her veil around her,
> her canopy dark waters and thick clouds.
> ¹⁶ She reached down from on high, she took me;
> she drew me out of the multitude of water.
> ¹⁷ She delivered me from my strong enemy,
> and from those who hate me;
> for they were too mighty for me.

2 Thessalonians 2:1 We beseech you all, sisters and brothers, with regard to the coming of our Redeemer Jesus Christ and our being gathered together to him: ² Be not quickly shaken in mind or alarmed, neither by spirit nor by word nor by letter, seeming to have come from us, claiming the day of the Savior is here now. ³ Let no one deceive you all in any way. For it will not come unless the rebellion first and the revealing of the lawless one, the one born for destruction. ⁴ Standing in opposition to and self-exalted above every designated god or sacred thing, sitting down in the temple of God, self-proclaimed to be God. ⁵ Do you all not remember that I told you these things when I was still with you? ⁶ And now you all know what it is restraining that one, until the time of their revelation. ⁷ For the conspiracy of lawlessness is already at work, but only until the one who now restrains it is removed. ⁸ And then the lawless one will be revealed, whom the Messiah Jesus will destroy with the breath of his mouth, reducing that one to nothing by the manifestation of his coming.

Luke 12:4 [Jesus said:] I say to you all my friends, fear not those who kill the body and after that I have no remaining power to do anything. ⁵ But I will show you all who you should fear; fear the one who, after having killed, has power to cast into hell. Yes! I am telling you all, fear that one! ⁶ Are not five sparrows sold for two copper coins? And not a single one of them is forgotten before God. ⁷ And yet even the hairs of your head are all counted. Fear not; you all are worth more than many sparrows.

PROCLAMATION

Text Notes

The readings this week begin with a passage from Baruch Jeremiah's companion and scribe, who occupies a liminal space in the scriptures of the First Testament and the traditions about it in Judaism and Christianity. Baruch is identified as a prophet in the Babylonian Talmud, *Megillah* 14 a-b, though his writings are only preserved in the Greek version of the First Testament where it immediately follows Jeremiah with which it shares its content and setting. The climax of the book of Jeremiah, of the prophecies of Jeremiah, is the destruction of the temple, devastation of Judah, abduction of the upper classes of Judean society into Babylonian captivity, and the forced exile of Jeremiah and Baruch into Egypt with some few who had escaped their would-be Babylonian captors; see Jeremiah 39:1–10; 40:1–7; 43:1–7. A purported epistle from Jeremiah constitutes the sixth chapter of Baruch, though in some bibles it is presented separately. The first reading of the following Sunday will come from the pseudepigraphal epistle as it shares the same context. Both are congruent with Jeremiah's message, that destruction and exile are inevitable and survival depends upon accepting their fate as a consequence of their failures. Baruch and the Epistle connected with it were in the earliest Bibles of the early church and remain in the Bibles of the larger Christian world; they are only missing from Protestant Bibles.

In Baruch 2:15, I provide the names of the matriarchs who proceed and accompany "Israel" for a fuller recitation. The "monarch" of verse 19 is identified as the royal pair, mother and son, Queen Mother and King, the ruling structure unique to ancient Judah (not shared by the northern monarchy before its destruction) that endured until the end of the independent sovereignty of Judah.

In Psalm 18:2, I draw the divine name from Deuteronomy 32:18, "You neglected the Rock that gave birth to you; you forgot the God who writhed in birth-labor for you."

In 2 Thessalonians 2:7, *musterion*, which means "mystery" or "secret," has the sense of a secret plan; thus, I translate it as "conspiracy."

The crowd in Luke 12 is made up of every type of human; in the world of the text they are women, children, and men. Jesus's address to his "dear ones," his *philois* in Luke 12:4, includes the women who followed him. *Philois* are not casual friends but rather persons who are beloved.

Preaching Prompts

The horror of the Babylonian contact shapes the entirety of the Hebrew Scriptures and what will become Judaism. The prophetic books build toward the Babylonian captivity and even as later writings celebrate the defeat of Babylon at the hands of Persia, the bleak conditions during the return point back to the loss of prosperity and security as a result of the Babylonian blitzkrieg. These readings require those who hear and preach them to put themselves in the perspective of a people whose sole identity is religious and cultural and has been upended because their political and geographical world has been upended. Their connection to the land that formed the heart of their sacred stories and provided the proving ground for God's faith to their ancestors had been brutally severed.

The psalm is set before the fall of the temple. It is striking that the psalter mixes these hymns of praise, petition, and lamentation almost without regard to their originating context. It is clear the people found solace in praying and chanting these songs and poems set to music. Harkening back to an image of God's power and glory displayed in similar majesty as that in which God appeared during the wilderness was both comforting and likely understood as a sign of God's continuing power, no matter how much the current circumstances veiled it.

The community of believers in Thessalonica were in a different set of circumstances but also living under foreign rule in their own land. They had more than the scriptures and songs of old to comfort them. They had the writings of new and emergent leaders in the Jesus movement, including Paul and those writing in his name (it is unclear which is the case with 2 Thessalonians), along with dissenting voices. Here the "word" is more than one of faithfulness and endurance; it is a promise that God will demonstrate the same kind of power that the psalmist memorialized. Those who usurp God's place or attempt to do so will come to their end. God has not overlooked them, has not forgotten them, and will deliver them.

In the Gospel reading Jesus also makes the point that God is deeply aware of the lives and deaths, sorrows and struggles, joys and difficulties of her people. God is attentive down to the very hairs of our heads—or lack thereof. All of these readings share a certain grittiness. It is possible that persons in each of these circumstances will die without having seen the promise or deliverance of God. Even in this most difficult circumstance, Jesus bids us "fear not."

There will be those who have come to the United States from political conflicts and warfare who will readily identify with these readings. The primary themes are trust in God, persevere in faithfulness, and hope for the fulfillment of God's promise to gather her people and restore them. Readers and hearers in the relative comfort of the United States may need some guidance to identify with the social and political context of these readings and by extension the larger canon of scriptures. Yet there are those among us for whom life under occupation—even while in the United States—is a daily experience. But are we as the Church listening to them and hearing the scriptures through their experiences?

Migration born of desperate circumstances and forced migration, occupation, and colonization all take a heavy toll on women and their children, resulting in poverty and often sexual violence and exploitation. Those stories of the people of Israel and their Judean survivors are not told and must be imagined. Those who have come to this country through similarly dreadful circumstances will not have to imagine. One of the layers of complexity in our society that is not always well represented in our churches or in our conversations is the presence and stories of immigrants. Womanism models for us the holding of all human complexities together to provide multifaceted lenses through which to read the scriptures. Gender and sexuality, class, privilege, and power, ability and disability, migration status and country of origin are only a few of the ways in which our humanity is expressed.

FEAST OF MARY MAGDALENE, JULY 22

Genesis 16:10–13; Psalm 68:4–11; Romans 16:1–16; John 20:1–2, 11–18

Genesis 16:10 The messenger of the WELLSPRING OF LIFE said to Hagar, "Greatly will I multiply your seed, so they cannot be counted for multitude." [11] Then the messenger of the FOUNT OF LIFE said to her,

> "Look! You are pregnant and shall give birth to a son,
> and you shall call him Ishmael (meaning God hears),
> for the FAITHFUL ONE has heard of your abuse.
> [12] He shall be a wild ass of a man,
> with his hand against everyone,
> and everyone's hand against him;
> and he shall live in the sight of all his kin."

[13] So Hagar named the LIVING GOD who spoke to her: "You are El-ro'i"; for she said, "Have I really seen God and remained alive after seeing God?"

Psalm 68:4–11

> [4] Sing to God, sing praises to her Name;
> exalt her who rides upon the clouds;
> HOLY is her Name, rejoice before her!
> [5] Mother of orphans and defender of widows,
> is God in her holy habitation!
> [6] God settles the solitary in a home, bringing prisoners into prosperity;
> while the rebellious shall live in a wasteland.
> [7] God, when you marched before your people,
> when you moved out through the wilderness,
> [8] the earth shook, even the heavens poured down,
> at the presence of God, the One of Sinai,
> at the presence of God, the God of Israel.
> [9] Rain in abundance, God, you showered abroad;
> when your heritage grew weary you prepared rest.
> [10] Your creatures found a dwelling in her;
> God, you provided in your goodness for the oppressed.
> [11] The AUTHOR OF LIFE gave the word;
> the women who proclaim the good news are a great army.

Romans 16:1 I commend to you all our sister Phoebe, a deacon of the church in Cenchreae, [2] so that you all may receive her in Christ as is worthy of the saints, and stand by her in whatever thing she may need of you, for she has been a benefactress of many, and of myself as well.

³ Greet Prisca and Aquila, my coworkers in Christ Jesus, ⁴ and who for my life risked their necks, to whom not only I give thanks, but also all the churches of the Gentiles, ⁵ and the church in their house. Greet Epaenetus my beloved, who was the first fruit in Asia for Christ. ⁶ Greet Mary, who has worked much among you all. ⁷ Greet Andronicus and Junia, my kin and my fellow prisoners; they are eminent among the apostles, and they were in Christ before I was. ⁸ Greet Ampliatus, my beloved in Christ. ⁹ Greet Urbanus, our coworker in Christ, and Stachys my beloved. ¹⁰ Greet Apelles, who is proven in Christ. Greet those who belong to Aristobulus. ¹¹ Greet Herodion, my kinsman. Greet those who belong of Narcissus in Christ. ¹² Greet Tryphaena and Tryphosa who toil in Christ. Greet the beloved Persis who has worked much in Christ. ¹³ Greet Rufus, chosen in Christ, and greet his mother who is also mine. ¹⁴ Greet Asyncritus, Phlegon, Hermes, Patrobas, Hermas, and the sisters and brothers [or friends and kin] who are with them. ¹⁵ Greet Philologus and Julia, Nereus and his sister, and Olympas, and all the saints with them. ¹⁶ Greet one another with a holy kiss. All the churches of Christ greet you.

John 20:1 Now it was the first day of the week. Mary Magdalene came, early on while it was still dark, to the tomb and saw the stone removed from the tomb. ² So she ran and went to Simon Peter and to the other disciple, the one whom Jesus loved, and said to them, "They have taken the Messiah out of the tomb, and we do not know where they have laid him."

¹¹ Now Mary stood outside, facing the tomb, weeping. As she wept, she bent down to see in the tomb. ¹² Then she saw two angels in white sitting, one at the head and the other at the feet, where the body of Jesus had been lying. ¹³ They said to her, "Woman, why do you weep?" She said to them, "Because they have taken my Savior, and I do not know where they have laid him." ¹⁴ Having said this, she turned around and saw Jesus standing, but she did not know that it was Jesus. ¹⁵ Jesus said to her, "Woman, why do you weep? For whom do you look?" Thinking that he was the gardener, she said to him, "Sir, if you have carried him away, tell me where you have laid him, and I will take him away." ¹⁶ Jesus said to her, "Mary." She turned and said to him in Aramaic, "Rabbouni!" (which means Teacher). ¹⁷ Jesus said to her, "Do not hold me, because I have not yet ascended to the Father. Rather, go to my brothers and say to them, 'I am ascending to my Abba and your Abba, to my God and your God.'" ¹⁸ Mary Magdalene went and announced to the disciples, "I have seen the Savior"; and she told them that he had said these things to her.

PROCLAMATION

Text Notes

The language of Hagar's annunciation parallels the promise to Abraham in Genesis 13:16 closely; each is promised that their "seed" (or offspring) will be numerous beyond counting. Hagar is the first woman in scripture granted an annunciation, the unnamed mother of Samson follows in Judges 13:3–7, followed in turn by Mary the mother of Jesus. Hagar and Rebekah (Genesis 24:60) are the only women in the canon credited with their own seed/offspring; the language is usually reserved for men (Rebekah's seed is blessed by her matrilineal family; her father Bethuel ben Milcah bore his mother's name, not his father's.) Notably, God speaks to Abraham *about* Sarah in Genesis 17:15–16, as do the divine messengers in Genesis 18:9–10, even when she is within hearing; none speak to her.

Hagar's abuse or affliction, more rightly, Sarah's abuse of Hagar in verse 11, is articulated with a verb that encodes both physical and sexual violence; the verb is also used of the abuse the Israelites suffered at the hands of the Egyptians. Some translate Ishmael's fate as living "in opposition," i.e., conflict, with his kin rather than "opposite," i.e., in their sight or presence; the verb has both senses.

The "we" in John 20:2 likely refers to other women with Mary Magdalene at the tomb. Other resurrection accounts include Mary the mother of James and Salome from Mark 16:1 and Joanna (with Mary Magdalene and James's mother) in Luke 24:10. Yet other possibilities include Jesus's aunt—the unnamed sister of Mary—with Mary the wife of Clopas, present at his crucifixion in John 19:25, and Susanna, who with other women supported Jesus financially, from Luke 8:3.

Mary Magdalene "messages," *aggellō*, the gospel of Christ's resurrection. The verb shares the root of messenger, one who announces, *aggelos*, commonly rendered "angel," though the term is not restricted to divine beings. Both she and the divine messengers she encountered are angels. See the use of "angel" as church leader in Revelation 2:1, 8, 12, 18; 3:1.

Preaching Prompts

For this feast of the disciple Orthodox Christians call the Apostle to the Apostles, the readings focus on women's proclamations to and about God, including their work in shaping the early church that speaks for them. Hagar is the only person in the scriptures to name God. She is a matron saint for this project in which I too name God, using God's characteristics revealed in the texts and in the experiences of its readers and hearers to render the unpronounceable name.

Hagar tells God who She is in her, Hagar's, experience and perception. In Psalm 68:12 at the command of God, an army of women proclaim the good news of God's care for her people. The language for that good news, *basarah* in Hebrew, *euaggelia* in Greek, becomes "gospel" in English, the gospel of the risen Christ that Mary Magdalene proclaimed to the absent male disciples and apostles. The women church leaders acknowledged by Paul spread that good news through Asia, though their words are lost to us.

The Magdalene texts are extensive: Matthew 27:55–61; 28:1–10; Mark 15:40–41, 47; 16:1–8 [9–11]; Luke 8:1–3; 23:55–56; 24:1–10; John 19:25; 20:1–2, 11–18. The fifty-seven verses tell a story of discipleship and faith that is virtually without peer among male disciples yet is not unique to this one woman, for there were other women at the cross and tomb who followed Jesus in life, attended him in death, and proclaimed him in resurrection. Yet she is distinguished by the preservation of her name and frequency of appearance. Mary the mother of Jesus and Mary Magdalene are the only women represented in all four Gospels, even considering the difficult to separate and identify Marys, even with multiple traditions about which Mary anointed Jesus.

Peeling back the traditions accreted around her, some of which—like the red egg—may be useful, she remains a disciple, functionally an apostle, preacher, eyewitness of the Passion, conversant with angels, benefactrix, burial attendant, healed/transformed/exorcised, messenger (angel) of the gospel.

PROPER 12 (CLOSEST TO JULY 27)

*Baruch 6:1–7; Psalm 106:1–6, 40–47; Colossians 2:9–14; Luke 21:20 –28

*The sixth chapter of Baruch is also known as the *Epistle of Jeremiah*. In some Bibles, the two are separated by Lamentations.

Letter of Jeremiah (Baruch 6) 1 A copy of a letter that Jeremiah sent to the women, children and men who would be led as captives into Babylon by the king of the Babylonians, to proclaim to them the message that God had commanded him:
² Because of the sins that you have sinned before God, you all will be taken to Babylon as captives by Nebuchadnezzar, king of the Babylonians. ³ Thus when you all go into Babylon, you will remain there for many years, for a long time, up to seven generations; after that I will bring you away from there in peace. ⁴ Now you all shall see in Babylon, gods made of silver, and golden and wooden, [carried] upon the shoulders, demonstrating the terror of the nations. ⁵ Be careful, therefore, lest you all be made to be like the foreigners or let fear of these gods seize and come upon you. ⁶ When you see the crowd before and behind them bowing down to worship them, say in yourself, "You are the [only] one to whom we must bow down to worship, Sovereign." ⁷ For my messenger is with you, and is watching over your lives.

Psalm 106:1–6, 40–47

¹ Hallelujah! Give thanks to the Ancient Of Days, for she is good;
for her faithful love endures forever.
² Who can utter the mighty acts of the Majesty of the Ages,
or disclose all her praise?
³ Happy are those who preserve justice,
doing righteousness at all times.
⁴ Remember me, Faithful One,
when showing favor to your people;
visit me in your saving work.

⁵ that I may see goodness attend your chosen ones,
　　that I may rejoice in the joy of your nation,
　　that I may proclaim praise along with your possession.
⁶ We have sinned along with our mothers and fathers;
　　we have committed iniquity, we have done wickedly.
⁴⁰ Then the anger of the DREAD GOD ignited against her people,
　　and she abhorred her possession.
⁴¹ She gave them into the hand of the nations;
　　they who ruled over them were they who hated them.
⁴² Their enemies oppressed them,
　　and they were humbled under their hand.
⁴³ Many times she delivered them,
　　yet they rebelled through their own design,
　　and were brought low through their iniquity.
⁴⁴ And she saw them through their distress
　　when she heard their cry.
⁴⁵ For their sake God remembered her covenant,
　　and showed compassion
　　according to the abundance of her faithful love.
⁴⁶ She caused them to be viewed tenderly
　　by all who held them captive.
⁴⁷ Save us, HOLY SHEPHERD, our God,
　　and gather us from among the nations,
　　that we may give thanks to your holy name
　　and rejoice in your praise.

Colossians 2:6 As therefore you all have received the Messiah, Jesus the God-born, in him continue to journey, ⁷ having been rooted and built up in him and having been confirmed in the faith, just as you were taught, abounding in thanksgiving. ⁸ [Therefore] see to it that no one takes you captive through philosophy and worthless deceitfulness, according to human tradition, according to the basic elements of the cosmos, and not according to the Messiah.

⁹ Now in the Messiah dwells the whole fullness of divinity, bodily. ¹⁰ And you all have in the Messiah come to fullness, the Messiah Jesus who is the head of every ruler and authority. ¹¹ In the Messiah also were you all circumcised without human hands, by putting off the body of the flesh in the circumcision of Christ. ¹² When you were buried with the Messiah in baptism, you all were also raised with the Messiah through faith in the power of God, who raised Jesus from the dead. ¹³ And when you all were dead in trespasses and the uncircumcision of your flesh, God brought you to life, together with the Messiah, forgiving us all our trespasses, ¹⁴ erasing the record that stood against us with its legal demands. God set this aside, nailing it to the cross.

Luke 21:20 [Jesus said to the women and men gathered near the temple:] When it happens that you see Jerusalem surrounded by armies, then you all shall know that its devastation has come near. ²¹ Then the women, children, and men in Judea must flee to the mountains, and the women, children, and men inside the city must leave it, and the women, children, and men out in the country must not enter the city. ²² These are days of retribution, as fulfillment of all that is written. ²³ Woe to those who are carrying in their wombs and to those who are nursing infants in those days! For there shall be great calamity on the earth and wrath against this people. ²⁴ And they shall fall by the edge of the sword and be taken captive into all nations, and Jerusalem shall be trampled on by the nations until the times of the [Gentile] nations are fulfilled.

²⁵ There will be signs in sun, moon, and stars, and on the earth distress among nations made anxious by the roaring of the sea and the waves. ²⁶ People shall lose heart from fear and expectation of what is coming upon the world, for the powers of the heavens will be shaken. ²⁷ And then they shall see *the Son of Woman coming in a cloud* with power and great glory. ²⁸ When these things begin, stand up and keep your heads up, because your redemption is drawing near.

PROCLAMATION

Text Notes

The Epistle of Jeremiah is most likely Deutero-Jeremiah, someone writing in his name, as with the later sections of Isaiah, Zechariah, and many of the New Testament epistles. As is the case with many of the psalms, what is marked as the first verse is an introductory statement. In the sixth verse of the Epistle of Jeremiah, the divine title used for the God of the Judean exiles is the Greek word that gives us "despot." I have elected to use a word that communicates a different kind of mastery or sovereignty. In verse 7, the word "messenger" can be either a divine messenger, an angel, or a human messenger, i.e., a prophet. There is insufficient information to make the determination so I keep the broadest meaning counter to NRSV, NRSVue, CEB and NETS. "Lives" at the end of the passage may also be understood as "souls."

In Psalm 106:46, "view tenderly" renders "view with/through mother-love" from the verb whose root is the womb. "Save us" in the following verse is the Hebrew expression that will become "Hosanna."

The setting for this passage is a conversation near the temple in Luke 21:1–5; that public space would have included women, children, and men. The identities and genders of those who raised the initial question with Jesus are not identified. Luke 21:27 quotes Daniel 7:13, which is in one of the Aramaic sections of the book. Here the expression translated "Son of Man" in the New Testaments of most editions of the Bible indicates a supernatural being with the appearance of a human person. In other places the phrase denotes mortality and Jesus uses it with regard to himself in both ways. (The King James is consistent in translating the related forms the same across both testaments while more contemporary Bibles have chosen to employ the translation for Jesus alone, resulting in a misunderstanding of the breath and of the expression across the testaments.)

Preaching Prompts

These readings are set in the kind of captivity many of us reading them millennia later have never experienced. In them, the God who accompanies her people into exile and captivity provides a word, a messenger, and perhaps an angel to speak on her behalf and to watch over her people. These lessons should remind us that the Israelites were a people perpetually under oppression and the Church began and flourished under that kind of oppression. We who read them now must ask ourselves how we translate these messages to people who are not living in those circumstances, and as citizens of nations with histories of inflicting oppression and in some cases the ongoing reality of citizenship in a nation that colonizes and takes captive in different ways.

In the Epistle written in Jeremiah's name, Judah has fallen, the temple has fallen, and the people are in exile. The miracles of old have dried up. God does not thunder against the invaders. The ground does not swallow them. There are no promises of miraculous deliverance. The people must learn to survive and thrive in the world as they know it. Many of us also live in intractable situations and pray for persons and circumstances for which there are no miracles. We have to learn how to live in this world as it is. And sometimes we are bent by this world or even have to make the difficult choice to bend ourselves to survive in circumstances that hold us and keep us from flourishing. And yet we are not alone. We are accompanied by God in all of our twisted and twisting and confining circumstances. God remains Immanuel, God with us to whom is our first loyalty even if it is not apparent to anyone else. And there is always someone through whom God speaks, messenger, prophet, or angel, God sends someone to watch over us as well.

The community of the psalmist is also in captivity. She reflects on the transgressions of generations past along with those of her own generation that led to their captivity, but she knows she serves a loving God who will not abandon her people. The psalmist longs for the gathering of the exiles when God will bring her people home from wherever they are. In verse 45 of the Psalm, God intervenes in the circumstances of their captivity to lighten the load, so much so that their captors began to view them favorably. But the psalmist will not accept a gentled captivity; she continues to long for the liberation that only God can bring.

The church to whom Paul writes was conceived under oppression and grew into its maturity in captivities of different sorts. But Paul is concerned with the captivity of the mind, the inner self. He understands that if a person is free in their mind, no captivity on earth can hold them. That is the lesson of generations of the enslaved who passed their faith down, though they never saw freedom themselves. They created spaces of liberation like the "hush harbors," where enslaved Africans gathered to preach a gospel not watered down by their captors.

In the Gospel, Jesus who lived under foreign occupation and oppression teaches that redemption in the material lives of the people will not come immediately and not without some of the worst that humankind does to one another. The miracle of his birth and life did not and would not dramatically change the world in which he and his disciples lived. They, like generations before them, would have to learn to flourish in the world as it is. But redemption is a sure and certain promise. Wait for it and keep your head up. The days of bending under the pressure of oppression and captivity are over. Jesus is coming with a power the oppressors of this world cannot imagine. He is coming back to free his people.

PROPER 13 (CLOSEST TO AUGUST 3)

Habakkuk 1:1–13; 2:1; Psalm 62:8–12; 2 Peter 3:1–11, 14; Luke 17:20–25

Note: The Habakkuk reading is divided into three speaking parts to convey the dialogue between the prophet and God more clearly. The first line is spoken by a narrator; the prophet follows and God responds. Italic font facilitates this tripart reading.

Habakkuk 1:1 The oracle that the prophet Habakkuk saw.
² HOLY ONE, how long shall I cry for help,
   and you will not hear?
   I cry out to you "Violence!"
   and you do not save.
³ Why do you make me see wrong-doing
   and behold trouble?
   Despoliation and violence are before me;
   litigation and contention arise.
⁴ So the law becomes powerless
   and justice has been aborted.
   The wicked surround the righteous—
   therefore judgment comes forth perverted.
⁵ *Look at the nations, and see!*
   Be astonished! Be astounded!
   For a work is being worked in your days
   that you would not believe if you were told.

⁶ *Look! It is I who rouses the Chaldeans,*
  that fierce and impetuous nation,
  that stomps through the breadth of the earth
  to seize dwellings not their own.
⁷ *Dreadful and frightful are they;*
  they invent their own justice and majesty.
⁸ *Swifter than leopards are their horses,*
  and more menacing than wolves at dusk;
  then their cavalry charges.
  Their cavalry comes from far away;
  they fly like an eagle swift to devour.
⁹ *They all come for violence,*
  advancing face front;
  they gather captives like sand.
¹⁰ *At royalty they scoff,*
  and of rulers they make sport.
  At every fortress they laugh,
  and heap up earth to take it.
¹¹ *Then a spirit swept them;*
  and they passed through and became guilty;
  they whose own strength was their god.
¹² Are you not from time-before-time,
  ANCIENT ONE, my God, my Holy One?
  You will never die.
  HOLY ONE, it is for judgment that you have marked them;
  O Rock, for discipline that you have positioned them.
¹³ Your eyes are too pure to behold evil,
  and you cannot look on wrongdoing;
  why then do you look on the treacherous,
  and are silent when the wicked swallow
  those more righteous than they?
²:¹ Upon my watchpost will I stand,
  and station myself on the rampart;
  Then will I keep watch to see what God shall say to me,
  and what God will answer concerning my charge.

Psalm 62:8–12

⁸ Trust in God at all times, O people;
  pour out your heart before her;
  God is a refuge for us. *Selah*

⁹ The woman-born are only futile,
  the children of earth, false;
  in the scales they ascend,
  less than a single breath.
¹⁰ Trust not in oppression,
  and set not your heart on robbery;
  if force bears fruit, do not set your heart on it.
¹¹ Once has God spoken;
  twice have I heard this:
  that power belongs to God.
¹² Faithful love belongs to you, Most High.
  For you repay to each one according to their work.

2 Peter 3:1 Now this, beloved, the second letter I am writing to you all; in them I am trying to arouse your genuine understanding by reminding you all ² that you should remember the words spoken in the past by the holy women and men who prophesied and the commandment of the Redeemer and Savior spoken through your apostles. ³ First of all know this, that in the last days will come scoffers scoffing and chasing after their own lusts ⁴ and saying, "Where is the promise of his coming? For, ever since our ancestors died, everything continues as from the beginning of creation!"

⁵ For they willfully forget this, that the heavens were of old, and from the waters and through water was formed by the word of God. ⁶ Because of which water the world then was deluged and destroyed. ⁷ Yet now the heavens and earth by the same word have been held in reserve for fire, kept until the day of judgment and destruction of the ungodly.

⁸ But this one thing, do not ignore beloved, that with the Most High one day is like a thousand years, and a thousand years are like one day. ⁹ The Most High is not slow about God's promise, as some think of slowness, but is patient with you all, not wanting anyone to perish, rather all to come to repentance.

¹⁰ But the day of the Most High will come like a thief and then the heavens with a loud noise will pass away; the elements will be dissolved, burned up and the earth and all her works—none shall be found. ¹¹ All these things are to be dissolved in this way. [Consider then,] what sort of persons you all ought to be in leading lives of holiness and godliness.

¹⁴ Therefore, beloved, while for these things you are waiting, strive so that without spot and being blameless is how you all are to be found by God in peace.

Luke 17:20 Jesus was asked one time, by the Pharisees, when would come the majesty of God and he answered, "The majesty of God is not coming with what can be perceived. ²¹ And people will not say, 'Look! Here!' or 'There!' For, see here, the majesty of God is among you all."

²² Then Jesus said to the disciples, "The days are coming when you all will long to see one of the days of the Son of Woman, and you will not see [one]. ²³ People will say to you all,

'Look! Here!' or 'There!' Do not go; do not chase after [them]. ²⁴ For just as the lightning flashes under the heavens from one place to another and blazes, so will the Son of Woman be in his day. ²⁵ But first he must suffer much [many things] and be rejected by this generation.

PROCLAMATION
Text Notes

Habakkuk's outcry is about physical violence (*chamas*), assault of all sorts, and interpersonal and martial conflict. In verse 4, the (little "t") torah has become powerless and ineffective. Lowercase "torah" refers to more than legal statutes; it includes the whole teaching of God through Moses with respect to the Torah and that that follows, including through the prophets.

In 2 Peter 3:1, *eilikrine dianoian* is "genuine" in the sense of both unadulterated and unpretentious, and "understanding" in the sense of comprehension and the intention to act on that understanding. In verse 2, "holy women and men who prophesied" renders and expands "holy prophets." "Scoffers scoffing" in verse 3 is a Hebraism; Hebrew (and Aramaic) roots form nouns and verbs—and sometimes adjectives. The nominal and verbal forms occur together but in inverse order, "they will come scoffing, scoffers." They're going "after their own lusts," here rendered "chasing after."

As is the case throughout the Gospels, and particularly in Luke, "disciples" should be presumed to include women, not limited to the twelve apostles. That is especially the case in public gatherings. Even at the temple where while women had their own space, upstairs in the Herodian temple, women and men mixed freely in the court of the Israelites where persons of any gender brought their offerings to be processed.

I use "majesty" throughout this work to indicate the grandeur of God-space and divine intent given the bloody imperial aspirations of kingdoms in the world of the text. In Luke 17:21, there is an interpretive choice as to whether the majesty of God is "among" the disciples or "within" them. Here, a theological understanding of God's work in the world as being communal rather than individualistic shapes the translation choice, see also NRSV and CEB. In verse 25, the text can be translated to say both that Jesus will suffer much and that he will suffer many things. I have given the reader the option of either or both.

Preaching Prompts

Habakkuk is unique among the prophets in that his message is his outcry to God on behalf of the people. The book does not start with God sending her servant a message to proclaim. It begins with Habakkuk asking God how long will the people be subject to horrific violence, verses 2–3. That is the famous and familiar, "How long, O Lord?" As with Job, God introduced into conversation with her child. God tells Habakkuk her plan to punish the Assyrians who have committed atrocities against the people by loosing the Babylonians (called Chaldeans) on them beginning in verse 5. Understandably, Habakkuk responds with skepticism in verse 12, daring to point out that God is immortal and not subject to the consequences of this unexpected plan. After some pointed questions in verse 13, Habakkuk decides to trust God, to wait and to watch in 2:1.

In the assigned portion of Psalm 62, the psalmist is also waiting for God to act, and urging the people not to turn to retaliatory violence themselves in verse 10. She ends (verse 11) with the powerful reminder that all power belongs to God.

The people who the person writing in Peter's name addresses are waiting in a different time and place. They are, as we are, waiting for the return of Jesus. Like the reign of God, the return of Christ is always "soon" and "at hand." The author of the Epistle invokes the sweep of history, as the Israelites told it, as a reminder that God does not measure time as we do. And that our responsibility is to wait in a way that is worthy of our calling so that when Jesus does return, he will have no reason to be ashamed of us.

In the Gospel, Jesus tells the disciples that the majesty of God is already among them. And he warns them against running after every misguided person (or perhaps every charlatan) to have special knowledge of what God is doing and where.

I imagine the confusion of the disciples—I don't have to imagine it because I share it—looking at the world around me, one every bit as violent as the one in which Habakkuk lived. Among us here? In this crucified and crucifying world? The promise of Jesus is that there is another day coming, set in motion by his suffering. And while we wait, as have all of the generations before us, the words of the psalmist, to cry out in prayer and the words of the anonymous author writing the earliest congregations of the Jesus movement, to live as Jesus taught us, remain unchanged, and stand the test of time.

PROPER 14 (CLOSEST TO AUGUST 10)

Ezekiel 14:12–22a; Psalm 124:1–8; Hebrews 11:29–12:2; Luke 17:26–37

Ezekiel 14:12 Now it was that the word of the JUDGE OF ALL FLESH was upon me:

¹³ Son of Woman, if a land sins against me by acting unfaithfully to commit a faithless act, and I stretch out my hand against her and break her staff of bread and send famine upon her and I cut off from her humankind and animalkind, ¹⁴ and were there these three men in her midst: Noah, Daniel, and Job; they through their righteousness would save only their lives,

an utterance of GOD WHOSE NAME IS HOLY.

¹⁵ If there were barbarous beasts that I sent through the land to bereave her, so that she became a desolation without anyone passing through because of the beasts, ¹⁶ these three men—were they in her midst, as I live—

an utterance of GOD WHOSE NAME IS HOLY:

They would save neither daughters nor sons; they alone would be saved yet, the land would become a desolation. ¹⁷ Or, if I brought a sword upon that land and I said, "Let a sword pass through the land," and I cut off from her humankind and animalkind; ¹⁸ these three men—were they in her midst, as I live,

> an utterance of God Whose Name is Holy:

They would save neither daughters nor sons for, they alone would be saved. ¹⁹ Or, were there a pestilence that I sent into that land, and I poured out my wrath upon her, in blood, to cut off from her humankind and animalkind; ²⁰ even if Noah, Daniel and Job were in her midst, as I live—

> an utterance of God Whose Name is Holy:

They would save neither daughters nor sons; they through their righteousness would save their lives.
²¹ For thus says God Whose Name is Holy:
More so [than these things] my four dreadful judgments I send upon Jerusalem—sword, famine, barbarous beasts, and pestilence—to cut off from her humankind and animalkind! ²² And look! There remain in her survivors who shall be left in her, bringing forth daughters and sons; they shall come out to you and you all shall see their ways and their deeds, and you all shall be comforted on account of the evil that I have brought upon Jerusalem, for all that I have brought upon her.

Psalm 124:1–8

¹ Were it not the Divine Warrior who was for us—
  Let Israel now say:
² Were it not the Divine Warrior who was for us—
  When people rose up,
³ then still alive they would have swallowed us up
  when their anger burned against us.
⁴ Then the waters would have swept over us;
  the torrent would have passed over us.
⁵ Then passing over us,
  the raging waters.
⁶ Blessed be the Holy Protector,
  who has not given us as prey to their teeth.
⁷ We like a bird have escaped from the snare of the fowlers;
  the snare is broken and we have escaped.
⁸ Our help is in the Name of God Who is Holy,
  who made the heavens and earth.

Hebrews 11:29 By faith women, children, and men passed through the Red Sea as though on dry land, but when the Egyptians chose to attempt it, they were drowned. ³⁰ By faith the walls of Jericho fell having been encircled for seven days. ³¹ By faith Rahab the prostitute did not perish with those who did not believe because she had received the spies with peace.

³² And what more should I say? For time would fail me to tell of Gideon, [Deborah,] Barak, Samson, Jephthah*, David, and Samuel and the women and men who were prophets. ³³ They who through faith subdued monarchies, did the work of justice, obtained promises, shut the mouths of lions, ³⁴ quenched mighty fires, fled to safety from the ravenous sword, were strengthened from weakness, became strong in battle, and felled encamped foreign armies.

³⁵ Women received their dead by resurrection. Others were tortured, not willing to receive release, in order a better resurrection to obtain. ³⁶ Yet others received the test of mocking and whipping and even chains and prison. ³⁷ They were stoned, cut apart, in a slaughter, they died upon the sword; they traveled around in sheepskin and goatskin hides; impoverished, oppressed, afflicted. ³⁸ Persons of whom the world was not worthy; in deserts they wandered and in mountains, and in caves and holes in the ground.

³⁹ Yet all these, martyred for their faith, they did not receive what was promised. ⁴⁰ For God, for us, provided something better so that they would not, apart from us, be made perfect.

¹²:¹ Therefore, since we have surrounding us so great a cloud of witnesses, let us also every weight throw off, along with the sin that distracts; through patience let us run the race that is set before us, ² looking to Jesus the foundation and fulfillment of our faith, who for the sake of the joy that was set before him endured the cross, its shame despising, and at the right hand of the throne of God, is seated.

*Some readers may choose to omit Jephthah, see Text Notes.

Luke 17:26 "Now just as it was in the days of Noah, thus shall it be in the days of the Son of Woman. ²⁷ Women and men were eating, drinking, marrying, being given in marriage—until the day Noah [and his wife and daughters and sons and daughters-in-law] entered the ark and the flood came and destroyed all of them [and their children]. ²⁸ Likewise, just as it was in the days of Lot: women and men were eating and drinking, buying and selling, planting and building. ²⁹ But on the day that Lot [and his wife and daughters] left Sodom, it rained fire and sulfur from heaven and destroyed all of them [and their children]. ³⁰ Accordingly shall it be on the day the Son of Woman is revealed. ³¹ On that day, anyone on the roof who has belongings in the house must not come down to gather them up and likewise, anyone in the field should not turn back. ³² Remember Lot's wife. ³³ The one who seeks to preserve their life will lose it, but the one who loses their life shall save their life. ³⁴ I tell you all, on that night there will be two in one bed; one will be taken and the other left. ³⁵ There will be two women grinding meal together; one will be taken and the other left." ³⁷ Then they asked him, "Where, Rabbi?" He said to them, "Where the corpse is, there the vultures will gather."

PROCLAMATION

Text Notes

The Hebrew and Aramaic expressions *ben adam* and *bar enosh* are the antecedents for the Greek expression *huios to anthropou*, all of which were traditionally translated as "Son of Man," (see Wycliffe, Geneva, Bishop, KJV, RSV). The JPS—which is a revision of an older translation by the same name—and NRSV and successive revisions forego that translation for "mortal" where CEB uses "human being." The effect (and perhaps intent) is to reserve the "Son of Man" title for Jesus. However, that erases the polyvalency of the term which means both "mortal" as throughout Ezekiel and Jesus's predictions of his death (Matthew 26:2; Mark 10:33; Luke 24:7) *and* an extraordinary being as in Daniel's vision (7:13) recast as Jesus's description of himself "coming with the clouds" (Mark 14:62).

The three virtuous men—Daniel, Noah, and Job—are ancestral figures of mythic time. "Danel" as it is spelled here is the Ugaritic character of mythic lore upon whom the Daniel story rests (the Rabbis corrected the spelling to the more familiar "Daniel"); thus, the biblical Daniel would not have been read as a literal character, and certainly not as a prophet as he appears in Christian canons—indeed, the text makes no such claim. Rather, he and the book that bears his name are ciphers for a subversive anti-imperial discourse against their current overlords (indicated by the numerous, almost comedic and thus likely intentional, historical errors, i.e., the names and sequence of rulers).

Psalm 124 is "a psalm of ascents," meaning a pilgrimage psalm, as the trip to Jerusalem is always described as "going up." That introductory line is the first verse in Hebrew, but Christians have separated from the rest of the psalm for many centuries and it is infrequently read in worship.

Some readers may choose to omit Jephthah* in Hebrews 11:32 given his faithlessness in distrusting the spirit of God that was upon him, and making and keeping a barbarous vow that resulted in him murdering his daughter, offering her as a human sacrifice to God. The omission of Deborah, behind whose skirts Barak hid, is rectified in an optional inclusion. In Hebrews 11:34, "weakness" can also mean "sickness."

In the Luke passage, I have included the family members who accompanied Noah and Lot as an option for the reader in brackets. I have also made clear that children suffered and were killed in each of these catastrophes.

Preaching Prompts

One of the dominant theologies in the Hebrew Bible is that God is responsible for evil, given God is responsible for all things including good and evil, and everything in between. Using the rhetorical form of a hypothetical argument punctuated by attestations of the divine authorship of the cataclysmic claims (the Greek word for the flood in the Gospel reading is *kataklusmos*), God calls God's own bluff, moving from a posture of total annihilation—with the exception of the three worthy ancestors—to a promise that God will not destroy everyone. A remnant shall remain. Though reduced in numbers, the community shall survive.

There will always be catastrophes and cataclysms, and people will struggle to make sense of them. Some will blame God. Some will blame people who are different from them as Pat Robertson blamed LGBTQIA people for hurricanes and other tragedies. At its heart, the story of God with the people of Israel and their descendants is one of survival in a situation that would cause anyone to despair. The psalmist has unshakable trust in that premise.

In the Epistle to the Hebrews—which very few serious critical biblical scholars attribute to Paul, and indeed was possibly written by Priscilla, making it the only book in the Christian testament with such a valid claim—the author catalogs the miraculous survival of lionized figures and ordinary folk among torrents of devastation *along* with the horrific deaths of the faithful. (Many of the church fathers rejected Pauline authorship, and starting with German scholar Adolf von Harnack in 1900, the case of Priscilla's authorship has been pressed. See the English translation in Lee Anna Starr, *The Bible Status of Woman* [Zarephath, NJ: Pillar of Fire, 1955[, 392–415, and Ruth Hoppin, *Priscilla's Letter: Finding the Author of the Epistle to the Hebrews* [Walnut Creek, CA: Lost Coast Press, 2020]). As verse 39 hopefully makes clear, having faith, having the "right" faith does not guarantee surviving difficult days. The world is not that simple and God is not that fickle. Rather, Hebrews is a testimony to fidelity and perseverance across time, the survival of a people as is the case in Ezekiel where the overthrow of the last monarchy, destruction of the temple, and deportation into Babylonian captivity circumscribed in every way the end of the people of Israel. But God's fidelity transcends political structures and geographical boundaries. One of the early messages of Ezekiel is that God is where her people are so God went into captivity and appeared to Ezekiel. This may be comforting as some of the political structures of US democracy crumble before our very eyes.

The message of Jesus, living under political, cultural, and religious oppression, is that the ancestral stories of nearly world-ending upheaval are preparation for the day on which Jesus, mortal and immortal, the fully incarnate Love and Word of God, will be revealed and our world will change again, and however terrifying that moment may be, whatever the inherent danger—don't risk your life for things or look back at your things like Lot's wife, or you may miss the revelation.

FEAST OF THE EVER-BLESSED VIRGIN MARY, AUGUST 15

Judith 13:18–20; Canticle 15, the Magnificat, Luke 1:46–55;
Revelation 21:1–7; Luke 1:26–38

Judith 13:18 Uzziah said to Judith, "O daughter, you are blessed by the Most High God above all other women on earth, and blessed be the Holy God, who created the heavens and the earth, who has guided you to cut off the head of the leader of our enemies. [19] Praise of you will never depart from the hearts of women and men who remember the power of God. [20] May God do these things for you as an eternal exaltation, and may God visit you with blessings, because you did not withhold your life when our nation was humiliated, rather you rallied against our demise, walking straight before our God." And all the people said, "Amen. Amen."

Canticle 15, the Magnificat, Luke 1:46–55

[46] "My soul magnifies the Holy One,
[47] and my spirit rejoices in God my Savior,
[48] for God has looked with favor on the lowliness of God's own womb-slave.
Surely, from now on all generations will call me blessed;
[49] for the Mighty One has done great things for me,
and holy is God's name.
[50] God's loving-kindness is for those who fear God
from generation to generation.
[51] God has shown the strength of God's own arm;
God has scattered the arrogant in the intent of their hearts.
[52] God has brought down the powerful from their thrones,
and lifted up the lowly;
[53] God has filled the hungry with good things,
and sent the rich away empty.
[54] God has helped God's own child, Israel,
a memorial to God's mercy,
[55] just as God said to our mothers and fathers,
to [Hagar and] and Sarah and Abraham, to their descendants forever."

Revelation 21:1 I saw a new heaven and a new earth, for the first heaven and the first earth had passed away, and the sea was no more. [2] And I saw the holy city, the new Jerusalem, descending heaven from God, prepared as a bride adorned for her beloved. [3] And I heard a loud voice from the throne saying,

"Look! The home of God is among the woman-born.
God will dwell with them as their God;

they will be God's peoples,
and selfsame God will be with them.

⁴ God will wipe every tear from their eyes.
Death will be no more;
grief and weeping and pain will be no more,
for the first things have passed away."

⁵ And the One who seated upon the throne said, "Look! I am making all things new." The One also said, "Write, for these words are trustworthy and true." ⁶ Then the One said to me, "It is done! I am the Alpha and the Omega, the beginning and the end. I will give to the thirsty from the spring of the water of life freely. ⁷ Those who overcome will inherit these things, and I will be their God and they will be my daughters and sons.

Luke 1:26 In the sixth month the angel Gabriel was sent by God to a town of Galilee, Nazareth, ²⁷ to a virgin betrothed to a man whose name was Joseph, of the house of David. And the name of the virgin was Mary. ²⁸ And the angel came to Mary and said, "Rejoice, favored one! The Most High God is with you." ²⁹ Now, she was troubled by the angel's words and pondered what sort of greeting this was. ³⁰ Then the angel said to her, "Fear not, Mary, for you have found favor with God. ³¹ And now, you will conceive in your womb and give birth to a son, and you will name him Jesus. ³² He will be great and will be called the Son of the Most High, and the Sovereign God will give him the throne of his ancestor David. ³³ He will reign over the house of Jacob forever, and of his sovereignty there will be no end." ³⁴ Then Mary said to the angel, "How can this be, since I have not known a man intimately?" ³⁵ The angel said to her, "The Holy Spirit, She will come upon you, and the power of the Most High will overshadow you; therefore the one born will be holy. He will be called Son of God. ³⁶ And now, Elizabeth your kinswoman has even conceived a son in her old age, and this is the sixth month for she who was called barren. ³⁷ For nothing will be impossible with God." ³⁸ Then Mary said, "Here am I, the woman-slave of God; let it be with me according to your word." Then the angel left her.

PROCLAMATION

Text Notes

In Judith 13:20, Judith's actions are described awkwardly as "rallying against" the "corpse" (understood as the eminent demise) of her people, i.e., taking action to oppose that which would end in their deaths.

In Mary's languages, Hebrew for prayer and religious texts and Aramaic for daily life, the Holy Spirit is feminine. The Greek scriptures use the neuter pronoun corresponding to "it." It is not until the production of the Vulgate and other Latin texts that the masculine pronoun is inserted. While the literary language is Greek, the translation choice reflects the underlying Semitic linguistic and cultural context. In verse 48 of the Magnificat, Mary uses the same slave language that Hannah does, "woman-slave of God," a common expression across the canon. When used with reference to reproduction, as here, I use womb-slave; the language of slavery pervades the scriptures and forms the rhetoric of the most familiar stories, often without examination. In verse 55 of the Magnificat, I have added Hagar as a witness to God's fidelity proclaimed in the verse.

Revelation 21 deploys a marriage metaphor that does not require a rigid gender binary or heteronormativity to be effective, so I have translated *aner*, "man," meaning "husband" in verse 2, as "beloved." *Nike* in verse 7 means to "overcome obstacles" or "prevail." To "be victorious" and "conquer" are also within the semantic range; however the latter two choices do not clearly indicate struggle, and "conquer" (as in NRSV) seems unnecessarily martial here.

Preaching Prompts

Like Judith, whose name can be translated "Jewish woman," Miriam, rendered "Mary" in English (along with other Hebraic names in the Second Testament to sound less Jewish), was a Jewish woman. Where Judith is an older widowed woman when she puts her body on the line to save her people, Mary, named for the prophet Miriam like all of the "Marys," was young and on the cusp of marriage. Each woman has her bona fides established in a lengthy genealogy. Judith's is the longest of any woman in the canon, stretching from the time of Nebuchadnezzar to Simeon, Leah's son by Jacob (Judith 8:1; 9:2), though some argue against her historicity. While Judith's husband is folded into *her* genealogy, "Her husband Manasseh, who belonged to her tribe and family," Mary's genealogy is *Joseph's* genealogy.

The patriarchal genealogy fails to tell the story of Mary and Jesus as descendants of Bathsheba and David, though it does so for Joseph (Matthew 1:1–17, see verses 6 and 16, and Luke 2:4), even while naming Tamar (I), Ruth, and describing Bathsheba as the wife of Uriah but without her name (Matthew 1:3, 5–6). Mary is *presumed* to be from Joseph's tribe, Judah, following the most common marital pattern and likely from a more closely related clan within the tribe. Mary is likely not Joseph's sister, though she could be his cousin; somewhere between Solomon in verse 7 and Mattan, Joseph's grandfather, in verse 15, Mary's genealogy is obscured.

Both Judith and Mary have their virtue attested—Judith's piety as a widow (Judith 8:4–6) and Mary's virginity (Luke 1:26ff)—and both will use their bodies in scandalous ways to effect salvation. Judith entices an enemy general who seeks to seduce her—but with a maid present to testify to her virtue—and beheads the man with his own sword (Judith 13:4–10). Mary agrees to the divine pregnancy, risking being ostracized and perhaps stoned for the appearance of breaking faith with Joseph. For some readers there will always be a question of the degree to which Mary was free to refuse. That she affirmatively consents is clear: "Let it be with me according to your word." But could she refuse? Before she consents, Gabriel says: "You will

..." The timing is crucial, helping readers and hearers grapple with consent issues in the text and the gulfs between ancient and contemporary ethical standards.

Mary and Judith are also linked in the words of blessing "among" and "above other" women in Judith 13:18 and Luke 1:42. Elizabeth, Mary's relative, could have chosen the blessing by drawing from her scriptures, from Judith, and from the words of Deborah's blessing on Jael in Judges 5:24: "Most blessed of women … of tent-dwelling women most blessed." (Judith was included in the Greek Jewish Bible and influential where not later canonical). Like her textual sisters, Jael's story is framed by scandal, assassinating an enemy general after welcoming him to hide there; a man who was so well known as a rapist his mother imagines his delay is caused by his proclivities (Judges 4:17–24; 5:24–30). His position at his death, between (not "at" per NRSV) Jael's legs, would seem confirmation.

The blessings of Jael and Judith with their histories of violence worry the innocence of the annunciation with the reminder of the violence to which Mary is at risk now and the violence she will live to see enacted on the body of her son. In the words of another holy person, "a sword will pierce her soul" (Luke 2:35).

John (1:1) says, "The Word became flesh and dwelled, *eskēnōsen*, among us." If Jesus is the heir of Bathsheba and David according to the flesh; it is through Mary's flesh, the matrix of the Incarnation, that God comes to dwell with us. That verb, *skēnoō*, "to dwell" is also used in the second reading chosen for today: "God will dwell with them as their God." The Feast of the Ever-Blessed Virgin Mary affords an opportunity to reflect on the ways in which God dwells with us and is a model of hospitality.

PROPER 15 (CLOSEST TO AUGUST 17)

Ezekiel 19:1–3; 10–14; Psalm 30:1–12; Romans 12:14–21; Luke 6:17–25

Ezekiel 19:1 All of you, raise a keening for the royal seed of Israel, ² and say:
   What a lioness was your mother among lions!
   Among young lions she lay, raising her cubs.
³ She raised up one of her cubs; who became a young lion,
   who learned to catch prey, who devoured the woman-born.
¹⁰ Your mother was like a vine in a vineyard planted by the waters,
   fruitful and full of branches from abundant water.
¹¹ She had mighty branches for a ruler's scepter;
   she grew tall, her height among the clouds,
   and was seen because of her height
   and because of her many branches.
¹² Then she was uprooted in a rage, she was thrown to the ground,
   the east wind withered her fruit, they were stripped off;

her strongest stem was withered, then consumed by fire.
13. Now she is planted in the wilderness,
in a dry and thirsty land.
14. Now fire has gone out from her staff, and has devoured her branches, her fruit,
now there is no mighty branch within her, no scepter for ruling.
This is a keening-lament, and it is used for lamentation.

Psalm 30:1–12

1. I will exalt you, ARK OF SAFETY, because you have pulled me up
and have not let my enemies rejoice over me.
2. HEALING ONE, my God, I cried to you for help,
and you healed me.
3. EVER-LIVING GOD, you brought my soul up from Sheol;
you preserved my life from descent to the Pit.
4. Sing praises to the FAITHFUL GOD, you her faithful;
give thanks remembering her holiness.
5. For her fury is a moment, her favor a lifetime.
Weeping may pass the night, yet in the morning, joy.
6. Now I, said in my prosperity,
"I shall never be shaken."
7. MAJESTIC ONE by your favor you established me as a mighty mountain;
you hid your face, I was terrified.
8. To you MOST HIGH I call,
and to you my sovereign I appeal:
9. "What profit is there in my [shed] blood, in my descent to the Pit?
will the dust praise you, declare your faithfulness?
10. Hear, HOLY ONE, and have mercy upon me;
HOLY ONE OF OLD, be my help.
11. You have turned my wailing into dancing;
from me you have taken my sackcloth and you have clothed me with joy.
12. So that my glory might praise you and not keep silent;
GLORIOUS ONE, my God, forever will I praise you.

Romans 12:14 Bless the ones who persecute you; bless and do not curse. 15. Rejoice with the ones who rejoice, weep with the ones who weep. 16. With one another, be harmonious; be not arrogant, but associate with the humble. Do not make yourselves [out] to be wiser than you are. 17. Evil for evil you shall not repay anyone; consider before time what is good in the sight of all. 18. If possible from your ability, with every human person, live in peace. 19. Do not avenge yourselves beloved rather, leave space for the wrath [of God]; for it is written, *"To me belongs vengeance; I will repay, says the Holy One."* 20. No, *"If your enemy hungers, feed* them; if they thirst, give them something to drink; for by so doing, burning coals shall you heap on their head." ²¹ Do not be overcome by evil rather, overcome evil with good.

Luke 6:17 Now Jesus came down with his apostles and stood on a level place, with a great crowd of his disciples, women and men, and a great multitude of people—women, children, and men—from all Judea, Jerusalem, and the coast of Tyre and Sidon; ¹⁸ who had come to hear him and to be healed of their diseases, and those who were troubled with unclean spirits were cured. ¹⁹ And all in the crowd were trying to touch him, for power came out from him and cured all of them.

²⁰ Then Jesus looked up at the women and men who were his disciples and said:
"Blessed are the poor,
for yours is the majesty of God.
²¹ Blessed are those who are hungry now,
for you all shall be fed.
Blessed are you who weep now,
for you all shall laugh.

²² Blessed are you when people hate you all and when they ostracize you, revile you, and spit out your name on account of the Son of Woman. ²³ Rejoice in that day and leap for joy, for surely your reward is great in heaven; for that is what their ancestors did to the women and men who were the prophets then.

²⁴ But woe to you who are rich,
for you all have received your consolation.
²⁵ Woe to you who are full now,
for you all shall be hungry.
Woe to you who laugh now,
for you all shall mourn and weep."

PROCLAMATION

Text Notes

The central figure of Ezekiel 19 is described as a lioness and a tree in feminine language throughout (compare CEB with NRSV, which shifts to "it" in verses 11ff counter to the Hebrew). It is a lament over the decline and fall of the Judean monarchy, that last vestige of a self-governing Israel; the individual cubs are the sons of Josiah, enthroned and dethroned at the whims of their conquerors, Nebuchadnezzar and Pharaoh Neco. The lioness, singular, conflates the last two queen mothers, Nehusta and Hamutal, or may represent Judah, uncommonly in feminine language (versus the more familiar [male] lion of Judah). Because the fall of Judah did not only affect royal sons, I use the more inclusive "royal seed" in verse 1. For the peril faced by the last princesses of Judah, see Jeremiah 41:10; 43:5–7 and my discussion of them and the queen mothers in *Womanist Midrash: A Reintroduction to the Women of the Torah and of the Throne.* The translation "vine in a vineyard" comes from a widely accepted correction to the original text, "vine in your blood."

Romans 12:16 uses a verb that means "condescend" to describe Paul's instruction that Christians spend time with the "lowly." I translate it "sit with" here. Verse 19 quotes Deuteronomy 32:35, in part, by corresponding to the first phrase in Hebrew then loosely following a combination of the LXX and MT. Verse 20 quotes Proverbs 25:21–22, following LXX nearly exactly; the sole divergence is the word used for "hunger."

Luke 6:17 describes a great crowd of disciples in addition to the disciples, apostles who were appointed in the previous verse; throughout Luke the disciples—when not limited to the apostles—include women and men. And "prophet" without further delineation is an inclusive group across both testaments.

Preaching Prompts

These lessons tell the stories of the kind of reversals that all of us face without regard to our circumstances, power, and privilege. The first lesson tells the story of the rise and fall of the last Judean dynasty presented as a lamentation that might well have been sung (lamentations were normally sung by women with the famous exception of David's lament for Saul and Jonathan). The psalmist comforts herself with the knowledge that God is her deliverance and that seasons of sorrow are seasonal; weeping does not last forever. In Romans 12, the perspective shifts from first person to third. Followers of the way of Jesus are to accompany one another in seasons of sorrow and suffering, weeping with those who weep and rejoicing with those who rejoice. Underlying the Epistle is the uniting theme for these readings that joy and sorrow in series are part of the human condition. The Gospel, in conversation with the Epistle, teaches that followers of Jesus should not expect to be exempt from that reality. Jesus teaches that the reversals will prove not to have been random over the grand sweep of time. Those with power and privilege will find themselves for rest. Those who have been oppressed will find themselves empowered. More than that, Jesus centers his teaching on the poor, hungry, and the sorrowful.

The idea that Christians should be happy all the time is a dangerous one that persists, as does the notion we should not express our grief or sorrow. Grief and its regular antecedents, death and loss, are difficult topics. It is hard to sit with someone in their sorrow, and their dying, in their extended painful illness, like Job's silence, or at least without ordering some inane pietism. Pastors and clinically trained chaplains learn about "ministry of presence" that can be practiced by anyone. Just be present. Be present for one another, and be present with yourself in your own grief. These are some of the lessons of the combined readings.

Reading with a gendered lens, in the Ezekiel lesson the lioness represents the queen mother as the queenly figure; in Judah is the mother and not the wife of the monarch. It is a reminder that patriarchy does not exist without women, whether upholding it or exercising power within its constraints. The kind of ministry of presence to which Paul calls the church is not gendered or hierarchical. It does not belong to clergy. The poor in Jesus's time and our own are overwhelmingly women and children—with the addition in our time of trans teens and black women in the trans community—being subject to extreme and life-threatening poverty.

Lastly, "blessed are the poor" is not a blessing of poverty which so often exists because of the intentionally oppressive and exploitative actions of the rich. Similarly, "you shall always have the poor with you" (Matthew 26:11; Mark 14:7) does not intend to convey God-ordained poverty. The persistence and perpetuation of poverty is a sign of the unredeemed world that will be transformed for the last time on the last day.

PROPER 16 (CLOSEST TO AUGUST 24)

Ezekiel 22:1–8, 12; Psalm 50:1–6; Hebrews 10:26–31; John 5:19 –24

Ezekiel 22:1 And it was that the word of GOD WHO DWELLS ABOVE THE CHERUBIM came to me saying: ² You, child of earth and Eve, will you judge? Will you judge the city of blood? Then, make known to it all its abominations. ³ So shall you say: Thus says the Holy GOD: Oh city! Shedding the blood of its own; its time has come! It makes idols for itself, defiling itself.

⁶ The leaders of Israel among you, each one wielded their power within you for the purpose of shedding blood. ⁷ Mother and father are treated with contempt within you: against the immigrant in your midst they commit violent acts of extortion; orphan and widow are subjected to violence within you. ⁸ My holy things have you despised and my sabbaths you have profaned.

¹² Bribes they take in you, to facilitate the shedding of blood. You take both interest (in cash) and collateral (goods), and you have violently defrauded your neighbors by extortion. Moreover, you have forgotten me, says the Holy GOD.

Psalm 50:1–6

Psalm 50:1 God of gods, the MAKER OF ALL,
  speaks and summons the earth
  from the dawning of the sun to its setting.
² From Zion, the perfection of beauty,
  God shines forth.
³ Our God comes and does not keep silent,
  before her is a devouring fire,
  and a whirling (wind) surrounds her.

⁴ She summons the heavens above—
    and the earth—in order to judge her people:
⁵ "Gather to me my faithful ones,
    who made a covenant with me by sacrifice."
⁶ The heavens declare her righteousness,
    for God, she is the one who judges. *Selah*

Hebrews 10:26 Indeed, if we willfully sin after receiving the knowledge of the truth, no longer is there a sacrifice for sins. ²⁷ Rather, [there is] an expectation of judgment and a zealous fire that will devour those opposed [to God]. ²⁸ Anyone who rebelled against the teaching of Moses without mercy, *on the testimony of two or three witnesses*, died. ²⁹ How much, do you suppose, even worse punishment will be deserved by those who the Child of God, they put under their feet and the blood of the covenant, they treat as a common thing—that by which they were sanctified—and the Spirit of grace they mocked?

³⁰ For we know the one who said:

Mine is vengeance, I will repay.

And again:

The Holy One will judge the people of God.

³¹ A fearful thing it is to fall into the hands of the living God.

John 5:19 Jesus answered [the Judeans in Jerusalem] and said to them, "Truly, truly, I say to you all, the Son can do nothing alone, but only what he sees the Father doing; for whatever that one does, the Son does likewise. ²⁰ The Father loves the Son and shows him all that he is doing and will show him greater works than these, so that you all will be astonished. ²¹ For just as the Father raises the dead and gives them life, so also the Son, to whomever he wishes, gives life. ²² No one does the Father judge; rather, all judgment has been given to the Son, ²³ so that all may honor the Son just as they honor the Father. Anyone who does not honor the Son does not honor the Father who sent him. ²⁴ Truly truly, I say to you all, anyone who hears my word and believes him who sent me has eternal life, and does not come under judgment, but has passed from death to life.

PROCLAMATION

Text Notes

In Ezekiel 22:2, I translate *ben adam* as "child of earth and Eve" to maintain the sense of mortality, connection to first parents, and the Earth. *To'evah*, the infamous word denoting some male-male homoerotic activity in Leviticus 19, no longer includes those acts; in fact, it is never used that way again in the Hebrew Bible (i.e., when it recurs in Proverbs, it refers to lying, deception and wickedness, see

Proverbs 3:32; 6:16; 8:7; 11:1, 20; 12:22; 20:10, 23). Here, it refers to extreme acts of violence and extortion and the violent deprivation of livelihood from the most vulnerable members of the community. In the omitted intervening verses, a catalog of sexual transgressions is also named; all of them are acts of sexual violence by men against women, including their own relatives.

In Hebrews 10, verses 26 and 27 are one long continuous sentence broken here for ease of reading and comprehension with the continuing verb in verse 27 made apparent in brackets. Similarly, in the same verse, the adjectival form of "opposition, against" requires a noun, "God," also in brackets. There are quotations from the Hebrew Bible in verses 28 and 30; respectively, they are: Deuteronomy 17:6; Deuteronomy 32:35; Deuteronomy 32:36.

Preaching Prompts

There is much talk about "biblical values" in some Christian communities in the United States, often by those with ready access to political and financial power, and loud certitude about their own virtue along with the singular correctness of their biblical interpretations, which are generally not acknowledged as being interpretations. Each of these readings includes words of indictment, words of justice, and words spoken by or embodied by one who is living Word in the flesh, or on high.

In the Ezekiel reading, the community that is subject to the depredations of others in colonizing imperial violence is also guilty of its own depredations against the most vulnerable of its people. It is a reminder that people can be on the margins actively marginalizing others; they can be privileged and at peril at the same time: queer folk can be racist and sexist; some black folk can be patriarchal and ableist; some women can be transphobic and classist, etc. In the psalm, the God who judges the nations will judge her own people. Choosing this God, and entering into covenant with her, comes with the responsibility to live according to her values or face her holy, righteous judgment. Ezekiel has given voice to her values.

The author of the Epistle to the Hebrews, perhaps Priscilla as thought by some Second Testament scholars, warns that God will hold her people to the covenant inscribed in the blood of Jesus just as she held her children of old to account, to the covenant inscribed in stone and Torah uttered by the lips of Moses. Following the ancient teaching about the forgiveness of sin being available for unintentional sin, but the one who chooses to sin is at the mercy of God—this is the theological premise of Yom Kippur, the Day of Atonement and the ancient practice of casting willful sins upon a goat sent into the wilderness to be consumed.

In the Gospel, John asserts that God's standards of justice are unmediated and unattenuated in Jesus: 1) They hold the same standards because they are parent and child and more than parent and child. 2) There is a cosmic, salvific balance in which resurrection and eternal life are bestowed. That means, 3) there is a possibility they will not be bestowed in some cases. This last reading argues against interpretations that sever Jesus from his Jewish culture and Torah, that try to create a "legalistic Old Testament"—as if legalisms, adhering closely to the laws of God, was something to be condemned rather than commended. That is an antisemitic and anti-Judaistic reading; here, the Gospel of John is firmly against such.

Together these lessons are a rebuke to the kind of theology in which folk can claim the benefits of being a covenant partner, of being "saved," and then behave in whatever way they see fit because they have redemption and resurrection in their pocket. The god of old is still on the throne of judgment and we shall all be held to account. The indictments are coming to the scriptures: abuse and exploitation of the poor and the immigrant. And in a rare declaration, the sexual abuse of girls and women is articulated as an indictment against the people of God.

PROPER 17 (CLOSEST TO AUGUST 31)

Obadiah 1:1–4, 10–15; Psalm 7:8–11, 17; James 4:5–11; Luke 17:1–4

Obadiah 1 The vision of Obadiah:
Thus says the Sovereign HOLY ONE to Edom:
We have heard a message from the ALL-SEEING GOD,
and from an envoy sent among the nations:
"Rise up! Let us rise against Edom for war!"
² See here! Least shall I make you among the nations;
despised shall you be, utterly.
³ The proudness of your heart has deceived you;
you who dwell in the clefts of Sela, the rock city,
with your habitation on high.
You say in your heart,
"Who will bring me down to earth?"
⁴ Though you soar like the eagle,
though among the stars is your nest set,
from there shall I bring you down,
                                        an utterance of FIRE OF SINAI.
¹⁰ For the violence done to Jacob, [the child of your mother],
shame shall cover you and you shall be cut off forever.
¹¹ On the day you stood on the frontline,
on the day strangers looted his wealth,
and foreigners entered his gates
and for Jerusalem cast lots,
you too were like one of them.

12 You should not have just watched on the day your twin—
   on the day of your twin's misfortune;
   you should not have rejoiced over the people of Judah—
   women, children, and men—on the day of their devastation;
   you should not have flapped your lips on the day of distress.
13 You should not have entered the gate of my people
   on the day of their calamity;
   you should not have just watched
   even you! over Judah's disaster,
   on the day of their calamity.
   You should not have sent for their goods
   on the day of their calamity.
14 You should not have stood at the crossroads
   to cut off their refugees;
   you should not have shut out over their survivors
   on the day of distress.
15 For the day of the RIGHTEOUS ONE is near against all the nations.
   As you have done, it shall be done to you;
   your recompence shall be returned on your own head.

Psalm 7:8–11, 17

8 The RIGHTEOUS GOD judges the peoples;
   grant me justice, RIGHTEOUS ONE, according to my righteousness
   and according to my integrity.
9 May it come to an end, the wickedness of the wicked,
   yet establish the righteous,
   you who test the minds and hearts, righteous God.
10 My shield is God,
   who saves the upright in heart.
11 God is a righteous judge,
   and a God who is indignant every day.
17 I will give thanks to the JUDGE OF ALL FLESH according to her righteousness,
   and I shall sing praise to the Name of the HOLY GOD, the Most High.

James 4:5 See here! Do you all suppose that in vain the scripture says, "God jealously longs for the God-crafted spirit settled within us"? 6 Rather, God gives great grace; therefore it says,

God opposes the proud,
but to the humble grants grace.

7 Submit yourselves therefore to God. Oppose the devil and it will flee from you all. 8 Draw near to God and God will draw near to all of you. Cleanse your hands you sinners,

and purify your hearts, you double-minded. ⁹ Lament and mourn and weep. Let your laughter be turned into mourning and your joy into sorrow. ¹⁰ Humble yourselves before the Holy One and God will exalt you all. ¹¹ Speak not ill against one another sisters and brothers. One who speaks ill against a sister or brother or judges another speaks ill against the law and judges the law. Yet if you judge the law, you are not a doer of the law but a judge. ¹² There is one lawgiver and judge who is able to save and to destroy. So who, then, are you to judge your neighbor?

Luke 17:1 Now Jesus said to his disciples, "It is not possible that things that will trip you up and lead you to stumble into sin will not come, but woe to the person on whose account they come! ² It would be better if a millstone were hung around their neck and they were thrown into the sea than for them to cause one of these little ones to stumble into sin. ³ Guard yourselves! If a sister or brother sins, you must rebuke them, and if there is repentance, you must forgive them. ⁴ And if seven times a day they sin against you and turn back to you seven times and say, 'I repent,' you must forgive them."

PROCLAMATION

Text Notes

In verse 1 of Obadiah, there is a royal, divine "we." There, God refers to themselves in the first person plural. Ancient readers might well envision God seated at the divine council with lesser divine beings in attendance, see Job 15:8 and Psalms 82:1 and 89:7. In verse 3, "Sela," which means rock is unlikely to refer to any generic rocky peak; rather, it may refer to the Edomite fortress city carved out of a rocky cliff face, generally identified with Petra. The tone of the piece is one of outrage that the kinship bonds between Jacob and Esau, referring to their descendants, have been broken and disregarded. In keeping with the aims of this project, in verse 10 I make that bond explicit through their shared mother in place of "your brother Jacob." Similarly, I characterize the fraternal bond as a "twin" bond in verse 12 in lieu of "brother."

James 4:5 cites an unknown verse. Verse 6 quotes Proverbs 3:34. Throughout this project, I employ the gender neutral pronoun "it" to refer to the devil, Satan, etc., as in verse 7. Here I use the stronger and more active "oppose" (rather than the more familiar "resist") for *antistete*. "Law" in verse 11 includes the Torah and the broader Israelites/Jewish legal tradition extant at that time.

In Luke 17:1 and in verse 2, the word *skandala* means to stumble and is used as a metaphor for falling into sin; I make all of that explicit in my translation. In verse 1, it is combined with a word that refers to a trap for a small land animal or bird. The NRSV inexplicably shifts the third-person address of the text to second person as does the NRSVue.

Preaching Prompts

The prophecy of Obadiah, whose name means "servant of God" and may therefore be a pen name, is a retaliatory call for war and retribution set on divine lips in response to the devastation of the Babylonian assault on Judah, Jerusalem, and the Israelite temple. The rage and pain it communicates is palpable and raw. As I write this, the world is watching in horror as Hamas launches a strike on Israel and we await Israel's response; both framed as retaliations. The rage and pain is palpable and raw. The stories are not the same and yet, these modern warring peoples are in some ways, direct and indirect, related to those ancient warring peoples. The current horror serves as a window into the horror communicated by this ancient text.

The heart of this powerful prophetic poem is the condemnation of Edom, Israel's sibling nation with whom they shared the heartbeat of their figurative mother Rebekah, for joining forces with Babylonian shock troops to pillage and plunder their kin, and in some cases, hand them over to captivity and block their escape. The refrain "you should not have..." is hammered, ringing out over and over and over again, eight times. The use of the personal name "Jacob" and the kinship language in verse 10 presents this conflict as a rupture and betrayal in a family without regard to the centuries of relational and geographical distance between the nations that have arisen from these two ancestral figures, Jacob and his twin Esau (unnamed here), represented by "Edom." Verse 15 calls for retributive violence of which the world has grown so weary but in which we, particularly as Americans and European Western nations, participate through our tax dollars, military equipment and personnel, governmental policies and actions shared with the world and sometimes within the borders of our own nations.

The cry that God do to "them" what they have done to "us" is an ancient and unending plea on the lips of persons and peoples around the globe from time immemorial. What shall we say to this? Is there anything we can say to the Palestinian mother in the rubble clutching her child's smoking remains or to the kidnapped Israeli child covered with the blood of playmates? What shall we say to the government leaders who will use these images of pain to justify the next round of violence? Speaking through the traumatized prophet—if indeed he or she was a firsthand witness to the atrocities described in such vivid detail—God proclaims that this violence will rebound to its perpetrators in verse 17. As they have done, so shall it be done to them. The challenge of this text is that it evokes perpetual war, perpetual retaliation. Yet this malediction is scripture and the rage of its prophet is honest if not holy. The cry of the conquered, colonized, and occupied prophet will not be easy to preach with integrity for those who are not or have not been subject to the violent control of another population. There is no happy ending for this passage and it should not be given one.

The psalmist who composed Psalm 7 could be a survivor of the assault Obadiah describes. Or she could be a survivor of ancient Israel's last assault on Edom. Her prayer is that God, the righteous Judge, who knows the hearts and minds of all persons, will judge rightly and put an end to the wickedness of the wicked (Psalm 7:9). Her hope is firm that it is God and God alone who saves (verse 10). Her insistence that God is "indignant" at such wickedness is the source of her confidence that God will act (verse 11).

In the Epistle, another subjugated population contends with internal conflict on an entirely different scale, yet the looming shadow of a militant persecuting empire signals that the personal and communal are not separate from the political. The emotional ups and downs of James 4:9 may seem almost trite, yet they sketch out the fullness of a human life, the life of a community, the life of a nation. In that common life—the passage moves from plural language to singular forms—James calls us to actively submit ourselves to God in all things and resist and oppose the devil, perhaps best understood as the forces of evil within and without the person and the community. Those calls to submission and resistance are plural; none of us can do so alone. For the reader interested in gender matters, it is notable that for James God is the only one to whom submission is due; James does not have a hierarchy of subordination structured around class (enslavement) or gender. Brother James draws the same conclusion as the psalmist: God is our only hierarch.

Each of these readings features conflict, pain, and betrayal in different ways. The Gospel speaks of the hard work of forgiveness and when read with each of the previous lessons and psalm, speaks to different contexts for the work of forgiveness. In the opening verses of Luke 17, Jesus teaches that life is going to go wrong, that it is not even possible to have a life and not stumble over something that can lead you into sin (Luke 17:1). At quite some distance from Obadiah, Jesus says what matters when the provocation arises is how you respond. Jesus speaks as to an individual person: "you" (singular) are responsible for all of the harm that happens as a result of your response, your retaliation, no matter the provocation, verse 2. Jesus also teaches a model of forgiveness that does not neglect the harm done to the wronged person, or the oppressed people. He calls for rebuke—let us reconsider Obadiah's holy rebuke of Edom—and Jesus insists that the prerequisite for forgiveness when one has wronged another is repentance. Forgiveness is gracious and abundant and beyond numbering, represented by the multiplication of sevens in verse 4. What would it look like if our individual, communal, and multinational conflicts were responded to and governed by these passages? What would it look like if the Church's response to the harm it has inflicted upon women and children, nonbinary and trans folk and men and boys governed by these passages?

PROPER 18 (CLOSEST TO SEPTEMBER 7)

Isaiah 40:6–11; Psalm 43:1–5; 2 Thessalonians 2:13–17; John 11:1–6, 17–27

Isaiah 40:6 A [heavenly] voice says, "Cry out!"
    And I said, "What shall I cry?"
    [The voice replied] All people are grass,
    their fidelity is like the flower of the field.
  ⁷ The grass withers, the flower fades
    when the breath of the Fire of Sinai blows upon it;
    surely the people are grass.
  ⁸ The grass withers, the flower fades;
    but the word of our God will stand forever.
  ⁹ Climb a high mountain,
    O woman of Zion who proclaims good news!
    Raise your voice with power,
    O woman of Jerusalem who proclaims good news!
    Raise it, daughter! Fear not, daughter!
    Say to the cities of Judah, daughter,
    "Here is your God!"
  ¹⁰ See, the Sovereign Redeemer comes with might,
    whose arm rules for God;
    whose reward is with God,
    and God's reparation comes before.
  ¹¹ She will feed her flock like a shepherd;
    she will gather the lambs in her arms,
    and carry them in her bosom,
    and gently lead the mother sheep.

Psalm 43:1–5

  ¹ Deliver for me justice God and defend my case
    from a people devoid of lovingkindness;
    from the deceitful and iniquitous deliver me!
  ² You are my God; my refuge;
    why have you rejected me?
    Why must I walk about mourning
    because of the oppression of the enemy?
  ³ Send forth your light and your truth;
    let them lead me;
    let them bring me to your holy mountain
    and to your dwelling-place.

4 Then shall I go to the altar of God,
  to God my joy, my delight;
  and I will praise you with the harp,
  O God, my God.
5 Why, my soul, do you despair,
  and why are you disquieted within me?
  Hope in God; for again shall I praise her,
  my salvation and my God.

2 Thessalonians 2:13 Now we are bound to give thanks to God always on your account, sisters and brothers [or friends and kin], beloved by the Messiah, because God chose you as the first fruits for salvation through sanctification by the Spirit and through belief in the truth. 14 For this purpose God called you through our proclamation of the gospel that you may obtain the glory of our Savior Jesus Christ.

15 Now then, friends and kin [or sisters and brothers], stand firm and hold fast to the traditions that you were taught by us, either by [spoken] word or by our letter. 16 And now, may our Savior Jesus Christ himself and God our Maker, who loved us and through grace gave us eternal comfort and good hope, 17 comfort your hearts and strengthen them in every good work and word.

John 11:1 Now then a certain man was sick, Lazarus of Bethany, the village of Mary and her sister Martha. 2 And Mary was the one who anointed the Messiah with perfume and wiped his feet with her hair; her brother Lazarus was sick. 3 So the sisters sent a message to Jesus, "Listen! Teacher, the man (your friend) who you love is sick." 4 Yet when Jesus heard it, he said, "This sickness is not unto death; rather it is for the glory of God so the Son of God may be glorified through it." 5 Though Jesus (dearly) loved Martha and her sister and Lazarus, 6 after hearing that Lazarus was sick, Jesus then stayed longer in the place where he was, two days.

17 When Jesus arrived he found that for four days Lazarus had already been in the tomb. 18 Now Bethany was near Jerusalem, about two miles away. 19 So, many of the Judeans had come to Martha and Mary to console them about their brother. 20 When Martha heard that Jesus was coming, she met him; however, Mary remained at the house. 21 Martha said to Jesus, "Rabbi, if you had been here, my brother would never have died. 22 Yet even now I know that whatever you ask of God, God will give you." 23 Jesus said to her, "Your brother will rise." 24 Martha said to him, "I know that he will rise in the resurrection on the last day." 25 Jesus said to her, "I am the resurrection and the life. The one who believes in me, even though they die, they will live, 26 and everyone who lives and believes in me will never die. Do you believe this?" 27 She said to him, "Yes, Rabbi, I believe that you are the Messiah, the Son of God, the one who comes into the world."

PROCLAMATION

Text Notes

Bat Zion (or Jerusalem) can mean both Daughter Zion, the city, *or* a daughter of Zion, a woman from the city. In Isaiah 40:9, reading "daughter of" reveals a female prophet crying out to Jerusalem. In keeping with the larger prophetic tradition and given the possibility created by the grammar, it is sensible to understand the text referring to a prophet proclaiming good news to Zion. Because the addressee is feminine, all of the verbs to her are also feminine. I reproduce "daughter" in places where English masks the frequency of feminine address.

To bear good news or "tidings" is to proclaim them, not hold them. The semantic range includes "near news/tidings," usually good, occasionally poor as in loss of a battle/war and "proclaim or preach that news," which can include divine salvation. In Isaiah 40:9, *mebasseret*, "she-who-bears-good-news," has been translated as Zion/Jerusalem being the proclaimer (CEB, NRSV, RSV, KJV, Geneva, and Bishop's Bibles), or as a proclaimer *to* Zion/Jerusalem (the *Dead Seas Scroll Bible*, JPS and Wycliffe Bibles, along with the LXX and Bibles dependent on it, Vulgate and Douay). Grammar dictates that the proclaimer is feminine, as are cities in Hebrew; if not the city, the proclaimer is a woman, likely a prophet. The verb *b-s-r* is *euaggelizo* in Greek and becomes the primary verb for proclaiming the gospel; it is so used in Matthew 26:13 about the actions of the woman who anoints Jesus. Isaiah 40:9 could well be translated in part "you good-news-preaching-woman of Zion/Jerusalem."

In Isaiah 40:9, I use the rare feminine pronoun for God outside of the songs as articulated in the front matter of this project. I place it here because of the alliteration, and to reproduce the phenomenon of God and the prophet sharing a single gender. (The masculine pronoun confusion of the biblical text is legendary.)

In the Epistle, I offer an alternative to the traditional binary translation, sisters and brothers, meant to encompass all believers using familial language, friends and kin. The underlying term is *anthropos*, "brothers" or "kindred," which includes female siblings (and relatives when being used more broadly).

In John 11:3, Mary uses the verb *phileo,* which denotes the close companionable love of friends; in verse 5, the narrator articulates Jesus's love for Mary and Martha with the verb *agapao*, a stronger, deeper love. Some may know these verbs from John 21 where Jesus asked Peter "Do you love me deeply?" and he keeps replying, "Jesus, I love you like a friend." That deeper *agapao* love also characterizes God's love for the world, most famously in John 3:16.

Martha's statement to Jesus in John 11:21 is stronger than it has often been translated. Not "my brother would not have died," but "my brother would *never* have died." That same "never" is included by Jesus in his response, "Everyone who lives and believes in me will never die."

Preaching Prompts

The God disclosed in Isaiah 40 is a God who knows her peoples' suffering, the captivity of the Judean remnant of ancient Israel in Babylonian exile, under Babylonian oppression. Her instruction to her prophet is to comfort her people in their present circumstance with hope for the redemption and deliverance that is soon coming. The image in the concluding verse of the passage is meant to evoke God leading the people back to their previous home, thereby promising an end to Babylonian domination in the world as they knew it. The psalm is an exilic one, in which an individual person representing the larger people gives voice to their longing to return to the land from which they were stolen. The world of 2 Thessalonians is one in which the fledgling community of Jesus followers is under cultural occupation. The temptation to conform is ever-present. The word of the apostle—Pauline authorship is disputed—to them is to hold fast to the traditions that have been passed down and reassurance of the comfort of God who is with them in their present circumstances.

In the Gospel, Jesus shockingly passes up an opportunity to heal his friend of his illness and leaves him to die. Mary and Martha are bereaved and looking for comfort from their friend and teacher, Jesus. His denial of the seemingly inescapable fact of Lazarus's death while making a theological point would seem to belie the love he holds for Lazarus, Mary, and Martha. Clearly, on one level, the intended message is that God does not always answer our prayers. When God does not respond to our prayers, God is doing something on a much grander scale for her own purposes that will bring her glory in the end. This is a hard lesson when the textbook is the life and death of someone you love. The story of Lazarus's resurrection is powerful and many of bereaved persons might wish for their beloved to be called back from the sleep of death. But even Lazarus will die later, as do we all, with no miracle. The comfort offered through this passage is not the nearly unobtainable miracle but the sure promise of the resurrection for all.

It is not difficult to conjure real-life and real-world examples of individuals and communities in need of comfort. In each one of these passages, the source of comfort is knowledge of God, God's work in the world, and God's love for humanity, individually and collectively manifested in the death-shattering eternal life God offers us through the unending life of Jesus. We are called to hold fast to that like the community in Thessalonica and proclaim that word of comfort to one another like the daughter of Zion in Isaiah.

PROPER 19 (CLOSEST TO SEPTEMBER 14)

Isaiah 43:1–3a, 5–7; Psalm 36:5–10; Titus 2:11–14; Luke 19:1–10

Isaiah 43:1 And now, thus says the MAKER OF ALL,
   the one who created you, Jacob [Rebekah's seed],
   the one who formed you, Israel [of Sarah's line]:
   Fear not, for I have redeemed you;
   I have called you by name, you are mine.
² For when you pass through the waters, I will be with you;
   and through the rivers, they shall not overwhelm you;
   even when you walk through fire you shall not be burned,
   and the flame shall not scorch you.
³ For I am the INCOMPARABLE ONE your God,
   the Holy One of Israel, your Savior.
⁵ Fear not, for with you am I;
   from the east will I bring your seed,
   and from the west will I gather you.
⁶ I will say to the north, "Release them!"
   and to the south, "Do not keep [them];
   bring my sons from far away
   and my daughters from the end of the earth."
⁷ Everyone who is called by my name,
   whom I created for my glory,
   whom I formed and made.

Psalm 36:5–10

⁵ HOLY ONE, throughout the very heavens is your faithful love,
   your faithfulness beyond the clouds.
⁶ Your righteousness is like the eternal mountains,
   your judgments are like the mighty deep;
   you save humankind and animalkind alike, FAITHFUL ONE.
⁷ How precious is your faithful love, O God!
   All the woman-born take shelter in the shadow of your wings.
⁸ They feast on the abundance of your house,
   and you give them drink from the river of your delights.
⁹ For with you is the fountain of life;
   in your light we see light.
¹⁰ Extend your faithful love to those who know you,
   and your justice to the upright of heart!

Titus 2:11 For the grace of God has appeared, bringing salvation to all persons, ¹² instructing us to reject ungodliness and worldly passions, living wisely, justly, and godly in the present age, ¹³ while we wait for the blessed hope and the manifestation of the glory of our great God and Savior, Jesus the Messiah. ¹⁴ It is Jesus who gave himself for us that he might redeem us from all iniquity and purify for himself a people of his own who are zealous for good works.

Luke 19:1 Now Jesus entered Jericho and was passing through it. ² There was a man named Zacchaeus and he was a chief tax collector and was rich. ³ He was seeking to see who Jesus was, but was not able to on account of the crowd, because he was short in stature. ⁴ So he ran ahead and climbed a sycamore to see him, because he was going to pass that way. ⁵ Now when Jesus came to the place, he looked up and said to him, "Zacchaeus, hurry and come down; for I must stay at your house today." ⁶ So Zacchaeus hurried down and welcomed him, rejoicing. ⁷ All who saw it began to grumble and said, "To a sinner has he gone to be a guest." ⁸ Zacchaeus stood there and said to the Messiah, "Look, half of my possessions, Anointed One, to the poor will I give, and if have defrauded anyone, I will pay back four times as much." ⁹ Then Jesus said to Zacchaeus, "Today salvation has come to this house, because he too is a child of Abraham. ¹⁰ For the Son of Woman came to seek out and to save the lost."

PROCLAMATION

Text Notes

In Isaiah 43:1, "Rebekah's seed" and "of Sarah's line" are offered in brackets to modify "Jacob" and "Israel."

In the psalm, the noun *el*, God, is used as an adjective describing the mountains in verse 6.

In Titus 2:12, the verb translated "instructing" has the sense of teaching with a moral purpose, similar to catechizing but rather than focusing on belief, it refers to teaching moral conduct.

In Luke 19:9, Jesus addresses Zacchaeus, perhaps facing him, but speaks to those around him referring to Zacchaeus in the third person. It is not Zacchaeus who needs to be reassured about who he is.

Preaching Prompts

In all these lessons, in different ways, God announces salvation beginning with the remnant of Israel in Isaiah 43:1 and extending to the entire world in Isaiah 43:7. Awfully, at the end of the first verse, God proclaims that redemption has already taken place. We are a living analog of that passage. Redemption has taken place, yet we live in a world with warfare all around us and the ruination of its devastation in every different direction. Those we have lost are gone and the grief indoors. Those who have been harmed live with the consequences of their injuries, physical, emotional, psychological, spiritual, and moral. Our nation has not fallen to external conquest, but its internal upheavals have been deadly. In verses 5 and 6, the prophet talks about the ongoing work of God. Redemption has taken place, yet the people are unwillingly dispersed, living in situations that induce great trauma. And God is doing her good work, gathering her children from every corner of the world in which they have been exiled, deported, kidnapped, taken hostage, enslaved, and trafficked. Might we consider that God is still doing that work as all of those horrors continue to be visited upon her children. If so, then we must acknowledge that everyone will not be brought home, everyone will not survive the trip, and some have already fallen.

In Psalm 36, God's salvation extends from humankind—"All the woman-born" in verse 7—to animalkind. In Titus 2, salvation comes to "to all persons." In these lessons, salvation extends from the survivors of Israel and Judah to every person and every creature, then, in the Gospel, to one particular person about whose merit there is some doubt for some folk. But his merit neither qualifies nor disqualifies. Salvation comes "to his house"; he is part of the family of God, as are we, humankind and creaturekind.

We still live in a world where people are told they are not eligible for salvation because of who they are and even what they have done. It is doubtful Zacchaeus succeeded in his job without defrauding his impoverished, oppressed people. He may well have employed threats of violence and orchestrated actual violence by means of his Roman overlords and their brutal soldiers, ready and willing to enforce the emperor's punitive tax laws. Zacchaeus was complicit with evil, with empire. Some people always are. There are always those of a subject population who work for the colonizers. They do not always have a choice. The choice between death and complicity is no choice.

A final note: often the women who make that difficult negotiation are celebrated in the stories of the conquering people and reviled by their own people. Consider the way Rahab becomes a de facto Israelite hero and by saving herself and whatever family she could from destruction leaving her people to nearly complete annihilation. Consider Matoaka of the Powhatan people popularized as Pocahontas. Consider Marina Malintzin, known as La Malinche, and Hernán Cortés. As suggested in the Rahab story and documented in those of Matoaka and Malintzin, the bodies of native and indigenous women are often used as the bridge between colonizer and colonized. What degradations might Zacchaeus have had to suffer in his position? While there is no suggestion he was used sexually, the cultural use of "whore language" to signify betrayals of any sort, real and imagined, might mean that he, like so many women, was called a Roman whore.

But this day, salvation came to his house. No one is beyond the saving grace of God. Indeed, as the poet or poetess writing in Isaiah's name declared, redemption is an accomplished fact.

PROPER 20 (CLOSEST TO SEPTEMBER 21)

Zechariah 7:8–14; Psalm 10:1–14; James 2:14–19, 24–26; John 5:25–29

Zechariah 7:8 And it was that the word of the JUST ONE came to Zechariah, saying: ⁹ Thus says the RULER of the Multitudes of Heaven:

True justice shall you all administer justly, loving kindness and mother-love shall you all offer one to another. ¹⁰ And the widow, the orphan, the immigrant, and the one made poor through oppression, you all must not oppress (further); and wickedness—one person against another—do not scheme in your hearts.

¹¹ Yet they refused to listen and turned a stubborn shoulder and plugged up their ears so as not to hear. ¹² And they made their hearts like flint so as not to hear the law and the words that the SOVEREIGN of the vanguard of heaven sent through God's own spirit through the former prophets, women and men. Thus a great wrath came from the SOVEREIGN of the vanguard of heaven. ¹³ And it was just as when God called, they would not hear, so when they called, I would not hear, says the SOVEREIGN-COMMANDER of winged warriors. ¹⁴ Then I scattered them with a whirlwind among all the nations whom they knew not known. Thus the land was desolate in their wake, so that no woman, man, or child passed over it, and a pleasant land was made desolate.

Psalm 10:1–14

¹ Why, COMPASSIONATE ONE, do you stand afar?
  Why do you hide yourself in hard times?
² In arrogance the wicked harass the poor;
  let them be caught in the schemes they have devised.
³ For the wicked praise their [every] inmost desire,
  extorts gain and blesses those who despise the CREATOR OF ALL.
⁴ The wicked turn up their nose and do not seek [God];
  There is no God in all their thoughts.
⁵ Their ways prosper all the time;
  your judgments are on high, beyond them;
  all their foes scoff at them.
⁶ They say in their heart, "We shall not be shaken;
  nor [see] evil down through the generations."
⁷ Cursing fills their mouths along with and deceit and oppression;
  under their tongues are trouble and iniquity.

⁸ They sit in ambush in the villages;
   in hiding places they murder the innocent.
   Their eyes surveil the vulnerable.
⁹ They lie-in-wait in secret like a lion in its den;
   they lie-in-wait that they may snatch the poor;
   they snatch the poor and drag them off in their net.
¹⁰ They stoop, they crouch,
   and the vulnerable fall prey through their might.
¹¹ They say in their heart, "God has forgotten,
   she has hidden her face, she will never see it."
¹² Rise up, FAITHFUL GOD; dear God, lift up your hand;
   forget not the oppressed.
¹³ Why do the wicked despise God,
   and say in their hearts you shall not find out?
¹⁴ You see, you regard trouble and grief,
   to take [it] into your hands.
   Upon you the vulnerable entrust themselves;
   to the orphan you have ever [only] been their helper.

James 2:14 What benefit is it, my sisters and brothers, if faith you say you have, but do not have works? Is faith able to save you? ¹⁵ If a sister or brother is naked and lacks daily food, ¹⁶ and one of you says to them, "Go in peace; warm yourself and eat your fill," and you all do not provide what is necessary for the body, what is the benefit of that? ¹⁷ And thus faith, if it has no works, is dead by itself.

¹⁸ Yet someone will say, "Faith you have faith and works I have." Show me your faith separately from your works, and I through my works will show you my faith. ¹⁹ You believe that God is One; you do well. Even the demons believe and they tremble.

²⁴ You see that by works is a woman or man shown to be righteous and not by faith alone. ²⁵ And likewise, was not Rahab the prostitute, by works, also shown to be righteous when she welcomed the messengers and sent them out by another road? ²⁶ For just as the body without the spirit is dead, so then faith without works is also dead.

John 5:25 [Jesus said to the women and men gathered around him at the temple:] Truly, truly, I tell you all, the hour is coming, and is now here, when the dead will hear the voice of the Son of God, and those who hear will live. ²⁶ For just as the Living God has life within, just so God has granted the Son to have life within. ²⁷ And God has given the Son authority to render justice, because he is the Son of Woman. ²⁸ Do not be astonished at this; for the hour is coming when all who are in their graves will hear his voice ²⁹ and will come out— those who have done good, to the resurrection of life, and those who have done evil, to the resurrection of judgment.

PROCLAMATION

Text Notes

In Zechariah 8:10, an orphan is a fatherless child, which is why the vulnerable poor are so often described as a widow and orphan together. In this same verse, the root of the verb "mother-love" is the noun that means "womb"; the tender emotion emanates from the womb and is only described as pertaining to God and women. In 8:13, the verb and its associated pronoun for "when God called" is indeed third person masculine, though other translations render it in the first person, see NRSV and CEB contra JPS; it is not uncommon for the divine address to shift between first and third person throughout the canon.

There are a number of difficulties with the text in Psalm 10. Robert Alter and JPS annotate them. "Hard" times in verse one of this song refers to drought. The use of "hard" here signifies both the hardened earth and the resulting difficult economic times. An alternate reading for the last line of verse 2 is that they, the poor, have been caught in the schemes of the wicked. "Turn their nose up" in verse 4 is a nearly literal translation of the disjointed "like a height, their nose (or countenance)." "They do not seek" lacks an object; I have supplied "God," because the verb is used primarily to seek God and the last phrase. The second phrase of verse 6 lacks a verb.

In verse 12 of the psalm, the psalmist calls God to rise and act using the language that Moses used whenever the Ark of the Covenant would be lifted up to go before the people, *qumah Adonai*, see Numbers 10:35. The Numbers verse is an important part of Jewish liturgy in response to which the congregation rises as God rose. The expression is evoked repeatedly in the psalms: Psalms 3:7; 7:6; 9:19; 10:12; 17:13; 74:22; 82:8; 132:8. (Psalm 44:26 is a partial match lacking the Divine Name.)

The setting for this passage is Jesus's encounter in the temple with a man he had previously healed in John 5:14 (see vv. 2–8 for the healing; vv. 14–18 for his conversation with the man). The main courtyard of the temple including its porticos were shared space in which women, children, and men were present. In John 5:27, the work of justice is more than passing a sentence; rather "judging" or "executing judgment" or "rendering a verdict" are but one dimension of justice work. Jesus is "the Human One" "the Mortal One," "Woman-Born," or "the Son of Woman" (or "Man" in antiquated translations); *huios tou anthroupou* includes all of those meanings, its primary route is the same as "anthropology," the study of all humanity.

Preaching Prompts

It is important for contemporary readers, hearers, and interpreters of scripture to hold before them that Israelite sacred literature is literature of resistance, written under oppression, and written under the memory of oppression and its lingering effects. Poverty, in the sequential worlds of the text, is a justice issue as it is in our world. The poverty of the people to whom Zechariah prophesied was a human-made circumstance, the result of a devastating occupation that razed arable land and took hostage or into slavery those with income-generating skill. Upon their Persian metered and tightly controlled return to the land, there was an income gap between those who came with even modest wealth and income generated under Persian patronage and those who would be described as so desperate for grain that they would sell their daughters as described in Nehemiah 5:1–5. It is useful to remember that the books of Haggai and Zechariah and Ezra and Nehemiah are a quartet occurring in the same time period.

The psalmist could well be in the community Zechariah describes or the one to which James writes or even in our own. In the language of my people, the psalmist gives God a piece of her sanctified mind, meaning she tells God off: What are you doing? Why are you not acting? Let me tell you what these people are doing, etc. And dramatically calling God to action in verse 12. Underlying the outcry of the psalmist over fiscal inequity that results in poverty as the work of the wicked and God's lack of action is a belief that such an equity is an offense to God, that God is a God of justice, that God cares for the poor, and that God hears prayer.

PROPER 21 (CLOSEST TO SEPTEMBER 28)

Isaiah 51:1–6; Psalm 92:1–5, 12–15; 1 Corinthians 3:1–9; John 4:7–26

Isaiah 51:1 Listen to me, all you that pursue righteousness,
   all you that seek the AUTHOR OF LIFE.
   Look to the rock from which you were hewn,
   and to the quarry from which you were dug.
² Look to Abraham your father,
   and to Sarah who writhed-in-labor for you all;
   he was just one when I called him,
   but I blessed him and made him many.
³ For the GOD WHO SAVES has comforted Zion;
   she has comforted all her waste places.
   And she shall make her wilderness like Eden,
   her desert like the garden of the CREATOR OF ALL;
   joy and gladness will be found in her,
   thanksgiving and the sound of song.
   [Sorrow and mourning will flee away.]
⁴ Listen to me, my people,
   and my nation, to me give heed;
   for a teaching shall from me go forth,

and my justice for a light to the peoples.
I will do so suddenly.
⁵ My deliverance is near,
my salvation has gone forth
and my arms will govern the peoples;
for me the coastlands wait,
and upon my arm they await.
⁶ Lift up your eyes to the heavens,
and look to the earth below.
For the heavens like smoke will vanish,
the earth like a garment will wear out,
and those who live on it will die like gnats;
yet my salvation will be forever,
and my deliverance will never be broken.

Psalm 92:1–5, 12–15

¹ It is good to give thanks to the AGELESS GOD,
to sing praises to your name Most High;
² to declare your faithful love in the morning,
and your trustworthiness by night,
³ upon the ten strings and the harp,
upon the murmurings of the lyre.
⁴ For you have made me glad,
WELLSPRING OF LIFE, by your work;
at the works of your hands I sing for joy.
⁵ How great are your works, WOMB OF CREATION!
Your designs are so very profound.
¹² A righteous woman or man flourishes like a palm tree,
and grows like a cedar in Lebanon.
¹³ They are planted in the house of SHE WHO IS HOLY;
in the courts of our God, they flourish.
¹⁴ Still producing fruit in their elder years;
fat with sap and ever green.
¹⁵ They declare that the MIGHTY GOD is upright;
she is my rock, and there is no unrighteousness in her.

1 Corinthians 3:1 Now sisters and brothers [or friends and kin], I could not speak to you all as spiritual, but rather as carnal, as infants in Christ. ² I fed you all with milk, not solid food, for you were not yet ready for solid food. Even now you are still not ready, ³ for you all are still carnal. Given there is still jealousy and discord among you, are you not carnal, and going around as merely human? ⁴ For when one says, "I am Paul's," and another, "I am Apollos," are you not merely human?

⁵ What then is Apollos? What is Paul? Ministers through whom you came to believe, as the Messiah granted to each person. ⁶ I planted, Apollos watered, but God produces growth. ⁷ Therefore neither the one who plants nor the one who waters is anything, rather it is God who produces growth. ⁸ The one who plants and the one who waters are alike, and each will receive wages according to their labor. ⁹ For we are God's coworkers, working together; you are God's cultivation, God's construction.

John 4:7 A Samaritan woman came to draw water. Jesus said to her, "Give me a drink." ⁸ Now his disciples had gone to the city to buy food. ⁹ The Samaritan woman said to him, "How are you, a Judean, asking a drink of me, a woman of Samaria?" (Judeans do not share things in common with Samaritans.) ¹⁰ Jesus answered and said to her, "If you knew the gift of God and who is the one telling to you, 'Give me a drink,' you would have asked him, and he would have given you living water." ¹¹ The woman said to him, "Sir, you have no bucket, and the well is deep. From where do you get that living water? ¹² Are you greater than our ancestor Jacob, the one who gave us the well, and with his daughters and sons and his flocks drank from it?" ¹³ Jesus answered and said to her, "Everyone who drinks of this water will thirst again. ¹⁴ But the one who drinks of the water that I will give will never thirst. The water that I will give will become in them a fount of water springing up into eternal life." ¹⁵ The woman said to him, "Sir, give me this water, that I may never thirst or keep coming here to draw water."

¹⁶ Jesus said to her, "Go, call your husband, and come [back] to this place." ¹⁷ The woman answered and said to him, "I have no husband." Jesus said to her, "You said rightly, 'I have no husband.' ¹⁸ For five husbands have you had, and now the one you have is not your husband. What you have said is true!" ¹⁹ The woman said to him, "Sir, I see that you are a prophet. ²⁰ Our mothers and fathers worshiped on this mountain, yet you say in Jerusalem is the place where people must worship." ²¹ Jesus said to her, "Believe me, woman, the hour is coming when neither on this mountain nor in Jerusalem will you worship the Sovereign God. ²² You all worship what you do not know; we worship what we know, for salvation is from the Judeans. ²³ But the hour is coming, and now is, when the true worshipers will worship the Sovereign God in spirit and truth, for these are the worshippers the Sovereign God seeks. ²⁴ God is spirit, and those who worship God must worship in spirit and truth." ²⁵ The woman said to Jesus, "I know that the Messiah is coming" (the one who is called Christ). "When he comes, he will proclaim all things to us." ²⁶ Jesus said to her, "I am, the one who is speaking to you."

PROCLAMATION

Text Notes

Sarah's labor in Isaiah 51:2 is described with a verb that means "writhe" and "twist" in birthing, and in some cases, dancing, as in Psalm 150:4. In verse 3, God has already begun to comfort Zion (see JPS); the future tense translation of NRSV and KJV neglect the immediate nature of God's response. The tense changes in the third verse, emphasizing the ongoing work of God (JPS keeps the passage in the past tense). The last line of verse 3 comes from the Great Isaiah Scroll of the Dead Sea collection, 1QIsa^a; the reader may choose to omit it. While some unnecessarily move the last verb constituting the final line of verse 4 to verse 5 (NRSV, CEB, Alter), it is entirely comprehensible in its place.

I use "murmuring" in Psalm 92:3 to render *higgion*; the wider semantic range includes melodic speech, song, the sound of instruments, and murmuring (Psalms 9:16 [v. 17 in Hebrew]; 19:14; 92:3; Lamentations 3:62). "Elder years" in verse 14 is *sevah*, "gray hair."

In John 4:26, Jesus says, *ego eimi*, "I am," echoing God's self-identification in Exodus 3:14, or in some other translations, "I am [he]"—the masculine pronoun is missing.

Preaching Prompts

Each of these lessons presents salvation as flourishing. In Isaiah 51:3 salvation is restoration expressed in ecological terms. While the ecological language is metaphorical, it is not only metaphorical. Restoration of people necessarily means restoration of the war-ravaged land in a wholistic view of salvation, which the scriptures offer with some regularity. In Psalm 92:12–15, God's people are an oasis hand planted by God; here the language of flourishing is explicit in verse 12. This flourishing results in a full life and the potential of children in the latter years. This indicates safety and sufficient nutrition. In the contemporary world, it is in stark contrast to the shortened life expectancy of black men in comparison to their white counterparts, and entire zip codes based on income levels and other factors such as environmental racism, i.e., proximity to chemical waste and other pathogens.

Beginning with infancy, the beginning of a Christian life, because one cannot flourish if one does not receive proper nutrition in infancy and childhood, the Epistle focuses on the source of the flourishing, God. Again, there is a parallel to our world in which some children's future is threatened because of the poverty of their families resulting in insufficient nutrition to form a solid foundation from which to grow and flourish. Shifting the focus to God who is the source of life and its flourishing, Paul also seeks to undermine cliquishness and the kind of divisions the Church was not able to avoid.

The native peoples of this land have reminded us that "water is life." In the Gospel, the woman who has been described variously as moving from man to man, or as having been abandoned seriously because Jewish women could not initiate divorce, she needed water to live and had no choice but to face public scrutiny, ridicule, and commentary every day. Then Jesus offered her water that would change her life, through which she would flourish in a way that transcended her circumstances even if they did not change. The first change was that she became a preacher of the gospel, bringing people to Jesus in the verses that follow this reading for next Sunday. And yet, her preaching ministry and her evangelistic ministry have been discounted by misogynistic, paternalistic, and patriarchal interpreters of scripture. Those kinds of interpretations don't just undermine the flourishing of women, nonbinary persons, and anyone else deemed not suitable for the ministry of the word, they undermine the flourishing of the entire Church.

But in the portion of the Gospel assigned for this day, the discussion of the ancient disaffection between those who descended from Samarian Israelites who had multiethnic ancestry as well because of being mixed with all of the other peoples conquered by the Assyrian empire and the Judeans reveals the power of the water of life. It washes away the divisions caused by the distinctions between persons and peoples.

PROPER 22 (CLOSEST TO OCTOBER 5)

Isaiah 52:7–10; Psalm 118:14–26; 1 Peter 1:10–12; John 4:27-30, 39-42

Isaiah 52:7 How beautiful upon the mountains
  are the feet of one who brings good news,
  proclaiming peace,
  bringing good news,
  proclaiming salvation,
  who says to Zion, "Your God reigns, daughter."
⁸ Daughter, the sound of your sentinels, lifting their voice!
  As one they sing for joy;
  for from one eye to another they see
  the return of the HOLY ONE OF SINAI to Zion.
⁹ Revel! Raise a song together,
  you ruins of Jerusalem.
  For the HOLY ONE OF OLD has comforted God's people,
  God has redeemed Jerusalem.
¹⁰ The MIGHTY GOD has bared a holy arm
  before the eyes of all the nations;
  and all the ends of the earth shall see
  the salvation of our God.

Psalm 118:14–26

¹⁴ The MIGHTY GOD is my strength and my might
  and has become my salvation.

15 The sound of song and of salvation is in the tents of the righteous:
    "The right hand of the MOST HIGH is mighty;
16 the right hand of the MIGHTY GOD is exalted;
    the right hand of the MOST HIGH is mighty."
17 I shall not die, but I shall live,
    and recount the deeds of the ANCIENT OF DAYS.
18 The MERCIFUL GOD has punished me severely,
    but to death did not hand me over.
19 Open to me the gates of righteousness,
    that I may enter through them
    and give thanks to the FOUNT OF JUSTICE.
20 This is the gate of the LIVING GOD;
    the righteous shall enter through it.
21 I thank you for you have answered me
    and have become my salvation.
22 The stone the builders rejected
    has become the chief cornerstone.
23 This is the MIGHTY GOD's doing;
    it is marvelous in our eyes.
24 This is the day that the CREATOR OF ALL has made;
    let us rejoice and be glad in it.
25 Save us, we pray, SAVING ONE!
    GENEROUS ONE, we pray, grant us prosperity!
26 Blessed is the one who comes in the name of GOD WHO IS HOLY.
    We bless you from the house of the EVER-LIVING GOD.

1 Peter 1:10 Concerning this salvation, the women and men who prophesied of the grace that was to be yours searched diligently and inquired earnestly, ⁱⁱ discerning with regard to the time that the Spirit of the Messiah within them made known when testifying before time of the sufferings and following glory of the Messiah. ¹² It was revealed to the women and men who prophesied that they were serving not themselves but you all, in regard to the things that have now been announced to you through those who brought you good new—gospel—by the Holy Spirit sent from heaven; these are things into which angels long to look!

John 4:27 Now, the disciples of Jesus came while [he was speaking to the woman at the well] and they were astonished that he was speaking with a woman, yet no one said, "What do you want?" or "Why are you speaking with her?" ²⁸ The woman left her water jar and went back to the city and she said to the people, ²⁹ "Come and see a man who told me everything I have ever done! Might he be the Messiah?" ³⁰ They left the city and were on their way to him. ³⁹ Many Samaritan women and men from that city believed in him because of the woman's testimony, "He told me everything I have ever done." [40] So when the Samaritans came to Jesus, they asked him to stay with them and Jesus stayed there two days. [41] And many more believed because of his word. [42] They said to the woman, "It is no longer because of your report we believe, for we ourselves have heard and we know that this is truly the Savior of the world."

PROCLAMATION
Text Notes

Addresses to Zion and Jerusalem are often in the feminine as they are here. I use "daughter" to make the occurrences visible to the English reader where it is not explicit. Verses 7 and 8 address the feminine singular Daughter Zion, and in verse 9, it is the plural "ruins of Jerusalem" that are addressed. In verse 8, "sentinels" is a synonym for prophets.

Verses 14–16 of the psalm quotes Miriam's song in Exodus 15:2 and are also found in Isaiah 12:2. "God's faithful love endures forever" is one of the oldest liturgical refrains in the Hebrew Bible: see the opening and closing of Psalm 118. (Though omitted above, the difficulty of rendering the assonant and alliterative poetry of Psalm 118:25 is worth mentioning given its import in in the Palm Sunday liturgy: *Ana Ya hoshia na; Ana Ya chatzlicha na*. The familliar "hosanna" pronunciation comes from the Greek transliteration of the Hebrew.)

Given the presence of women and men among the prophets in the testaments, I have expanded "prophets" in 1 Peter 1:10 and in verse 12 to reflect that.

In John 4:42, the woman's discourse, *lalian*, is articulated with a word that has a sense of disreputable, or even gossip. The choice may have been intended to convey disrespect for and distrust of a woman's word.

Preaching Prompts

In the multifaceted tradition of the Black Church when one has survived difficult and or dangerous times, events, and circumstances, including death and disease, it is common to say, "She's got a testimony." The community of the poet-prophet who donned the name Isaiah for her proclamations is part of the generation that survived and saw the end of Babylonian captivity and the return to Zion. Time had folded back on itself and God had set her people free again, as in of old. God had shown that her might power is undiminished. These testimonies of deliverance form the foundation of faith in God as Liberator. And they stand as bedrock, not worn down by time for us today. The God of liberation is unchanged.

The psalm is the liturgy of return. Whether it was used in that first procession to the newly built second temple is unclear, but it is clear that once it came into use, it served to reenact that moment and marked festival processions on designated holy days, including during Passover. The psalm is framed as the testimony of an individual, a single person who has been delivered counter to the broader Israelite tradition of salvation being a corporate act.

The Epistle is a look back at the kind of difficult days from which the first lesson and psalm celebrate God's deliverance. It serves as a testimony to the God who spoke words of hope and promise to sustain the people during the years, decades, and even centuries when liberation was but a faint hope and salvation an unfulfilled promise. The author of 1 Peter wants her congregation to know that they are at the fruit of salvation and that the workings of their salvation, both celestial and terrestrial, are a mystery so great that not even angels apprehend them. Testimony is so important because the world in which salvation is accomplished is the same world desperately in need of redemption. It doesn't look like a Savior has come. But this group of believers is the fruit of the promise of God through the power of the Holy Spirit. That same promise has come to the world in our present circumstances. For the early church that was under Roman oppression, for this world it is under all of the oppressive ideologies and the policies that derive from them and their consequences under which salvation continues to be born and proclaimed.

In the Gospel, the testimony of a woman who was doubly less than credible because of her gender and her culture and because of her familial circumstances, fodder for gossip, took her testimony to the streets. It was powerful and persuasive enough that her townsfolk overlooked her as the source of it and went to see for themselves. In some ways, this is a more difficult salvation to preach because it doesn't come with the defeat of the Romans or the restoration of Israel as a self-governing entity. We face the same difficulty. The mighty God has come to us in an unexpected way, offering life and liberation, transformation in our circumstances. That is a different kind of testimony, but no less powerful.

PROPER 23 (CLOSEST TO OCTOBER 12)

Isaiah 61:1–4, 8–10; Psalm 133:1–3; 2 Corinthians 2:14–16; Mark 14:3–9

Isaiah 61:1 The Spirit of the Sovereign GOD is upon me,
   because the HOLY GOD has anointed me.
   God has sent me to declare good news to the oppressed,
   to bind up the brokenhearted,
   to proclaim liberation to the captives,
   and freedom to the prisoners;
² to proclaim a year of the MOST HIGH God's favor,
   and the day of vengeance of our God;
   to comfort all children, women, and men who mourn;

³ to provide for those women, children, and men who mourn in Zion;
to give them glory instead of ashes,
the oil of gladness instead of mourning,
the mantle of praise instead of a faint spirit.
They will be called oaks of righteousness,
the planting of the MOST HIGH,
for God to display God's own glory.
⁴ They shall build up the ancient ruins,
they shall raise up the former devastations;
they shall restore the ruined cities,
devastations across generations.
⁸ For I, the ETERNAL GOD, am the One who loves justice,
and the One who hates robbery sacrificed as a burnt offering;
I will faithfully give them their recompense,
and I will make an everlasting covenant with them.
⁹ Their descendants shall be known among the nations,
and their offspring among the peoples;
all who see them shall recognize
that they are a people whom the HOLY ONE has blessed.
¹⁰ I will greatly rejoice in the MOST HIGH God,
my soul shall exult in my God;
for God has clothed me in garments of salvation,
God has covered me with a robe of righteousness,
as a bridegroom vests himself with a garland,
and as a bride adorns herself with her jewels.

Psalm 133

¹ Look! How precious and how lovely
when [friends and] kin live together as one!
² Like the precious oil on the head,
running down upon the beard,
on the beard of Aaron,
running down over the collar of his robes.
³ Like the dew of Hermon,
That falls on the mountains of Zion.
For there the WOMB OF CREATION commanded her blessing,
life eternal.

2 Corinthians 2:14 Thanks be to God, who parades us in triumph in Christ, and through us makes known in every place the scent that comes from knowing Christ. ¹⁵ For we are the fragrant aroma of Christ to God among those who are being saved and among those who are perishing. ⁱ⁶ To the one, a scent from death to death, to the other a scent from life to life. Who indeed is sufficient for these things?

Mark 14:3 Now Jesus was at Bethany in the house of Simon who had a skin disease; as he reclined at table, a woman came with an alabaster vessel of pure nard ointment – very expensive – she broke open the alabaster and poured it on his head. ⁴ But some being angry said among themselves, "For what was the nard wasted? ⁵ For this ointment could have been sold for more than three hundred denarii, [three hundred days' wages] and given to the poor." And they were indignant with her. ⁶ But Jesus said, "Leave her alone! Why do you trouble her? A good work has she done for me. ⁷ For always shall you have the poor with you and whenever you wish you can do good by them; but me, you shall not always have. ⁸ What she had it to do, she did; she has anointed my body beforehand for its burial. ⁹ Truly I tell you all, wherever the gospel is proclaimed in the whole world, what she has done will be told in remembrance of her."

PROCLAMATION

Text Notes

In Isaiah 61:1, "vests" has a liturgical sense. The actual verb is a form of the word for "priest"; the bridegroom dresses himself just as a priest puts on his ornaments.

In the first two verses of the psalm, the basic and utilitarian adjective "good" serves to describe both the feeling of community and the quality of the anointing oil. "Precious" fits both contexts.

The verb signifying "parading" and "triumph" in 2 Corinthians 2:14 is unclear here but can include a celebratory parade and one in which the conquered are put on display.

In the ancient world, the term "leprosy" was used to refer to a host of diseases (and in the Hebrew Bible to some infestations affecting objects). "Skin disease" covers the range of possibilities with out reducing the unknown condition to Hansens disease, modern leprosy.

Preaching Prompts

Oil had profound cultural value and was indispensable in the ancient Afro-Asiatic world. It had mundane (grooming), lifecycle (birth, death), medicinal, and religious uses. The good stuff also had financial value, likely due to rare or valuable spices and other aromatics (Exodus 25:6 mentions "spices" to be used in the anointing oil for the dedication of the wilderness, sanctuary, and ordination of Israel's first priests, including Aaron.) Athalyah – the only woman to rule as "king" (2 Kgs 11:2; 2 Chr 22:12) – would have been anointed upon her ascension, but not many other women, if any.

The head was a site of honor for crowns and wreaths and garlands as at the end of the Isaiah 61 reading; the horns of animals often signify glory and honor. Oiling the head and hair, "greasing the scalp," are enduring social and cultural practices in the African diaspora. It is also somewhat common in some Black American Christianities to refer to persons with spiritual anointings like the subject of Isaiah 61 as, "oily," like Aaron at his ordination (Ex 29:7; he was further sprinkled with blood and blood mixed with oil, vv 20-21, and rubbed with fat from a fresh slaughter).

Reading Isaiah 61 in its own context yields a reminder that God does not just call Jesus to the work of liberation. The poet-prophet says, "The Spirit is upon *me*" for this same work centuries before Jesus. The work is contextual and concrete. The physical and financial costs of Israelite subjugation will be reversed; liberation is all encompassing, physical as well as spiritual. Indeed, the work of liberation is dangerous because of its very contextualization. The powers of empire that seek to subjugate, degrade and exploit are lethal, as the anonymous woman who bestows her touch on Jesus in Mark makes visible with her fragrant, precious offering. The fragrant offering of the early followers of Jesus in the epistle is their willingness to die like Jesus, and pending the uncertain grammar, the lead in a mocking procession which for them would be a triumphal procession.

PROPER 24 (CLOSEST TO OCTOBER 19)

Isaiah 62:1–7, 10–12; Psalm 18:2–11, 16–19;
2 Corinthians 6:2–10; John 6:35–40, 54–57

Isaiah 62:1 For the sake of Zion I will not keep silent,
  and for the sake of Jerusalem I will not keep still,
  until her vindication shines out like blazing light,
  and her salvation like a flaming torch.
² The nations shall see your vindication, daughter,
  and all the monarchs your glory;
  and you shall be called by a new name
  that the mouth of the Living God will grant.
³ You, daughter, shall be a crown of beauty in the hand of God Most High,
  and a royal diadem in the hand of your God.
⁴ Daughter, no more shall you be called Forsaken,
  and no more shall your land be called Devastated;
  but you shall be called My Delight Is in Her,
  and your land, Married;
  for the Faithful God delights in you,
  and your land shall be married.

⁵ For as a young man marries a virgin girl,
   so shall your builder marry you, daughter,
   and as the bridegroom rejoices over the bride,
   so shall your God rejoice over you.
⁶ Upon your walls, daughter Jerusalem,
   I have posted sentinels;
   all the day and all the night,
   they shall never be silent.
   You who remind the God Who Sees,
   take no rest for yourselves,
⁷ and give God no rest
   until God establishes Jerusalem
   and makes it renowned throughout the earth.
¹⁰ Go through, go through the gates!
   Prepare the way for the people!
   Build up, build up the highway;
   throw away (the loose) stones,
   lift up a banner over the peoples.
¹¹ Look! The God Who Saves has made it heard
   to the end of the earth:
   Say to Daughter Zion,
   "See, your salvation comes;
   bringing reward and recompense first."
¹² They shall call them, "The Holy People,
   The Redeemed of the God Who Saves";
   and you, daughter, shall be called, "Sought Out,
   A City Not Forsaken."

Psalm 18:2–11, 16–19

² The Rock Who Gave Us Birth is my rock,
   and my fortress, and my deliverer,
   my God, my rock in whom I take refuge,
   my shield, and the horn of my salvation, my stronghold.
³ I call upon the Holy One, may she be praised,
   and from my enemies I shall be saved.
⁴ The snares of death encompassed me;
   the rivers of wickedness assailed me.
⁵ The snares of Sheol encircled me;
   the snares of death confronted me.

⁶ In my distress I called upon SHE WHO HEARS;
to my God I cried for help.
From her temple she heard my voice,
and my cry came before her, to her ears.
⁷ Then the earth shuddered and quaked;
the foundations also of the mountains trembled
and were shaken because of her anger.
⁸ Smoke went up from her nostrils,
and consuming fire from her mouth;
burning coals blazed forth from her.
⁹ She spread out the heavens, and descended;
thick darkness was under her feet.
¹⁰ She mounted up on a cherub, and flew;
she soared upon the wings of the wind.
¹¹ She made darkness her veil around her,
her canopy dark waters and thick clouds.
¹⁶ She reached down from on high, she took me;
she drew me out of the multitude of water.
¹⁷ She delivered me from my strong enemy,
and from those who hate me;
for they were too mighty for me.
¹⁸ They confronted me in the day of my calamity;
yet the SHELTERING GOD was my support.
¹⁹ She brought me out into a broad place;
she delivered me, because she delights in me.

2 Corinthians 6:2 God says,

At an acceptable time have I hearkened to you,
and on the day of salvation have I helped you.

Look! Now is the acceptable time; see, now is the day of salvation! ³ In no way, none, are we giving cause for offense, so there will be no reproach against ministry. ⁴ Rather, in every way have we commended ourselves as servants of God: through much endurance, in tribulations, in distress, in calamities, ⁵ in beatings, in imprisonments, in tumults, in labors, in sleepless nights, in hunger; ⁶ in purity, in knowledge, in patience, in kindness, in holiness of spirit, in love without pretense, ⁷ in truthful speech, and in the power of God; with the weapons of righteousness for the right hand and for the left; ⁸ amid honor and dishonor, amid slander and renown; as deceitful and yet genuine; ⁹ as unknown, and yet well known; as dying, and look! We are alive; as punished, and yet not killed; ¹⁰ as sorrowful, yet always rejoicing; as poor, yet making many rich; as having nothing, and yet possessing everything.

John 6:35 Jesus said to [to his disciples asking about eternal life], "I am the bread of life. The person who comes to me will never be hungry and the one who believes in me will never be thirsty. ³⁶ Rather I said to you all that you have seen me and yet you all do not believe. ³⁷ Everything that the Creator gives me will come to me and anyone who comes to me I will never drive away. ³⁸ That is why I have come down from the heavens, for this reason, not to do my own will, but the will of the one who sent me. ³⁹ And this is the will of the one who sent me, that out of all that God has given me I should lose nothing, but rather raise it up on the last day. ⁴⁰ This is indeed the will of my Abba, that all who see the Son and believe in him may have eternal life, and I will raise them up on the last day.

⁵⁴ "The one who eats my flesh and drink my blood has eternal life and I will raise that one up on the last day. ⁵⁵ For my flesh is true food and my blood is true drink. ⁵⁶ The one who eats my flesh and drinks my blood abides in me, and I in that person. ⁵⁷ Just as the living Creator sent me and I live because of the Creator, and so then will that one who eats me live because of me."

PROCLAMATION

Text Notes

The use of "daughter" in Isaiah 62 makes the divine address to a feminine subject, Zion, in verses 1–6 accessible to English readers as it is to those who read in Hebrew. The end of verse 6 addresses the people, or some among them, as a collective.

The poetry of verse 4 is impossible to replicate in English; note the four assonant three-syllable words: *Azuvah, Shamamah, Hephzibah,* and *Be'ulah* (not Beulah) and the corresponding lack of rhyme or rhythm in their translations: "Forsaken," "Devastated," "My Delight Is in Her," and "Married." The pattern recurs in verse 12 with *D'rushah* and *Ir Lo Ne'etzavah*, "Sought Out," and "A City Not Forsaken."

The verb marry in Isaiah 62:4–5 is *ba'al*, which also means lord/master as a noun. (It may be familiar as the divine title for the god Ba'al whose proper name is not used.) While the verb suggests a very hierarchal understanding of marriage it is rarely used in the canon, five times for humans and in eleven divine metaphors. Sentinels, as in Isaiah 62:6, are often synonymous for prophets.

In Psalm 18:2, I draw the divine name from Deuteronomy 32:18, "You neglected the Rock that gave birth to you; you forgot the God who writhed in birth-labor for you." The occasion of Psalm 18 is David's escape from Saul; that introduction takes up the first verse in Hebrew. The psalm proper begins with "He said," often included with the introductory verse. David's "love" in what is now verse 1, as Christian translations number the psalms, is *racham*, mother-love, love that is rooted in the womb, *rechem*, and otherwise used only by God to express her love. From David, we should perhaps read it as gesturing toward a reciprocal love that originates deep within.

Verse 3 of the psalm has the passive "be praised" without supporting grammar. Other translators have added "*worthy to* be praised." Some translations render verse 3 in the future (see NRSV and KJV). However, the introduction makes clear David is reflecting on his past deliverance. The imperfect here is more present, i.e., because of God's faithfulness, whenever I call on God as before, I shall be saved.

The Epistle quotes Isaiah 49:8 from the Septuagint.

"Abba" is a familial and familiar term for "father" in Aramaic and Biblical Hebrew and, in Modern Hebrew as well. No small number of Jewish children call their fathers "Abba."

Preaching Prompts

The abundance of images for God in these readings are nearly dizzying: parent and protector, shelter and salvation, birthing rock and living bread. Each of these is relational and intimate. God is with us as she has been with her people through all the ages. Jerusalem figures prominently in the first lesson and psalm as the home of the temple wherein God could be found at any time. Though the scriptures will not continue to tie God to a specific place, God's people will always know where she may be found, wherever it is that they are, in whatever circumstance.

In Isaiah 62 Jerusalem represents Judah, unnamed, which is at this point the remnant of the people of Israel. Vindicating Jerusalem, the people and the land means delivering them from their captivity and restoring them to their former home. It is a matter of honor, God's honor. In the world of the Hebrew Scriptures, the fall of Jerusalem was perceived as God's failure to keep her people safe. That is why the opening verses of the psalm refer to God's saving acts being in full view of the nations who may have come to doubt her power or think her people were available for the picking.

In the psalm the God of all the ages reveals herself to be a God of all power who harnesses the forces and elements of the heavens to create her own transportation in which to come to the rescue of her children when they are in danger. Where God marshals her forces to save the whole people in the first lesson, in the psalm God comes to the rescue of a single soul in danger.

In the Epistle the people who make up the burgeoning Jesus movement are connected to many lands and in their persecution, often cut off from those lands. Salvation is portrayed as endurance through a different kind of captivity. One might imagine these new followers of the Way being encouraged by the poetry of Isaiah 62. Though the bodies of her members be destroyed, the Church cannot be destroyed because it is the body of Jesus whom death could not destroy.

In the Gospel the way of salvation is a table with strange fare: the body and blood of Jesus. At that meal we internalize his death and his life and a mystery happens. The meaning of the Eucharist and its understanding varies enough across the communions who may pick up this volume that I dare not say what it means in my understanding as though it were true for all. But I will say accepting the invitation to that table and sharing in that meal make us more than recipients of salvation but also participants.

Women and girls are present in each of these layers of scripture, though they may be hidden by grammar and recoverable (with a willing translator) as in the first lesson. They may also be unspoken, buried in generic language for people groups as in the bulk of these readings. Yet in times of conflict and catastrophe, it is women and girls on the front lines, picking up the pieces and holding their families together and figuring out what to put on the table, whether in captivity or in the underground churches of the first century through those of my enslaved ancestors. And women were often unnamed disciples in the crowds, in the rooms and at the tables—especially when the tables were in their houses or they were paying for the food on those tables. There is no Church without women and girls. And the Church cannot be saved without women and girls. The salvation of the Church is not only tied up with the fate and welfare of women and girls, I argue it is dependent upon it.

PROPER 25 (CLOSEST TO OCTOBER 26)

Isaiah 66:7–13; Psalm 139:1–14; 1 Peter 1:3–9; John 3:1–10

Isaiah 66:7 Before she writhed-in-labor, she gave birth;
   before her pain came upon her, she delivered a boy-child.
⁸ Who has heard of such as this?
   Who has seen (things) such as these?
   Shall a land be born in one day?
   Shall a nation be birthed in one moment?
   Yet as soon as she writhed-in-labor,
   Zion gave birth to her children.
⁹ Shall I open the womb and not midwife? says the WOMB OF CREATION;
   shall I, the one who midwifes, shut the womb? says your God to you, daughter.
¹⁰ Rejoice with Jerusalem, and celebrate with her
   all you who love her; rejoice with her in joy,
   all who mourn deeply over her;
¹¹ in order that you all may nurse and be satisfied
   from her comforting breast;
   that you all may drink deeply and delight yourselves
   from the glory of her breast.
¹² For so says the HOLY ONE OF OLD:
   Watch! I will extend to her flourishing like a river,
   and the wealth of the nations like an overflowing stream;

and you all shall nurse and be carried on her arm,
and you all shall be bounced on her knees.
13 As a mother comforts her child,
so will I comfort you all;
you all shall be comforted in Jerusalem.

Psalm 139:1–14

1 SOURCE OF LIFE, you have searched me and known me.
2 You know my sitting down and my rising up;
you comprehend my thoughts from afar.
3 My journeying and my resting you watch over,
and with all my ways are you acquainted.
4 When there is no word is on my tongue,
Behold! ALL-SEEING GOD, you know everything.
5 Behind and before you surround me,
and lay upon me your hand.
6 Beyond wonderful is this knowledge to me;
so exalted I am unable to approach it.
7 Where can I go from your spirit?
Or where from your presence can I flee?
8 If I ascend to the heavens, there you are;
if I recline in Sheol, see, it is you!
9 If I take up dawn's wings
if I settle at the farthest reaches of the sea,
10 even there your hand shall lead me,
and your right hand shall hold me fast.
11 If I say, "Surely darkness shall cover me,
and night will become light behind me,"
12 even darkness is not dark to you;
night is as daylight,
for dark is the same as light.
13 For it was you who crafted my inward parts;
you wove me together in my mother's womb.
14 I praise you, for I am awesomely and marvelously made.
Wonderous are your works;
that my soul knows full well.

1 Peter 1:3 Blessed be the God and Father of our Redeemer Jesus Christ who in great mercy has engendered a new birth for us into a living hope, through the resurrection of Jesus Christ from the dead, 4 into an inheritance that is incorruptible, undefiled, and unfading, kept in the heavens for you all, 5 who in the power of God are kept through faith for a salvation ready to be revealed in the end time. ⁶ In this you rejoice even when necessary for you to suffer various trials, ⁷ in order that the examination of your faith, more precious than gold, which though perishable is tested by fire, may be found yielding praise and glory and honor when Jesus Christ is revealed. ⁸ You have not seen him, yet you love him. You do not see him now, yet you believe in him and rejoice with a joy glorious and beyond words. ⁹ You are receiving the completion of your faith, the salvation of your souls.

John 3:1 Now there was a member of the Pharisees, Nicodemus was his name, a leader of the Jewish people. ² He came to Jesus by night and said to him, "Rabbi, we know that you came from God as a teacher for no one has the power to do these signs that you do without God (being) with them." ³ Jesus answered him, "Truly truly, I say to you, if a person is not born again, from above, they will not be able to see the majesty of God." ⁴ Nicodemus said to Jesus, "How can a person be born after having become old? Surely no one is able to enter a second time into the belly of their mother and be born?" ⁵ Jesus answered, "Truly truly, I say to you, no one can enter the majesty of God without being born of water and Spirit. ⁶ Whatever (or whoever) is born of flesh is flesh and what is born of spirit is spirit. ⁷ Do not marvel that I say to all of you, 'You must be born again, from above. ⁸ The wind (like a spirit) blows where it chooses and you hear the sound of it, but know not from where it comes or where it goes. So it is with everyone who is born of the Spirit." ⁹ Nicodemus replied and said to Jesus, "How are these things possible?" ¹⁰ Then Jesus replied and said to him, "Are you a teacher of Israel and these things you know not?

PROCLAMATION

Text Notes

In Isaiah 66:7, the word underlying "boy-child" is "male"; I made this choice for smoother English grammar. In verse 9 the word "womb" is implied and supplied both times as is common in other translations. The depiction of God as "midwifing" stems from the causative (Hiphil) conjugation of the verb "to give birth." (In its nominal form, the noun "midwife" is a participle in the intensive Piel conjugation functioning as a noun.) The poet responsible for this chapter seems to have reached beyond the Hebrew language for the expression "glory of her breast" in verse 11. The underlying expression "teat" or "udder of glory" may well have come from Akkadian and has an Arabic cognate (see the corresponding entry in the *Dictionary of Classical Hebrew*). In verse 12, "flourishing" is a better, less materialistic reading of *shalom* than "prosperity."

The one comforted by their mother in Isaiah 66:13 is a man; the grammar of his passive comforting relegates his mother to the end of the sentence and makes him the focus: "As a man is comforted by his mother . . ." Common convention (JPS, NRSV, CEB) inverts the sentence, "As a mother comforts . . ." Mother-love in

Psalm 103:13 is attributed to a father: "As a father mother-loves his children" (using the verbal form of the noun "womb"). The verse could be translated: "As a father loves his children with a mother's love . . ." As with Isaiah 66, the maternal image, here womb-love, is also attributed to God.

In Psalm 139:13, "inward parts" are "kidneys" signifying internal organs. And in verse 14, "marvelous" and "wondrous" are the same word. I alternate them for alliteration to give a sense of the poetry.

"Engendered" in 1 Peter 1:3 translates *anagennao*, "causing to be born." Were it in the feminine, it might be "conceived." "Engendering" more broadly describes the result of the biological male in the generation of new life whereas "conceive" and "conception" tend to be reserved for biological females, animal and human.

In the first verse of John 3, I render "the Jews" as "the Jewish people" to avoid the translation that has served as a polemic, especially on Christian lips. In verses 3 and 7, I include both components of the underlying word, *anothen*, "born from above" and "born again." Nicodemus' second question in verse 4 includes a negative particle that is not commonly translated; however, it gives a bit of flavor to this discussion between learned figures who hold respect for each other. This entire discourse should be read as any other rabbinic discourse in which the questions being asked are part of the teaching being given. Also, in verse 4, Nicodemus uses the generic word for "stomach" or "belly" rather than the specific word for "womb." In verse 7, Jesus shifts his address to the previously unacknowledged audience of followers and disciples, a gathered crowd that is not identified. If the narrative of John 3 is intended to continue the narrative of John 2, then Jesus is in Jerusalem, teaching in public and the audience would be women, men, and children whether on the streets or in the courtyard or porticos of the temple. The translation in verse 8 makes the duality of the word *pnuma* clear to the English reader and hearer, as it means both "wind" and "spirit." The use of capital letters varies throughout this passage. The lowercase "S" on "Spirit" in verse 6 is intentional to reflect "Spirit" as a generic category; elsewhere the capital letter indicates the Spirit of God.

Preaching Prompts

These readings themselves use multiple genders present in the text along with traditionally gendered practices, mixed and remixed to tell a story of God that is helpful and hopeful in a world in which gendered terms and their use and meaning are reimagined and reinterpreted in new ways of telling the human story, genderqueer and trans stories of God and their people.

At one level, birthing is a basic human function long tied to women and viewed with mixtures of wonder and utilitarianism and sorrow across the ages. These intimate functions of women's bodies have often been culturally controlled by men, whether in terms of honor-based societal controls limiting the movement and sexual choices of women, medicalization of birth, or the restriction of reproductive rights and choices. At this level, fear and sorrow are never far away: fear of inability to conceive and the ensuing consequences in the world of the text, sorrow over lost pregnancies and children uniting women and their partners and families across time. At another level, birthing is mysterious: the work of the gods, the work of the God of Israel, and a metaphor for God's work in the world, including the birth of the land and people of Israel in Isaiah 66. In these few verses, God is birthing, midwifing, and grandfathering; the language for the former in the text is feminine and in the latter masculine. At the same time, none of this was considered literal. Here it is important to remember that this is poetry and each line has its own metaphor and they do not necessarily blend seamlessly into one portrait and verse numbers and breaks between individual lines are all postbiblical and acts of interpretation themselves.

Who is the one who gives birth to the boy child in Isaiah 66:7? My reading is that it is God who gives birth to a son identified as both land and nation in the middle lines of verse 8; otherwise the text would have Zion, traditionally identified as God's daughter, giving birth to the land and nation of Israel of which Zion—Jerusalem—is a part in some sort of mystical time loop. The next line tells the same story differently, as is common in Israelite poetry; now the grammatically feminine birth-giver is Zion, giving birth to her many children, the people of Israel. Here, God who is portrayed with masculine grammar, "midwifes," (in a verbal form) bringing the child of God's Daughter Zion into the world. Would that not make the people of this new land God's grandchildren in this verse? Does the poet expect the reader and hearer to imagine Zion is something other than God's daughter as in all other prophetic discourse, including the earlier sections of this prophetic compilation, one of which this poet-prophet imitates while adding her contribution? (For the possibility to likelihood of the author of the section of Isaiah being a woman, see my *Daughters of Miriam: Women Prophets in Ancient Israel*.)

In the psalm, God is intimately present with every human person at every moment along their journey to and through life and in the afterlife as understood by this psalmist. For some, God's "weaving" or "knitting" the internal organs of the psalmist in her mother's womb is biblical or theological evidence for a particular understanding of the human person from conception that has contentious political and legislative implications. For others, the poetry is no biological or theological textbook nor legal codex resolving the question of "ensoulment" or whether or when the divine handicraft is yet or will become a human person, a living soul.

In the Epistle, God who fathered Jesus without masculine organs creates a new kind of birth through the resurrection of Jesus. Considering his resurrection to be a tangible mystery, his body still marked by wounds of the Arch-Sacrament. One might imagine those bloody wounds as matrices of this new birth as did so many medieval artists, portraying the wounds of Christ remarkably similar to labia.

And in the Gospel, Jesus insists that his audience (likely enjoying his teaching discourse with Nicodemus, and Nicodemus as well), and with them all of us, must be born through his second other mystical parent, the Spirit which on his lips and those of everyone in his culture was grammatically feminine in contrast to the neuter presentation in Greek. That birth in which "again" and "above" cannot be unraveled any more than "Spirit" and "wind" is the only passage into holy sanctified majestic realm that is God-space into which we are received as beloved children of a God who transcends and transgresses gender as do the human beings, the living souls created in their image.

FEAST OF ALL SAINTS, NOVEMBER 1

Isaiah 25:1, 4a, 6–10a; Psalm 67; Romans 15:7–13; Matthew 27:50–56

Isaiah 25:1 Holy One of Old, you are my God;
   I will exalt you, I will praise your name,
   for you have worked wonders,
   ancient counsel, faithful and trustworthy.
 4 For you are a refuge to the poor,
   a refuge to the needy in their distress,
   a shelter from the storm and a shade from the heat.
 6 The Commander of heaven's legions will make for all peoples on this mountain,
   a feast of rich food, a feast of well-aged wines,
   of rich food prepared with marrow, of refined well-aged wines.
 7 And God will destroy on this mountain
   the shroud that shrouds all peoples,
   the veil that veils all nations.
 8 God will swallow up death forever.
   Then the Sovereign God will wipe away tears from every face,
   and will sweep aside the shame of God's people from the whole earth,
   for God Whose Name is Holy has spoken.
 9 It will be said on that day,
   Look! This is our God; in whom we hope, and who saved us.
   This is the Creator of All in whom we hope;
   let us be glad and rejoice in God's salvation.
 10 For the hand of the Ancient Of Days shall rest on this mountain.

Psalm 67

 1 May God be merciful to us and bless us,
   show us the light of her countenance and come to us.

² Let your ways be known upon earth,
   your saving health among all nations.
³ Let the peoples praise you, O God;
   let all the peoples praise you.
⁴ Let the nations be glad and sing for joy,
   for you judge the peoples with equity
   and guide all the nations upon earth.
⁵ Let the peoples praise you, O God;
   let all the peoples praise you.
⁶ The earth has brought forth her increase;
   may God, our own God, give us her blessing.
⁷ May God give us her blessing,
   and may all the ends of the earth stand in awe of her.

Romans 15:7 Accept one another, therefore, just as Christ has accepted you, for the glory of God. ⁸ I tell you that the Messiah has become a servant of the circumcised for the sake of truth, to confirm the promises given to the mothers and fathers, ⁹ and in order that the Gentiles might glorify God on account of God's mercy. As it is written,

"Therefore, I will confess you among the Gentiles,
and sing praises to your name,"

¹⁰ and again it says,

"Rejoice, O Gentiles, with God's people,"

¹¹ and again,

"Praise the Most High, all you Gentiles,
and let all the peoples praise God,"

¹² and again Isaiah says,

"The root of Jesse shall come,
and the one who rises to rule the Gentiles,
in whom the Gentiles shall hope."

¹³ May the God of hope fill you with all joy and peace in believing, so that you may abound in hope by the power of the Holy Spirit.

Matthew 27:50 Jesus cried again with a loud voice and relinquished his spirit. ⁵¹ Then, look! The curtain of the temple was torn from top to bottom in two. And the earth was shaken, and the rocks were split. ⁵² And the tombs were opened, and many bodies of the saints who had fallen asleep were raised. ⁵³ Then after his resurrection they came out of the tombs and entered the holy city and appeared to many. ⁵⁴ Now when the centurion and those with him, who were standing guard over Jesus, saw the earthquake and what took place, they were terrified and said, "Truly this man was God's Son!"

⁵⁵ Now there were many women there, from a distance watching; they had followed Jesus from Galilee and had ministered to him. ⁵⁶ Among them were Mary the Magdalene, and Mary the mother of James and Joseph and the mother of the sons of Zebedee.

PROCLAMATION

Text Notes

Division of verses for Isaiah 25 varies among translations. I follow the Masoretic Text and Jewish Publication Society here. Similarly, the flexibility of Hebrew tenses can place God's salvific actions in the past or future. The past tense emphasizes God's past faithfulness, laying the ground for a reasonable hope in continuing faithfulness.

Since *pateron* in Romans 15:8 can be inclusive of "ancestors" or "fathers" and God's promises were not and are not limited by gender, I use the most inclusive option. In verse 9, Christ takes up the same diaconal ministry with which the women who follow him are credited. Verses 9–12 quote Psalm 18:49, Deuteronomy 32:43, Psalm 117:1, and Isaiah 11:10 from the LXX. There are some variances between the Greek and Hebrew of Deuteronomy 32:43. In the Hebrew text, "the nations, God's people" are called to rejoice, while in the Greek, the heavens are called to rejoice *with* God's people. (For more on the divergence between the manuscript traditions on this verse, see the annotations and comparisons in *The Dead Seas Scrolls Bible*, ed. Abegg, Flint, and Ulrich.)

The women who "ministered" to Jesus, *diakoneo*, have been understood as providing for Jesus (NRSV), serving him (CEB), and ministering to him (KJV); all are viable, however, breadth in translation rather than specificity would seem to be called for.

Preaching Prompts

For the Feast of All Saints, this lectionary turns to declarations of God's faithfulness to all peoples and nations. This passage of Isaiah speaks repeatedly to "all peoples" and "all nations" in verses 6–7, all of whom will benefit from God's death-destroying salvific work. Similarly, in the psalm, God's salvation is for all nations with all peoples invited to join in the praise of God. The Epistle focuses on the acceptance of God's gift of salvation by the Gentile nations. The Gospel takes us back to that saving work in the life and death of Jesus, hinting at the resurrection to come with the resurrection of saints who preceded Jesus in death, at the moment of his death. Meanwhile, the saints who stood bearing witness would become second-class saints in the eyes of many, excluded from ministry, ordination, and leadership based on their gender. Perhaps ironically, and almost certainly intentionally, the reduction of their ministry to open checkbooks exploits and limits their gifts at the same time.

PROPER 26 (CLOSEST TO NOVEMBER 2)

Daniel 5:1–12; Sirach 1:14–20; 1 Corinthians 1:26–31; Luke 21:9–19

Daniel 5:1 Belshazzar the king made a great feast for a thousand of his nobles and in the presence of the thousand he was drinking wine. ² Belshazzar commanded, in a wine haze, that they bring the vessels of gold and silver that his father Nebuchadnezzar took from the temple that was in Jerusalem, so that the king and his nobles, his consorts and his concubines might drink from them. ³ And so they brought in the vessels of gold that were taken from the temple, the house of God in Jerusalem, and the king and his nobles, his consorts and his concubines drank from them. ⁴ They drank the wine and gave praise to the gods of gold and silver, bronze, iron, wood, and stone.

⁵ In that moment the fingers of a human hand appeared, writing on the plaster of the wall of the palace of the king across from the lampstand; the king watched the hand, palm and all, as it wrote. ⁶ Then the countenance of the king changed and his thoughts made him afraid. The joints of his hips loosened and his knees knocked together. ⁷ The king cried out forcefully to bring in the conjurers, the Chaldeans and the diviners and the king said to the sages of Babylon that "any person who can read this writing and tell me its interpretation shall be clothed in purple, have a chain of gold around their neck and rank third in the kingdom." ⁸ Then all the king's sages came in, but they could not read the writing or tell the king the interpretation. ⁹ Then King Belshazzar became greatly terrified and his countenance changed and his nobles were perplexed.

¹⁰ The queen, on account of the discussion of the king and his nobles, came to the banqueting hall. The queen said, "O king, forever may you live! Let not let your thoughts make you afraid or your countenance change. ¹¹ There is a person in your kingdom who has a spirit from the holy gods in him. And in the days of your father, enlightenment, understanding and wisdom like the wisdom of the gods was found in him. Your father, King Nebuchadnezzar—chief of the magicians, conjurers, Chaldeans, and diviners, your father the king made him. ¹² All because of what was an extraordinary spirit, knowledge, and understanding to interpret dreams, explain riddles, and unravel problems, was found in him, in Daniel, who the king named Belteshazzar. Now let Daniel be called and he will declare the interpretation."

Sirach 1:14–20

¹⁴ The beginning of wisdom is awe of the Holy One;
 with the faithful in the womb she was created, together with them.
¹⁵ With humankind she built her roost, an eternal foundation,
 and among their descendants, she will be trusted.
¹⁶ The fullness of wisdom is to reverence the Holy One;
 she inebriates mortals with her fruits.
¹⁷ Every house of theirs she fills whole with desirable things,
 and their storehouses with her produce.

¹⁸ A crown of wisdom is the awe of the Holy One,
   sprouting peace and wholeness, healing.
¹⁹ Skill and knowledge, understanding she rained down,
   and she exalted the reputation of those who hold her.
²⁰ The root of wisdom is to reverence the Holy One,
   and her branches are length of days.

1 Corinthians 1:26 Now look to your own call, sisters and brothers [or friends and kin]: not many of you were wise by mortal standards, not many were powerful, not many were highborn. ²⁷ Rather, God chose what is foolish in the world to shame the wise and God chose what is weak in the world to shame the strong. ²⁸ And what is insignificant in the world and what is despised God chose, to eradicate what is, ²⁹ so that no mortal can boast in the presence of God. ³⁰ God is the source of your life in Christ Jesus, who became for us Wisdom from God, and righteousness and sanctification and redemption, ³¹ in order that, as it is written, "Let the she or he who boasts, boast in the Messiah."

Luke 21:9 [Jesus said to the women and men gathered near the temple:] When you all hear of wars and riots, be not terrified; for these things must come into being first, but the end will not be immediately.

¹⁰ Then Jesus said to them:

Nation will rise against nation, and monarchy against monarchy. ¹¹ Great earthquakes shall there be, and in various places, famines and plagues and terrors, and from heaven, there will be great signs. ¹² But before all this, they will lay their hands upon you and persecute you all; they will hand you over to synagogues and prisons, and you will be brought before monarchs and governors because of my name, ¹³ an opportunity for you all to testify. ¹⁴ So fix your hearts not to prepare your self-defense in advance. ¹⁵ For I shall give you a mouth [to speak] and a wisdom that they will be able to withstand or contradict, not a single one of your opponents. ¹⁶ You all shall be betrayed even by mother and father and sister and brother, by kin and friends, and they will put some of you to death. ¹⁷ You all will be hated by all because of my name. ¹⁸ Yet not a hair of your heads will perish. ¹⁹ By your endurance you will gain your souls.

PROCLAMATION

Text Notes

The first lesson comes from one of the Aramaic portions of Daniel. In Daniel 5:2–3, there is a category of royal women translated as "consorts" here and in JPS and CEB, but "wives" in NRSV and NRSVue who may be best understood as royal hostages or captives given its verbal root, *shegal* as "rape" or given the noun form is used exclusively as a title for foreign royal women. It may be derogatory, slut shaming, as it is used in Jeremiah 3:2 to describe Israel's prostitution. The Masoretes consider the word so obscene they replace it with the verb "to sleep/have sex" there. The title form is also used in Psalm 45:9 for the royal bride from Tyre who is understood to be Jezebel. The Babylonian royal culture differs from Israelite and Judean culture in that the senior royal wife in Babylon is called a "queen" in Daniel 5:10, and there are concubines, verses 2–3. In the Hebrew Bible, among royal women the title "Queen" (from the same Hebrew root as "King") is not used for spouses; in Judea, the mother of the king is known as "the Great Lady," usually translated as "Queen Mother." There is no Hebrew term that corresponds to the Aramaic term for "concubine" used in this passage. In Israelite culture, "secondary wives" are often mistranslated as concubines in JPS and NRSV, corrected in CEB and NRSVue. There is a pun in verse 11 in which "the holy gods" can also mean "the holy God." *Elohim* takes a plural form whether it means gods, plural, or the singular Israelite God. Thus, the author has placed a pun on the lips of the queen. She speaks of her many Babylonian gods but has unwittingly given voice to the singular Israelite deity.

This week, the response to the first lesson is a canticle, a wisdom hymn from Sirach. In Sirach 1:14 I use "awe" rather than the more common "fear" of God; the underlying word includes both as well as reverence for the infinitive form in Sirach 1:16 and 20. Given these options, whether a translator chooses awe/reverence or fear speaks to one's theology, perhaps more so than to who God is. Wisdom is more than personified in Sirach 1. She builds a nest in verse 15, suggesting avian qualities.

In 1 Corinthians 1:25 just prior to this reading, Paul uses *anthroupou*, "human," to emphasize the limitations of mortal human wisdom and strength; verses 26 and 29 use *sarx*, "flesh," in the same manner. In each case, "mortal" conveys the sense. In verse 31, he refers to, but does not directly quote, Jeremiah 9:24: "Let those who boast, boast in this, that they understand and know me, that I am the HOLY ONE."

The setting for Luke 2 passage is a continued conversation near the temple (beginning in Luke 21:1–5) in a public space that would have included women, children, and men. In Luke 21:12, "lay hands" is much more like the African American Vernacular English (AAVE) "throw hands."

Preaching Prompts

The theme uniting these readings is wisdom. In each case, wisdom has its origins with God. And in each reading (excepting the canticle) those to whom God reveals wisdom are imperiled in some way. They include the young Daniel, a foreign queen, and everyone who is in on the gag that Daniel is not really about the Babylonians. In the Epistle, it is the members of the burgeoning Jesus movement who are imperiled, persecuted, and prosecuted as predicted by the Gospel reading.

Daniel is resistance literature, a story invoking an ancient and legendary character whose origins lie with or beyond the Ugaritic character D'nil, centuries before the first Israelite stories were told or put to parchment. In all of the Daniel stories, Daniel is young and wise beyond his years because he is "God's judge," the meaning of his name. In the biblical story, none of the learned men around the king are able to decode his dream or have the first idea of where to seek help. These Babylonian mystics and sages are out-thought by the young Daniel with whom God's spirit of wisdom resides, and by their queen, uninvited to the deliberations, who keeps her ear to the ground as well as to the doors of rooms to which she is uninvited. As a narrative of resistance, the Babylonians stand in for the current oppressors during the time in which this story was crafted, perhaps recrafted to ridicule Israel's Greek oppressors by using stories and characters from their past. Only the current Israelites would be wise enough to know the subtext of the narrative.

The wisdom of Sirach stands in sharp contradiction to the wisdom of the world and those whom the world reckons as wise. In this canticle, it is revealed that wisdom is the inheritance of every human soul, engrafted in the womb. But only activated, if you will, by the proper posture toward God, reverence and awe (in other translations, "fear").

The earliest followers of the Jesus movement were simple people, enslaved persons, women, and—from the perspective of the earliest Jewish followers—foreigners. They would have been regarded as a motley assortment even including some high status Jewish and Greek followers. None of their compatriots, fellow citizens, or communal denizens would turn to them for wisdom; rather, the Greek and Roman philosophers were the esteemed examples of wisdom in their world. But Paul writes to them that they are precisely who God chose to reveal wisdom into this world along with their brother and Redeemer, Jesus, who shares their ignoble circumstances and disrepute in the world.

Wisdom in the portion of Luke 21 read on this day has a narrow meaning: how to respond when put on trial for following Jesus. That wisdom will come straight from heaven and be placed on the tongue of those who are persecuted and prosecuted for following Jesus. The setting is apocalyptic. In this age when so much of are fiction and films are post-apocalyptic, it is important to remember that Jesus prepares us for cataclysms to come. Even then in those most extreme circumstances, God will be with us. Those who confess Jesus will need to hold on to that because they will find that discipleship is expensive. Regardless of your status in the world, the time will come when confessing Jesus may not seem wise to the world. Should we persist, we will find not only a divine word on our tongues but a holy companion on the journey wherever it leads. As Americans, or Westerners more broadly, we will not likely share the real expectation that our faith might lead to our prosecution or even our death. But some of us have found in taking to the streets and other acts of civil disobedience, that standing up for the values of our faith can indeed be costly. Wherever our faith leads us, God goes with us and meets us there; God's wisdom is a whisper away if and when we are called to account for our faith should the day come when it costs us something.

PROPER 27 (CLOSEST TO NOVEMBER 9)

Malachi 2:13–16; Psalm 37:1–2, 7–9, 27–28, 35–40;
2 Timothy 2:8–13; Luke 18:9–14

Malachi 2:13 This you all do repeatedly: covering in tears the altar of the Faithful God, weeping and groaning because God no longer even turns toward the offering or receives it with favor at your hand. 14 You ask, "On what account?" On this account, because the Judge of all Flesh was a witness between you and the wife of your youth, in which you betrayed her, yet she is your partner and wife of your covenanting. 15 Did not the One make [her], and [is not] the spirit of the one who is left God's? And what does the One desire? Godly offspring. So guard your own spirits, and against the wife of one's youth, let no one betray. 16 For the One despises divorce, says the God Who is Love, the God of Israel, and [the One also despises] covering one's garment with violence, says the Commander of heaven's legions. So guard your own spirits and do not betray.

Psalm 37:1–2, 7–9, 27–28, 35–40

1 Be not angry on account of the wicked,
   be not envious of wrongdoers;
2 for they will soon wither like the wild grass,
   and fade like the planted grass.
7 Be still before the Most High, and wait patiently for her;
   be not angry on account of those who prosper on their path,
   or the one who carries out plots.
8 Let go of anger and forsake wrath;
   be not angry; it leads only to evil.
9 For the wicked shall be cut off,
   but those who hope in the Fount of Justice shall inherit the land.
27 Turn from evil, and do good
   and you shall abide forever.
28 For the Faithful One loves justice;
   and will not forsake God's faithful ones.
   For all time shall they be guarded,
   yet the children of the wicked shall be cut off.
35 I have seen the wicked oppressing,
   and spreading themselves out like a native green tree.
36 They passed on, and suddenly! They were no more;
   though I sought them, they could not be found.
37 Regard the blameless and behold the upright,
   for there will be a future for the peaceable.

38 But transgressors shall be utterly destroyed together;
 the future of the wicked shall be cut off.
39 The salvation of the righteous is from the Ever-Present God;
 she is their stronghold in the time of trouble.
40 The Redeeming God helps them and delivers them;
 she delivers them from the wicked, and saves them,
 because they take refuge in her.

2 Timothy 2:8 Remember Jesus Christ, raised from the dead, from the line of David [and Bathsheba]; that is my gospel, ⁹ for which I suffer hardship, even to chains, like a criminal. But the word of God is not chained. ¹⁰ Because of this, therefore I endure everything for the sake of the elect, in order that they may also obtain salvation in Christ Jesus with eternal glory. ¹¹ This is a trustworthy saying:

For if we die together, we will also live together;
12 if we endure, we will also reign together;
 if we deny [Christ], he will also deny us;
13 if we are faithless, faithful he remains,
 for he cannot deny himself.

Luke 18:9 Jesus also told this parable to certain folk who trusted in themselves that they were righteous and despised everyone else:

¹⁰ Two persons went up to the temple to pray, the one a Pharisee and the other a tax collector. ¹¹ The Pharisee, was standing by himself praying thus, "God, I thank you that I am not like other people—thieves, crooks, adulterers, or even like this tax collector. ¹² I fast twice a week; I give a tenth of everything I acquire." ¹³ But the tax collector, standing far off, would not raise his eyes to heaven, rather was beating his breast and saying, "God, be merciful to me, a sinner!" ¹⁴ I tell you, this one went down to his home, made righteous, rather than the other; for all who exalt themselves will be humbled, but all who humble themselves will be exalted.

PROCLAMATION

Text Notes

The Hebrew of Malachi 2:15 is obscure and resolved in different ways among each major translation, KJV, NRSV, CEB, JPS, and Robert Alter. The opening phrase is "did not one make . . . ?" The next pair of words, *sh'ar ruach*, means something like "remnant of spirit." While the first word of the pair has the same consonants as the word meaning "flesh," yielding translations such as NRSV "flesh and spirit," the two nouns are in construct, meaning the word "of" joins the pair, e.g., "house of God." "Flesh of spirit" is not tenable. The DCH offers as one of the meanings, "ones who are left," used to refer to the remainder or "remnant" of Israelites (and others) after the Babylonian invasion and other catastrophes; see Isaiah 10:20–22; 11:11–16; 17:3; 28:5; Nehemiah 10:29; 11:20 (David J. A. Clines, ed. *The Dictionary of Classical Hebrew* [Sheffield: Sheffield Phoenix Press, 2011], 221).

The subject of verse 16 is inferred from the verbs, which have the same grammar as the verbs associated with "the One" of the previous verse. Some translations, NRSV and JPS, shift to the first person, which is unnecessary here. Moses's divorce of his wife is accomplished with the same verb found in Malachi 2:16. However most translators soften it with "send away/back," the broader meaning of the verb: see KJV, NRSV, JPS and CEB; Alter acknowledges it means divorce but insists it *must* have some other meaning for Moses and Zipporah. (See Robert Alter, *The Hebrew Bible: A New Translation with Commentary*.)

The language of Psalm 37:1 is somewhat stronger than the traditional "fret not" found in KJV and NRSV. Rather, it is the verb for burning anger that often discloses divine wrath. Verse 2 uses two different words for grass, with the latter sometimes having the sense of cultivated grass. To be "still" in verse 7 is also to be "silent," as in Aaron's silence in Leviticus 10:3 (elsewhere, Jeremiah 47:6; 48:2; Ezekiel 24:17; Amos 5:13; Psalms 4:4; 30:12; 31:17). The word used for "hope" in verse 9 can also mean "wait"; some translators (KJV, NRSV) use "wait" here while others (CEB, Alter) use "hope" to distinguish it from "wait" in verse 7, a separate word (where JPS uses "look to"). The Hebrew of verse 35 is awkward but not untenable. There is no need to replace the MT with the LXX as do the NRSV and CEB.

Many translations of 2 Timothy 2:11–13 add "with him" throughout for poetic balance; the object and preposition are not present. Verse 12 requires an object for the verb; I have supplied "Christ" from verse 10.

Adikoi in Luke 18:11 is an adjective behaving as a noun, meaning "unjust ones" or "crooked ones," hence my "crooks."

Preaching Prompts

The readings for this week consider fidelity, particularly fidelity in marriage and between intimate partners, as a measure of our fidelity to God, and a signifier of our own righteousness or journey to it. The unit from Malachi 2 on marriage and divorce has been understood in multiple ways given the difficulty of some of the Hebrew. In addition, a number of ancient sources have different readings; very much like today, people interpreted the text quite differently. (The *Jewish Study Bible* annotates some of these in its commentary on the passage.) This week I invite reflection on the text, reading it as a critique of betrayal in marriage, using the example of husbands in the ancient Israelite context who could initiate divorce at a whim, leaving women socially ostracized and financially vulnerable. This contemporary reading focuses on betrayal in our intimate lives; and the understanding that we cannot understand ourselves to be faithful to God if we betray those closest to us. This reading also invites consideration of the normalization of adultery and intimate abuse of women and girls that are no longer considered scandalous or even serious enough, in some cases, to reflect on one's standing in the community or before God. To that end, I invite consideration of the psalm as the cry of an abandoned and betrayed woman.

Psalm 37 is a psalm of frustration. It explores the perennial question of why the wicked get away with their wickedness. While the psalm focuses on poverty-inducing oppression, the word wickedness, literally "evil," knows no limitation. In the world of the psalm, as well as in the world in which we read and chant the psalm, those most affected by disparate economic policies, institutionalized poverty, and paycheck-to-paycheck vulnerability are women and their children. Divorce and abandonment are equally impoverishing. As we reflect on what wickedness looks like in our world, let us not neglect interpersonal wickedness while condemning the wickedness of empire. There is a caution to be had, recognizing that divorce and separation are complex issues and every situation should not be papered over with the label "wickedness." The reading I propose is rooted in the primary verb of the Malachi passage, "to betray" or "act treacherously (against)."

While the first lesson and the psalm focus our attention on the one who is betrayed, the Epistle has a word for those who have committed betrayal: "If we are faithless, Christ remains faithful" (2 Timothy 2: 13). Calling attention to human failing is not to shame or humiliate but rather, to ameliorate the consequences, mitigate harm, and offer grace and pardon with repentance.

The Gospel reading speaks to those who think they have no need of repentance, who do not acknowledge the wickedness in their lives or consider the various betrayals of human failing they have committed to be of consequence. In Luke 18:9, Jesus is subtweeting—a practice in which one responds to something of which one has knowledge without specifying the original circumstance; persons who are aware of the circumstance will recognize what is being addressed even though it is not said explicitly. We are to understand self-righteous persons are in the crowd, perhaps looking Jesus in the face as he tells this parable. In my sanctified imagination, I hear Jesus putting emphasis on the word "persons." The most obvious point of the parable is no one is righteous, yet those who know they are sinners and confess it are further on the path to righteousness than perhaps they know. In terms of the larger suggested theme, we might consider that we as church and society are unrighteous, that we have not yet repented as long as we participate in and construct systems that trap some women and their children in poverty and in which betrayals and intimate violations do not rise to a level of concern.

PROPER 28 (CLOSEST TO NOVEMBER 16)

Malachi 3:1–7; Psalm 84:1–12;
Revelation 22:1–5, 16–17, 20–21; Luke 24:44–53

Malachi 3:1 Look here! I am sending my messenger who will smooth the way before me, and the suddenly Sovereign whom you all seek will come to the temple belonging to the Sovereign. The messenger of the covenant in whom you delight—see now!—that one is coming, says COMMANDER of heaven's legions. ² But who can endure the day of that one's coming, and who can stand when that one appears?

For that one is like refining fire and like cleaners' soap. ³ That one will sit refining and purifying silver and will purify the descendants of Levi—women and men—and refine them like gold and silver, until they present offerings to the HOLY ONE OF OLD in righteousness. ⁴ Then the offering of Judah and Jerusalem will be pleasing to the HOLY ONE OF SINAI as in the days of old and as in former years.

⁵ Then will I draw near to you for judgment; I will be a witness who hastens [to testify] against those who practice sorcerers, against those who commit adultery, against those who swear falsely, against those who oppress, [cheating] the wage-earners of their wages as well as [oppressing] the widow and the orphan, against those who push aside the immigrant, and do not revere me, says the COMMANDER of heaven's vanguard.

⁶ For I GOD WHOSE NAME IS HOLY do not change; therefore you all, children of Rachel, Leah, Bilhah, and Zilpah, have not been finished off. ⁷ From the days of your mothers and fathers you have turned away from my statutes and have not kept them. Return to me and I will return to all of you, says the SOVEREIGN of the vanguard of heaven of hosts. But you say, "How shall we return?"

Psalm 84:1–12

¹ How beloved is your dwelling place,
   SOVEREIGN of the vanguard of heaven!
² My soul longs, truly she faints
   for the courts of the GOD WHO DWELLS ABOVE THE CHERUBIM;
   my heart and my flesh sing for joy
   to the living God.
³ Even the sparrow finds a home
   and the swallow a nest for herself,
   where she may lay her young
   at your altars RADIANT ONE,
   my Majestic One and my God.
⁴ Blessed are those who dwell in your house;
   forever they praise you. *Selah*

⁵ Blessed is the child of earth and Eve whose strength is in you,
  in whose heart are the [pilgrim] highways.
⁶ As they pass through the valley of Baca
  springs they make it.
  Even more, blessings! Covering it with the early rain.
⁷ They go from strength to strength.
  The God of gods will be seen in Zion.
⁸ MAJESTY OF THE HEAVENS, hear my prayer;
  incline your ear, O God of Rebekah's lineage! *Selah*
⁹ Behold our shield, O God;
  look on the face of your anointed.
¹⁰ For better is a day in your courts
  than a thousand (anywhere else).
  I (would) choose to be a doorkeeper in the house of my God
  than dwell in the tents of wickedness.
¹¹ For sun and shield is the RESPLENDENT God;
  The GLORIOUS ONE bestows grace and honor.
  She withholds no good thing
  from those who walk blamelessly.
¹² COMMANDER of heaven's legions,
  blessed is child of earth who trusts in you.

Revelation 22:1 The angel showed me the river of the water of life, bright as crystal, coming from the throne of God and of the Lamb ² through the middle of the street. On each side of the river is the tree of life with its twelve kinds of fruit, producing its fruit each month, and the leaves of the tree are for the healing of the nations. ³ There will no longer be any accursed thing. But the throne of God and of the Lamb will be in it, and God's servants will worship God; ⁴ they will see God's face, and God's name will be on their foreheads. ⁵ And night will be no more; they need no light of a lamp or of the sun, for the Holy God will be their light, and they will reign forever and ever.

¹⁶ "I, Jesus, sent my angel to you all to testify to this for the churches. I am the root and the descendant of David, the bright morning star."

¹⁷ The Spirit and the bride say, "Come."
  And let whoever hears say, "Come."
  And let whoever thirsts come.
  Let whoever wishes take the water of life as a gift.

²⁰ The one who bears witness (to the point of martyrdom) to these things says, "Yes! I am coming soon."
  Amen. Come, God-born Jesus!
²¹ The grace of the Savior Jesus be with all the saints. Amen.

Luke 24:44 Jesus said to [the two disciples], "These are my words that I spoke to you while I was still with you all, because everything must be fulfilled in the teaching of Moses, the prophets, and the psalms written about me." [45] Then he opened their minds to understand the scriptures. [46] Then he said to them, "So it is written, the Messiah is to suffer and to rise from the dead the third day, [47] and repentance and forgiveness of sins is to be preached in his name to all nations, beginning from Jerusalem. [48] You are witnesses of these things. [49] Now look! I am sending you the promise of my Father. You all stay in the city until you have been clothed with power from on high."

[50] Then Jesus led them out as far as Bethany, and lifting his hands, he blessed them. [51] While he was blessing them, Jesus retreated from them and was carried up into heaven. [52] And they worshiped him, and returned to Jerusalem with great joy; [53] and they were in the temple every day blessing God.

PROCLAMATION

Text Notes

The messenger of Malachi 3:1 can be a human being or a divine being so I have used neutral language to preserve the ambiguity. The actions on "the way" the messenger is to undertake is expressed with the verb "turn," often translated "prepare" or "clear." "Smooth" contains the notion of turning over the soil to smooth the surface. In verse 3, I specify women and men because the passage addresses the Levites and not just the priests and because women and men could and did present their own offerings (with the presentation being distinct from committing ritual sacrifice). Verse 6 refers to the Israelites as "the children of Jacob," I refer to them as the children of the matriarchs with whom Jacob fathered those children, including the two he enslaved.

Psalm 84 uses the kind of language lovers use for each other; Robert Alter finds it almost erotic (see his accompanying text notes on the psalm.). In verse 5, I use "child of earth and Eve" for *adam*, "human person" with the earth from which we were created, *adamah*, signified by the same root. A descriptor for the "highways" is lacking; there is broad agreement the pilgrim highways to Jerusalem are meant. "God of Rebekah's lineage" replaces "God of Jacob" in verse 8. The language of 10 is stronger than traditionally translated, "I (would) choose" rather than "I (would) prefer."

In Luke 24:44 the evangelist introduces an early canon of scripture consisting of Torah, Prophets and the Psalms. This suggests that the remainder of books in the category now known as "Writings" in the Jewish tripartite canon were not yet widely accepted as scripture.

In Revelation 22:22, the verb that means "to bear witness" or "to testify" means to do so at the point of one's life and shares of the same as the word "martyr." I have included the nuance in parentheses for the reader.

Preaching Prompts

This is the last Sunday of Ordinary Time before the commemoration of the Majesty of Christ leading us back into Advent. Each of these readings marks the end of things as they are known and understood while looking forward with hope to a promised future. The Malachi reading is from the last chapter of the Christian ordering of the First Testament (Jewish Bibles end with Chronicles, or occasionally, Ezra-Nehemiah.) The psalm is a Korahite psalm (one of the liturgical guilds), one perhaps marking the end of the world in which the Jerusalem temple towered and one in which God and her people would surely return to Zion. The New Testament reading comes from the last chapter and last verses of Revelation, the last book of the Christian Bible and the Gospel from the last verses of the last chapter of Luke, the Gospel assigned to this year, Year C.

Malachi 3 promises the arrival of a messenger whose nature is unknown, whether human or supernatural, who will purify and prepare God's people for the future that is to come, the beginning in the House of Levi, the keepers of the secret things, those with whom God dwells most intimately. The language "Levites" and that of older translations "sons of Levi" as in Handel's Messiah, neglect the daughters of Levi who had their own sacred roles largely lost to us. However, they, like their brothers, were able to dine at God's table, consuming the holy food unlike other women in Israel, including their mothers—if their mothers were not themselves daughters of Levi. I suggest in *Womanist Midrash: A Reintroduction to the Women of the Torah and the Throne* (Fortress, 2017, p. 114) that it was the daughters of Levi who inspected the bodies of Israelite women for signs of skin disease and other quarantining issues rather than their male kin because of the modesty and honor customs that shaped Israelite society.

If the psalm is a love song, it is a heartsick one written to a distant lover in a long distance relationship. (It is useful to remember that Ezekiel's proclamation that God accompanied her people into exile was revolutionary and unimaginable. Most of the survivors of Judah would have felt cut off from God without the temple, that the now-homeless God would have abandoned the Earth.) Yet the psalmist chooses to hope in a future where the living God returns to her abode. In the face of utter destruction and the glittering temples of false gods, the psalmist chooses service in a temple that can no longer be seen rather than any of those attempting to seduce her away from her Love.

The reading from Revelation also promises a temple that cannot be seen. As is the case with the psalm, the temple is not the point, but a sign of the matter at heart, God's reunion with her people, healing every hurt, wiping away every tear, the joyous reunion of distant lovers reunited after what has felt like eons.

The temple stands in the Gospel, but the reader knows it will not for long. Just as it had fallen previously, it will fall again. Its rise and fall have ceased to be a priority for the followers of the Jesus movement. For even with God in its midst, it was made by human hands; not even the wealth, power, and might of a king can keep a physical building from crumbling. Rather, the disciples—including perhaps a married couple—mourned the destruction of the precious body of Jesus, his life and all that he meant to them, and all of the hopes they had invested in him. And yet, as did God of old in ages past accompany her people through the valley of sorrow and death, so too did the risen Jesus accompany his unknowing disciples to their reunion banquet feast with their beloved.

MAJESTY OF CHRIST (CLOSEST TO NOVEMBER 23)

2 Kings 24:8, 11–17; Psalm 47; Hebrews 1:1–9; Matthew 27:11–14, 27–37

2 Kings 24:8 Jehoiachin was eighteen years old at his reign. He reigned three months in Jerusalem and the name of his mother was Nehushta daughter of Elnathan of Jerusalem.

¹¹ Now King Nebuchadnezzar of Babylon came to the city while his troops were besieging it. ¹² Then King Jehoiachin of Judah surrendered to the king of Babylon, himself and his mother and his slaves and his officers and his officials. The king of Babylon took him [captive] in the eighth year of his reign.

¹³ He brought out from there the treasures of the house of the HOLY ONE OF OLD and the treasures of the king's house; he cut up all the vessels of gold in the temple of the HOLY ONE which King Solomon of Israel had made, just as the HOLY ONE had spoken. ¹⁴ Nebuchadnezzar took into exile all Jerusalem, all the officials, all the warriors, ten thousand exiled women and men, all the artisans, and the smiths; no one remained except the poorest people of the land. ¹⁵ He took Jehoiachin into exile to Babylon; the king's mother, the king's women, his officials, and the elite of the land he took into exile from Jerusalem to Babylon. ¹⁶ The king of Babylon took into exile to Babylon all the valiant warriors, seven thousand, the artisans and the smiths, one thousand, all of them strong and fit for war. ¹⁷ The king of Babylon made Mattaniah, Jehoiachin's uncle, king in his place and changed his name to Zedekiah.

Psalm 47

¹ All you peoples clap your hands;
 shout to God with a joyful sound.
² For the SOVEREIGN GOD, the Most High, is awesome,
 a great governor over all the earth.
³ She subdued peoples under us,
 and nations under our feet.
⁴ She chose our heritage for us,
 the pride of Rebekah's womb whom she loves.

⁵ God has gone up with a shout,
   SINAI'S FIRE with the sound of a trumpet.
⁶ Sing praises to God, sing praises;
   sing praises to our Sovereign, sing praises.
⁷ For God is Sovereign over all the earth;
   sing praises with a psalm.
⁸ God is ruler over the nations;
   God is seated on her holy throne.
⁹ The nobles of the peoples gather,
   the people of the God of Hagar and Sarah;
   for to God belong the shields of the earth,
   she is highly exalted.

Hebrews 1:1 Many times and in many ways God spoke to our mothers and fathers through the prophets, female and male. ² In these last days God has spoken to us by a Son, whom God appointed heir of all there is, and through whom God created the worlds. ³ The Son is the brilliance of God's glory and reproduction of God's very being, and the Son undergirds all there is by his word of power. When the Son had made purification for sins, he sat down at the right hand of the Majesty on high, ⁴ having become as much greater than the angels as the name he inherited is more excellent than theirs.

⁵ For to which of the angels did God ever say,
   "You are my Child; today I have begotten you"?
   Or this,
   "I will be their Parent, and they will be my Child"?
⁶ Then again, when God brings the firstborn into the world, God says,
   "Let all the angels of God worship him."
⁷ On the one hand of the angels God says,
   *"God makes winds into celestial messengers,
   and flames of fire into God's ministers."*
⁸ But of the Son God says,
   *"Your throne, O God, is forever and ever,
   and the righteous scepter is the scepter of your realm.*
⁹ *You have loved righteousness and hated lawlessness;
   therefore God, your God, has anointed you
   with the oil of gladness beyond your companions."*

Matthew 27:11 Now Jesus stood before the governor and the governor questioned him saying, "Are you the King of the Jews?" Jesus said, "You say so." ¹² And when he was accused by the chief priests and elders, he did not answer. ¹³ Then Pilate said to him, "Do you not hear how many accusations they make against you?" ¹⁴ And he did not answer him, not one word, so that the governor was greatly astonished.

²⁷ Then the soldiers of the governor took Jesus into the governor's command post, and they gathered the whole cohort around him. ²⁸ They stripped him and put a scarlet robe on him. ²⁹ And having woven a crown from thorns, they put it on his head along with a reed in his right hand and they knelt before him and mocked him, saying, "Hail, King of the Jews!" ³⁰ And they spat on him, and took the reed and struck him on his head. ³¹ After mocking him, they stripped him of the robe and put his clothes [back] on him. Then they led him away to be crucified. ³² Now going out, they found a Cyrenian man named Simon; this man they conscripted to carry his cross.

³³ And coming to a place called Golgotha (which means Skull Place), ³⁴ they offered him wine mixed with vinegar to drink; but when he tasted it, he would not drink. ³⁵ And when they had crucified him, *"they divided his clothes"* among themselves by *"casting lots."* ³⁶ Then they sat down and kept watch over him there. ³⁷ Now they placed over his head his charge, written as, "This is Jesus, the King of the Jews."

PROCLAMATION

Text Notes

Nebuchadnezzar's troops are called "slaves" in 2 Kings 24:11. The king's surrender in verse 12 is articulated ironically with the primary verb of the exodus, *y-tz-'*. Likewise, Nebuchadnezzar "bought out" the riches of the Jerusalem temple in verse 13 just as God brought out the Israelites. The ranks of deportees include women and men. The first accounting includes the Queen Mother, second in authority to the king (listed in that order in verse 12) and the entire senior administrative team, which would have likely included women in some roles (indicated by seals from royal women and female administrators before and after the fall of Jerusalem). The second reckoning in verse 14 repeats and numbers the officials and warriors at ten thousand, and craftspersons and smiths; the former would have included women, as potting and weaving were traditionally female occupations. A third reckoning in verse 15 circles back to the surrendering of the Queen Mother and adds the royal women, wives, and other women, including royal daughters and likely the surviving wives of previous monarchs, then repeats the officials a third time and adds all of the nobles. A fourth accounting in verse 16 numbers the warriors at seven thousand and one thousand war-ready artisans and smiths. These different accountings suggest chaos and confusion rather than specificity in spite of the recorded numbers. The broader sense is that everyone who was anyone was exiled except the almost overlooked "poor of the land," tucked away at the end of verse 14, not mentioned again.

In Psalm 46:4, the "pride of Rebekah's womb" is "the pride (or majesty) of Jacob." In verse 6, "the God of Hagar and Sarah" is "the God of Abraham."

In Hebrews 1:1, the explication of prophets as female and male reminds the reader/hearer of the gender diversity in Israel's prophetic ranks. *Megalōsynēs*,

"Majesty," in Hebrews 1:3, as a feminine noun, marks a rare use of feminine language to describe God or her attributes in the New Testament.

The following verses quote the earlier scriptures widely and often out of context: Hebrews 1:5 quotes Psalm 2:7, where the anonymous psalmist says God told them they were God's begotten child, probably initially heard with regard to David. The next quote is from 2 Samuel 7:14 (and its duplicate, 1 Chronicles 17:13), where the promise of God to be a parent to a future monarch is to one of David's descendants. Given the difficulty of asserting biological gender for heavenly beings, I use the neuter "child" and "parent" in verse 5. Verse 6 quotes Deuteronomy 32:43 and Psalm 97:7 from Greek, where the original "gods" were replaced by "angels" to correct toward a pure monotheism. Verse 7 quotes Psalm 104:4, playing on the primary meaning of angel, "messenger." Verses 8–9 quote Psalm 45:6–7, where the first verse refers to God, but the second refers to the king whose wedding psalm it is (Ahab, since Jezebel is the only princess of Tyre to marry into Israel).

"Astonished" in Matthew 27:14 can also mean "impressed." Verse 31 ends "to crucify" with no object; some translations add "him" there. Verse 35 quotes the LXX language for dividing garments and casting lots in Psalm 22:18 exactly.

Preaching Prompts

The liturgical year ends with a reflection on the Majesty of Christ as the Church prepares to begin a new year, remembering his first advent while preparing for his next. As the weeks reviewing the rise and fall(s) of Israel's monarchies during Ordinary Time have made abundantly clear, monarchy is, as all human institutions, an enterprise that is doomed to fail. Yet monarchy and its conventions have given us language for God, imperfect but familiar, as the psalm amply demonstrates. Jesus takes that language and those conventions and inverts them; the reign of God and its majesty are very different from the splendor of the world's sovereigns.

To the fallen Judean monarchy and their Babylonian colonizers and occupiers, Jesus says the poor of the land who were deemed not worth the labor to even deport are at the heart of the reign of God. The majesty of Christ is not found in treasures of temple or palace, burgled and broken apart, but in a crown of thorns beaten in by bullies and in his battered and denuded body. This human, mortal, woman-born Jesus is the glory and majesty of God; in the words of the Epistle to the Hebrews, "the brilliance of God's glory and reproduction of God's very being." That humanness, shared with every girl and woman, boy and man, nonbinary child and adult, is also the majesty of Christ and our own.

APPENDIX
DIVINE NAMES AND TITLES*

FIRST TESTAMENT

AGELESS GOD
AGELESS ONE
ALL-KNOWING GOD
ALL-KNOWING ONE
ALL-SEEING GOD
ALMIGHTY
ANCIENT OF DAYS
ANCIENT ONE
ARK OF SAFETY
ARCHITECT OF HEAVEN
AUTHOR OF LIFE
BREATH OF LIFE
COMMANDER of heaven's legions
COMMANDER of heaven's vanguard
COMPASSIONATE GOD
COMPASSIONATE ONE
CREATOR
CREATOR OF ALL
DIVINE WARRIOR
DREAD GOD
ETERNAL
ETERNAL ONE
EXALTED
EVER-LIVING GOD
EVER-PRESENT GOD
FAITHFUL ONE
FAITHFUL GOD
FEARSOME GOD
FIRE OF SINAI
FOUNT OF JUSTICE
FOUNT OF LIFE
FOUNT OF WISDOM
GENEROUS ONE
GLORIOUS ONE
GOD WHO DWELLS ABOVE THE CHERUBIM
GOD WHO HEARS
GOD WHO IS HOLY
GOD WHO IS LOVE
GOD who is MAJESTY
GOD WHO IS MYSTERY
GOD WHO PROVIDES
GOD WHO REDEEMS
GOD WHO SAVES
GOD WHO SEES
GOD WHO THUNDERS
GOD WHOSE NAME IS HOLY
GRACIOUS GOD
GRACIOUS ONE
HEALING ONE
HEAVENLY MIDWIFE
HOLY GOD
HOLY ONE
HOLY ONE OF OLD
HOLY ONE OF SINAI
HOLY PROTECTOR
HOLY SHEPHERD
INSCRUTABLE GOD
INCANDESCENT ONE
INDOMITABLE GOD

---

* This list of divine titles intentionally exceeds the number of those used in this volume. These titles are offered to enrich the liturgical lexicons of those who pray, preach and preside, in public or in private.

Judge of all the Earth
Judge of all Flesh
Just God
Just One
Living God
Loving God
Magnificent One
Majestic One
Majesty
Majesty of the Ages
Majesty of the Heavens
Maker of All
Merciful God
Merciful One
Mighty God
Mighty One
Most High
Mother of All
Mother of Creation
Mother of the mountains
Mother of Wisdom
One
One God
One Who Is
Radiant God
Radiant One
Redeemer
Redeeming God
Redeeming One
Resplendent One
Righteous God
Righteous One
Rock Who Birthed Us
Rock Who Gave Us Birth
Ruler of All
Ruler of the Multitudes of Heaven
Saving God
Saving One
Sheltering God
Shepherding God

She Who Birthed the Earth
She Who Hears
She Who Provides
She Who Is
She Who Is Delight
She Who Is Exalted
She Who Is Faithful
She Who Is Glory
She Who Is God
She Who Is Holy
She Who Is Majesty
She Who Is Mighty
She Who Is Peace
She Who Is Power
She Who Speaks Creation
She Who Is Strength
She Who Is Wisdom
She Who Is Worthy
She Who Reigns
She Who Saves
She Who Sees
She Who Speaks Life
She Who Thunders
Sinai's Fire
Source of Life
Sovereign
Sovereign of All
Sovereign-Commander of winged warriors
Sovereign God
Sovereign One
Sovereign of heaven's vanguard
Sovereign of the vanguard of heaven
The I Am
Too Holy to be Pronounced
Thunder of Sinai
Thundering God
Warrior Protectrix
Wellspring of Life
Wisdom

Wisdom of the Ages
Womb of Creation
Womb of Life
Worthy One
You Who Are

SECOND TESTAMENT
Jesus/Christ

Anointed
God-born
Messiah
Rabbi
Redeemer
Savior
Son of Woman
Teacher
Woman-Born

God

Creator
Creator of All
Dread God
Faithful One
Father
Holy One
Living God
Majesty
Maker
Most High
One Parent
Provider
Reconciler
Shepherd-Of-All
Sovereign
Weaver (of lights)

BIBLIOGRAPHY

Abegg, Martin, Peter Flint, and Eugene Ulrich. *The Dead Sea Scrolls Bible: The Oldest Known Bible*. San Francisco: HarperSan Francisco: 1999.

Aland, Barbara, Kurt Aland, et al. *Novum Testamentum Graece*. Stuttgart: Deutsche Bibelgesellschaft, 2017.

Alter, Robert. *The Hebrew Bible: A Translation with Commentary*. New York: W.W. Norton and Company, 2019.

The Anchor Yale Bible Commentaries. Garden City, NY: Doubleday, 1964–Present.

Ariel, Israel. *Carta's Illustrated Encyclopedia of the Holy Temple in Jerusalem*. Jerusalem: Coronet Books, 2004.

Arndt, William, F. Wilbur Gingrich, Frederick William Danker, and Walter Bauer. *A Greek-English Lexicon of the New Testament and Other Early Christian Literature*. 3rd ed. Chicago: University of Chicago Press, 2000.

Aymer, Margaret, *Acts of the Apostles*. Edited by Carol A. Newsom, Sharon H. Ringe, and Jacqueline E. Lapsley. *Women's Bible Commentary*. 3rd ed. Louisville: Westminster John Knox Press, 2012.

Barth, Markus. *Ephesians. Introduction, Translation, and Commentary*. The Anchor Bible, vol. 34. Garden City, NY: Doubleday, 1974.

Bassler, Jouette M. "First Corinthians." In *Women's Bible Commentary*, edited by Carol A. Newsom, Sharon H. Ringe, and Jacqueline E. Lapsley, 558–66. 3rd ed. Louisville: Westminster John Knox Press, 2012.

Berlin, Adele, and Marc Zvi Brettler. *The Jewish Study Bible*. 2nd ed. Oxford: Oxford University Press, 2004.

Bloch, Ariel, and Chana Bloch. *The Song of Songs: The World's First Great Love Poem*. Modern Library Classics. New York: Random House, 1995.

Briggs Kittredge, Cynthia, and Claire Miller Colombo. "Colossians." In *Philippians, Colossians, Philemon*, edited by Mary Ann Beavis, 124–201. Wisdom Commentary, vol. 51. Collegeville, MN: Liturgical Press, 2017.

Brooten, Bernadette. *Women Leaders in the Ancient Synagogue*. Brown Judaic Studies 36. Chico, CA: Scholars Press, 1982.

Brown, Raymond F. *The Epistles of John: A New Translation with Introduction, Notes and Commentary*. The Anchor Bible, vol. 30. Garden City, NY: Doubleday, 1982.

Budge, E. A. Wallis. *The Queen of Sheba and Her Only Son Menyelek (I): Being the 'Book of the Glory of Kings' (Kebra Nagast) a Work which is Alike the Traditional History of the Establishment of the Religion of the Hebrews in Ethiopia, and the Patent of Sovereignty which is Now Universally Accepted in Abyssinia as the Symbol of the Divine Authority to Rule which the Kings of the Solomonic Line Claimed to have Received through their Descent from the House of David*. London: Oxford University Press, H. Milford, 1922.

Byron, Gay L., and Vanessa Lovelace. *Womanist Interpretations of the Bible: Expanding the Discourse*. Atlanta, GA: Society for Biblical Literature, 2016.

Clines, David J.A. *The Dictionary of Classical Hebrew*. Rev. ed. Sheffield: Sheffield Phoenix Press, 2018.

Common English Bible. Nashville, TN: Common English Bible, 2011.

Cooper, Kate. *Band of Angels: The Forgotten World of Early Christian Women*. New York: Overlook Press, 2013.

Dickerson, Febbie. *Luke, Widows, Judges, and Stereotypes*. Lanham, MD: Lexington Books/Fortress Academic, 2019.

Edelman, Diana. "Mephibosheth." *The Anchor Bible Dictionary, Volume 5*. Edited by David Noel Freeman et al. New York: Doubleday, 1992.

Falk, Marcia. *The Song of Songs: Love Lyrics from the Bible*. Brandeis Series on Jewish Women. Waltham, MA: Brandeis University Press, 2004.

Fitzmyer, Joseph. *The Acts of the Apostles: A New Translation with Introduction and Commentary*. The Anchor Bible, vol. 31. Garden City, NY: Doubleday, 1998.

———. *First Corinthians: A New Translation with Introduction and Commentary*. The Anchor Yale Bible, vol. 2-2. New Haven, CT: Yale University Press, 2008.

———. *The Gospel According to Luke I–IX. Introduction, Translation and Notes*. The Anchor Bible, vol. 28. Garden City, NY: Doubleday, 1981.

Fox, Everett. *The Early Prophets: Joshua, Judges, Samuel, and Kings: A New Translation with Introductions, Commentary, and Notes by Everett Fox*. The Schocken Bible, vol 2. New York: Schocken Books, 2014.

———. *The Five Books of Moses: Genesis, Exodus, Leviticus, Numbers, Deuteronomy: A New Translation with Introductions, Commentary, and Notes*. The Schocken Books, vol 1. New York: Schocken Books, 1995.

———. *Give Us A King!: Samuel, Saul, and David: A New Translation of Samuel I and II, with an Introduction and Notes by Everett Fox*. 1st ed. New York: Schocken Books, 1999.

Freedman, David Noel. *The Anchor Bible Dictionary*. New Haven, CT: Yale University Press, 1992.

Freeman, Lindsay Hardin. *Bible Women: All Their Words and Why They Matter*. Cincinnati, OH: Forward Movement, 2014.

Frick, Frank. "Israel? A People and a Land: Joshua and Judges." In *A Journey Through the Hebrew Scriptures*, 240–62. Belmont: Wadsworth Publishing, 2002.

Gafney, Wilda. *Daughters of Miriam: Women Prophets in Ancient Israel*. Philadelphia, PA: Fortress Press, 2008.

———. *Nahum, Habakkuk, Zephaniah*. Edited by Barbara E. Reid, OP. Wisdom Commentary, vol. 38. Collegeville, MN: Liturgical Press, 2017.

———. *Womanist Midrash: A Reintroduction to the Women of the Torah and the Throne*. Lexington, KY: Westminster/John Knox Press, 2017.

Henderson, J. Frank, Jean Campbell, Ruth Fox, and Eileen M. Schuller. *Remembering the Women: Women's Stories from Scripture for Sundays and Festivals*. Chicago: Liturgy Training Publications, 1999.

Huizenga, Annette Bourland. *1–2 Timothy, Titus*, Wisdom Commentary Series. Collegeville, MN: Liturgical Press, 2016.

Ilan, Ṭal. *Mine and Yours Are Hers: Retrieving Women's History from Rabbinic Literature*. Leiden: Brill, 1997.

The Inclusive Bible: The First Egalitarian Translation. Lanham, MD: Rowman and Littlefield, 2007.

Johnson, Luke Timothy. *The Letter of James: A New Translation with Introduction and Commentary*. The Anchor Bible, vol. 37. New York: Doubleday, 1995.

Kol HaNeshamah. Elkins Park, PA: Reconstructionist Press, 2000.

Kramer, Ross. "Nympha." In *Women in Scripture: A Dictionary of Named and Unnamed Women in the Hebrew Bible, the Apocryphal/Deuterocanonical Books, and the New Testament,* edited by Carol L. Meyers, Toni Craven, and Ross Shepard Kraemer, 132–33. Boston: Houghton Mifflin, 2000.

Lamsa, George. *The Holy Bible from the Ancient Eastern Text: George M. Lamsa's Translations from the Aramaic of the Peshitta*. San Francisco, CA: Harper and Row, 1985.

Levine, Amy-Jill, and Marc Brettler. *Entering the Passion of Jesus: A Beginner's Guide to Holy Week*. Nashville, TN: United Methodist Publishing, 2018.

———. *The Jewish Annotated New Testament*. New Revised Standard Version. Oxford: Oxford University Press, 2011.

Magiera, Janet. *Aramaic Peshitta New Testament Translation: Messianic Version*. San Diego, CA: LWM Publications, 2009.

Marcus, Joel. *Mark 1–8: A New Translation with Introduction and Commentary*. The Anchor Bible, vol. 27A. Garden City, NY: Doubleday, 2008.

———. *Mark 8–16: A New Translation with Introduction and Commentary*. The Anchor Yale Bible, vol. 27B. New Haven, CT: Yale University Press, 2009.

McCarter, P. Kyle. *II Samuel: A New Translation with Introduction and Commentary*. The Anchor Bible, vol. 9. New York: Doubleday, 1984.

Meyers, Carol L., Toni Craven, and Ross Shepard Kraemer. *Women in Scripture: A Dictionary of Named and Unnamed Women in the Hebrew Bible, the Apocryphal/Deuterocanonical Books, and the New Testament*. Boston, MA: Houghton Mifflin, 2000.

Moore, Carey A. *Tobit: A New Translation with Introduction and Commentary*. The Anchor Bible, vol. 40, part 1. New York: Doubleday, 1996.

Murdock, James. *Murdock's Translation of the Syriac New Testament. Translated into English from the Peshitto Version by James Murdock*. Boston: Scriptural Tract Repository, 1892.

New Revised Standard Version. Washington, DC: National Council of Churches, 1989.

Newsome, Carol, Sharon H. Ringe, and Jacqueline Lapsley. *Women's Bible Commentary*. 3rd ed. Louisville: Westminster John Knox Press, 2012.

Page, Hugh. *Israel's Poetry of Resistance: Africana Perspectives on Early Hebrew Verse*. Minneapolis: Fortress Press, 2013.

Rashkow, Ilona. *Taboo or Not Taboo: Sexuality and Family in the Hebrew Bible*. Minneapolis: Fortress Press, 2000.

Scholz, Susanne. *Introducing the Women's Hebrew Bible: Feminism, Gender Justice, and the Study of the Old Testament*. New York: Bloomsbury T & T, 2017.

Smith, Mitzi J. *I Found God in Me: A Womanist Biblical Hermeneutics Reader*. Eugene, OR: Cascade Books, 2015.

Soggin, J. Alberto. *Judges: A Commentary*. Translated by James Bowden. Philadelphia: Westminster, 1981.

Stamm, Johann, Ludwig Köhler, and Walter Baumgarner. *The Hebrew and Aramaic Lexicon of the Old Testament*. Leiden: Brill Academic Press, 1994.

Stein, David. *The Contemporary Torah: A Gender-Sensitive Adaptation of the JPS Translation*. Philadelphia, PA: Jewish Publication Society, 2006.

Tal, Abraham. *The Samaritan Pentateuch*. Tel-Aviv: Tel-Aviv University, 1994.

Tanakh: The Holy Scriptures: The New JPS Translation According to the Hebrew Text. Philadelphia, PA: Jewish Publication Society, 1985.

Thurston, Bonnie. *The Widows: A Women's Ministry in the Early Church*. Philadelphia: Fortress Press, 1989.

Trible, Phyllis. *God and the Rhetoric of Sexuality*. Overtures to Biblical Theology 2. Philadelphia: Fortress Press, 1978.

———. *Texts of Terror: Literary-Feminist Readings of Biblical Narratives*. Overtures to Biblical Theology, no. 13. Philadelphia: Fortress Press, 1984.

Westbrook, April D. *"And He Will Take Your Daughters . . .": Woman Story and the Ethical Evaluation of Monarchy in the David Narrative*. New York: Bloomsbury T & T Clark, 2015.

Wills, Lawrence M. "Mark." In Levine and Brettler, *Jewish Annotated New Testament: New Revised Standard Bible Translation*. Oxford: Oxford University Press, 2011. 69-109

Winter, Miriam Therese. *The Gospel According to Mary: A New Testament for Women*. New York: Crossroad, 1993.

———. *WomanWisdom: A Feminist Lectionary and Psalter: Women of the Hebrew Scriptures, Part One*. New York: Crossroad, 1991.

———. *WomanWitness: A Feminist Lectionary and Psalter: Women of the Hebrew Scriptures, Part Two*. New York: Crossroad, 1992.

———. *WomanWord: A Feminist Lectionary and Psalter: Women of the New Testament*. New York: Crossroad, 1990.

Wisdom Commentary Series. Barbara E. Reid, OP, General Editor. Collegeville, MN: Liturgical Press, 2015.

Witherington, Ben. *A New English Translation of the Septuagint (and Other Greek Translations Traditionally Included Under That Title)*. New York: Oxford University Press, 2000.

SCRIPTURE INDEX

YEAR A	First Reading	Psalm	Second Readings	Gospel	YEAR A
Advent I	Genesis 1:1-5	8	Romans 8:15-25	Matthew 24:32-34	Advent I
Advent II	Isaiah 54:1-8	113	Hebrews 11:8-13	Luke 1:5-17, 24-25	Advent II
Advent III	Ruth 4:11-17	78:1-8	Galatians. 4:1-7	Matthew 1:1-16	Advent III
Advent IV	Susannah 1-31-45	34:1-9	Titus 3:4-7	Matthew 1:18-25	Advent IV
Christmas I	Isaiah 26:16-19	68:4-11	1 Thessalonians. 4:13-18	Luke 2:1-14 or 1-20	Christmas I
Christmas II	Isaiah 66:10-13	103:1-17	1 Peter 1:22-2:3	Luke 2:1-7 (8-20)	Christmas II
Christmas III	Wisdom 9:1-6, 9-11	33:1-9	Colossians 1:15-20	John 1:1-14	Christmas III
First Sunday After Christmas	Proverbs 23:22-25	8	1 John 5:1-5	Luke 2:25-38	First Sunday After Christmas
Feast of the Holy Name	Isaiah 7:3-16	89:1-8, 14	Philippians 2:5-13	Luke 2:15-21	Feast of the Holy Name
Second Sunday After Christmas	Hosea 11:1-4, 7-9	68:18-20, 22, 24-27, 31-33	Hebrews 11:23-28	Matthew 2:13-18	Second Sunday After Christmas
The Epiphany	Isaiah 60:1-6	67	2 Timothy 1:5-10	Matthew 2:1-12	The Epiphany
I Epiphany	Isaiah 2:1-5	57	2 Peter 1:16-21	Matthew 3:1-17	I Epiphany
II Epiphany	Isaiah 9:2-7	36:5-10	Romans 15:8-13	Matthew 4:18-25	II Epiphany
Feast of the Presentation	Leviticus 12:1-8	Psalm 48:1-3, 9-14	1 John 5:1-5	Luke 2:22-38	Feast of the Presentation
III Epiphany	Tobit 13:11-17	22:23:31	1 Timothy 3:14-16	Matthew 4:18-25	III Epiphany
IV Epiphany	Isaiah 42:1-5, 10-16	107:1-9, 19-22	James 1:17-21	Matthew 8:14-22	IV Epiphany
V Epiphany	2 Kings 5:1-4, 9-14	30	Acts 16:16-24	Matthew 9:18-26	V Epiphany
VI Epiphany	Isaiah 62:1-7, 12	146	Revelation 12:1-6, 13-17	Matthew 11:7-19	VI Epiphany
VII Epiphany	Isaiah 61:1-4, 8-10	Song of Songs 3:1-11	1 Corinthians 9:1-10	John 2:1-11	VII Epiphany
VIII Epiphany	Isaiah 6:1-7	29	Revelation 4:2-11	John 1:1-5	VIII Epiphany
Epiphany Last	Leviticus 19:1-2, 9-18	77:13-20	Romans 12:1-13	Matthew 17:1-9	Epiphany Last
Ash Wednesday	Joel 2:1, 12-17, 21-22	90:1-10, 12	1 Corinthians 15:45-49	Matthew 6:1-6, 16-18	Ash Wednesday
Lent 1	Genesis 2:7-9, 15-17, 21-25; 3:1-7	51:1-17	Revelation 22:1-5, 16-17	Matthew 3:1-6	Lent 1

353

YEAR A	First Reading	Psalm	Second Readings	Gospel	YEAR A
Lent II	1 Kings 17:8-16	111:2-10	2 Corinthians 9:6-13	Matthew 14:13-21	Lent II
Lent III	Numbers 5:5-10	32:1-7	James 5:13-18	Matthew 5:21-16	Lent III
Lent IV	Genesis 31:25-27, 43-50	144:3-4, 12-15	1 John 4:13-21	Matt: 12:46-50	Lent IV
Lent V	Numbers 11:4-15	104:1-4, 10-15, 27-30	1 Corinthians 3:1-9	Matthew 15:2-39	Lent V
The Annunciation	Zephaniah 3:14-20	Canticle 15	2 Corinthians 6:16-18	Luke 1:26-38	The Annunciation
Palm Sunday					
Liturgy of the Palms		118:19-29		Matthew 21:1-11	
Palm Sunday Liturgy of the Word	Isaiah 49:5-16	22:1-11	Galatians. 3:23-4:7	Mark 14:32(53-) 15:47	
Monday in HW	Jeremiah 31:81-13	22:19-31	Hebrews 1:1-9	John 12:1-7	Monday in HW
Tuesday in HW	Isaiah 49:1-6	123	Philippians 3:17-21	Matthew 21:12-17	Tuesday in HW
Wednesday in HW	Ezekiel 17:22-24	36:5-10	1 John 2:7-14	Matthew 23:37-39	Wednesday in HW
Maundy Thursday	Exodus 15:11-21	136:1-16	Hebrews 11:23-28	Matthew 26:17-56	Maundy Thursday
Good Friday	Judges 11:29-40	22	Hebrews 12:1-4	Luke 22:14-23, 56	Good Friday
Holy Saturday	Job 14:1-14	31	Philippians 2:1-8	Matthew 28:8-10, 16-20	Holy Saturday

Great Vigil of Easter

Great Vigil Lessons & Canticles	Vigil Lesson	Vigil Canticle/ Psalm	Canticle Name
A God-Crafted Creation	Genesis 1:2, 26-27; 2:1-4	Daniel (LXX) 3:52-60	Canticle of the Three Young Men
The Salvation of Hagar and Ishmael	Genesis 21:1-2, 8-21	Psalm 27:5-7, 10-14	
From Slavery to Freedom	Exodus 14:26-29; 15:20-21	Exodus 15:1-3, 11, 13, 17-18	The Song of Miriam and Moses
Rahab's Salvation	Joshua 2:1–7, 12–14; 6:15–17, 23	Wisdom 5:1-5; 6:6-7	
Deborah Saves the People	Judges 4:1-10, 23	Judges 5:1, 4–7, 12, 24, 31	Canticle of Deborah
Judith Saves Her People	Judith 8:9-10, 32-34; 13:3-14, 17-18	Judith 16:1-6, 13	The Song of Judith

YEAR A	First Reading	Psalm	Second Readings	Gospel	YEAR A
Vigil Epistle & Gospel			Acts 16:13-15	Matthew 28:1-10	
Easter Day - Early Service	Choose from Great Vigil Lessons				Easter Day - Early Service
Easter Day - Principal Service	Isaiah 49:1-13	18:2-11, 16-19	Hebrews 11:1-2, 23-24, 28-39	Matthew 28:1-10 OR John 20:1-10 (11-18)	Easter Day - Principal Service
Easter Day - Evening Service	Isaiah 25:6-9	118:14-26	2 Tim 2:8-13	Luke 24:13-35 or 13-27	Easter Day - Evening Service
Monday in Easter Week		16:8–11	1 Peter 1:3-9	John 20:19-23	Monday in Easter Week
Tuesday in Easter Week		18:1-6	1 Corinthians 15:3-7	Luke 24:36-43	Tuesday in Easter Week
Wednesday in Easter Week		30:1-5	1 Corinthians 15:12-20	Luke 24:44-53	Wednesday in Easter Week
Thursday in Easter Week		49:5-15	1 Corinthians 15:35-44	John 21:4-14	Thursday in Easter Week
Friday in Easter Week		86:8-13	Romans 6:5-11	Mark 16:9-15, 19-20	Friday in Easter Week
Saturday in Easter Week		116:1-9	Acts 13:29-38	Matthew 28:8-20	Saturday in Easter Week
Second Sunday of Easter	Acts 1:3-5, 12-14 (or Sirach 1:14-20)	Psalm 111	1 John 5:1-6	John 20:19-31	Second Sunday of Easter
Third Sunday of Easter	Acts 1:6-8 (or Sirach 4:11-16)	Psalm 34:1-14	Hebrews 5:7-14	John 5:25-29	Third Sunday of Easter
Fourth Sunday of Easter	Acts 5:12-16 (or Sirach 15:1-6)	Psalm 119:97-103	Romans 6:5-11	Matthew 22:23-33	Fourth Sunday of Easter
Fifth Sunday of Easter	Acts 17:1-4, 10-12 (or Wisdom 6:12-19)	Psalm 63:1-8	1 Peter 1:3-9	John 11:17-27	Fifth Sunday of Easter
Sixth Sunday of Easter	Acts 17:22-34 (or Sirach 14:20-27)	Psalm 19:7-10	Philippians 3:7-11	Matthew 27:45-54	Sixth Sunday of Easter
Ascension Sunday	Acts 1:1-11	Psalm 24	Revelation 3:20-22	Luke 24:46-53	Ascension Sunday
Seventh Sunday of Easter	Acts 3:18-26 (or Sirach 51:13-21)	Psalm 27:1-2, 4-5, 7, 10, 13-14	1 Peter 3:13-22	Luke 14:7-14	Seventh Sunday of Easter

Scripture Index

YEAR A	First Reading	Psalm	Second Readings	Gospel	YEAR A
Pentecost Sunday					Pentecost Sunday
Vigil (or Early Service)	Joel 2:27-32	Exodus 19:1-19	Psalm 139:7-14	Acts 2:1-18	Vigil (or Early Service)
Principal Service	Acts 2:1-17 (or Isaiah 44:1-8)	Psalm 104:1-4, 10-15, 27-30	Romans 8:14-17, 22-27	John 14:8-17	Principal Service
Trinity Sunday	Hosea 11:1–4	Psalm 130:5–8; 131:1–3	2 Peter 1:16–18	Matthew 28:16–20	Trinity Sunday
Season after Pentecost					Season after Pentecost
Proper 1 (Closest to May 11)	Judges 9:1-6, 22, 50-56	Psalm 29	Acts 17:1-7	Matthew 14:1-12	Proper 1 (Closest to May 11)
Proper 2 (Closest to May 18)	Ruth 1:1-14	Psalm 69:1-3, 13-17, 30-34	Acts 2:43-47	Matthew 10:40-42	Proper 2 (Closest to May 18)
Proper 3 (Closest to May 25)	Ruth 1:15-22	Psalm 115:9-18	Acts 4:32-35	Matthew 11:7-19	Proper 3 (Closest to May 25)
Proper 4 (Closest to June 1)	Ruth 2:1-16	Psalm 9	Acts 5:1-11	Matthew 12:46-50	Proper 4 (Closest to June 1)
Proper 5 (Closest to June 8)	Ruth 3:1-18	Psalm 65:5-13	Acts 5:12-16	Matthew 13:31-35	Proper 5 (Closest to June 8)
Proper 6 (Closest to June 15)	Ruth 4:9-17	Psalm 78:1-8	1 Timothy 5:1-8	Matthew 15:1-9	Proper 6 (Closest to June 15)
Proper 7 (Closest to June 22)	1 Samuel 1:1-6, 9-18	Psalm 113	Colossians 4:10-17	Matthew 15:21-28	Proper 7 (Closest to June 22)
Proper 8 (Closest to June 29)	1 Samuel 1:19-28	Canticle of Hannah: (1 Samuel 2:1-10)	1 Corinthians 3:1-9	Matthew 15:29-39	Proper 8 (Closest to June 29)
Proper 9 (Closest to July 6)	1 Samuel 2:18-21, 26	Psalm 111	1 Thessalo-niansalonians 2:1-8	Matthew 18:23-35	Proper 9 (Closest to July 6)
Proper 10 (Closest to July 13)	1 Samuel 2:12-17, 22-25	Psalm 49:5-15	1 Timothy 6:6-16	Matthew 19:16-30	Proper 10 (Closest to July 13)
Proper 11 (Closest to July 20)	1 Samuel 8:1, 4-18	Psalm 99	Revelation 19:5-9	Matthew 20:1-16	Proper 11 (Closest to July 20)
Feast of Mary Magdalene 22 July	Genesis 16:10-13	Psalm 68:4-11	Romans 16:1-16	John 20:1-2, 11-18	Feast of Mary Magdalene 22 July
Proper 12 (Closest to July 27)	1 Samuel 9:1-3, 15-18, 10:1	Psalm 96	Acts 13:16-23	Matthew 4:1-11	Proper 12 (Closest to July 27)
Proper 13 (Closest to August 3)	1 Samuel 15:1-3, 8, 10-17, 24-25	Psalm 7:1-8, 17	Romans 2:1-11	Matthew 5:21-26	Proper 13 (Closest to August 3)
Proper 14 (Closest to August 10)	1 Samuel 17:1-7, 12-16, 24-27	Psalm 108:1-6, 11-13	Ephesians 6:10-17	Matthew 5:43-48	Proper 14 (Closest to August 10)
Feast of the Ever-Blessed Virgin Mary 15 August	Judith 13:18-20	Canticle 15, the Magni-ficat, (Luke 1:46-55)	Revelation 21:1-7	Luke 1:26-37	Feast of the Ever-Blessed Virgin Mary 15 August

YEAR A	First Reading	Psalm	Second Readings	Gospel	YEAR A
Proper 15 (Closest to August 17)	1 Samuel 17:55-18:9	Psalm 78:68-72	Romans 1:1-8	John 7:37-44	Proper 15 (Closest to August 17)
Proper 16 (Closest to August 24)	1 Samuel 14:49-51, 18:17-21, 29	Psalm 62	Romans 12:9-21	Matthew 7:15-20	Proper 16 (Closest to August 24)
Proper 17 (Closest to August 31)	1 Samuel 25:14-19, 23-25, 32-34, 42-43	Psalm 25:4-12	1 Corinthians 7:1-9	Matthew 5:38-42	Proper 17 (Closest to August 31)
Proper 18 (Closest to September 7)	1 Samuel 27:1-3, 8-12	Psalm 72:1-4, 12-14, 18-19	Romans 2:12-16	Matthew 18:1-7	Proper 18 (Closest to September 7)
Proper 19 (Closest to September 14)	1 Samuel 30:1-8, 17-19	Psalm 13	Hebrews 2:10-13	Matthew 18:10-14	Proper 19 (Closest to September 14)
Proper 20 (Closest to September 21)	2 Samuel 1:17-27	Canticle Mater Tua Leaena (Ezekiel 19:1-3, 10-14)	Revelation 21:1-7	Matthew 5:1-9	Proper 20 (Closest to September 21)
Proper 21 (Closest to September 28)	2 Samuel 11:2-15	Psalm 38:1-9, 11, 18, 21-22	Colossians 3:5-11	Matthew 15:10-11, 15-20	Proper 21 (Closest to September 28)
Proper 22 (Closest to October 5)	2 Samuel 13:1-16, 21-22	Psalm 27:1-14	1 Corinthians 5:9-11	Matthew 25:31-46	Proper 22 (Closest to October 5)
Proper 23 (Closest to October 12)	2 Samuel 20:1-2, 14-22	Proverbs 8:1-4, 10-17	1 Corinthians 12:4-11	Matthew 13:54-58	Proper 23 (Closest to October 12)
Proper 24 (Closest to October 19)	2 Samuel 21:1-14	Psalm 94:1-15	1 Timothy 1:12-17	Matthew 5:38-42	Proper 24 (Closest to October 19)
Proper 25 (Closest to October 26)	1 Kings 1:1-5, 11-18, 29-31	Psalm 61	James 5:1-6	Matthew 6:19-27	Proper 25 (Closest to October 26)
Feast of All Saints 1 November	Isaiah 25:1, 4a, 6-10a	Psalm 67	Romans 15:7-13	Matthew 27:50-56	Feast of All Saints 1 November
Proper 26 (Closest to November 2)	1 Kings 2:10-24	Psalm 72:1, 5, 8-11, 15, 17	Revelation 15:2-4	Matthew 12:38-42	Proper 26 (Closest to November 2)
Proper 27 (Closest to November 9)	1 Kings 5:1-6, 13-14	Psalm 148	Revelation 21:10, 22-27	Matthew 6:28-34	Proper 27 (Closest to November 9)
Proper 28 (Closest to November 16)	1 Kings 11:26-39	Psalm 46	Hebrews 12:18-24, 28-29	Matthew 19:27-30	Proper 28 (Closest to November 16)
Majesty of Christ (Closest to November 23)	2 Kings 24:8, 11-17	Psalm 47	Hebrews 1:1-9	Matthew 27:11-14, 27-37	Majesty of Christ (Closest to November 23)

YEAR B	First Reading	Psalm	Second Readings	Gospel
Advent I	*Isaiah 12:1–5*	Psalm 65:1–13	Romans 1:7–8, 14-17	Mark 1:1–13
Advent II	*Genesis 16:7–13*	Psalm 48:1–3, 9–14	Romans 10:9–13	Mark 1:14–28
Advent III	*Genesis 20:1–7, 9, 11-12, 14, 17*	Psalm 147:1–7	Acts 16:16–24	Mark 1:29–45
Advent IV	*Isaiah 52:7–10*	Psalm 118:14–26	1 Peter 1:10–12	Luke 1:26–38
Christmas I	Isaiah 26:16-19	68:4-11	1 Thessalonians 4:13-18	Luke 2:1-14 or 1-20
Christmas II	Isaiah 66:10-13	103:1–17	1 Peter 1:22-2:3	Luke 2:1-7 (8-20)
Christmas III	Wisdom 9:1-6, 9-11	33:1-9	Colossians 1:15-20	John 1:1–14
First Sunday After Christmas	*Isaiah 40:1–8*	Psalm 69:30–36	Galatiansatians 4:1—7	Luke 2:25–38
Feast of the Holy Name	Isaiah 7:3-16	89:1-8, 14	Philippians 2:5-13	Luke 2:15-21
Second Sunday After Christmas	*Hosea 11:1–4, 7–9*	Psalm 71:15–23	2 Thessalonians 2:13–17	Matthew 2:13–18
The Epiphany	Isaiah 60:1-6	67	2 Timothy 1:5-10	Matthew 2:1-12
I Epiphany	*Isaiah 51:4–8*	Psalm 85	Hebrews 2:1–11	Mark 2:1–12
II Epiphany	*Proverbs 4:1–13*	Psalm 25:4–12	Galatiansatians 1:6–12	Mark 2:13–28
Feast of the Presentation	Leviticus 12:1-8	Psalm 48:1-3, 9-14	1 John 5:1-5	Luke 2:22-38
III Epiphany	*2 Kings 5:1–4, 9–14*	Psalm 103:1–17	1 Corinthians 12:1, 4–11	Mark 3:1–12
IV Epiphany	*Jeremiah 9:17–22*	Psalm 34:1–14	Romans 16:1–16	Mark 3:13–35
V Epiphany	*Isaiah 6:1–10*	Psalm 119:33–40	1 John 5:18–20	Mark 4:1–20
VI Epiphany	*Job 38:1–3, 8–11, 16–18, 28–29*	Psalm 107:1–3, 19–32	James 1:2–7	Mark 4:30–41
VII Epiphany	*Isaiah 38:16–20*	Psalm 30:1–5, 8–12	2 Corinthians 4:7–12	Mark 5:21–43
VIII Epiphany	*Proverbs 23:22–26*	Psalm 111	1 John 5:18–21	Mark 6:1-13
Epiphany Last	*Judges 5:1–7*	Psalm 102:12-21	2 Peter 1:16–21	Mark 6:14–29
Ash Wednesday	Joel 2:1, 12-17, 21-22	90:1-10, 12	1 Corinthians 15:45-49	Matthew 6:1-6, 16-18
Lent 1	*Judges 5:24–31*	Psalm 25:1–7	Romans 12:14–21	Mark 6:14–29
Lent II	*Proverbs 28:20–25*	Psalm 50:1–15	1 Timothy 5:1–4, 8	Mark 7:1–15
Lent III	*Joshua 6:15–17, 23, 25*	Psalm 146	James 2:14–19, 24–26	Mark 7:24–30
Lent IV	1 Kings 17:8–16	Psalm 145:8–10, 14–19	1 Corinthians 3:1-9	Mark 8:1-21

YEAR B	First Reading	Psalm	Second Readings	Gospel
Lent V	Genesis 4:17–25	Psalm 128	1 Corinthians 7:1–17	Mark 10:1–16
The Annunciation	Zephaniah 3:14-20	Canticle 15	2 Corinthians 6:16-18	Luke 1:26-38
Palm Sunday				
Liturgy of the Palms		118:19-29		Matthew 21:1-11
Palm Sunday Liturgy of the Word	Isaiah 49:5-16	22:1-11	Galatians. 3:23-4:7	Mark 14:32(53-)15:47
Monday in HW	Jeremiah 31:81-13	22:19-31	Hebrews 1:1-9	John 12:1-7
Tuesday in HW	Isaiah 49:1-6	123	Philippians 3:17-21	Matthew 21:12-17
Wednesday in HW	Ezekiel 17:22-24	36:5-10	1 John 2:7-14	Matthew 23:37-39
Maundy Thursday	Exodus 15:11-21	136:1-16	Hebrews 11:23-28	Matthew 26:17-56
Good Friday	Judges 11:29-40	22	Hebrews 12:1-4	Luke 22:14-23, 56
Holy Saturday	Job 14:1-14	31	Philippians 2:1-8	Matthew 28:8-10, 16-20

Great Vigil of Easter

Great Vigil Lessons & Canticles	Vigil Lesson	Vigil Canticle/ Psalm	Canticle Name	
A God-Crafted Creation	Genesis 1:2, 26-27; 2:1-4	Daniel (LXX) 3:52-60	Canticle of the Three Young Men	
The Salvation of Hagar and Ishmael	Genesis 21:1-2, 8-21	Psalm 27:5-7, 10-14		
From Slavery to Freedom	Exodus 14:26-29; 15:20-21	Exodus 15:1-3, 11, 13, 17-18	The Song of Miriam and Moses	
Rahab's Salvation	Joshua 2:1–7, 12–14; 6:15–17, 23	Wisdom 5:1-5; 6:6-7		
Deborah Saves the People	Judges 4:1-10, 23	Judges 5:1, 4–7, 12, 24, 31	Canticle of Deborah	
Judith Saves Her People	Judith 8:9-10, 32-34; 13:3-14, 17-18	Judith 16:1-6, 13	The Song of Judith	
Vigil Epistle & Gospel			Acts 16:13-15	Matthew 28:1-10
Easter Day - Early Service	Choose from Great Vigil Lessons			
Easter Day - Principal Service	Isaiah 49:1-13	18:2-11, 16-19	Hebrews 11:1-2, 23-24, 28-39	Matthew 28:1-10 OR John 20:1-10 (11-18)
Easter Day - Evening Service	Isaiah 25:6-9	118:14-26	2 Tim 2:8-13	Luke 24:13-35 or 13-27
Monday in Easter Week		16:8–11	1 Peter 1:3-9	John 20:19-23
Tuesday in Easter Week		18:1-6	1 Corinthians 15:3-7	Luke 24:36-43

YEAR B	First Reading	Psalm	Second Readings	Gospel
Wednesday in Easter Week		30:1-5	1 Corinthians 15:12-20	Luke 24:44-53
Thursday in Easter Week		49:5-15	1 Corinthians 15:35-44	John 21:4-14
Friday in Easter Week		86:8-13	Romans 6:5-11	Mark 16:9-15, 19-20
Saturday in Easter Week		116:1-9	Acts 13:29-38	Matthew 28:8-20
Second Sunday of Easter	Acts 1:3–5, 12–14 (or Proverbs 9:1–6)	Psalm 104:1–4, 10–15, 27–30	2 Corinthians 9:6–10	John 14:1–5
Third Sunday of Easter	Acts 5:12–16 (or Isaiah 43:1–3a, 5–7)	Psalm 50:1–6	Ephesians 1:7–14	John 5:25–29
Fourth Sunday of Easter	*Acts 6:1–7 (or Jeremiah 7:1–7)*	Psalm 68:4–11	1 Timothy 5:1–4, 8	John 14:18–24
Fifth Sunday of Easter	Acts 8:1–12 (or Isaiah 52:7–10)	Psalm 71:15–23	Romans 10:9–15	John 4:24–29
Sixth Sunday of Easter	Acts 9:36–42 (or Isaiah 26:16–19)	Psalm 36:5–10	Romans 8:11–17	John 6:35–40
Ascension Sunday	Acts 1:1-11	Psalm 24	Revelation 3:20-22	Luke 24:46-53
Seventh Sunday of Easter	Acts 8:26-39 (or Deuteronomy 25:5–9)	Psalm 45:6–10	1 Corinthians 7:32–40	Mark 12:18–27
Pentecost Sunday				
Vigil (or Early Service)	Joel 2:27-32	Exodus 19:1-19	Psalm 139:7-14	Acts 2:1-18
Principal Service	Acts 2:1-17 (or Isaiah 44:1-8)	Psalm 104:1-4, 10-15, 27-30	Romans 8:14-17, 22-27	John 14:8-17
Trinity Sunday	Hosea 11:1–4	Psalm 130:5–8; 131:1–3	2 Peter 1:16–18	Matthew 28:16–20
Season after Pentecost				
Proper 1 (Closest to May 11)	Genesis 1:1–5	Psalm 31:1–5, 15, 18–19	Romans 5:1–5	Mark 1:9–13
Proper 2 (Closest to May 18)	Proverbs 4:1–10	Psalm 111:1–10	1 Corinthians 1:26–31	Matthew 11:7–19
Proper 3 (Closest to May 25)	2 Kings 4:1	Psalm 94:1–15	James 2:5–13	Matthew 5:1–9
Proper 4 (Closest to June 1)	Isaiah 51:1–8	Psalm 92:1–5	1 Corinthians 3:1–9	Mark 4:30–34
Proper 5 (Closest to June 8)	1 Samuel 28:5–17	Psalm 95:1–7	1 John 4:1–6	Mark 5:1–20
Proper 6 (Closest to June 15)	Numbers 11:4-15	Psalm 147:7–14	1 Timothy 6:6–16	Mark 6:30–44
Proper 7 (Closest to June 22)	1 Kings 19:19–21	Psalm 23	1 Peter 2:21–25	Mark 8:27–38
Proper 8 (Closest to June 29)	Genesis 2:4b:–7	Psalm 139:1, 7–14	Ephesians 1:3–9	Mark 9:33–37, 42
Proper 9 (Closest to July 6)	1 Samuel 8:1, 4–18	Psalm 72:1–4, 12–14, 18–19	1 Timothy 2:1–6	John 6:14–20

YEAR B	First Reading	Psalm	Second Readings	Gospel
Proper 10 (Closest to July 13)	Esther 1:1–11	Psalm 62:5–12	James 5:1–6	Mark 10:17–31
Proper 11 (Closest to July 20)	Ruth 1:1–14	Psalm 80:1–7	1 Thessalonians 5:12–24	Mark 12:41–44
Feast of Mary Magdalene 22 July	Genesis 16:10-13	Psalm 68:4–11	Romans 16:1-16	John 20:1-2, 11-18
Proper 12 (Closest to July 27)	Isaiah 61:1–4, 8–10	Psalm 133:1–3	2 Corinthians 2:14–16	Mark 14:3–9
Proper 13 (Closest to August 3)	Ruth 1:15–22	Psalm 44:1–4, 8, 17, 23–26	Acts 6:1–6	Luke 18:1–8
Proper 14 (Closest to August 10)	Ruth 2:1–16	Psalm 112	2 Corinthians 8:1–5	Luke 12:13–21
Feast of the Ever-Blessed Virgin Mary 15 August	Judith 13:18-20	Canticle 15, the Magnificat, (Luke 1:46-55)	Revelation 21:1–7	Luke 1:26-37
Proper 15 (Closest to August 17)	Ruth 3:1–18	Psalm 65:1–13	2 Corinthians 9:6–13	Luke 8:1–3
Proper 16 (Closest to August 24)	Ruth 4:9–17	Psalm 107:1–9, 19–22	1 Corinthians 12:14–26	Matthew 5:43–48
Proper 17 (Closest to August 31)	2 Chronicles 28:1, 5, 8–15	Psalm 106:1–6, 40–47	Ephesians 4:1– 8	John 4:7 –26
Proper 18 (Closest to September 7)	2 Kings 17:21–28, 42	Psalm 34:1–14	1 Peter 5:6–11	John 4:27 –29, 39-42
Proper 19 (Closest to September 14)	1 Samuel 1:1–6, 9–18	Psalm 113	1 Thessalonians 2:9–12	John 16:16–22
Proper 20 (Closest to September 21)	1 Samuel 1:19–28	Canticle of Hannah (1 Samuel 2:1–10)	1 Corinthians 3:1–9	Matthew 10:34 –39
Proper 21 (Closest to September 28)	1 Samuel 2:18–21, 26	Psalm 144:3–4, 12–15	1 Peter 2:4–10	Mark 9:14–29
Proper 22 (Closest to October 5)	1 Samuel 4:19–22	Psalm 74:1–12	Revelation 21:10, 22–27	Mark 13:1–8
Proper 23 (Closest to October 12)	1 Samuel 15:1–3, 8, 10–17, 24–25	Psalm 25:1–11	Ephesians 4:25–32	Mark 11:12–14, 20–25
Proper 24 (Closest to October 19)	1 Samuel 14:49–51	Psalm 3:1–8	Romans 5:6–11	Mark 4:21–25
Proper 25 (Closest to October 26)	1 Samuel 25:14–19, 23–25, 32–34, 42–43	Psalm 37:1–2, 7–11, 16, 35–40	2 Corinthians 8:1–9	Matthew 5:38–42
Feast of All Saints 1 November	Isaiah 25:1, 4a, 6-10a	Psalm 67	Romans 15:7-13	Matthew 27:50-56
Proper 26 (Closest to November 2)	2 Samuel 11:2–15	Psalm 32:1–7	2 Peter 3:1–4, 8–9	Matthew 15:10–20
Proper 27 (Closest to November 9)	1 Kings 5:1–6, 13–14	Psalm 72:1–4, 12–14, 18–19	Philippians 4:1–7	Matthew 6:28–34
Proper 28 (Closest to November 16)	2 Kings 24:8, 11-17	Psalm 47	Hebrews 1:1-9	Matthew 27:11-14, 27-37
Majesty of Christ (Closest to November 23)	2 Kings 24:8, 11-17	Psalm 47	Hebrews 1:1-9	Matthew 27:11-14, 27-37

YEAR C	First Reading	Psalm	Second Readings	Gospel
Advent I	Zechariah 8:1-13	Psalm 46:1–11	1 John 4:13–21	Luke 1:5-19
Advent II	*Isaiah 41:4-10, 17-20*	Psalm 27:4-5, 8-14	1 Peter 3:13–17	Luke 1:26-38
Advent III	*Isaiah 12:1–6*	Psalm 118:1–9, 14–21	Revelation 1:4–6, 8, 12–18	Luke 1:39–45
Advent IV	Exodus 20:1–21	Psalm 91	Romans 8:14–27	Luke 1:46–56
Christmas I	Isaiah 26:16-19	68:4-11	1 Thessalonians 4:13-18	Luke 2:1-14 or 1-20
Christmas II	Isaiah 66:10-13	103:1–17	1 Peter 1:22-2:3	Luke 2:1-7 (8-20)
Christmas III	Wisdom 9:1-6, 9-11	33:1-9	Colossians 1:15-20	John 1:1-14
First Sunday After Christmas	1 Kings 8:12–13, 27–30, 41–43	Psalm 143	1 Corinthians 6:12–20	Luke 2:41–51
Feast of the Holy Name	Isaiah 7:3-16	89:1-8, 14	Philippians 2:5-13	Luke 2:15-21
Second Sunday After Christmas	Wisdom 3:13b–15, 4:1-2	Psalm 143	1 Corinthians 6:12–20	Luke 3:1–6, 15–23</CST
The Epiphany	Isaiah 60:1-6	67	2 Timothy 1:5-10	Matthew 2:1-12
I Epiphany	Genesis 21:14–19	Psalm 34:1–14	2 Corinthians 9:6–13	Luke 4:1–15
II Epiphany	1 Kings 17:8–16	Psalm 40:1–11, 13, 16–17	Romans 12:9–18	Luke 4:16–27
Feast of the Presentation	Leviticus 12:1-8	Psalm 48:1-3, 9-14	1 John 5:1–5	Luke 2:22-38
III Epiphany	Isaiah 2:1–5	Psalm 119:10–18	1 Peter 1:22–25	Luke 4:38–44
IV Epiphany	1 Kings 17:17–24	Psalm 146	1 Corinthians 15:12–26	Luke 7:11–17
V Epiphany	Proverbs 8:1–4, 10–17	Psalm 111	James 3:13–18	Luke 7:18–35
VI Epiphany	Numbers 5:11–24, 27–28	Psalm 7:1-8, 14-17	1 Corinthians 7:1–17	Luke 7:36–50
VII Epiphany	Genesis 47:13–25	Psalm 107:1–3, 35-43	Acts 5:1–11	Luke 8:1–15
VIII Epiphany	Isaiah 11:1–5	Psalm 33:6–9, 13–22	Romans 15:7–13	Luke 9:18–27
Epiphany Last	*Judges 4:5–10*	Psalm 46	2 Peter 1:16–21	Luke 9:28–36
Ash Wednesday	Joel 2:1, 12-17, 21-22	90:1-10, 12	1 Corinthians 15:45-49	Matthew 6:1-6, 16-18
Lent 1	Ezekiel 37:1–14	Psalm 49:1–2, 5–15	Ephesians 1:15 –21	John 3:1–8
Lent II	Genesis 31:25–29, 43–50	Psalm 144:3–4, 12–15	Romans 8:18–25	Luke 8:40–55
Lent III	Exodus 16:2–18	Psalm 65:5–13	Acts 27:1, 27–38	Luke 9:12 –17
Lent IV	Numbers 26:33, 27:1–11	Psalm 56:1–13	Acts 18:1-3, 18-20, 24-28	Luke 10:38–42

YEAR C	First Reading	Psalm	Second Readings	Gospel
Lent V	1 Kings 10:1–10, 13	Psalm 131:1-3	1 Thessalonians 1:2–10	Luke 11:27–32
The Annunciation	Zephaniah 3:14-20	Canticle 15	2 Corinthians 6:16-18	Luke 1:26-38
Palm Sunday				
Liturgy of the Palms		118:19-29		Matthew 21:1-11
Palm Sunday Liturgy of the Word	Isaiah 49:5-16	22:1-11	Galatians. 3:23-4:7	Mark 14:32(53-)15:47
Monday in HW	Jeremiah 31:81-13	22:19-31	Hebrews 1:1-9	John 12:1-7
Tuesday in HW	Isaiah 49:1-6	123	Philippians 3:17-21	Matthew 21:12-17
Wednesday in HW	Ezekiel 17:22-24	36:5-10	1 John 2:7-14	Matthew 23:37-39
Maundy Thursday	Exodus 15:11-21	136:1-16	Hebrews 11:23-28	Matthew 26:17-56
Good Friday	Judges 11:29-40	22	Hebrews 12:1-4	Luke 22:14-23, 56
Holy Saturday	Job 14:1-14	31	Philippians 2:1-8	Matthew 28:8-10, 16-20

Great Vigil of Easter

Great Vigil Lessons & Canticles	Vigil Lesson	Vigil Canticle/ Psalm	Canticle Name	
A God-Crafted Creation	Genesis 1:2, 26-27; 2:1-4	Daniel (LXX) 3:52-60	Canticle of the Three Young Men	
The Salvation of Hagar and Ishmael	Genesis 21:1-2, 8-21	Psalm 27:5-7, 10-14		
From Slavery to Freedom	Exodus 14:26-29; 15:20-21	Exodus 15:1-3, 11, 13, 17-18	The Song of Miriam and Moses	
Rahab's Salvation	Joshua 2:1–7, 12–14; 6:15–17, 23	Wisdom 5:1-5; 6:6-7		
Deborah Saves the People	Judges 4:1-10, 23	Judges 5:1, 4–7, 12, 24, 31	Canticle of Deborah	
Judith Saves Her People	Judith 8:9-10, 32-34; 13:3-14, 17-18	Judith 16:1-6, 13	The Song of Judith	
Vigil Epistle & Gospel			Acts 16:13-15	Matthew 28:1-10

Easter Day - Early Service	Choose from Great Vigil Lessons			
Easter Day - Principal Service	Isaiah 49:1-13	18:2-11, 16-19	Hebrews 11:1-2, 23-24, 28-39	Matthew 28:1-10 OR John 20:1-10 (11-18)
Easter Day - Evening Service	Isaiah 25:6-9	118:14-26	2 Tim 2:8-13	Luke 24:13-35 or 13-27
Monday in Easter Week		16:8–11	1 Peter 1:3-9	John 20:19-23
Tuesday in Easter Week		18:1-6	1 Corinthians 15:3-7	Luke 24:36-43

Scripture Index

YEAR C	First Reading	Psalm	Second Readings	Gospel
Wednesday in Easter Week		30:1–5	1 Corinthians 15:12–20	Luke 24:44-53
Thursday in Easter Week		49:5-15	1 Corinthians 15:35-44	John 21:4-14
Friday in Easter Week		86:8-13	Romans 6:5-11	Mark 16:9-15, 19-20
Saturday in Easter Week		116:1-9	Acts 13:29-38	Matthew 28:8-20
Second Sunday of Easter	Acts 1:3–8, 12–14 (or Judith 8:1–17)	Psalm 6:1–10	Romans 8:31–39	Luke 18:18–30
Third Sunday of Easter	Acts 8:1–12 (or Judith 9:1–14)	Psalm 74:1–12	Ephesians 6:10–18	Luke 12:49–53
Fourth Sunday of Easter	Acts 12:6–17 (or Judith 10:1–8)	Psalm 69:1–3, 13–17, 30–34	Philemon 1:1–2, 7–16	Luke 13:10–17
Fifth Sunday of Easter	Acts 16:13–23, 40 (or Judith 13:1–16)	Psalm 102:17–21, 25–28	Colossians 4:10–17	Luke 15:1–10
Sixth Sunday of Easter	Acts 17:1–4,10–12 (or Judith15:8-13)	Psalm 9:1–14, 18–20	Titus 3:1–8	Luke 18:1–8
Ascension Sunday	Acts 1:1–11	Psalm 24	Revelation 3:20–22	Luke 24:46–53
Seventh Sunday of Easter	Acts 17:22–18:4 (or Judith 16:18-25)	Psalm 149:1–6	Romans 16:1–16	Luke 13:18–30
Pentecost Sunday				
Vigil (or Early Service)	Joel 2:27-32	Exodus 19:1-19	Psalm 139:7-14	Acts 2:1-18
Principal Service	Acts 2:1–17 (or Isaiah 44:1-8)	Psalm 104:1-4, 10-15, 27-30	Romans 8:14-17, 22-27	John 14:8-17
Trinity Sunday	Hosea 11:1–4	Psalm 130:5–8; 131:1–3	2 Peter 1:16–18	Matthew 28:16–20
Season after Pentecost				
Proper 1 (Closest to May 11)	Jonah 3:1–10	Psalm 85:1–13	1 Peter 3:8–12	Luke 16:19–31
Proper 2 (Closest to May 18)	Amos 2:6–13	Psalm 105:1–15	Ephesians 2:11:–22	Luke 13:22–30
Proper 3 (Closest to May 25)	Hosea 1:1–10	Psalm 8:1–10	1 Peter 2:1–15	Luke 18:15–17
Proper 4 (Closest to June 1)	Hosea 2:1, 14–20	Psalm 104:1–4, 10–15, 27–30	Ephesians 1:3–14	Luke 12:22–28
Proper 5 (Closest to June 8)	Micah 2:6–12	Psalm 80:1–7	1 Thessalonians 5:12–24	Luke 4:40–43
Proper 6 (Closest to June 15)	Micah 4:1–10	Psalm 22:22–31	Revelation 15:2–4	Luke 14:1, 12–24
Proper 7 (Closest to June 22)	Isaiah 8:1–8	Psalm 34:11–22	1 John 3:1–3	Luke 9:38–48
Proper 8 (Closest to June 29)	Jeremiah 9:17–22	Psalm 126:1–6	Revelation 21:1–7	Luke 23:26–31
Proper 9 (Closest to July 6)	Jeremiah 29:1–14	Psalm 33:8–22	James 5:7–11	Luke 21:29–36

YEAR C	First Reading	Psalm	Second Readings	Gospel
Proper 10 (Closest to July 13)	Jeremiah 31:2-6, 8-11, 13-17	Psalm 118:14-26	James 5:1-6	Luke 13:31-35
Proper 11 (Closest to July 20)	Baruch 2:11-23	Psalm 18:2-11, 16-17	2 Thessalonians 2:1-8	Luke 12:4-7
Feast of Mary Magdalene 22 July	Genesis 16:10-13	Psalm 68:4-11	Romans 16:1-16	John 20:1-2, 11-18
Proper 12 (Closest to July 27)	Baruch 6:1-7	Psalm 106:1-6, 40-47	Colossians 2:9-14	Luke 21:20-28
Proper 13 (Closest to August 3)	Habakkuk 1:1-13; 2:1	Psalm 62:8-12	2 Peter 3:1-11, 14	Luke 17:20-25
Proper 14 (Closest to August 10)	Ezekiel 14:12-22a	Psalm 124:1-8	Hebrews 11:29-12:2	Luke 17:26-37
Feast of the Ever-Blessed Virgin Mary 15 August	Judith 13:18-20	Canticle 15, the Magnificat, (Luke 1:46-55)	Revelation 21:1-7	Luke 1:26-37
Proper 15 (Closest to August 17)	Ezekiel 19:1-3, 10-14	Psalm 30:1-12	Romans 12:14-21	Luke 6:17-25
Proper 16 (Closest to August 24)	Ezekiel 22:1-8, 12	Psalm 50:1-6	Hebrews 10:26-31	John 5:19-24
Proper 17 (Closest to August 31)	Obadiah 1:1-4, 10-15	Psalm 7:8-11, 17	James 4:5-11	Luke 17:1-4
Proper 18 (Closest to September 7)	Isaiah 40:6-11	Psalm 43:1-5	2 Thessalonians 2:13-17	John 11:1-6, 17-27
Proper 19 (Closest to September 14)	Isaiah 43:1-3a, 5-7	Psalm 36:5-10	Titus 2:11	Luke 19:1-10
Proper 20 (Closest to September 21)	Zechariah 7:8-17	Psalm 10:1-14	James 2:14-19, 24-26	John 5:25-29
Proper 21 (Closest to September 28)	Isaiah 51:1-8	Psalm 92:1-5	1 Corinthians 3:1-9	John 4:7-26
Proper 22 (Closest to October 5)	Isaiah 52:7-10	Psalm 118:14-26	1 Peter 1:10-12	John 4:27-30, 39-42
Proper 23 (Closest to October 12)	Isaiah 61:1-4, 8-10	Psalm 133:1-3	2 Corinthians 2:14-16	Mark 14:3-9
Proper 24 (Closest to October 19)	Isaiah 62:1-7, 10-12	Psalm 18:2-11, 16-19	2 Corinthians 6:2-10	John 6:35-40, 54-57
Proper 25 (Closest to October 26)	Isaiah 66:7-13	Psalm 139:1-14	1 Peter 1:3-9	John 3:1-10
Feast of All Saints 1 November	Isaiah 25:1, 4a, 6-10a	Psalm 67	Romans 15:7-13	Matthew 27:50-56
Proper 26 (Closest to November 2)	Daniel 5:1-12	Sirach 1:14-20	1 Corinthians 1:26-31	Luke 21:9-19
Proper 27 (Closest to November 9)	Malachi 2:13-16	Psalm 37:1-2, 7-9, 27-28, 35-40	2 Timothy 2:8-13	Luke 18:9-14
Proper 28 (Closest to November 16)	Malachi 3:1-7	Psalm 84:1-12	Revelation 22:1-5, 16-17, 20-21	Luke 24:44-53
Majesty of Christ (Closest to November 23)	2 Kings 24:8, 11-17	Psalm 47	Hebrews 1:1-9	Matthew 27:11-14, 27-37